'An exemplary study of social class and its ramifications for the lives of people, this book is an all-too-rare example of sociological research that systematically weaves together quantitative and qualitative data with both macro- and micro-analysis. The result is a complex, multidimensional understanding of how class works. It should be read not only by people specifically interested in the dynamics and dilemmas of contemporary South Africa, but by anyone interested in the problem of class in the contemporary world.'

— *Erik Olin Wright, Vilas Distinguished Professor of Sociology, University of Wisconsin-Madison, President of the American Sociological Association*

'This is research of a scale, ambition and rigour unusual in South African sociology. The team provides a conceptually innovative analysis of class in Soweto to argue that township residents have multiclass identities, that subjective conceptions of class are shaped by indigenous languages, and that the working class and poor together constitute an internally differentiated proletariat. It is an impressive work that sets a benchmark for further research, nuanced analysis and vigorous debate, not only for South African social science but also for global debates.'

— *Karl von Holdt, Director: Society, Work and Development Institute, University of the Witwatersrand*

'The Class in Soweto research project has already resulted in important journal articles and an outstanding documentary film. The team has now gathered their research together into a wonderful book that will transform how we understand social change in contemporary South Africa.'

— *Jeremy Seekings, Director: Centre for Social Science Research, University of Cape Town*

Class in Soweto

Peter Alexander, Claire Ceruti, Keke Motseke,
Mosa Phadi and Kim Wale

UKZN PRESS University of KwaZulu-Natal Press

First published 2013 by
University of KwaZulu-Natal Press
Private Bag X01
Scottsville, 3209
South Africa
Email: books@ukzn.ac.za
Website: www.ukznpress.co.za

ISBN: 978-1-86914-220-9

Managing editor: Louis Gaigher
Editor: Glenda Younge
Proofreader: Sally Hines
Indexer: Abdul Bemath
Typesetter: Patricia Comrie
Cover design: Nicolene van Loggerenberg/ IdeaExchange

Printed and bound by Interpak Books, Pietermaritzburg

Contents

Abbreviations

ACDP	African Christian Democratic Party
AIC	African Independent/Indigenous Church
AMPS	All Media Products Survey
ANC	African National Congress
BEE	black economic empowerment
COSATU	Congress of South African Trade Unions
CPS	Current Population Survey
CSR	Centre for Sociological Research
DA	Democratic Alliance
EC	employment category
ICLS	International Conference of Labour Statisticians
ID	Independent Democrats
IFP	Inkatha Freedom Party
ILO	International Labour Organisation
LFS	Labour Force Survey
LSM	Living Standards Measure
NRF	National Research Foundation
OHS	October Household Survey
OKM	Operation Khanyisa Movement
ONS	Office of National Statistics
QLFS	Quarterly Labour Force Survey
RDP	Reconstruction and Development Programme
RCSC	Research Chair in Social Change
SACP	South Africa Communist Party
SAL	small-area layer
SCA	Soweto Civic Association
SECC	Soweto Electricity Crisis Committee
SOYCO	Soweto Youth Congress

Stats SA	Statistics South Africa
UCC	United Congregational Church
UCKG	Universal Church of the Kingdom of God
UDF	United Democratic Front
UDM	United Democratic Movement
UJ	University of Johannesburg
Wits	University of the Witwatersrand
ZCC	Zionist Christian Church

Acknowledgements

The principal funder of the Classifying Soweto project was the Rosa Luxemburg Foundation, which provided generous backing from beginning to end, enabling us to employ researchers and an administrator. From Dr Arndt Hopfmann, Dr Gert Stephan and Dr Armin Osmanovic, the foundation's successive regional directors, and Rose Khumalo, its local project officer, we received intellectual engagement, patience and sympathy, as well as a steady flow of funds. In addition, we received financial support from a National Research Foundation (NRF) focus-area grant, and over the past two years we benefited from association with the South African Research Chair in Social Change (RCSC), which is funded by the Department of Science and Technology and administered by the NRF. Thanks are due to taxpayers in Germany and South Africa who sustain these institutions.

The project was located at the University of Johannesburg (UJ), which gave space, time and administrative support. We are particularly obliged to Profs Derek van der Merwe and Adam Habib, the two deputy vice chancellors with whom we have worked, and Prof. Rory Ryan, the dean of the Faculty of Humanities. Staff from the university's research office, and finance and human resource sections provided efficient and friendly administration. Dr Riette Eiselen, Neelis Potgieter and Anneli Hardy of UJ's Statkon gave valuable advice and practical support. The project was first located in the Department of Sociology, then the Centre for Sociological Research (CSR), and finally the RCSC. We are grateful for collegiality in each of these units, and in particular for the constant support and solidarity of Dr Marcelle Dawson, who stayed with us during all these moves.

Prof. Peter Alexander conceived and led the project. He was joined by Claire Ceruti and Rudzani Mudau in 2005, but the latter moved on to greener pastures in 2007. Mosa Phadi joined the group and continued to be employed as a researcher until 2010. Kim Wale was a researcher from 2008 until she left in 2010, and Keke Motseke filled her position. Mosa and Kim continued to be part of our team even after they had moved to work on their doctorates. Early in 2012, as the project wound down, Claire started to work full time on her doctorate and Keke became a researcher in a commercial organisation. Along the way, Owen Manda, Sibongile Mazibuko and Siniko Qingqwa joined us on the project. Sadly, Siniko died while conducting exciting research on – of all things – funerals in Soweto. In the first two years, Claire Ceruti doubled up as our finance and administration officer, but later we were joined by Lucinda Landen, who spent 50 per cent of her time on Classifying Soweto and the other 50 per cent working for the CSR/RCSC. She was a mainstay of the project.

Peter, Claire and Rudzani constructed the sample frame and questionnaire for the 2006 survey. Claire coordinated the fieldwork and Rudzani and Dr Leo Zeilig managed work on the ground. Prudence Makhura provided backup with logistics. Our fieldwork supervisors were Chantelle Pepper, Simon Nhlapo, Sandile Ndingi, Lyson Mutinhidzo, Sibongile Mazibuko, Simba Mlilwana, Rejoice Shumba, Olufisayo Orimohoye, Nhlanhla Msweli and Zinzile Masango. The fieldworkers were Mashudu Mashamba, Wiseman Mgaga, Milicent Mbuyane, Sekko Mphaka, Masechaba Nkomo, Arthur Lekalake, Tlamelo Ntshekang, Mbaili Mpungose, Herman Pharasi, Ngiphiwe Nkwe, Andrena Mohlathe, Primrose Behane, Cynthia Tshitanye, Mosa Phadi, Moses Lukhwareni, Shonisani Ndou, Samuel Mfuba, Johanna Mhlongo, Siniko Qingqwa, Tshiveaho Mulaudzi, Hulisani Nemanahi, Fumane Seale, Nokuthula Vilikai, Mandisa Gumada, Ntsiki Morrison, Godfrey Magota, Emily Mabunda, Comfort Phokela, Dorah Pholo, Botsang Mmope, Solani Mhlanga, Colbert Sinthumule, Samuel Seshibe, Sizwe Mhlongo, Cibile Hlophe, Borman Tsela, Daniel Similane, Sbonisiwe Mhlongo and Nomaswazi Ngwane. In the last days of the fieldwork we were assisted by several colleagues, particularly Tshidiso Matsidisho. Nhlanhla, Rejoice and Linda Hlongwane worked on coding, cleaning and checking. Mosa and Siniko helped with processing the data. Analysis was undertaken mainly by Claire and Mosa.

A short survey to check the population's gender balance was undertaken by Mosa, Siniko and Comfort. The semi-structured interviews were led by Sibongile, who was supported by Mosa, Kgopotso Khumalo, Comfort, Siniko and Tshidiso. Kim, Mosa and Claire analysed the data. Keke's interviews on religion were undertaken by her, Bongani Xezwi, Lufuno Gogoro, Jabulile Msimang and Gugu Khubali. Mosa undertook research for the film *Phakhati*, which she made with Eyelight Productions, and she completed a master's dissertation based on data from the project. Tapiwa Chagonda completed a linked doctoral thesis on the Zimbabwean working class and Claire is in the final throes of completing a related doctorate on public sector workers' strikes. These dissertations were supervised by

Peter, together with Claire, and Profs David Moore and Bridget Kenny. Profs Kenny and Cecilia van Zyl-Schalekamp and Owen undertook a parallel project on the East Rand, which included a survey undertaken by Social Surveys.

We are much obliged to Profs Kenny, Liz Stanley, Satish Deshpande, Erik Olin Wright and Immanuel Wallerstein, and Colin Barker, who joined us for research workshops and offered comradely and incisive advice. Erik's contribution took the form of a memorable seminar that moved around Soweto and stopped at interesting locations for fascinating discussions. Other advice was provided by Profs John Goldthorpe, Owen Crankshaw, Jeremy Seekings, Thea de Wet, Phil Bonner and Eddie Webster, by Drs Blade Nzimande, Claudia Ortu and Grace Khunou, and by Trevor Ngwane.

Peter and Prof. Marcel van der Linden organised a workshop in Amsterdam on 'What is the Working Class? in 2006 and we held an international conference on 'Understanding Class' at UJ in 2009. For the latter, we received stimulating keynote addresses from Profs Wright, Deshpande, Seekings, Alex Callinicos, Mike Savage and José Alcides Figuiredo Santos. Some of the papers from this event were published in a special issue of *South African Review of Sociology* 42(3) (2010), which was edited by Peter, Prof. Deshpande and Kim, with support from the journal's editors, Drs Shireen Ally and Dawson and Prof. Kenny. We also organised an 'Academics and Activists Workshop on the Rebellion of the Poor' at UJ in 2011, with Dr Luke Sinwell as co-convenor.

Conference and seminar presentations and film showings based on our research have taken place in South Africa, Germany, Britain, Turkey, India, Portugal, Russia and the US. We are grateful to the organisers of these events and to participants who gave us advice and provoked us to think more deeply. Some of the material that appears in this book has been published elsewhere. This includes Ceruti (2009) and Ceruti (2011), which appeared in *Review of African Political Economy*; Ceruti (2010); Alexander (2010) and Phadi and Manda (2010), which appeared in *South African Review of Sociology*; and Phadi and Ceruti (2012), which appeared in *African Sociological Review.* We are obliged to reviewers and editors of these publications for sharpening our thinking. The reviewers of the original manuscript of this book provided encouragement and detailed comments, and we are grateful to them.

Editing was a collective activity involving all five of the final members of the team, and the task was completed by Peter and Kim. Alex Potter copy-edited the pre-submission manuscript and Glenda Younge edited the revised version. Thanks to both of them. Louis Gaigher was a patient and supportive managing editor.

Special thanks are due to friends, families and lovers who nourished us with ideas, encouragement and practical support of various kinds. These included Caroline O'Reilly, John and Ivy Alexander, Meisie Jemina Phadi, Mmaletstasi Tsiane Maria Phadi, Ncotsho Pakade, Leo Zeilig, Cheryl Bongers, Anton Wale and Ruth Warren.

Finally, we are immensely grateful to the people of Soweto who inspired our research and took time to answer our questions. Without you this book would not have been possible.

1

Affordability and action

Introduction and overview

Peter Alexander

'The discrepancies in livelihoods across the world are so large that they are without historical precedent and without conceivable justification' (Pieterse 2002: 1–2). This gulf has fed commentary about 'class' both in the popular media and among political analysts. In many countries, the expansion of a new middle class has attracted attention, and this has sometimes been matched by concern about the plight of the poor and the working class. Academic research on class has lagged behind, but even here there has been renewed interest over recent years. However, this scholarship emanates overwhelmingly from the global North, where class structures and social dynamics are different from those in the majority of the world. This book enriches the debate through a study conducted in Soweto, South Africa's largest black township, which provides a home for about one in 30 of the country's 50.6 million inhabitants (Stats SA 2011a).[1]

In South Africa, income inequality and unemployment have reached extreme levels. In terms of Gini co-efficients for income, it is the most unequal country in the world (with the exception of a few with small populations), and Johannesburg – which is where Soweto is located – is the most unequal major city (with a Gini co-efficient of 0.75) (UN HABITAT 2010: 73, 193). The county's unemployment levels are also among the worst in the world, with the official figure standing at 24.9 in early 2012 (Stats SA 2012b). However, a very high proportion of adults is 'not in the labour force', so excluded from this statistic, and others are engaged in survivalist activities. All this may lead one to dismiss South Africa as so exceptional that its class structures and identities can be written off as unique, and thus extraneous to a wider analysis of class. Our view, however, is that the intensity of the contrast between rich and poor in South Africa and the magnitude of joblessness in Soweto and elsewhere, can assist us to comprehend the class nature of those who are excluded by occupation-related analyses or marginalised by a focus on direct relationships to production. In other words, it can contribute to the study of class, not only in lower-income countries, but also in much of the global North, where unemployment and underemployment are now significant issues, both socially and theoretically. In Spain, the second quarter 2012 official rate of unemployment was 24.6 per cent, only 0.3 per cent lower than South Africa's for the same period (*Washington Post* 2012). The urgency of such analysis was underlined by, for instance, the 2011 'riots' in Britain, in which the majority of the participants were outside the labour force and viewed their actions in terms that were diametrically opposed to the majority of the population (Roberts 2011: locations 545, 638).

Our research was motivated by two concerns. In addition to interest in the impact of heightened inequality, there was a related political question. While this had broader implications, we posed it locally. Earlier research had revealed that the more radical of South Africa's social movements were composed overwhelmingly of people who were jobless (Alexander 2006a: 49). In contrast, trade union membership invariably excludes those without jobs. Since 2004 this gap has been highlighted by the development of, on the one hand, 'a rebellion of the poor', in which workers are peripheral, and, on the other hand, a level of strike action that, measured in days lost per capita, was among the highest in the world. Furthermore, there have been political differences between leaders of the Congress of South African Trade Unions (COSATU) and the social movements, and there has sometimes been friction between employed workers and rebelling youth. In this context, we pondered the following question: Is it possible that workers and the poor constitute distinct classes?

We have called this book *Class in Soweto*, a title intended to convey a sense of how people see themselves in class terms, as well as the differences in employment, housing, income and culture we discerned as researchers. The project from which the book emanates was known as 'Classifying Soweto', with this name embodying an understanding of 'classifying' in line with academic usage that signals the importance of social class for analysis of social change. Recognising that apartheid discourse still has purchase and that 'classifying' might be acssociated with racial classification, we decided on a new title. The chapters in this volume were written by different authors, all of whom were engaged in the project and participated in discussions on how to interpret its findings. This opening chapter outlines the project's theoretical and methodological framework, comments on some relevant literature, summarises the various chapters, and then draws on all of these to highlight novel aspects of our account.

The book is innovative in a number of respects. With 69 per cent of adult Sowetans either not in the labour force, unemployed or engaged in survivalist activities, traditional occupation-based categorisation had limited value. Instead we developed nine *employment categories* that reflected different relationships to production (mostly indirect). Each individual could be allocated to an employment category (EC), which was valuable, because it is individuals who engage in different kinds of economic activity, participate in struggle and hold particular identities. This takes us to the second innovation. Unlike previous studies of class identity, and in line with the recognition that people have multiple identities, we permitted respondents to describe themselves using more than one class label. That is, they could say they were middle class or working class, but they could also describe themselves as middle class *and* working class. It turned that out that more than 90 per cent of Sowetans could identify themselves using class terms, but only 38 per cent used a single label.[2] Most Sowetans had *multiple* class identities. We found that there was a material basis for the different class labels. A close association existed between regular employment and 'working-class' identity, and people described as 'lower class' or 'poor' (the two terms were virtually synonymous) tended to suffer greater deprivation than other Sowetans. We also discovered that distinctions between lower-, middle- and upper-class labels were based mainly on a notion of *affordability*, a term derived from popular perceptions that linked identity with EC. When it came to *action*, strikes mobilised people who generally regarded themselves as working class and the rebellion involved mainly people who were not workers, a high proportion of whom were regarded as lower class. However, the distinction was about 'relationships to means and ends of protest', rather than class in any fundamental sense, and we reached the conclusion that, in class terms, Soweto was best understood as a 'differentiated proletarian unity'.

Theoretical and methodological framework

Erik Olin Wright (2005: 180) once asked: 'If "class" is the answer, what is the question?' His point was not only that definitions of class are embedded in distinct theoretical approaches, but also that these approaches are anchored in different kinds of question. Each approach has a primary anchor that establishes the main criteria that 'class' as a concept is designed to fulfil, one or more secondary anchors that help delineate the theoretical reach of the concept, and, in most cases, further questions that are empirically relevant but do not impinge on the definition of class. Wright (2005: 180–92) then sketches out six key questions that, depending upon one's approach, could be regarded as a primary anchor, a secondary anchor or merely empirically relevant. These six questions are about distribution of inequality, subjective location, life chances, antagonistic conflict, historical variation and emancipation. He proposes that the last of these provides Marxism (and himself) with its primary anchor, arguing that, within this tradition, 'class contributes to the critique of capitalist society rather than just to description and explanation'. This book derives from a project animated by just this position – it stimulated the founding questions and it grounded my conceptualisation. But there have also been secondary anchors. Like Wright, we have been concerned with antagonistic conflict. Unlike him, we also prioritised subjective location (and I will return to this later).[3]

Extending Wright's metaphor just a little, an anchor prevents a boat from drifting out to sea, but it allows that boat to rise with the tide and sway with the wind. Our researchers did not have to swear an oath of allegiance to Karl Marx when they were appointed, and discussions between colleagues over theory and over interpretation of data have been part of the pleasure of this project (and, one hopes, these have improved our analysis). We gained a great deal from the work of scholars strongly influenced by Max Weber and we read Pierre Bourdieu's *Distinction* as a team. This affected the design of our questionnaire, and it has flavoured our conclusions. However, the more I have reflected on our findings, the less explanatory value I have found in the work of these two great writers. Of course this is partly, or even largely, because the opening questions had Marxist anchors, but there is more to it than that. Critically, the assumption of relatively stable boundaries implicit in the key concepts of *status group* (Weber) and *habitus* (Bourdieu) make better sense in the contexts in which these terms were developed (respectively, early twentieth-century Germany and 1960s France), than in Soweto at the end of the first decade of the twenty-first century.[4] Had we looked at South Africa when it was more rigidly divided along racial lines, or even, perhaps, if we had considered the whole country today (rather than one large township), it might have been necessary to nuance this point. But the Soweto we researched was the product of rapid social change, and within it there was a good deal of social fluidity and blurring of boundaries. I make use of the term 'poor', deploying it analytically in contradistinction to 'workers', but am not suggesting that the poor constitute a status group (even if we allow for the possibility that a status group can be negatively privileged). A worker might be materially and culturally 'better off' than somebody regarded as 'poor', but workers and the poor tend to share households and neighbourhoods, a person can be a worker one day and 'poor' the next (and vice versa), and disposable income is linked to household demographics. The idea of *habitus* fits, at best, uncomfortably with people holding multiple class identifications, which is what we found (see also Phadi and Ceruti 2011: 91).

There are three theoretical issues that require clarification before proceeding. First, one of the strengths of Marx's 'class' is that it was principally an abstraction (part of his theorisation of the laws of motion of the capitalist mode of production and a prediction about a socialist future). In this sense, there were 'two great classes', capitalists and workers, each internally united by their antagonistic relationship to exploitation. Because class was abstract and exploitation remains central to social dynamics in capitalist society, the concept has continuing salience in the form in which it was initially advanced. However, Marx never formally defined 'class', and he (and Frederick Engels) also used the same word in ways that were historically specific (that is more sociologically and/or politically concrete) (see also Wolpe 1986).[5]

The second issue is this. At the more concrete level, class is about production, but it is also about aspects of social reproduction.[6] The importance of reproduction was acknowledged, especially by Engels (1884: preface), and Marx (1954: 603) writes, for example, about the way the unemployed were 'thrown' onto the 'shoulders' of the working class and *lower middle class*. Today, there is often a larger gap than in Marx's time between classes defined in terms of (1) production and (2) distinctions within the space of reproduction (that is, consumption as well as the reproduction of labour). This arises from a growth in the size of the middle classes, and, in cases like South Africa, an increase in the proportion of people who are either unemployed or underemployed. Consumption can encourage quiescence, but absence of things such as housing of a certain quality can be an important source of struggle. Action may occur in the sphere of production (for instance, a strike) but may also occur in the sphere of reproduction (such as a service delivery protest). Understood in this way, Marxism provides us with the greater flexibility we need to make sense of contemporary society.

The third issue concerns the importance of subjectivity (which Wright does not stress but we do). Here my concern has three components. (1) Changing the world involves agency, and to address this we need to understand how people see themselves consciously and behave unconsciously in class terms. The emphasis on agency derives from the weight Marx and Engels placed on working-class action. This comes, in particular, in the formulation: 'the emancipation of the working class must be the act of the working class itself' (Engels 1969: preface to the English edition of 1888, though similar formulations exist elsewhere). (2) As Alex Callinicos (2006: 2–3) argues, Marx's distinction between class-in-itself and class-for-itself is closely related to one between class as something objective, what Callinicos terms simply 'class', and subjectivity. In this formulation, subjectivity could include subjectivities related to race, gender and so on, but we focused narrowly on class subjectivities. (3) Formulations that clearly distinguish between objective and subjective aspects of class discourage slippage into assumptions that capitalism leads inevitably to socialism, and instead opens possibilities for researching the nature of the relationship between the two dimensions.

We started from the principle that there is value in undertaking an empirical study of class. In order for Marx to theorise the centrality of the working class, he first had to experience it as a collective subject. For this there was probably a seminal moment in August 1844, when he wrote glowingly about Parisian workers and Silesian weavers, and Frederick Engels joined him fresh from Manchester (where he was working on *The Condition of the Working Class in England*).[7] Marx and Engels reflected on what they witnessed, and interpreted this by drawing on their existing theoretical positions. The aim in this project was to proceed in a similar manner, albeit in a more consciously sociological way. In a parallel project, summarised in Chapter 10, we look more directly at contemporary struggle, doing so through the lens of the 'rebellion of the poor'. In neither of these projects has our interest extended to what I defined above as the abstract level of Marx's theory, which was certainly beyond our reach.

What we have done is investigate the interplay between an objective marker of class related to production (what we termed 'employment categories'), some aspects of reproduction (particularly housing and household composition) and subjectivity. The last of these might be further divided into questions of identity (both identity labels and the way in which people describe themselves within broader systems of meanings), culture (subjectivity practised in everyday life) and conflict (how people organise in relation to class struggles). This gives us five main themes, which, in short-hand, we can refer to as production, reproduction, identity, culture and struggle. While chapters cut across themes, Chapters 4 and 5 are mainly about production-related questions, Chapter 3 deals with issues related to reproduction, Chapters 6 and 8 are about identity, and Chapters 7 and 9 look at culture (though in very different ways). The fifth theme, conflict, forms the background to the book and is discussed in Chapter 10. None of this sits perfectly or fully with distinctions outlined above, which have emerged from an attempt to integrate empirical evidence with my own pre-existing theoretical assumptions. The outcome is complex and somewhat messy, but that is the nature of empirical research.

We operationalised our key concepts in various ways. For our 'production' theme, we introduced the notion of *employment category* (EC). Given that some ECs are associated with lack of employment, the term might seem like a misnomer, and it is not ideal, but we used it for want of something better. We consciously avoided 'occupation category' and 'class location', and we did not regard ECs as 'classes' (in any sense). While there was a theoretical basis to the ECs, they were modified to some extent by an iterative engagement with the data. One can see them as defined in terms of relationships to production, whether direct or indirect, and of relationships between the different categories. However, the categorisation should be regarded as provisional, because an acceptable theorisation would require a broader frame of reference, both geographically and in terms of the questions being posed. A further explication of the distinctions and the procedure for allocating individuals to the various categories – a complex and time-consuming process – is provided by Claire Ceruti in Chapter 4.

We ended up with nine ECs. First, there are the *capitalists*, the exploiters. Secondly, there are *regularly employed* workers who stand on the other side of the main class divide within capitalist society. We lumped all workers together, whether or not they directly produce surplus value. The third group, *managers and supervisors*, were employees who exercised some measure of control and surveillance over workers (albeit, in practice, with limited powers). Fourthly, there was the *petty bourgeoisie* (which included self-employed workers), who owned their own business but exploited themselves and employed no more than a handful of staff (commonly family members). The fifth group, the *unemployed*, resemble Marx's 'reserve army of labour' (see Chapters 4 and 10). The next two groups are akin to that part of Marx's 'surplus population' engaged in some kind of work (so not actually part of the reserve army). They include the *survivalist self-employed*, who, unlike the *pretty bourgeoisie*, would have preferred to be regularly employed. Then there are partial workers, whose precise relationships to exploitation varied, but whose conditions were always inferior to those of the regularly employed. In practice, most were engaged on a short-term basis (for example, as day labourers), but we also included people working just a few hours per week, who might, literally, be regularly employed, but were actually unemployed for more than half of what one can regard as a normal working week (that is, 40 hours). Finally, there were two groups that were outside the labour force (in other words, neither employed nor available for employment). These were, eighthly, *students* and, ninthly, *pensioners* and others not in the labour force (for instance, disabled). In some respects these two categories were similar, but they had contrasting expectations of joining the labour force (that is, making themselves available for exploitation).

For our identity theme, we learned from initial qualitative research that people could hold more than one class identity. While this was a surprise, it seemed plausible theoretically.[8] For the survey, the discovery enabled us to ask our key identity question in a novel way – one that moved beyond expecting respondents to select just one identity from a predetermined list. We asked 'would you call yourself . . .

[followed, in turn, by one of eight labels, all of which were derived from the qualitative interviews]'. Our other themes do not require further elucidation at this stage. For 'reproduction' and 'culture', colleagues drew together responses to several, sometimes many, questions in our survey. This was linked with data from qualitative interviews.

A case study of the kind undertaken was suitable for developing and testing concepts and relationships, which is what we needed in order to provide a response to our opening questions. But, why select Soweto? Firstly, it was accessible (indeed, during most of the research, our team was situated on the university's Soweto campus). Secondly, linked to this, we had some prior knowledge of the township's geography and political life. Thirdly, its size, location, leadership and past events meant that it was – and still is – politically important. Fourthly, related to this, there was literature that helped with historical context. Fifthly, its size also meant that it provided a reasonable cross-section of class backgrounds (although this proved to be more limited than anticipated). Sixthly, we wanted to undertake a study that was comprehensive and representative, and Soweto is sufficiently compact and geographically defined to make this possible. Lastly, it provided the possibility to, albeit cautiously, draw out some implications for South Africa as a whole.

Appendix 1 provides a detailed account of our research design and its implementation. The main component was a survey conducted in Soweto in June and July 2006 (which covered adults of sixteen years and over). This included a representative sample of 2 340 respondents and had a response rate which exceeded 90 per cent (that is, very high). Quantitative research was sandwiched between two main rounds of qualitative fieldwork (with some chapters, especially the one on churches, involving further research). Additional data was collected for our research documentary, *Phakathi*. We regarded our approach as broadly Marxist, albeit heterodox. It was intended to capture a particular situation in which those officially regarded as employed were a minority of the adult population (less than one-third if one excludes the underemployed). However, we planned the survey in a way that left open a range of interpretations.

What were the limitations? Firstly, we did not survey Johannesburg's 'suburbs'. This has three significant implications. (1) In the course of our research, it became clear that there had been significant out-migration of better-paid Sowetans, and these were not captured in the survey.[9] (2) There were no white or Indian respondents in our survey and only a few so-called 'coloureds', so the significance of racial differences is largely absent. (3) The research misses out on the wealthy in general and capitalists specifically (though this would probably have been true of any survey-based project). Secondly, we administered our questionnaire and conducted interviews in or outside people's homes, and our findings about identity may have been different had we undertaken research in workplaces. However, one of our researchers conducted preliminary fieldwork in two factories, and his interviewees tended to stress workers' lower-class – as distinct from working-class – identity (Manda 2009). Thirdly, we cannot say anything about the rural areas (including former homelands, farms and mines), the population of which constitutes nearly half the country's total (Gaffney Group 2012: 130). The fourth limitation is that our survey provided a snapshot of a particular moment in time. One significant change was that in 2009, mainly as a consequence of the global financial meltdown, nearly one million jobs were lost in South Africa.[10] In addition, while the 2011 local government election showed that the African National Congress (ANC) remained the dominant political force in Soweto, the proportion of the township's residents who were 'unhappy' with service delivery had increased significantly and many participated in strikes and urban unrest.[11] Despite these limitations, we feel that the class structure and dynamics around class subjectivity that we have revealed have broader relevance, especially for South Africa. Beyond the country's borders, our research will expand the geographical scope of scholarship on class, providing pointers for ongoing theoretical debate.

Some relevant international literature

This section offers reflections on theoretical work that had direct implications for concepts we have used or arguments we have advanced. It is also aimed at establishing a foundation for demonstrating the originality of our findings, analysis and theorisation, which is advanced later in this chapter. A fuller reflection on the literature is available elsewhere (Alexander 2010b). Studies on class in South Africa have more immediate significance and will be considered in the section that follows.

Much debate on class in the 1980s and 1990s pitted Wright, champion of the neo-Marxists, against John Goldthorpe, standard-bearer for the neo-Weberians. Wright's (1978: 30–110) initial attempt to apply Marxism to the class relations of advanced capitalism led him to distinguish six categories associated with control over production.[12] With a concern to place greater weight on disaggregating the middle class, he subsequently developed a scheme that had twelve class locations, with these defined by relations to authority and to scarce skills, as well as means of production (Wright 2000: 15–26). In contrast, Goldthorpe's approach was initially founded on assessments of common life chances that were related to market and work situations, but in a further iteration he stressed the importance of employment relations (distinguishing, on the one hand, employees who are tightly supervised and paid a wage, and, on the other hand, cases in which work requires greater autonomy, and pay and conditions reflect the need for loyalty) (2000: 206–29). Arguably, Wright moved closer to Weberian formulations and Goldthorpe shifted nearer to Marxism (Roberts 2001: 27–31). While Wright's revised approach has, perhaps, made less impact than the earlier one (Roberts 2001: 37; Seekings 2005: 27–8), Goldthorpe's new scheme has had significant influence in Britain, shaping the socio-economic classes used by its Office of National Statistics (ONS). The ONS, however, made one important change. It added an eighth category to Goldthorpe's seven (ONS 2008). This included the long-term unemployed and students, a so-called 'residual', thus recognising the growing importance of these segments of the population and the need to move beyond specific employment relationships. The approaches of both Wright and Goldthorpe have merits. The former contributes to our understanding of class conflict and social transformation, while the latter reveals the extent to which educational achievement, social mobility and voting behaviour are linked to 'class'. However, both have the limitation of seeing class as something rooted only in work relationships, what Rosemary Crompton (2008) termed an 'employment aggregate approach'.

In contrast, there is 'culturalist class analysis', influenced to a greater or lesser degree by different readings (perhaps misreadings) of Bourdieu (who actually placed a good deal of emphasis on production relations) (for example, 1984: 372). The value of this literature is that it challenges one to think about the way in which culture marks out class boundaries, albeit in ways that are often 'ambiguous' and 'fuzzy' (Skeggs 2004: 5). While methodologies have generally been ethnographic – limited in scope, if insightful – Tony Bennett et al. (2009) drew on some of Bourdieu's quantitative work to produce a statistically sophisticated study, conducted in 2003/04, which covered the whole of Britain. They found that cultural variables – covering participation, knowledge and taste – were associated with respondents' 'class', gender and age. While there were no *homologies* (that is, clearly defined groupings of a Bordieuvian kind), the categorical midpoints were distinct in each case.[13] The class model that best fitted the data – that is, that best described how people in Britain practice class – was one that distinguished the middle class, an intermediate class and the working class. The research found that the working class 'neither likes nor is interested in legitimate [high] culture' (Bennett et al. 2009: 252) and that the middle class, especially its higher levels, simply engages in more cultural activity (its members are 'omnivores'). In reading this account, one might conclude that the lack of homologies and the need for an intermediate class reflect the importance of 'ambivalence' (the same might be said of 'fuzziness').

In response to culturalist approaches, Goldthorpe and Tak Wing Chan (2007; Chan and Goldthorpe 2010: 12) argue that we should distinguish, along neo-Weberian lines, between class positions (particularly employment relations) and status order (expressed in a hierarchy of lifestyles associated in particular with 'who eats with whom and who sleeps with whom').[14] Goldthorpe (2008: 351) concludes:

> . . . when we look at things like risk of unemployment or the long-term lifetime development of earnings, class not status is important. If we shift, however, to another field, that of cultural consumption – the extent to which people participate in various forms of music, theater, dance, cinema, and the visual arts – we get the reverse result.

Given that Bennett et al. (2009) use Goldthorpian economic categories (albeit modified), it is perhaps hardly surprising that their conclusions had much in common with those advanced by Goldthorpe. Moreover, both are consonant with a model that recognises that, while people in Britain frequently have difficulties in consciously positioning themselves (in other words, they are often ambivalent), their cultural practices still recognise a distinction between working class and middle class.

In terms of class identity labels, the existing literature makes interesting reading. From 1983 until 1991 the British Social Attitudes Survey (BSAS) included a question about the class people 'belonged' to (Jowell et al. 1993). In 1991 the figures were 29 per cent for the middle classes, 64 per cent for the working classes, and 4 per cent for 'poor'. Regrettably, the series was discontinued, but more recent studies still show that a majority of Britons regard themselves as working class.[15] The US data is better. For instance, American National Election Studies (2010) has asked about class identification since 1956. It requests respondents to select one of four classes, with the followings result in the most recent survey: average working class – 41 per cent; upper working class – 10 per cent; average middle class – 39 per cent; upper middle class – 10 per cent. While the numbers contradict much public discourse about the archaic nature of working-class identification, they go some way to explaining why politicians, especially in the US, but now also in Britain, are concerned about the working-class vote.[16]

However, simple choices of the kind offered in these studies miss the problem of 'ambivalence', discussion on which was initiated by Mike Savage (2000). His interpretation of 200 interviews conducted in Manchester was that, although about two-thirds of respondents could define themselves in class terms, 'identification is usually ambivalent, defensive and hesitant' (see also Savage, Bagnall and Longhurst 2001). He argued: 'class does not seem to be a deeply held personal identity, nor does "class belonging" appear to invoke strong senses of group or collective allegiance. In so far as class is significant, it is largely with respect to politics.' However, Geoff Payne and Clare Grew (2005) re-evaluated the Manchester data and combined this with their own fieldwork, which used similar questions but was conducted in a rural area. They concluded that hesitations and qualifications do not reflect unease about class as such, but rather the genuine difficulties that exist in reaching conclusions about a complex phenomenon. For their respondents, they argued, class was not a simple matter of occupations, but involved assessments about income, attitudes, housing, education and much more.

Discussion about the nature of such ambivalence was taken up in a US study by Michael Hout (2008), which draws on data from the General Social Survey.[17] In this he distinguishes between people who were unambiguously working or middle class and those whose class position was ambiguous. The latter included individuals who were 'living on the border', that is, lower professionals, routine white-collar workers and self-employed manual workers, and/or those subject to 'status inconsistency', such as people with a low-status job and a high income. Among employed people who were unambiguously working class, 71 per cent identified themselves as working class, with a further 8 per cent saying they were lower class; and among those in unambiguously middle-class positions, 77 per cent said they were middle class, with a further 9 per cent self-identifying as upper class. For those in ambiguous positions, the split was 47 per cent middle class, 53 per cent working class and less than one per cent for each of the other two options. Thus, Hout's study suggests that class ambiguity is an important source of ambivalent class identity.

A further twist is provided by Paula Surridge (2007), who probed responses to a question on self-identity asked in the 2003 BSAS. This offered respondents a list of sixteen possible identities from which they were asked to choose three, placing them in order of importance. While those who were most obviously disadvantaged were strongly attracted to a working-class identity, the 'salariat' had a preference for non-class identities. This should be linked with evidence from Bennett et al. (2009: 178), who observed that, while the higher echelon of the middle class was culturally dominant, it rejected any clear class identity, as doing so might invite 'contestation'.[18] So, one might hypothesise that in Britain there is a tendency for different classes to be constituted differently. From a functionalist perspective, this would make sense. For workers, an emphasis on economic boundaries adds legitimacy to arguments on the injustice of domination by a rich minority and, by contrast, the middle class benefits from the outward fuzziness, inner cohesion and confidence associated with cultural capital. However, British reluctance to claim a middle-class identity can be contrasted with the position in the US, where, according to Fiona Devine (2005: 161), people from all economic backgrounds spoke freely about their class identity (with 'middle class' seen as an inclusive category, rather than an exclusive one, as in Britain).

This rich body of international literature has undoubted strengths. In particular, while the importance of culture has been highlighted, the continuing salience of employment relations in shaping critical aspects of social life is also apparent. Further, while research on identity is underdeveloped, what does exist has tended to show that in Britain and the US, class identification retains significance in people's lives, even if this is complicated by ambivalence about what 'class' means. The way class is practised and the extent to which it is verbalised are different in the two countries, and in Britain there is variation between classes. Thus, we are alerted to the need for textured and context-specific analysis if we are to make sense of class, and class identity in particular. However, there are gaps. Most importantly, leading sociological journals have carried few articles on the character of class in the global South and prominent scholars on class appear to be innocent of the theoretical implications of the kinds of structures and identifications that exist outside the North (see Alexander 2010b).[19] In this book, we offer a contribution that addresses this parochialism.

Some views of class in South Africa

The purpose of this review of local literature is broader than our brief reflection on international texts above. In addition to providing a basis for showing how our work builds upon and moves beyond existing scholarship, the aim is to expose South African debates to a wider audience and sketch out some pertinent historical context. There are, of course, ties to the international literature. Marx and Weber have both been influential, and Wright, and, to some extent, Goldthorpe have also made an impact. There have also been moments when South African scholarship has had a resonance internationally, especially through discussion of race and class. Within the local literature, four main problematics can be discerned and are considered below. These are, firstly, the general structure of class relations, including what might be termed the 'white worker debate'; secondly, the contours of class relations in townships; thirdly, the African petty bourgeoisie; and, lastly, class analysis and the poor.

Structure of class relations and the white working class

Initially, discussion about apartheid, which was imposed from 1948 onwards, hinged on the idea of 'caste', seen by Weber (2010) as an extreme form of *Stand* (usually translated as status group). In an early contribution, Leo Kuper (1949: 152–3) wrote about the '"caste-like" characteristics of the social structure', concluding: 'Race factors restrict the rational development of capitalism, by imposing the non-rational use of subordinate labour.' He added:

> . . . the criterion of 'propertylessness' is insufficient to establish the class situation of workers: race is an integral factor, securing and reinforcing non-ownership of productive property as a determinant of the class position of the Native worker, but tending to identify the white non-owner with the owner group.

Pierre van den Bergh (1965: 52–9) reasoned along similar lines, arguing that '"race" is by far the most important criterion of status' and that four 'colour castes' (whites, coloureds, Indians and Africans) were each sub-divided by class. Asserting that there was a lack of class consciousness among white workers, he dismisses – in one sentence – the applicability of a Marxist theory of class to South Africa, adding that the South African labour movement 'has always defined its function as that of protecting the White manual worker against non-White competition'.[20] While 'race' posed a challenge for Marxist analysis, Van den Bergh misread the labour history, which shows that white trade unionists, many of them Marxists, frequently acted in sympathy with black workers (see Alexander 2000: 63, 120–3).

As Jeremy Seekings (2009: 877) observes, in the early 1970s 'Weberian social science was eclipsed, totally and quickly'. It collapsed under pressure from a Marxist critique, which demonstrated that, rather than apartheid being 'non-rational', it was functional to the development of capitalism. The migrant labour system had delivered 'cheap labour' to South African employers and institutionalised racial divisions among workers, thereby boosting profits (Wolpe 1972; Johnstone 1976). The problem for the Weberians was largely political: following Weber, race and class inhabited separate domains, and in the South African case the former was said to be undermining economic development associated with the latter. As a consequence, the Weberians appeared to be shielding capital at a moment when class struggle was growing in importance and when solidarity movements were challenging international businesses that had South African interests.[21]

But how would Marxists handle historical divisions between black and white workers? One approach treated white miners as foremen and then assumed them to be stereotypical of white workers (Simson 1973); another argued that a petty bourgeois component of the 'white wage-earning classes' received some of the surplus extracted from black labour, with these holding sway over the 'white working class proper' through 'ideological class practices' (Davies 1973, 1979: 25); and a third distinguished free white labour and unfree black labour (Johnstone 1976).[22] In contrast, Harold Wolpe (1976) offered a more orthodox Marxist position that emphasised class differences among white 'employees' and criticised writers who exaggerated the political and ideological determinants of class. By 1980 the debate had become scholastic, and a vibrant new labour history was highlighting considerable complexity in the matters at hand (for example, Webster 1978; Marks and Rathbone 1981).[23] Moreover, while white workers were declining – both numerically and in political influence – black workers were growing in number and developing new unions that played an increasingly important role in the struggle against apartheid.

By the mid-1980s, Wolpe (1986) had developed a critique of 'economistic' theories of class. He argued that, in constructing 'class' in purely economic terms, these approaches – whether Weberian or Marxist in origin – assumed either that class relationships were irrelevant to an explanation of apartheid or that an explanation of apartheid could be reduced to class interests (including the interests of different class fractions). Actually, Wolpe's own earlier account of apartheid – emphasising the benefits of apartheid for capitalism – was itself economistic (and, as a consequence, obscured the potential for the system to unravel). His new position, with which I concur, took a different tack:

> . . . while at one level classes must be conceived of as unitary entities, concretely, to the contrary, their internal unity is always problematic. In the sphere of production and exchange, classes exist in forms which are fragmented and fractured by politics, culture, ideology and, indeed, the concrete organisation of production and distribution itself . . . One might say that class unity, when it occurs, is a conjunctural phenomenon (Wolpe 1986: 121).

An abstract analysis of class is required, because it can reveal processes that are otherwise hidden, but it is not sufficient. The significance of Wolpe's approach is not only historical (associated with the 'white working class' and so on), but also relates directly to our own study. That is, one should not expect to find a direct and simple relationship between class – as something objective – and its subjective manifestations (whether self-identity, culture or struggle).[24]

Class in the townships

Alongside this theoretical debate, a series of rich ethnographic monographs was providing a picture of stratification in South African townships in the 1950s, 1960s and 1970s. As Seekings (2009: 871) observes: '[T]hese studies . . . were important in breaking with anthropological scholarship that prioritised either ethnicity or rural-urban differences.' They included books by Monica Wilson and Archie Mafeje (1963), whose fieldwork in Langa was undertaken between 1955 and 1962; Leo Kuper (1965), who did research in Durban between 1958 and 1961; Mia Brandel-Syrier (1971), who worked on an East Rand township between 1958 and 1967; Thomas Nyquist (1983), who conducted fieldwork in Grahamstown in 1966/67 and 1975; and Philip Mayer (1977), whose research in Soweto was undertaken in 1965 and again in 1975/76.

The subject matter of these accounts was similar, although the terminology varied. Wilson and Mafeje write about 'class'; Kuper was particularly interested in the way that status (meaning 'prestige') was associated with occupation, but he is not consistent and also talks about 'class'; Brandel-Syrier's account is about strata, but she generally refers to 'class' or 'status' (which she used interchangeably); Nyquist's study ranks people according to occupation; and Mayer (1977: 16) analyses 'class' perceptions, which he said were 'basically perceptions of status groups'.

Wilson and Mafeje (1963: 13–46) show people distinguishing between three groups: migrant labourers, semi-urbanised folks and 'townsmen'. The latter group included 'decent people' (who ranged from university students, through secretaries, nurses, ministers of religion and teachers, to lawyers and doctors), other respectable people (mainly small traders), and a younger generation of 'location boys' and 'girls' that included factory workers. Kuper (1965: 127–9) includes a survey of 99 teachers, 77 of whom thought that 'class differences' existed. Of these, 34 said there were three classes, sixteen said there were two and fourteen said four. His sample was small and selective, but the proportions are remarkably similar to those we found in Soweto. The way people justified these numbers varied greatly, but most included an educated grouping – similar to the 'decent people' – as the top class. Brandel-Syrier's (1971: xxvi–vii) informants generally offered a three-class model as well, but, she notes, the classificatory indicators varied, with locals offering finer distinctions than Africans with a 'national point of view'. In Nyquist's (1983: 21–5) study, 86 per cent of 301 respondents said that there were three 'levels' among Africans in Grahamstown (the high, the middle and the low). Those regarded as having a 'high' ranking were, once more, similar to Wilson and Mafeje's 'decent people' (with doctors at the top), but they also included carpenters; the 'middle' class included other artisans, police constables, shop assistants, waiters, petrol attendants and, interestingly, domestic servants; and the 'lower' class comprised herbalists, labourers, shebeen queens and, at the very bottom, latrine workers.

Mayer's analysis, which is particularly pertinent (and is considered again in Chapters 2 and 8), adds a new dimension to Brandel-Syrier's notion of 'point of view'. He shows that, whereas the 'class model' – which identified an exploitative relationship between white capitalists and black workers – was articulated by 'ordinary working people', educated respondents tended to express themselves in terms of racial domination (Mayer 1977: 23–32).[25] Within Soweto, working people saw themselves as near the 'middle', but the educated and better off also placed themselves at the centre, pushing 'ordinary people' towards the bottom (Mayer 1977: 123–4). The 'educated rich' were sometimes distinguished from the 'rich rich', referred to as 'tycoons', who, Mayer (1977: 106) writes, were often no more than shopkeepers. Lower down the hierarchy than factory workers came labourers and domestic servants, who considered themselves, and were considered by others, to be 'poor people'; and beneath them there were the 'very poor', the destitute, 'people who live through suffering' (Mayer 1977: 111).[26]

We can add a few further points that provide valuable context for understanding Soweto today – sometimes suggesting a counterpoint, more often a continuity. Firstly, in all these cases, prestige was linked more to education than to money, but in practice the better off were nearly always the better educated (although this was already changing in Soweto before 1976). Moreover, education and income were related to occupation, so one can have sympathy for writers who, in neo-Weberian terms, muddled class and status.[27] Secondly, the top stratum was marked off by two kinds of cultural difference: (1) refinement, in particular the use of English (even for conversations between friends), and (2) conspicuous consumption in the form of housing, cars, furniture, fashionable clothes and appearance (for instance, hair straightening) (for examples, see Wilson and Mafeje 1963: 137–8; Kuper 1965: 112, 138; Brandel-Syrier 1971: 87, 94; Mayer 1977: 68). Traders might have the income required for consumption, but they rarely achieved refinement. Thirdly, this top stratum was small. In Brandel-Syrier's (1971: 94) case, the educated elite was as small as half a per cent of the township's total population and the business elite was smaller still. Numerically, teachers were the largest educated group, but there were social distinctions among them and not all were considered part of the elite (Brandel-Syrier 1971: 64–5; Nyquist 1983: 44). Fourthly, while small, the elite – at least at its higher level – was relatively cohesive, engaging in common social activities and often intermarrying (Wilson and Mafeje 1963: 138–40; Nyquist 1983: 96–110). The elite generally preferred the old mission churches (Methodist, Anglican, Catholic, etc.), which had higher status than the Zionist and Ethiopian churches

(Kuper 1965: 99, 137; Nyquist 1983: 69). Fifthly, the unemployed are barely mentioned in these studies – which is not surprising, given that unemployment had not yet become a visible problem – but Mayer (1977: 102) notes that 'the poor suffer from spells of unemployment'. Lastly, with the exception of a few activists, class divisions among Africans were regarded as separate from those among whites and only a few Africans were better off than the poorest whites.

The reader will find commonalities between these accounts and our own, including the prevalence of a three-class model, the association between church type and status, the use of the word 'tycoon' and the prevalence of the phrase 'live through suffering'. These studies also show that there is nothing new about consumerism, even if its relative importance has increased as a marker of status; this at the expense of education, which, though, is still important. The combination of exploitation and hierarchical models of class remains widespread in Soweto.

African petty bourgeoisie

As contestation over the 'white working class' waned, interest in the African petty bourgeoisie expanded. Again, the debate had political significance; this time because of implications for how one characterised the leadership of the liberation struggle and for the kind of class alliances that should be supported. By 'petty bourgeoisie' writers mean something analogous to those defined above as 'decent', or 'elite,' or 'top stratum', or 'better off' (and sometimes 'bourgeoisie' or 'upper class'). While 'petty bourgeoisie' is subjective, it is more precise than 'middle class', a vague identity term claimed by a much larger number of Africans (and, of course, others generally).

From historical and ethnographic accounts it is clear that, until the 1970s, the petty bourgeoisie was numerically small yet consistently provided leadership for urban Africans in general and the ANC in particular. As part of a social history of the Transvaal Native Congress in the years 1917–20, Philip Bonner proposed that the petty bourgeoisie – whether professionals or owners of small businesses – could be pulled either in the direction of capital or that of labour, and the way this was resolved related to place and time. In his case, the 'place' was a colonial setting where the petty bourgeoisie was 'stunted and repressed' and the boundary between it and the working class was blurred; and the 'time' was one of an 'immensely powerful upsurge of working-class agitation' (Bonner 1982: 305). The outcome, Bonner (1982: 305) shows, was a leadership that had its own 'sectional interests' and placed its own 'stamp on events', but 'were not mere manipulators'. They were 'radicalised' though also 'fragmented' by events going on around them. Bonner's was an insightful application of a Marxist conception of class to an important phenomenon at a particular conjuncture. In other moments, the petty bourgeoisie might be differently formed, come under different influences and play a different role in history.[28]

His account was followed by a more theoretical dispute about the growth of the African petty bourgeoisie from the 1960s onwards. In attempting to assess the extent and character of this expansion, Owen Crankshaw (1986) engaged with contrasting theories offered by Wright and Nicos Poulantzas. We have already encountered the former. The upshot of Poulantzas's (1975) position was that all those not engaged in direct production of surplus value – including, for instance, routine white-collar workers – should be included as part of a 'new petty bourgeoisie'.[29] Crankshaw's (1986) estimate was that this 'new petty bourgeoisie' numbered about 35 per cent of wage earners by 1983. According to him, Wright would have placed all but about 9 per cent of these among the proletariat or 'semi-autonomous employees'. The wider significance of the argument was that, if one accepted the broad (that is, Poulantzian) definition, it helped justify the working class holding back on its own demands in order to develop a broader alliance. Actually, many of the 'semi-autonomous employees' could have been included as part of the proletariat. This was specifically true of school teachers, who, by 1980 – following the massification of African schooling and the transformation of teaching into a mainly black occupation – were busy converting professional associations into unions (Crankshaw 1997: 89; Amoako 2012).[30] A further problem with the statistics is that they refer to employees, thus excluding the unemployed, and hence giving an inflated impression of the proportion of the African population who could be regarded as petty bourgeois under any definition.

Bonginkosi 'Blade' Nzimande (1990; 1991) advanced the debate by distinguishing divergent interests within the African petty bourgeoisie. For Nzimande (1990: 181–209), there were four 'strata' (his term). The first was the *bureaucratic petty bourgeoisie*, the senior functionaries in the Bantustans and townships. Secondly, there was the *civil petty bourgeoisie*, that is, state employees (mostly teachers, nurses and clerks), which was the largest of the four strata. Thirdly, there was a *corporate petty bourgeoisie*, which 'closely identifies with a free market', was hostile to the apartheid state and under pressure from the militancy of the working class. Finally, there was the *trading petty bourgeoisie*, which included one component that was closely associated with the bureaucratic petty bourgeoisie and another that was said to be 'autonomous'.[31] Under the right conditions, the civil petty bourgeoisie, part of the corporate petty bourgeoisie and the autonomous trading petty bourgeoisie might ally with the working class. Nzimande's categorisation had much to offer. In particular, it took us beyond the horizons of the township, created a better sense of diversity within the African petty bourgeoisie, and drew attention to the impact of the state, as well as capital and labour. However, fundamental changes have occurred since the study was completed in 1991, and one doubts whether the 'African petty bourgeoisie', in the form described by Nzimande, still exists in a meaningful way. While one element emerged as capitalists and rulers, a much larger component is identifiable as workers.[32]

Recent academic research on the petty bourgeoisie is limited. However, an interview-based study of black corporate managers by Geoffrey Modisha (2007) yielded insights that are particularly relevant for our own account. All the managers lived in the suburbs, but whereas the more junior ones came from trade union backgrounds, lacked formal qualifications and had parents in traditional working-class occupations, the more senior had formal qualifications and most had parents in professional positions. An important experience that most of these managers had in common, and which distinguished them from their white colleagues, was a need to negotiate relationships with kin who were generally poorer and living in townships. One explained: 'I can't actually get rich in a short period of time, because I share the money with members of my extended families because they are not working.' Respondents who maintained links with their families living in townships said things like: 'People are always looking for employment from me . . . Some people are crying in front of me.' By contrast, the managers who came from a professional background tended to cut ties with their relatives, with one explaining: 'I struggle to live with those people because of my interpretation of reality.'

Modisha's analysis recognises the importance of 'levels' within corporate hierarchies, and his contrast between black and white managers shows how people from dissimilar backgrounds experience the same class location in different ways. Thus, he adds further complexity to the account of politically salient class characteristics provided by Bonner, Nzimande and others. In sum, one's specific 'position' within the petty bourgeoisie shapes one's judgements, but so too does personal history and the 'pull' of external forces (capital, labour and the state). In the second decade of the twentieth century and in the 1980s, powerful working-class movements were able to radicalise important sections of the petty bourgeoisie, but is the working class still sufficiently coherent to have a similar impact today?

Unemployment and class analysis

Modisha's interviews point to the anguish and suffering associated with poverty and unemployment. Thus, he takes us to matters at the heart of South Africa's social crisis and to the main focus of current debate around class.

The problem of unemployment did not become apparent until the 1970s. This was largely because influx controls ensured that jobless Africans were hidden away in the Bantustans, mainly in rural resettlement slums. Urban unemployment had been 'displaced', to quote Charles Simkins (1981). He and Cosmas Desmond (1978: vii) state bluntly that from 1960 South African unemployment never fell below one million. The rate rose steeply from the last years of the decade, dipped in the mid-1970s, and then rose continuously through the 1980s (Crankshaw 1997: 104–5).[33] Unemployment underpinned the 1970s and 1980s struggle against apartheid in two ways. Firstly, it provided a critical mass of young recruits for township resistance. Secondly, the increased burden of unemployment wiped out the benefit of improved wages, pushing workers to fight for higher pay, leading in turn to stronger union organisation and heightened class consciousness. According to official statistics, the expanded rate of unemployment (that is, including discouraged job seekers) stood at 28.6 per cent in 1994; it peaked at 41.8 per cent in 2002; then went down, but up again following the slump of 2008/09, reaching 33.8 per cent in early 2012 (a figure that represented 6.9 million adults of working age) (Altman 2003; Stats SA 2012a, 2011a). South Africa's level of unemployment is worse now than at any time under apartheid and is more pronounced than anywhere else in the world.

The unemployed – and the 'poor' more generally – highlight a problem for occupation-based class analysis: how does one 'class' people who have no occupation? In the South African context, where the issue is presented in stark relief, this conundrum has been addressed by some of the country's leading sociologists. My comments here are reinforced in Chapter 4 by Ceruti.

An important contribution to this debate was made by Seekings and Nicoli Nattrass (2005), who began their analysis with Goldthorpe's revised scheme, and modified this to take account of South African conditions. Their main theoretical innovation was to move from an assessment based on individuals to one based on households, which they justified by reference to Wright's notion of mediation. Everybody in a household was allocated to the occupation of its 'dominant' member. This was modified to take account of household income from wealth and entrepreneurial activity (so long as this was greater than a government pension).[34] This left a residual category that included households in which nobody was employed and where income from these other sources was negligible. From here, Seekings and Nattrass (2005) mapped the 'class structure', which they presented in the form of a pyramid with three layers, and then used this model to summarise changes that occurred with the ending of apartheid. They found that the top layer became deracialised and better off; the middle, which included the 'core working class', was also generally better off, but had declined in size; and the bottom (which included the 'marginal working class' and the residual category) was mostly worse off and had grown in size.[35] The approach is responsive to South African conditions, and as a means of describing significant aspects of social transformation it is helpful. But if one wants to explore the relationship of 'classes' to subjectivities, we need an account that recognises that people are individuals as well as members of households. Further, the dominance principle undervalues the size and impact of poverty by allocating many of the unemployed, for instance, to a 'higher' class. Moreover, what individuals can 'afford' will be determined by the composition of the whole household (particularly its size and number of income earners) and not just the occupation of its dominant member and income from wealth and entrepreneurship.

Seekings and Nattrass (2005) also took up the issue of whether or not part of the unemployed constituted an underclass. Their response disaggregated their residual, defining as 'underclass' only 'households with no employed members and thus no social capital' (Seekings and Nattrass 2005: 289). This solution is elegant but, as with Wright's (1978: 93) attempt to grapple with the same issue, it is also problematic.[36] Lack of employment in a household is not the same as absence of social capital – people can be jobless and still have friends, go to church, attend the weddings and funerals of their extended family, and receive remittances from a mother or father who works away from home.[37] Being part of a poverty-stricken household is likely to have an adverse impact on life chances, but poverty is widespread and cannot be reduced to households without any employed members. In a recent reflection, Seekings (2008a: 23) insists that there is 'a discrete "underclass" or lower class separate from the "working class" ', but acknowledges that this 'can be identified by any number of criteria' and 'the appropriate label for this class can be debated'. It would seem, then, that a problem remains. I would certainly not wish to suggest that this is an easy matter but, from the perspective of the questions we are asking, it is possible to simply recognise that some people are unemployed. Difficulties arise when one merges 'class' and what are essentially occupation-based categories.[38]

An alternative theorisation was advanced by Karl von Holdt and Edward Webster (2005), who represent their position diagrammatically in the form of an onion (reproduced in Chapter 4). This includes a core of full-time workers; a ring of outsourced, temporary, part-time and domestic workers; a further ring of informal workers; and an outer layer comprising the unemployed (Von Holdt and Webster 2005: 28; see also Webster 2006; May and Meth 2007). This model refocuses attention on individuals, it shows movement between the different layers and it avoids slicing off a separate underclass. However, while households are mentioned, they are not integrated into the model and the two in five South African adults 'not in the labour force' are missing. The strength of the argument – and it is considerable – is its concern with organisational questions. The limitation of trade unions (specifically COSATU) in failing to move beyond the core is recognised, and the authors advocate the importance of community-based movements that mobilise people outside the nucleus. For 'a counter movement to truly be effective', they argue, it should link workplace and community struggles, adding: 'in other words, uniting the trade union movement and social movements in a broad coalition against the destructive impact of the market on society' (Von Holdt and Webster 2005: 38). Unfortunately, their view of organisation is somewhat formalistic, with social movements seen as the equivalent of trade unions. Mass organisation among the jobless is far more difficult to sustain than among workers, and successful mobilisation tends to be short term, thus posing critical strategic and tactical dilemmas.

Von Holdt (2011: 6) has now broadened his analysis, proposing that 'a rapid process of class formation' is underway in South Africa. He points to an important shift: among black people, in particular, there is a growing gulf between those who, at the one end of the spectrum, have become part of the ruling class, either as capitalists (still far smaller in numbers and less wealthy than their white counterparts) or as part of the governing elite, and, at the other end, those who Von Holdt describes as the 'unemployed and precariously employed'. One aspect of this phenomenon is migration from townships to suburbs, involving, according to a 2008 study, some 12 000 black families per month, in the six largest cities alone (National Planning Commission 2011).[39] An associated process is access to better-performing schools, which has implications for entry to better-paid jobs (Simkins 2005). But it is difficult to see how these processes amount to the creation of new classes.

Main findings

We now consider how our own research adds to the literature discussed above.

In Chapter 2 Kim Wale provides an overview of the history of 'class' in Soweto. The township's origins were as a residential area designed mainly for workers living in married circumstances. In 1946 the council provided space for the educated elite in an area known as Dube, and from the late 1950s hostels were built for migrant workers, adding another component to Soweto's social mix. While restrictions on the development of the black middle class led to a measure of 'class compression', the Soweto uprising of 1976 was followed by attempts to improve the position of better-off urbanites and to lock the new unions, growing apace, into state-sponsored negotiating procedures. But the plan backfired. Throughout the 1980s, the elite provided leadership for a community whose school students and unemployed youth were becoming increasingly militant. Meanwhile, workers advanced a class struggle that merged with activity in the township to create a force that was central to the overthrow of apartheid. In the post-apartheid years, there has been significant class differentiation, with better-off people generally moving out of the township and increased poverty occurring within it. Before the end of apartheid, growing numbers of people were living in shacks, and many people still live in such conditions.

In Chapter 3 Ceruti paints a picture of contemporary Soweto that draws mainly on quantitative data, much of it gathered as part of our 2006 survey. She shows that the population of the township was growing, in part because of continuing in-migration. On a number of indicators, its residents tended to be a little better off than other South Africans, but the rates of unemployment were higher than the average for the country. Housing provides the main focus of the chapter. Here the evidence lends support to findings from other researchers that there is growing differentiation. A minority live in relatively costly new houses or in substantially improved older ones, while the majority reside in former council houses that have not been upgraded, backyard rooms, shacks and hostels. However, Ceruti cautions against an oversimplified view that equates better housing types with work status or higher income, showing that other factors contribute to the differentiation, including household size and when people came to Soweto. Significantly, people without work live in close proximity to others with regular salaries. Indeed, among our respondents, those living in backyard shacks were more likely to be receiving a regular wage than to be unemployed, and the proportion of unemployed was above average for Soweto among those living in unrenovated former council houses (which are superior in quality to shacks).

In Chapter 4 Ceruti extends her account onto the terrain of employment and unemployment. Drawing on the survey, she shows that only 24 per cent of Sowetans were 'regularly employed workers', with a further 7 per cent categorised as petty bourgeoisie, managers or capitalists. The remaining 69 per cent were either fully unemployed, engaged in survivalist activities, or outside the labour force by virtue of being students or pensioners. In these circumstances, an occupation-aggregate approach to class analysis is unhelpful, because it leaves a large majority of the population 'unclassed', unless, perhaps, they are treated as appendages of people with jobs (which, as we have seen, creates further problems). Ceruti opts for an approach that emphasises the 'community of fate' that exists between those who are employed and those without regular jobs. The critical issue is the role played by households in ensuring survival through the redistribution of resources, with the effect that the ratio of earners to dependants can have a considerable impact on experiences of poverty. Ceruti develops Marx's concept of the labour reserve and surplus population to propose a dynamic-systemic model of class, where different experiences of exploitation may be crosscut by common experiences of home life. For Ceruti, Soweto is overwhelmingly a *differentiated proletarian township*, where 'proletarian' is taken to mean 'those without property'. While differences between workers and the unemployed do not amount to class differences, differentiation tends to obscure commonality in the popular imagination.

Chapter 5 rounds off the discussion of class and employment. It does so through an analysis of 'underemployment' undertaken by Wale and myself. The 'underemployed' include two components: the survivalist self-employed and partial workers. We show that the households of the underemployed tend to be worse off than those of the unemployed. To explain this, we draw on an Indian aphorism that 'the poor are too poor to be unemployed'. That is, for most adults, unemployment is only possible if a member of one's family has some source of income, whether it is a wage or a grant of some kind. The implication is that government statistics for unemployment – even those based on the expanded measure – are an unsatisfactory indicator of social well-being. The labour absorption rate – the percentage of the working-age population in employment – is more useful, and for South Africa this is the lowest for any major country, at just over 40 per cent. But, on interrogating this figure further, we find that only 27 per cent of the working-age population is formally employed.

In Chapter 6 we move the focus to 'subjective' aspects of class as they were reflected in our survey and qualitative research in Chapter 6. The data presented by Mosa Phadi and Ceruti shows that a very high proportion of Soweto's adults have some class awareness. For instance, extrapolating from our survey, 93 per cent of Sowetans gave themselves at least one class label. However, only 38 per cent accepted *just* one label. The main forms of multiple class identity were (1) poor/lower combined with middle and (2) working combined with middle, both of which are reasonable responses in the context of what we came to know about class identity in Soweto. The dominant model was based on three classes, with some kind of upper, middle and lower (including poor) classes. 'Working class' was a supplementary identity. In qualitative interviews the upper class was pictured as comprising those with a 'luxury life', but in the survey those claiming the identity, a small minority, were not especially well off and were distinguished mainly by their self-confidence. The middle-class identity was nebulous. While it represented those who were neither 'upper' nor 'lower', the precise definitions varied. The poor or lower class – the two were used as synonyms – were indeed poorer than other people, and this included lower levels of educational attainment. Extrapolating from the survey, 66 per cent of Sowetans claimed a middle-class identity, with 'working class' coming second at 43 per cent.

In Chapter 7 Wale draws on her reading of interview transcripts to develop an argument that links the pivotal concept of affordability with different forms of class consciousness present in respondents' worldviews. She begins by reminding us that affordability mediates class as economic difference and class as cultural difference. Then, using the metaphor of a ladder, she argues that when people look 'upwards', they tend to emphasise cultural and individual expressions of class, but when they look downwards, poverty and lack of work come to the fore. Wale's account then moves to a discussion of competing worldviews and their relationship to the ladder. The implications of her account are contradictory. On the one hand, class difference is not necessarily seen as something bad: it may be associated with a system that is basically just, and is thus politicised in a way that reinforces the status quo. On the other hand, where mobility is stunted, either through economic impediments or through race, feelings of injustice increase and with them the potential that class, perhaps alongside race, can be mobilised by a counter-hegemonic movement. Thus, affordability matters, not only as a concept that permits a holistic understanding of class, but also as a reality that is pregnant with possibilities for social change.

In Chapter 8 Phadi and Owen Manda explore how Sowetans' understandings of class are shaped by terms available to them in their indigenous languages. Raymond Williams (1976), discussed by the authors, regarded 'class' as a 'difficult word'. In South Africa, difficulty is magnified by the interaction of indigenous terminology, originally constructed in particular rural contexts, with this already 'difficult word'. Two empirical issues are considered. Firstly, there is no general term that can be equated with 'class' as used in a primarily economic sense. The nearest counterparts convey implications of standing, status or level. Secondly, while there are no direct equivalents for specific class terms, several words are associated with poverty and a number are related to wealth. But 'middle class' poses a particular problem because the closest translation in indigenous South African languages means 'in the middle', creating possibilities for numerous interpretations. This helps to explain why such a high proportion of Sowetans consider themselves to be middle class. 'Working class' creates further 'difficulty', with people tending to translate it as meaning 'those who work', thus limiting the potential for developing a class vocabulary with broad emancipatory implications. This chapter has wider significance because it reveals the inadequacy of imposing an English-language template (with all its 'difficulty') on a non-English setting, where people are likely to be framing their worldviews according to different standards and where a common term – 'middle class', for instance – may have different meanings.

Chapter 9, by Keke Motseke and Sibongile Mazibuko, analyses the relationship between class and church. This is important because our survey showed that 87 per cent of Sowetans were Christians (more than the national average) and almost half the population had attended church in the previous seven days. In terms of affiliation, the mainline churches (such as Catholic and Anglican) have less support than reflected in ethnographic accounts reviewed above, with only 26 per cent of the population associating with them. These have been overtaken by the African Independent Churches (AICs) (27 per cent of the population), and the Pentacostals are growing (12 per cent). Firstly, as has been true historically, there is a tendency for poorer people to be attracted to the AICs and for those who are better off to associate with mainline churches. Secondly, while the significance of class was widely denied and in some churches wealthier congregants helped those who were poorer, class differences were often manifest in clothing, seating position and the kind of people who took leadership positions. The general proposition is that people attend a church where they feel socially accepted and where their needs and aspirations are nourished, and this means that class is implicated in church attendance.

Chapter 10 provides my conclusion. There are two appendices. In Appendix 1, Ceruti and I describe the methods used in this study. In particular, we provide details about the quantitative survey: definition of population, questionnaire design, sampling procedures, data collection, response rate and weighting. In Appendix 2, Ceruti provides additional information about Sowetans drawn from the survey. This includes demographics, levels of educational attainment, mother tongue and political support. Only 9 per cent of the population were members of a trade union, but 88 per cent 'felt close' to the unemployed. Finally, the film *Phakathi: Soweto's Middling Class* is available from the South African Research Chair in Social Change at the University of Johannesburg and can be viewed on www.youtube.com. This documentary, made by Phadi and others as part of the project, explores the reasons why such a high proportion of Sowetans regarded themselves as middle class.

Summary

The volume's conclusions are presented in the final chapter. Here I draw together aspects of the theoretical framework, relevant literature and chapter outlines as a means of signalling key issues.

Our 'anchoring question' was about emancipation – posed in the context of South Africa's acute social inequalities and intense but separate struggles by workers and the poor. The methodology, broadly Marxist in character, aimed at exploring the relationship between an objective marker of employment relations, aspects of social reproduction and various classed subjectivities. In Soweto, a large majority of the adult population is either unemployed, underemployed or not in the labour force, thus exposing the need for a model that moves beyond occupational classification. For us, assigning the class position of the 'dominant' member of a household to each member of that household did not provide a solution, because it is individuals, rather than households, who have class identities and engage in struggle. Our approach involved developing nine ECs, with these capable of accommodating the entirety of our sample.

Our questions on identity revealed that more than 90 per cent of Soweto's population could define themselves in class terms. Typically, people thought there were three classes – that is, some version of lower, middle and upper class – but, when asked about their own identity, the second largest number described themselves as working class. Initial qualitative research had led us to ask about identification in a way that was novel in two respects. First, the class labels offered were derived from interviews rather than preconceived, and, secondly, respondents could select more than one label. In practice, most people selected at least one such label (for example, poor and middle class or working class and middle class). One can hypothesise that an important reason for multiple class identification is that 'class' names two distinct experiences. It distinguishes a worker from those who benefit by exerting control over their labour, but it also distinguishes those regarded as in some measure better off from those who are less so (commonly producing three classes). Moreover, the boundaries within these experiences are often unclear. This can be true of relational class, especially in large corporations and the state, with their long chains of command and separation of management from ownership. However, it is particularly the case with hierarchical class, where the signifiers of difference are varied (such as income, education, housing, clothes, language/accent). People are making sense of different social realities, and thus identification with two or more classes is rational. That is, while people recognise the importance of class (however defined), they often have difficulty aligning themselves with a single class label because class identities are, genuinely and for good reason, associated with more than one phenomenon.

There is also an objective basis for class identities. 'Working class' was associated with having a job, and the most popular identity of regularly employed workers was 'working class'. By contrast, people describing themselves as 'lower class' tended to be more deprived than those who did not. Popular perceptions of class generally referenced 'affordability', a word used in English that also had mother-tongue equivalents.[40] For instance, the 'middle class' were said to be 'in the middle' between those who could *afford* everything (the upper class, rich, etc.) and those who were suffering (the lower class, poor etc.). 'Affordability' provides a link from subjective experiences (including classed culture and verbalised class identities), through income, to occupation (or lack of occupation). Thus, it connects consumption and production. In addition, while people mention individual attributes and cultural associations when they look 'upwards' in class terms, they refer to lack of basic resources when they look 'down'. This reinforces suggestions in some sociological literature that the way people define 'class' might be affected by their class location, with those defined as 'middle class' mainly concerned with cultural referents and the 'working class' and 'poor' emphasising the importance of economic markers.

An important twist in our account of class identity arose when considering the mother-tongue terms that were available when people were translating class-related words into English. Notably, this showed that when people use the term 'middle class', they are very often translating from a word that means 'in the middle', which is far more inclusive. This, in turn, helps to explain why 'middle class' was the most popular class identity.

With regularly employed workers tending to identify themselves as 'working class', and pensioners, the underemployed and unemployed more likely to describe themselves as 'poor', it might seem that there is a firm basis for distinguishing a working class from a poor or lower class. But this is not the position we adopted. Within Soweto, there was little evidence of antagonism associated with ECs or class identity, and better-off people were generally sympathetic to those who were poorer. This reflected life histories and the close physical proximity of workers and the unemployed. Households tended to re-distribute resources from better-placed family members to those who were poorer. Kin, friends, neighbours, churches and so on provided material support in the form of things like food, school fees and loans, but also, for instance, information about job opportunities. In terms of accommodation, there were no sharp divisions between the kind of housing occupied by, for example, the unemployed and the regularly waged. In terms of identity, most people were not either 'working class' or 'poor', rather they described themselves as 'middle class' or accepted more than one class label. So, while there is a gap between 'workers' and 'the poor', it is mitigated by a range of factors.

In the sense that Sowetans, bar a small minority, are either workers, 'wannabe' workers (including subsistence self-employed), retired workers or directly dependent on workers (including most students), Soweto is predominantly a proletarian township. However, there is considerable variation. It is a differentiated unity. Common interests are cut through by different daily experiences of work, survival and inter-personal relationships, and by the different capacities to mobilise to change those experiences. But the long-term interests of workers and the poor are similar, unlike those of workers and capitalists.

Our research was framed by concerns about divisions between workers and the poor that existed in the face of massive inequality, and it was informed by theoretical assumptions and a methodological stance derived from Marxism. How well does Marxism stand up to challenges posed by the findings and analysis presented in the chapters that follow? A response to this question is offered in Chapter 10. Here, though, we can acknowledge that for Marx and Engels tasks of the kind we have undertaken were not merely about defining and theorising problems, they were also about helping to chart a solution. Their conclusions recognised the importance of 'class' as part of the struggle for a classless society. We make no pretence to have produced a book with a different ending, but I hope the reader finds merit in the evidence and argument we use to get there.

Notes

1. This ratio assumes that the population of Soweto at the time of writing (August 2012) was nearly 1.5 million, which is a very rough approximation based on figures presented in Chapter 3 and a measure of subsequent growth similar to that for Gauteng (the province in which Soweto is located). More reliable numbers will be available once the results of the national census conducted in October 2011 are published. For the broader Johannesburg context, see Beall, Crankshaw and Parnell (2002b).
2. In a Cape Town study, where respondents were asked to choose between one of four classes, only 2 per cent failed to choose one of the four (Seekings 2007a: 14).
3. Wright regards 'life chances' as a secondary anchor, reflecting, perhaps, the influence of Max Weber.
4. There is no intention here to equate Weber's 'Class, status, party' and Bourdieu's *Distinction* (where the concepts of, respectively, 'status group' and 'habitus' are explained). The former is vast and unspecific in its reach (though short in length); the latter is time and place specific (though very long). 'Class, status, party' appeared as a chapter in *Economy and Society*, first published in 1921, but was probably written before the First World War according to Dagmar Waters et al. (Weber 2010). *Distinction* was not published until 1979 (in French), but it is based on survey data from 1963 and 1967–68 and, according to Richard Jenkins (2002: 74), Bourdieu's use of *habitus* dates from 1967. Bourdieu (1984: xi, 513), himself, drew attention to the fact that his survey 'measured relatively stable dispositions' and also to the 'Frenchness' of his book.
5. For instance, Engels's (1969) descriptions of various components of the working class in *The Condition of the Working Class in England*, his and Marx's (1965) discussion of 'petty-bourgeois socialism' in the *Communist Manifesto*, and Marx's (1954: 617) references to 'lower middle class housing'.

6. On production/reproduction I am not arguing anything different from many other Marxists (including Wolpe 1972; Cockburn 1977; Harvey 2012).
7. The references for this claim are as follows. By Marx: 'Critical notes on the article "The king of Prussia and social reform. By a Prussian"', *Vorwarts*, 7 August 1844; 'Letter to Ludwig Feuerbach in Bruckberg, 11 August 1844'; and 'Preface' to *A Contribution to the Critique of Political Economy*, 1859. By Engels: 'Ludwig Feuerbach and the end of classical German philosophy', 21 February 1881. I have used the versions of these sources available at http://www.marxists.org (accessed 29 June 2011). Engels reached Paris on 28 August 1844. In passing, it is worth noting that in his preface to the first German edition of *The Condition of the Working Class in England*, Engels (1845) recorded: 'I have continually used the expressions working men (Arbeiter) and working-class, propertyless class and proletariat as equivalents.'
8. The recognition that people hold multiple identities is now so well entrenched in sociological literature that we have been unable to cite an originating source. However, the basic idea is present in Antonio Gramsci's (1971: 333) invaluable concept 'contradictory consciousness'.
9. Combined, these three minorities comprise about 25 per cent of Johannesburg's population (Gaffney Group 2012: M289).
10. From 13 844 000 in 2008 fourth quarter to 12 803 000 in 2010 first quarter (Stats SA: 2009d; Stats SA 2010a).
11. Surveys conducted by TNS between February 2010 and May 2012 showed an expansion in the proportion of the eight metro populations who were 'unhappy' with service delivery, and, in the case of Soweto, the increase was from 49 per cent to 61 per cent (SA Local Government Briefing 2012: 32).
12. Wright's approach produced three 'unambiguous' classes (bourgeoisie, proletariat and petty bourgeoisie) and one contradictory class location positioned between each pair of these (that is, managers and supervisors, semi-autonomous employees and small employers). Our capitalists were, in Wright's (1978) terms, 'small employers'; and his 'semi-autonomous workers' were accommodated either as managers, petty bourgeoisie or regularly employed workers. The unemployed, pensioners and students do figure in Wright's (1978: 91–6) broader framework, but not as part of his main scheme.
13. Bourdieu (1984: 175) regards as 'homologous' the associations that exist across different 'areas of practice'. These homologies 'are all homologous to one another because they are all homologous to the structure of objective oppositions between class conditions'. According to Bourdieu, this alignment of classes across different areas of practice is a feature of class *habitus*.
14. In practice, status order was operationalised mainly by ranking jobs (which turns out to be correlated with class positions).
15. A 2006 survey by Future Foundation (2006) found that 53 per cent of Britons regarded themselves as working class and 43 per cent as middle class. The study had discouraged what it called 'shyness' by asking: 'Would you call yourself working class, middle

class or upper class?' Even so, it complained that there was 'confusion' among people about which class they belonged to (for example, bank managers who said they were working class) and it decried a tendency towards the 'muddle class' [sic]. Even so, people who said they were middle class had twice the level of savings and three times the level of investments than those who said they were working class. Unfortunately, the sample was small – only 1 000 people for the whole country – but the figures were similar to those of the British Household Panel Study.

16. This is not to say that a high level of working-class identification exists everywhere. For instance, it has been reported that in Japan, about 90 per cent of people regard themselves as middle class (Savage 2000: 35), while for India, Deshpande (2003: 129–31) suggests that 'middle class' is a desirable identity to which even those who are 'ineligible' lay claim. It is possible that, as in South Africa, language and translation play at least some part in the construction of class identity.
17. The General Social Survey poses the following question: 'If you were asked to use one of four names for your social class, which would you say you belong in: the lower class, the working class, the middle class, or the upper class?' According to Hout (2008: 29), for the years 2000–04 the question received a 99.4 per cent response rate and yielded the following replies: lower, 5 per cent; middle, 47 per cent; working, 44 per cent; upper, 4 per cent. Hout adds that when the exact same question was asked by Richard Centers in 1949, 49 per cent self-identified as working class and 45 per cent as middle class. It is remarkable how little US class identifications have changed over more than half a century.
18. Similarly, Deshpande (2003: 140) makes the point that 'the middle class more than any other is defined by its ownership and control of cultural capital'.
19. We might reasonably be criticised for underestimating the importance of southern literature in this introduction. However, the purpose here has been to consider the most influential texts. Separately, in 2009, we held a conference on 'Comprehending Class' in Johannesburg. This produced three volumes of papers and led to a special issue of the *South African Review of Sociology*, which included, in addition to two articles on South Africa (Phadi and Manda 2010; Moodie 2010), papers on Brazil, India and China (respectively, Santos 2010; Dhawan 2010; Chan 2010).
20. Van den Bergh was not always consistent. At one point, he envisions the possibility of a revolution led by the black proletariat, but adds, perspicaciously, that this was unlikely 'to result in rapidly rising living standards for the African masses . . . [and] the intelligentsia probably stands most to gain through change' (Van den Bergh 1965: 210).
21. Seekings (2009: 878) makes the further point that key figures either emigrated (including Kuper) or died. Sandwiched between the state and the movement, the environment was harsh for liberals, Weberians included.
22. I have argued against the free/unfree thesis elsewhere (Alexander 2006b). This distinction is not grounded in Marxism, and the account assumes, wrongly, that all black workers were like slaves or serfs.

23. This history was strongly influenced by Thompson (1968). Attempts to apply his notion of 'class experience' – which mediated consciousness and exploitation – could have made a valuable contribution to the debate (Alexander 1999: 32). The distinction between Marxists and Weberians – or, at least, between some Marxists and some Weberians – can be drawn too sharply. For example, the Weberian John Rex (1986: 66–7) distinguished between black workers and white workers in terms of a 'differential relationship . . . to the means of production', with the former 'unfree' and the latter '[part of a] community . . . able to defend real privileges'. This was only a shade different from the Marxism countered by Wolpe (1976: 200–3; Rex 1986: 68).
24. Unfortunately, Wolpe had blind spots. In particular, because he tended to be dismissive of history and loyal to the main wing of the liberation struggle, his analysis of conjuncture was impaired. His new thinking fed into a book, completed in February 1987, that reached a pessimistic conclusion about the possibility of ending apartheid rule, yet eight months later, and before the book was published (Wolpe 1988), he was himself involved in negotiations that would bring apartheid to an end (Alexander 2007: 114).
25. It is not always clear whether Mayer is writing about 1965 or 1976 or both, but here he is referring to 1965.
26. Mayer's monograph, which exists only as a manuscript, was not available to us when we completed our main fieldwork, so similarities between his findings and our own are all the more remarkable.
27. Weber's (1924: 181) *economic classes* consisted of 'people [who] have in common a specific causal component of their life chances, in so far as this component is represented exclusively by economic interests'. These economic classes were aggregated into four major *social classes*: the working class, petty bourgeoisie, technicians and lower managers, and propertied elite (Breen 2005: 32; Crompton 2008: 33). Seekings (2009: 868) notes: '[E]ven Weber himself tended to elide class and status in practice.'
28. The role of the petty bourgeoisie has been a continuing interest of Bonner's (see Bonner and Nieftagodien: 2008). For a history of the black petty bourgeoisie, see Alan Cobley (1990).
29. Although not discussed here, Poulantzas's work provided a point of departure for many South African Marxists, including Rob Davies (1979). In the 1980s, Wolpe (1988) came to see value in Poulantzas's approach, but was highly critical of Davies's interpretation.
30. According to Seekings and Nattrass (2005: 104), 'In greater Soweto . . . there were only eight secondary schools until 1972. By 1976 there were twenty, with three times as many students as in 1972. By the end of 1984 there were fifty-five [schools].' Transvaal African teachers had established their first association by 1920, and held a strike as far back as 1944 (Amoako 2012).
31. Nzimande (1990: 197) reports that there were 3 000 small shopkeepers in Soweto in the late 1980s.

32. For an appraisal of the relevance of Nzimande's categories in post-apartheid South Africa, see Roger Southall (2004).
33. For a review of the literature on apartheid unemployment, see Nattrass and Seekings (2005).
34. 'Dominant' is a non-gendered concept developed by Goldthorpe and others (Edgell 1993: 47).
35. By 2008, there had been further shrinkage in the size of the 'core working class' (that is, unskilled and semi-skilled manual workers outside agriculture and domestic work), and continued growth in the size of the bottom layer (Seekings 2011: 538).
36. For Wright (1978: 93) the temporarily unemployed could be equated to the reserve army and did not pose a 'special problem', but the permanently unemployed were 'more problematic', and, as far as I can tell, the problem was never resolved, other than by regarding them as an 'underclass'.
37. Moreover, the authors' own evidence contradicts their assumption. They include a table based on a 2000 Cape Town survey which shows that the main way people got their first job was through a friend or a relative in a different household (45 per cent), while getting it through a household member happened much less often (19 per cent) (Seekings and Nattrass 2005: 285).
38. Ben Roberts (2001: 110), who is open to the possibility that underclasses exist, makes the observation that, at least in Britain, 'as yet the best reason for having an underclass . . . is to maintain the (sociological) purity of the working class'.
39. The National Planning Commission cites the UCT Unilever Institute as its source.
40. For instance, the isiZulu *ngiyazikhona*, meaning 'I can afford'. Significantly, this word has a second meaning: 'I can take care of myself.' Thanks to Trevor Ngwane for clarifying this matter.

2

Historical introduction to class in Soweto

Kim Wale

This chapter provides a summarised history of Soweto. It does not provide new information on this history, but offers a general introduction for those who are not familiar with Soweto's origins and development.[1] The story of Soweto revolves around the push and pull between the state's attempts to segregate and control a black working class and the reaction to these attempts from below. The chapter begins with a discussion of Soweto's planning and origination from above (1902–60), then focuses on the development of a sense of Sowetan culture from within, which culminated in the Soweto uprising of 1976. It looks at the impact of reform policies and the development of organised popular resistance to apartheid within Soweto from 1979–90, and reflects on how Sowetans experienced the transition to democracy and the kinds of stratification that characterise the township today.

Origins and planning of Soweto (1902–60)

Soweto's origins, planning and transformation are intimately tied to the spatial ordering of the 'apartheid city'.[2] Like other townships bordering city centres in South Africa, Soweto was created as the geographical expression of apartheid's ideologies of racial segregation and influx control. While this vision was solidified in the apartheid period, its genesis lay in the racist segregation policies of the government of the Union of South Africa and its concern about the multiracial slum environment developing within Johannesburg.

Constructing Soweto: Slum clearance, segregation and control

As industry developed in Johannesburg following the end of the Anglo-Boer War in 1902, so did a multiracial working class who lived together in vibrant inner city slums (Proctor 1979: 52; Bonner and Segal 1998: 11). The British government and the newly formed Johannesburg municipal council strongly objected to the developing slum environment. As part of the attempts to clear the slums, the townships of Klipspruit (1904) and later Orlando (1931) were created to relocate Africans. The more public reason given for clearing the slums was that they posed a serious health threat (Parnell 1988: 116). However, social and political motivations reflected themselves in the ways in which communities were relocated through principles of segregation and control.[3] For instance, Keith Beavon (2004: 110) explains how the social intimacy shared by poor black and white workers, living side by side with one another in the slums, threatened to disintegrate racial boundaries within the working class.

Two Acts facilitated the lengthy process of slum clearance. The Natives Land Act, No. 27 of 1913, set down the legal foundation for residential segregation, later made compulsory in the Native Urban Areas Act, No. 21 of 1923, which emphasised the principle that Africans should be allowed in urban areas only insofar as they were needed to work for white industry (Kane-Berman 1978: 71; Mandy 1984: 175). Through this Act, employment became linked to the provision of racially segregated accommodation, which ensured that most Africans would not have residential rights in urban South Africa (Alexander and Chan 2004: 611). In line with the ideology of the Urban Areas Act, the construction of Soweto facilitated the state's project of ensuring that the African working class would be racially separate from the white working class; would be denied residential rights; and would remain under strict control and surveillance, not only in spaces of work, but also in spaces of residence.

Orlando was the first township constructed in the heart of what, from 1963, was called Soweto. It was designed to house Africans who had been removed from slum neighbourhoods. While advertised as a 'paradise' by the council, residents of the newly constructed Orlando township recalled the miserable conditions, poor standards of accommodation and community facilities, and loss of community spirit that characterised their experiences (Bonner and Segal 1998: 17–18). As a result of these unpleasant living conditions and the large distance between greater Johannesburg and the new township, Ellen Hellman describes the removal to Orlando as 'something akin to exile' (1971: 1). African families removed from slums did everything they could to resist being resettled there.

Soweto's working class grew significantly during the Second World War as influx controls were relaxed to allow an inflow of African workers for the demands of the war industry (Kane-Berman 1978: 73; Alexander 2000: 18). The Johannesburg council was unable to provide housing for these workers, however, due to wartime shortages of building materials. Instead they issued permits enabling tenants in Orlando to take in sub-tenants (Beavon 2004: 124), which resulted in serious overcrowding. It was from this lack of space and housing provided for African workers, that the squatter movements emerged. These movements began in 1944 when the charismatic, people's leader, James 'Safasonke' ('we shall all die together') Mpanza, led a group of sub-tenants to an area of open land in Orlando West, where they set up illegal hessian shelters (Stadler 1979: 31; Hirson 1989: 150). Mpanza took control of governing and policing the settlement, constructed his own courts, saw to the day-to-day needs of his people and sold traders' licences (Mandy 1984: 177; Bonner and Segal 1998: 23). Due to the defiant and illegal nature of these squatter spaces, the council hastily developed plans to set up temporary accommodation in the emergency camps of Jabavu (in 1944) and Moroka (in 1947). The council responded to the housing shortage through site-and-service schemes, providing sites in Soweto with basic services and facilities, such as sanitation, water, roads and refuse removal. Tenants were allowed to build shacks at the back of the site in anticipation of the erection of a proper house (Kane-Berman 1978: 58; Beavon 2004: 127).

The rising African unemployment, housing shortage and land invasions of the immediate post-war years highlighted the perceived problem of uncontrolled in-migration (Alexander 2000: 19, 99). Two reports were commissioned in an attempt to deal with African urbanisation. While the Fagan Report (commissioned in 1946) concluded that urbanisation was inevitable, but required regulation, the Sauer Report (commissioned in 1947) responded that it was undesirable and should be slowed down and eventually reversed (Hindson 1987: 59). In the context of rising white anxiety, the National Party came into power in 1948 on the back of the Sauer Report and its promises to address the failures of influx control.

Apartheid, influx controls and new divisions

While the landscape of urban South Africa had already been organised in terms of the principles of racial segregation, apartheid built this into a total system, which included the strengthening of influx control legislation and the creation of ethnically based 'homelands' constructed as separate and racially based administrative zones (Tomlinson et al. 2003: 6). Apartheid brought with it new kinds of class compression among urban Africans, as well as new types of division between urban and migrant Africans. While the slum clearance of the 1930s had focused attention on separating the African working class from the white working class, the 1950s saw a shift in policy focus towards the African middle classes. The apartheid government embarked on a project of class compression among urban Africans in terms of geography, housing and occupational class structure. Educational opportunities in the form of the mission schools, through which many of the more privileged urban Africans had gained their education, were removed and replaced with Bantu Education (Crankshaw 2005: 354). In terms of occupational structure, African businesses, as well as African employment in certain white-collar and skilled trade jobs, were restricted (Crankshaw 2005: 355). Perhaps the most brutal outcome of apartheid's focus on the African middle classes was the programmes of forced removal of property-owning Africans from their houses in the freehold townships of Sophiatown, Martindale and Newclare to the new townships of Meadowlands and Diepkloof in Soweto (Beavon 2004: 132).

In addition to the Natives Urban Areas Act, three new pieces of legislation contributed to creating internal divisions within Soweto. The Native Laws Amendment Act, No. 54 of 1952, the Abolition of Passes and Coordination of Documents Act, No. 67 of 1952 (commonly known as the Pass Laws Act) and the Natives Resettlement Act, No. 19 of 1954, were designed to deal with African urbanisation following the principles of the Sauer Report (Alexander and Chan 2004: 611–12). These Acts worked to exert strict controls on the influx and efflux of migrant labourers and to constitute class divisions between urban Africans who had residential rights and migrant Africans who were allowed in urban areas only when they were granted permission to remain for purposes of employment. The new Urban Areas Act prohibited Africans from staying in proclaimed urban areas for more than 72 hours unless they were classified as 'section tenners' on the basis of whether they had been born in urban areas and how long they had resided and worked there (Hindson 1981: 201). The Abolition of Passes and Coordination of Documents Act introduced a new pass book, known to most Africans as the *dompas* (stupid pass), which all Africans over the age of sixteen years would be expected to carry (Alexander and Chan 2004: 612). The pass was a small book that indicated, among other things, the bearer's identity, address, employment details and encounters with the police. A small group of elite Africans, such as chiefs, professors and medical doctors, were exempted from the requirements of the pass, but they still had to carry a document indicating this exemption (Alexander and Chan 2004: 612).

The Abolition and Coordination of Documents Act drew a clear line between urban Africans and migrant workers, and in Soweto this was further entrenched through the separate hostel dwellings for migrants and the family 'matchbox' houses for those with Section 10 rights (Beavon 2004: 133). Divisions within Soweto along migrant/urban and tribal lines were entrenched through the construction of hostels and the Natives (Urban Areas) Amendment Act of 1956, which compelled migrant workers who were living in the city to move to the newly constructed Dube Hostel in Soweto (Beavon 2004: 134). The pace of hostel construction increased in the late 1950s and 1960s; and, following the National Party's policy of entrenching tribal divisions, each hostel was reserved for a particular ethnic group (Bonner and Segal 1998: 39). Life was extremely harsh in the hostels, with little privacy and unhygienic living conditions (Beavon 2004: 135). The tribal segregation enforced by apartheid was also active in the ethnic zoning of permanent residents, justified through an argument that different ethnic groups naturally belong together and would want to live together. In practice this meant that houses were allocated according to ethnic group, traders could buy only from shops in their own ethnic area, and children were forced to attend schools for people of the same ethnic origin (Bonner and Segal 1998: 43). Naledi, Mapetla, Tladi, Moletsane and Phiri were areas within Soweto designated as Sepedi-, Sesotho- and Setswana-speaking zones; Chiawelo was set aside for Xitsonga- and Tshivenda-speaking people; and Dlamini, Senaoane, Zola, Zondi, Jabulani, Emdeni and White City were for isiZulu and isiXhosa speakers (Bonner and Segal 1998: 43).

Overall, the 1950s witnessed a deepening of the articulation of race with class, as the apartheid government extended its project of segregation to the black middle classes and removed their developing class privilege, while at the same time protecting white workers from African competition. Other kinds of divisions were also created in Soweto through apartheid legislation and the construction of hostels to house migrants who were not given the right of residence. Those classified as migrant labourers were restricted from entry into this urban working class and were allowed to remain in South Africa only if their labour was required by white bosses. By contrast, those classified as settled, urban Africans with residential rights were given job preference in order to reduce urban unemployment (Posel 1991: 82–5). The pass system profoundly defined the lived experience of apartheid and came to constitute the very symbol of oppression and abuse for Africans in urban areas (Breckenridge 2002: 1). It is not surprising, then, that these urban areas became sites of resistance through the 1950s up until 1960. This period of resistance came to a violent end, however, as the screws were tightened following the 1960s national anti-pass campaign mobilised by the African National Congress (ANC) and the breakaway Pan Africanist Congress. The protests were met by fierce opposition as police opened fire on African communities protesting the pass laws, the most famous example of which was in Sharpeville, where 69 men, women and children were killed (Mufson 1991: 6). The Sharpeville massacre, and the state of emergency that followed, resulted in the silencing of black opposition through the rest of the 1960s. Furthermore, the exemptions and distinctions built into the 1952 laws were removed and Section 10 rights were reduced.

Soweto's cultures of class (1960–78)

By 1964 apartheid's project of racial segregation and oppression was at its height. Attempts at resistance had been violently squashed and the leading resistance organisations were banned and went into exile. This section focuses attention on the forms of internal class and status differentiation that developed within Soweto during the lull of political activity following the Sharpeville massacre. Bonner and Segal (1998) have described the decade between 1965 and 1975 in Soweto as a 'loaded pause' as the pause gave rise to the famous Soweto uprising of 1976. This section outlines the developing forms of cultural class stratification within Soweto, and demonstrates how these became increasingly politicised alongside the rising black consciousness movement.

Stratification within townships

Three useful township ethnographies conducted in the 1960s offer insight into class stratification during this period. Phillip Mayer (1977; 1979) reports on local perceptions of class in Soweto, Ellen Hellman (1971) writes on her own observations of Soweto during this period, and Mia Brandel-Syrier (1971) conducted research on the elite in a township on the Reef named White Waters, which she calls 'Reeftown'. Both Mayer and Brandel-Syrier offer local models of class stratification, which, although different, share some noteworthy similarities.

Mayer's research shows the residents of Soweto dividing their population up into three or four classes. His three-class model – consisting of an upper, middle and lower class – is supported by the observations of Hellman (1971: 23). At the top of the class-status structure was the bourgeoisie or elite, the strata reflected in the pass law exemptions, which comprised professionals and businesspeople, many of whom lived in the prestigious sections of Dube, earning them the name 'Dubenheimers' (Hellman 1971: 24; Mayer 1977; Mayer 1979: 295). Below the elite were the 'better off', equivalent to a middle class, who included 'semi-skilled factory workers, drivers, policemen, teachers, sales representatives and clerks, up to professionals and businessmen' (Mayer 1979: 295). Entry into this middle class was made possible through education, money, occupation and degree of 'Westernisation' (Hellman 1971: 23). While occupation and income were key factors constituting this middle class, as Hellman (1971) demonstrates, this class was also constructed around a language of 'Westernisation' and 'civilisation'.

Finally, there was a lower class in Soweto, fashioned within the language of the 'ordinary working people' and the dissolute (Mayer 1977: 100–23). These were the majority of unskilled or semi-skilled workers in industry, commerce or domestic service. This class was further divided into the respectable poor and the dissolute.

The 'respectable poor' or 'ordinary labourers' often referred to themselves as the 'people who are in the middle' (*abantu abaphakathi*), because they had steady jobs and could cope economically, in comparison to those whom they saw as dissolute (Mayer 1977: 100; Mayer 1979: 295). Despite their lower-class status, the respectable poor in Soweto maintained the moral high ground, asserting that they were self-disciplined in practising the values of hard work and humanity, which they felt had been lost by the elite (Mayer 1977: 103). In contrast to these constructions of a respectable poor, there was also a perception of the very poor who lacked the moral values and decent behaviour of the ordinary working people. This bottom category was also referred to as 'the suffering', 'the lowest', 'the dissolute' and 'those who can't respect themselves' (Mayer 1977: 110).

In Brandel-Syrier's discussion of the different views of class stratification, she argues that in Reeftown there were also distinctions within the three main classes. From the local perspective, these included an upper-upper, middle-upper and lower-upper class; an upper-middle and ordinary-middle class; and an upper-lower and ordinary-lower class (Brandel-Syrier 1971: xxvi). These research results from Soweto and Reeftown demonstrate that despite attempts to compress class during this period, class stratification was clearly evident. Furthermore, we notice a certain language developing in the description of class difference, for example, the language of the 'ordinary' in both Mayer's and Brandel-Syrier's class models, and the language of the 'middle people' in Mayer's class model. These 'middle people' did not represent the middle class, but rather the so-called ordinary working classes, who come to represent the 'middle' of class status, located between those who are dissolute, on the one hand, and a better-off middle- and upper-class minority, on the other hand.

Consumption and status in Soweto

Moving the focus from local perspectives of class to local expressions of status and style allows an understanding of the changing role of politics within class cultures during this period. The spread of popular styles and tastes within Soweto in the 1960s and 1970s was made possible through the developing black press and the rising literacy rate. Advertisers sought to create and capitalise on a mass, black, urban market. The various black magazines and newspapers such as *Zonk*, *Golden City Post* and *Drum* functioned to create a consumer culture in Soweto that helped to forge a distinctive black, urban taste and style (Bonner and Segal 1998: 61). Perceptions of style and status influenced many aspects of Sowetan life, including language, dress and musical taste. Bonner and Segal (1998: 59–60) describe the different styles of the 'Ivies', the 'Hippies' and the 'Pantsulas', which had emerged by the end of the 1960s. The 'Hippies' style trademark was long bell-bottomed trousers. In contrast, the 'Ivies', who would wear their trousers high in the waist so that their socks would show, were invested in a dignified status identity and could be found at certain fashionable drinking and music spots, engaging in conversation about higher-class status symbols. Finally, the 'Pantsulas' embodied the style of a working-class culture, identified by their cotton caps, called 'sporties'. Despite their working-class status, 'Pantsulas' would wear very expensive clothes – especially expensive shoes – and had their own unique way of walking and talking.

In an interview with Peter Alexander, Joyce Siwane, who moved to Orlando West as a child in the mid-1940s and was politically active in Soweto from a young age, commented on her memories of class in the 1970s. She explained that due to the restrictions on investment opportunities for the urban black population, consumption became one of the few means through which class stratification could be expressed. Siwane described class differentiation in Soweto in the 1970s in terms of the isiZulu concept *dayazikhona* or 'being able to afford'. She explains the meaning of 'being able to afford' and how affordability was linked to consumption and self-expression as follows:

> Generally you could afford to provide for your kids, in terms of food and clothing – you could afford smart clothing for your kids and for yourself. In terms of the township fashion sense, you would be better dressed. Remember, because people didn't have investment opportunities, they used to dress very expensively, because that was the only way of self-expression.[4]

During the 1960s and 1970s, expressions of class position through consumer culture seemed to accept and express rather than subvert the class system. Despite the depoliticised appearance of these expressions of consumer culture, this practice of self-expression in urban black South Africa did come to play a profound role in the politics of township resistance. From 1965 the apartheid government began its strategy of de-urbanisation. Funds were now taken out of the development of Soweto and used to develop the homelands. At the same time, influx controls were tightened, lease-holdership rights within Soweto were removed and traders were further restricted (Bonner and Segal 1998: 70–1). Increased repression and a growing sense of urban identity were associated with rising resentment in Soweto. This was given expression through the teachings of Steve Biko, the charismatic leader of the South African Student Organisation, which was launched at the University of Natal in 1969. His philosophy of Black Consciousness spoke to the psychological oppression of apartheid and the need to foster positive feelings of self-worth within the black population in order to resist injustice.

The cultural expressions of style and class shifted from being apolitical expressions of the status quo to the subversive anti-racist fashions of 'black is beautiful'. One of Bonner and Segal's respondents describes the new politics of fashion developing in the townships during the period of Black Consciousness:

> It was the days of 'Black is Beautiful' and you would sport big Afro hair and African attire, that sort of thing. It all went to emphasise that we are black people. If you are going to be involved in any kind of politics, you have got to appreciate who you are and not only appreciate it, but be very proud of who you are (Sibongile Mkhabela quoted in Bonner and Segal 1998: 75).

The politics of Black Consciousness, which preached the liberation of the mind from the negative self-image of the oppressor, gave rise to active political resistance to the Bantu Education system and the Soweto uprising of 1976. Twenty thousand Soweto schoolchildren marched on the morning of 16 June 1976 in protest against the government's decision to enforce the use of Afrikaans as a language of instruction in secondary schools (Kane-Berman 1978: 1). The march began as a joyful and peaceful student protest, but when the police opened fire on the marchers, violence broke out between the police and the Soweto community, which lasted for a week and claimed at least 176 lives (Kane-Berman 1978: 1). The students' protest against the system was soon joined by young unemployed workers. Widespread mobilisation followed the uprising as calls on workers to engage in stay-away strikes often met with great success (Hirson 1979). The Committee of Ten arose out of the student protest as workers and parents sought to support and advise the student movement (Nthambeleni 1999). It was made up of prominent Sowetans, led by Dr Nthato Motlana, and was aimed at challenging the government-sponsored municipal authorities. The following section describes how the after-effects of this historic event resulted in a reversal of apartheid policies towards the urban black population in an attempt to quell the rising African resistance.

Reform and resistance (1979–90)

Two key historical events came together to usher in the era of reform in South Africa. The first was the aftermath of the Soweto uprising, which sent a strong message to government and capital about the threat that black resistance posed to political and economic stability. The second event was a shift in Afrikaner ideology, as the reformers (*verligtes*) came to the forefront, with P.W. Botha taking over as prime minister from the conservative John Vorster (Bonner and Segal 1998: 104).

In this context, Botha's 'total strategy' of reform was undertaken in order to re-establish control within African townships and security within the country, and to protect South Africa's capitalist economy. Despite these attempts, popular township resistance spread across the country, and Soweto's civics and youth organisations developed to form a key part of this resistance towards the end of the 1980s.

Reform policy and the new middle class in Soweto

The 'total strategy' of reform was largely based on two 1979 government-commissioned reports. The Wiehahn Report argued that because urban black workers were becoming a more permanent part of the urban economy they should be allowed to form trade unions under the Industrial Conciliation Act, No. 28 of 1956 (Callinicos 1988: 40). Alongside the Wiehahn Report, the Riekert Report similarly aimed to create a more quiescent working class, but also focused attention on developing and protecting an urban, black middle class so they could be in a position to bear the costs of running and maintaining the townships (Hindson 1987: 84). This report imagined a dual process of liberalising labour markets and the withdrawal of the state from townships. Furthermore, influx controls were relaxed for urban Africans, but intensified for rural Africans. As pass laws were lifted for urban Africans with Section 10 rights, so the costs of running the townships were imposed on them by the new, black local authorities through the rates and taxes levied on consumers, homeowners and African businesspeople (Hindson 1987: 84). Together these two reports aimed to develop both a 'responsible', settled, black working class who were less prone to resistance and also to separate out more established urban Africans from the rest. Afrikaans- and English-speaking capital needed a black middle class to 'act as a buffer between the white minority and the African masses' (Callinicos 1988: 3). However, this plan backfired and instead created more opportunities for organising resistance. The urban middle class was able to link with others in developing township organisation, while workers united to develop powerful trade unions.

Due to Soweto's propensity for resistance, it was a township specially earmarked for reform in order to foster a black middle class that would have too much to lose by participating in resistance. At the same time, shifts in the economy meant that there was an increasing demand for skilled and flexible labour (Beall, Crankshaw and Parnell 2003: 58). While the 1970s had been characterised by limited class differentiation, this began to change in the 1980s, with a few Sowetans joining the ranks of higher professionals. This is captured in Siwane's reminiscences:

> At that time too there were more nurses beginning to take a third programme, like psychiatric nursing and those kinds of things. Those opportunities were becoming open and in the 80s we began to see African senior nurses becoming matrons of hospitals.[5]

The increasing class differentiation among urban Africans of the 1980s was seen in the housing differentiation in black townships such as Soweto. State housing reforms from the early 1980s allowed the private sector to build and sell houses for ownership by those urban Africans who could afford them. These were therefore restricted to Africans employed in relatively well-paid occupations, such as supervisors, artisans, technicians, personal assistants, school teachers, nurses and police officers (Crankshaw 1997: 120). Bonner and Segal (1998: 105) show the different reactions with which people in Soweto experienced and expressed the rise of the new, black middle class. On the one hand, popular local magazines such as *Tribute* expressed a sense of pride in and support of this class by saying 'there is no pride in poverty' (Magubane 1990, cited in Bonner and Segal 1998: 105). At the same time, a certain level of judgement and criticism was expressed in the use of the term 'buppies', meaning black, upwardly-mobile professionals who drive fast cars, are arrogant and mimic Euro-American lifestyles.

In addition to this increasingly mobile black middle class, the effects of a withdrawal of state funding for housing meant there was also an increase of poor, fringe shack dwellers, backyard tenants and the urban unemployed (Beall, Crankshaw and Parnell 2003: 58). Owen Crankshaw (1997: 119) argues that in this context of the twin processes of African advancement and unemployment, racial categories became increasingly inadequate to understand social differentiation, and class categories became increasingly significant. However, despite the increased stratification within Soweto, a study conducted in 1980 on the quality of life in Soweto demonstrated that even among the more privileged group of urban, black South Africans in Soweto, their lived experience and values continued to be closely connected with the lower and working classes (Human 1981). Respondents in this study were individuals with higher incomes, occupations and education levels than the rest of Soweto, but continued to express a deep frustration with the status quo and a desire for and commitment to radical change. This demonstrates the failure of the reformist strategy to allow the aspirant, black, urban middle class to live the lifestyle they wanted. White-collar workers and professionals lived alongside the poor in overcrowded, underserviced housing.[6]

Township resistance

Reform policies had the unintended effect of creating spaces for the deepening of mass democratic mobilisation through unions and urban movements on a scale never seen before (Swilling and Phillips 1989: 68). Youth organisations and civics played a key role in mobilising and organising township resistance to the apartheid state in the 1980s. The civic movement was based in the new forms of resistance and self-governance that arose in the 1980s out of grassroots and community organisations mobilising on everyday issues faced by people in the townships (Adler and Steinberg 2000: 1). A key civic in Soweto was the Soweto Civic Association (SCA), the core of which consisted of the previous members of the Committee of Ten.[7] The SCA was launched in 1979 and set up branches throughout Soweto and proceeded to mobilise on issues of rent and service charges, and the recognition of Sowetans as permanent South Africans (Shubane 1991: 262). Another key political structure that formed after the uprising was the Congress of South African Students in 1979, which contributed to reviving the Charterist tradition and reintroducing ANC ideology in Soweto. Later, the Soweto Youth Congress (SOYCO) was launched in 1983 (Shubane 1991: 262–3).

By 1982 there were a series of calls for an umbrella body to help with the coordination and facilitation of urban resistance, and to link local struggles to the national resistance movement (Seekings 1992: 94). A significant shift in internal resistance politics came with the formation of the United Democratic Front (UDF) in 1983, when a number of different anti-apartheid groupings came together to resist the government's 'New Deal' decision to create three separate parliaments for the coloured, Indian and white populations (Seekings 1992: 95; Bonner and Segal 1998: 111). According to Jeremy Seekings (1992: 113), the main role played by the UDF was ideological as it set out to provide a national framework for local struggles and a set of leaders, symbols and spokespeople. Although the relationship between the UDF and the ANC in exile was complex, through its adoption of the Freedom Charter it contributed to the support of Charterism in townships. Within Soweto, the creation of the UDF strengthened local Charterist organisations such as SOYCO and the SCA (Shubane 1991: 165). The creation of the UDF coincided with an economic recession that worsened the already poor living conditions in the townships and reignited popular struggle (Bonner and Segal 1998: 112). By 1984 the unemployment rate in Soweto was at 53 per cent, and many of the energetic unemployed youth found a sense of purpose within SOYCO (Bonner and Segal 1998: 113). The more radical and militant members of this youth grouping became known as 'the comrades', a term meaning 'friends in the struggle' (Bonner and Segal 1998: 113).

Between 1984 and 1986 Soweto was less central in the uprising, which was blazing through townships across the country. Khehla Shubane (1991: 264–6) argues that the reason for this lull was to be found in the social cleavage caused by reform policies, which split the middle classes in Soweto into those who formed part of the anti-apartheid leadership and those who chose not to be involved in the struggle. Adding to this, political infighting emerged in the student movement between rival Charterist and Black Consciousness supporters. In July 1985, the government declared a state of emergency (lifted in March 1986, but re-declared in June 1986). Within this environment of intense repression, activists had to develop different forms of opposition, such as consumer boycotts. However, the increasing intimidation of the young and militant 'comrades' and the assaults inflicted on Sowetans who dared to shop at white shops undermined the boycott and forced the UDF leadership to find ways of containing the youth (Bonner and Segal 1998: 122–3). One of the solutions to the dangers posed by the radicalism of the comrades was the formation of street committees, in which the SCA took the lead. Street committees strengthened organisation at the grassroots level, with meetings held in people's homes, bringing leaders into closer contact with people's concerns. By the time the first state of emergency was lifted, Soweto's organisational capacity had greatly improved, allowing the SCA to organise marches to pressurise the Soweto Municipal Council (Shubane 1991: 267–8). By establishing street committees, the SCA was providing an alternative to state power. Through people's power, these local organisations assumed key state-like functions, such as taking over the running of services and playing a judicial role through the formation of people's courts (Rosenthal 2010: 251–2).

Until the middle of the 1980s, the unions had generally remained separate from political struggle and community-based resistance, but there were exceptions (Seekings 2000: 128). Eventually, from late 1988, anti-apartheid resistance inside South Africa was unified under the banner of the Mass Democratic Movement, within which the Congress of South African Trade Unions was centrally involved (SAHO n.d.). In Soweto, the political spirit was revived through the SCA's call for the boycott of rents and municipal service charges. By 1988 the rent boycott was supported by 95 per cent of the township, and the Soweto Municipal Council was in debt for R274 million (Bonner and Segal 1998: 130–1). The degree of community support and the spirit surrounding the boycott is emphasised by a Sowetan interviewed by Mareka Monyokolo (1990: 28) in December 1989:

> The boycott is taking up issues that we have been wanting to express but could not because as individuals we cannot make an impact on the council,

> but as a whole community and a whole township we can actually get the councillors to come down on their knees and address our problems in a satisfactory way . . . I personally think we are winning, we are making it.

Despite the class differentiation that was already evident through a rising, black elite within the township, the majority of Sowetans supported the rent boycott, albeit for different reasons. In a study of the relationship between class consciousness and the rent boycott, Monyokolo (1990) compared the views of residents in Pimville/Klipspruit in two distinct 'old' and 'new' areas. The old area was considered a predominantly working-class area with old, state-built 'matchbox' houses and the new area was considered middle class, with new, privately owned houses. While respondents based in the former said that they supported the boycott because the issues directly affected them, those residing in the latter said that the issues did not affect them, but they were pledging solidarity with the working-class struggle. Despite the focus on working-class issues, the boycott received support from differently classed areas within Soweto, as its ultimate aim was one of challenging the racial inequality of apartheid.

In place of the SCA, which had been restricted since 1987, a new body called the Soweto People's Delegation was formed to enter into negotiations with government (Zuern 2011: 86). Its demands included the radical call for a single tax base for Johannesburg and Soweto, an end to racial segregation and the creation of one city (Shubane 1991: 271; Bonner and Segal 1998: 131). The council finally gave in to all these demands and, with the approval of Soweto residents, the Soweto People's Delegation signed the famous Soweto Accord on 24 September 1990 (Zuern 2011: 87), which placed Soweto at the centre of the liberation struggle again, as it represented the first time that the apartheid government had given into the demands of black, urban Africans. The balance of power had shifted decisively, marking the beginning of the end of apartheid.

Negotiations and post-apartheid in Soweto (1990–2011)

The unbanning of black political parties and the release of Nelson Mandela in February 1990 sent a wave of joy and celebration through Soweto. Expectations soared as Sowetans came to believe that great changes would happen overnight. Instead, the ANC entered into drawn-out negotiations with the National Party, while Sowetans faced increasing brutality and insecurity. Political competition between the Zulu-nationalist Inkhata Freedom Party and ANC supporters became violent, and by August 1990 Soweto was 'engulfed in flames' (Bonner and Segal

1998: 148). Urban black South Africans expected that the change in power for which they had fought would result in substantial change in their own lives, but this has not been the case for many of the poor and working class in Soweto.

Negotiations, disillusionment and resistance

Towards the end of the 1980s, many of the youth had come to romanticise the ANC, but during the negotiations some felt betrayed. It was not only the decision to negotiate with the apartheid state that angered Sowetans, but also the related decision to suspend the armed struggle. Between 1991 and 1993 Monique Marks conducted qualitative research among the youth in Diepkloof, Soweto. Her respondents were young, working-class, unemployed and school-going youth between the ages of 14 and 28 years, who formed part of the Charterist movement in Soweto. In the early 1990s, these youth resisted the suspension of the armed struggle, arguing that violence continued to be a necessary means through which to become liberated. Furthermore, the move to suspend the armed struggle was seen as a dangerous one, leaving communities vulnerable to continued violence. These sentiments are expressed by one of Marks's respondents: 'It was a blunder for the ANC to suspend armed struggle because of violence, the killing of our people' (Marks 1995: 15). In general, the youth interviewed expressed a deep mistrust of the negotiation process.

Similarly, the Soweto-based activist Trevor Ngwane (2003: 41) recalled the feelings of disillusionment with the ANC's choice to enter into negotiations with the apartheid government:

> I remember turning on the radio and hearing: 'the ANC announced today that the armed struggle has been suspended'. We couldn't believe it – it was like chopping off an arm and a leg. Of course they never did anything much but we used to romanticise it, that little bomb at the Wimpy Bar won them so much support in the country. People wanted to trust them, naturally, but there was opposition to the direction the negotiations were taking.

Analysing the negotiations from a political economy point of view, Michael MacDonald (2006) argues that they resulted in a trade-off: the ANC traded in the people's dreams for social revolution and agreed to protect the imperatives of capital, and the National Party traded in its hopes for power sharing. Black South Africans became equal citizens under the law and were given access to democratic institutions, enabling them, as a majority, to elect black leaders to power. However, property rights had to be respected and orthodox economic policies adopted. While privileging local and global capital, these policies excluded the possibility of redistribution and functioned to work against the ANC's pro-poor promises (Terreblanche 2002). The neo-liberal path that resulted from the negotiation process has had severe implications for the lives of Sowetans, especially in the area of service delivery. In 1999 the City of Johannesburg publicised its plan to privatise services through its iGoli 2002 programme of cutbacks and putting services out to tender (Ngwane 2003: 44). iGoli 2002 was replaced by iGoli 2010 and then iGoli 2030. While iGoli 2010 emphasised government's commitment to creating an 'African world-class city', the mayor's review criticised this approach for trying to satisfy too many people, and the focus was turned to business – the aim of iGoli 2030 is to create a 'world-class business location' (Tomlinson et al. 2003: 18). iGoli 2030, therefore, shifted priorities even further away from the shortage of housing and services for the poor and onto the growth of business in Johannesburg.

The policies of the post-apartheid state and local government reinforce the economic, social and spatial separation in Johannesburg (Tomlinson et al. 2003: 18). The impact of this on the livelihoods of the poor can be seen at the everyday level of basic services, and it is also at this level that renewed political resistance has taken place. In Johannesburg, the Anti-Privatisation Forum (APF) was established in 2000 by activists involved in the struggle against iGoli 2002 and came to act as an umbrella organisation uniting struggles against privatisation in the workplace and communities (Dawson 2010: 272). The Soweto Electricity Crises Committee (SECC) is the Anti-Privatisation Forum's largest affiliate and was formed by Ngwane and other activists in 2000 with a focus on the issue of electricity as a means through which to engage Soweto's residents in a broader struggle against neo-liberalism (Alexander 2005). As a result of Eskom's[8] decision to change its pricing structure in 1999, from a flat rate to a rate per kilowatt hour, electricity prices rose by nearly 47 per cent in one year, and a survey conducted by Maj Fiil-Flyn showed that three-fifths of 200 Sowetans surveyed had experienced cut-offs in the previous year (2001: 2). The SECC has mobilised thousands of people on the issue of the privatisation of electricity and secured significant respect across Soweto. Kelly Rosenthal (2010: 260) points out the similarities that exist between the SCA of the 1980s and the SECC of post-apartheid South Africa, both in terms of the form of their organisation and the way in which Sowetans are mobilised on everyday issues affecting them. However, the ideology of the SECC diverges from the Charterist ideology of the past in its strong emphasis on socialism.

Stratification, class and material culture

In the everyday lives of Sowetans, the shift from apartheid has brought with it some improvements, but has also deepened inequalities. A significant policy feature of post-apartheid South Africa has been the attempt to deracialise capital by opening up new economic opportunities for black South Africans. While this process can be traced back to the era of reform during apartheid, the attempt to create a new black elite to join with the old white elite has been intensified through policies such as Black Economic Empowerment and Employment Equity. Although new opportunities have been opened up for black advancement, they are not open to the majority in the poor and working class, but rather favour those who have already advanced (Seekings and Nattrass 1996: 336). Many better-off Sowetans have chosen to move to the previously whites-only suburbs, to newly built suburbs outside Soweto and to the so-called 'suburbs' within the township. For example, Diepkloof Extension is an area within Soweto occupied by the new middle and upper classes; it has quiet roads, big houses, well-kept gardens, high fences and expensive cars.

Even for people who move out of Soweto, the connections pulling them back to the township remain strong (Mbembe, Dlamini and Khunou 2008: 246). Emotional and familial ties to the township continue to exist, although these are likely to wane with time. At the other end of the class divide, informal settlements such as Mosoaledi lie not too far away from Diepkloof Extension, and here one sees the intense poverty that continues to exist within Soweto, as well as elsewhere in South Africa. A marked aesthetics of inequality characterises Soweto. For example, standing among the tiny shacks and muddy streets of Mosoaledi, you can glance over the bridge to see Maponya Mall, one of South Africa's biggest shopping malls, an impressive symbolic structure of consumerism built by one of the most successful members of the black elite. The stark inequality that characterises Soweto today is traced through its housing structures by Jo Beall, Owen Crankshaw and Sue Parnell (2003: 200–1):

> In the 1950s, the vast bulk of Sowetans had no choice but to accept the standard 'matchbox' house. By the 1990s, however, state reforms that privatised the provision of housing meant that Sowetans lived under increasingly differentiated housing conditions. On the one hand, reforms that introduced homeownership offered the wealthy few the opportunity to purchase housing of a relatively high standard. On the other hand, the withdrawal of the state from low-cost housing provision led to overcrowding of formal houses and the proliferation of shacks in backyards on open land.

Continuing with the example of housing, a University of the Witwatersrand (Wits) survey conducted in Soweto in 1997 reported that approximately 57 per cent of Sowetans lived in council-built housing, 20 per cent in backyard shacks, 9 per cent in private houses, 6 per cent in informal settlements and 4 per cent in workers' hostels (Morris et al. 1999: 5). About one in five Sowetans lived in backyard shack accommodation, and these constituted one of the poorest segments of this population, earning an average of little more than R1 000 per month (Crankshaw, Gilbert and Morris 2000: 845–6). Beall, Crankshaw and Parnell (2003) argue that the trend of housing diversification has deepened with the changes brought about by the post-apartheid regime and characterises the growing class inequalities within Soweto.

In terms of the experiences of poverty in Soweto, Beall, Crankshaw and Parnell (2003: 206–9) asked people how they would most like their current situation to change. The issues of unemployment, housing, infrastructure and services emerged as the most important ones. The experience of poverty in Soweto often intersects with other forms of identity, such as gender, age and length of time spent in the township. The older generations focused more on the affordability of services, so that to be poor is to not be able to pay for services, resulting in the accumulation of huge debts for services and electricity. For the youth, poverty was associated with having nowhere to go and nothing to do, especially in terms of the lack of sports or recreational facilities (Beall, Crankshaw and Parnell 2003: 207). The gendering of poverty is emphasised in women's complaints about the stresses that accompanied having to find adequate shelter for their families and dependants, linking their own source of vulnerability and poverty to the responsibility they bear for their families (Beall, Crankshaw and Parnell 2003: 207). In terms of age and length of time spent in Soweto, these aspects influence housing relations, as it is the older residents of Soweto who have gained access to council housing, and the newer and younger residents who rent the backyard shacks attached to these houses (Beall, Crankshaw and Parnell 2003: 207). The significance of the relationship between length of time spent in Soweto and contemporary access to housing, further indicates how the historical privilege given to black South Africans with residential rights impacts on stratification today.

Another lens through which to understand the experience and expression of class in post-apartheid Soweto is through people's consumption patterns and social interaction with material culture. As we saw earlier in this chapter, consumption can be understood as a key aspect of the subjective experience of class and as a window through which to understand people's internalisation, expression and contestation of class differentiation. Helen Meintjies (2001) demonstrates the link between consumption, class and gender through her study on the symbolic associations of domestic appliances in Soweto. On the one hand, households contain a wide range of modern and expensive electrical appliances with the latest bells and whistles; on the other hand, when it comes to labour-saving devices such as washing machines, these were resisted as a symbol of the laziness of women who are seen to be 'too modernised' (Meintjies 2001: 347). The consumption practices and symbolic value of domestic appliances buy into a consumerist neo-liberal ideal up to a point, but also resist it in terms of a certain construction of 'proper' womanhood.

Taking a closer look at youth culture in Soweto, a picture emerges of the ways in which discourses of hope and marketing combine to create a form of youth identity that is constructed around the aesthetic form of the cell phone. Mbembe, Dlamini and Khunou (2008: 243) explain how cell phone advertisements sell the kind of lifestyle that was promised in the discourses of hope, opportunity and the 'Rainbow Nation' that dominated the constructions of a 'New South Africa':

> So, adverts are playing on ideas of desirability, accessibility, and opportunity. Everywhere you go in Soweto, for example, you will meet adverts for MTN and Vodacom cell phones, not to mention beauty products. They all sell a lifestyle, and in many ways, the youth are buying into it. Through acquiring these products, the youth want to be seen as connected and as beautiful. One can also see the 'rainbow nation', with its celebration of blackness as talented, wealthy, making it.

The cell phone, which is the accessory of the moment, is deemed to be a symbolic manifestation of status by the youth of Soweto. As Mbembe, Dlamini and Khunou (2008: 244) continue:

> A cell phone is the best accessory ever. Those without disposable income find ways of owning one and having airtime. A lot of the hip guys do not leave their cell phones in their cars or put them in their pockets. They hold them in their hands. Funny enough, as they walk in a crowd or in a public space, it starts ringing or they suddenly have to make a call.

Cell phones, then, represent one way in which the youth of Soweto can express a certain desire for consumption and thus position themselves within a system of status, regardless of their actual economic situation. If you are struggling to make ends meet, but find a way to have the latest cell phone, you are doing okay.

Conclusion

The main aim of this chapter is to outline the history of Soweto as a township constructed within the shifting ideologies and policies of apartheid, and to show how Sowetans experienced this township and responded to the oppressive environment imposed on them by the state. By bringing this history of class into the present context and reviewing some of the literature on class and stratification in Soweto, this chapter sets the stage for the following chapters. In Chapter 3 we look more closely at what this history means for stratification within the township today. The tendency to use housing structures as a proxy for inequality will be questioned by Claire Ceruti. Her analysis of the quantitative findings demonstrates the ways in which different dimensions of stratification (including housing) intersect with one another to produce the inequality we see in Soweto today. Chapter 4 moves the discussion from stratification to occupational class structure and develops a picture of what the class structure looks like in Soweto today, and asks what this means for political alliance and mobilisation. The second half of the book, from Chapter 6 onwards, focuses more on the way in which people in Soweto view the class structure and their position in it, thus adding to some of the literature cited above by shifting the focus onto questions of the experience and expression of class for Sowetans.

Notes

1. Due to constraints of space and the broad focus of this chapter many readers may find that certain themes do not make an appearance or are not adequately covered. For a fuller account of the history of Soweto, see Philip Bonner and Lauren Segal's 1998 book *Soweto: A History*.
2. For more on the apartheid city, see Christopher (1994), Davies (1981) and Seekings (2011).
3. For example, in her analysis of venereal disease, Karen Jochelson demonstrates how health-related objections to the slum environment were underpinned by fears that the multiracial environment posed a threat to the construction of white supremacy in South Africa (2001: 72).
4. Interview with Joyce Siwane conducted by Peter Alexander, September 2009.
5. Interview with Joyce Siwane conducted by Peter Alexander, September 2009.
6. I am grateful to Jeremy Seekings for highlighting this point in comments on this chapter.
7. According to Phil Eidelberg (1999: 57), the Soweto Civic Association, which provided community leadership across the township, 'appeared to have a largely middle-class, professional and white-collar membership'. Visiting Soweto in 1985, Peter Alexander remembers being struck by the elite character of this organisation's leadership.
8. Eskom is the South African parastatal electricity producer.

3

Contemporary Soweto

Dimensions of stratification

Claire Ceruti

A sense of place

One can make two superficial mistakes about contemporary Soweto. Visitors usually quickly dispose of the first myth – that it remains the overflowing slum built by apartheid[1] – only to replace it with a second fable, which is sustained by the swanky new shopping mall, substantial improvements to the main roads and tourist areas, shiny cars streaming in and out of the township on the weekends, and the refurbishment of many houses that started life as apartheid 'matchboxes'. Diepkloof Extension caricatures any myth of a socially flat township (see Photograph 3.1). This palpably wealthier area on the east edge of Soweto developed towards the end of apartheid. From here, the only thing that reminds you that you are in Soweto is the view of a dingy hostel beyond the tiny manicured lawns and across the vlei (marshy ground). Not far from some of Soweto's main roads lie pockets of poverty that shocked even our township-born, student fieldworkers. Most Sowetans are better off than this, but few have the wealth implied by the new Maponya Mall, and those with opportunities to get the shiny car have often seized the additional opportunity to leave the township. The township is neither homogeneously squalid nor generally rich.

It is obvious why Diepkloof Extension is widely recognised as a symbol of class in the rest of Soweto. It is a grassy suburb – in the Soweto sense of the word suburb – on the very eastern edge of the township. Outside the township, 'suburb' implies a formerly white area or an area very similar to a formerly white area. Meadowlands, Emdeni and Orlando in Soweto are not called suburbs. Naturena, an area just east of Soweto developed for middle-class blacks near the end of apartheid, is called a suburb. Parktown North in Johannesburg is a suburb. Within

Soweto, only Diepkloof Extension and sometimes Protea Glen –a newer area of Soweto characterised by commercially built private houses – are called suburbs. One woman observed that there is no one selling on the streets in Diepkloof. A Soweto street cleaner told us, 'Our places are not the same. Things are always cleaner there and there are wonderful houses', but the 'higher class' people living there 'don't even want to see you next to their gate. They don't even allow you to go to the toilet because they think you are dirty.' Diepkloof Extension stands out from the rest of Soweto in the 2001 census figures regarding employment, income and computer ownership. It has substantially more professionals and managers and more legislators than any other part of Soweto. I heard Diepkloof Extension referred to as *emakishini* (at the kitchens) – a term coined by domestic workers during apartheid days to refer to the then-white Johannesburg suburbs, which these workers knew most intimately through their kitchens.

Other places around Soweto also have class associations. Informal settlements were often a reference point when people were asked to describe the lower class. Certain zones of Pimville and Protea Glen are understood by most Sowetans to be above the average, sometimes called upper class, or more commonly middle class. These zones are marked by houses built to stock plans by private builders from the 1970s onward, in contrast to the 'matchbox' former council houses built by the apartheid state. Census figures show that these areas, too, deviate somewhat from the general picture on income and have higher employment levels than average for the rest of Soweto. The higher zones of Pimville stand way above the rest when it comes to tertiary studies, and Protea Glen is the home of technicians around Soweto. As a whole, Soweto was sometimes described as poor and frequently as 'mixed' in our exploratory interviews. We heard Rockville, greater Diepkloof, Naledi and Soweto as a whole described as 'a potpourri of the toppest of the top to the lowest of the low' and as 'both middle class and lower class – let me say, working class'. These popular geographies remind us that space is classed and class spatialised, as social geographers know. Place – which Doreen Massey (1994: 154) defines as 'a constellation of social relations, meeting and weaving together at a particular locus' – proves important for this book, because we tend to locate ourselves contextually when we class ourselves (Zussman 1985; see also Crompton 2008: 92; Bottero 2005: 240–2).

This chapter is devoted to placing Soweto in two ways. Firstly, it situates Soweto as a post-apartheid township in its geographic and social environment, thereby also situating our survey. How does Soweto compare with the rest of Johannesburg and the country on basic socio-economic indicators? How have larger forces and flows shaped the place we see today? Secondly, it aims to sketch the internal socio-economic contours of the place as revealed by our survey and other data, looking in particular at the extent and distribution of various kinds of heterogeneity and homogeneity in the township.

The second aim simultaneously lends itself to assessing whether housing type works as a proxy for socio-economic or class stratification. A study of class in Soweto needs to evaluate this not only because the only other major survey of class in Soweto – the 1997 University of the Witwatersrand (Wits) survey (Morris et al. 1999; see also Beall, Crankshaw and Parnell 2002a, 2002b) – used housing type as a proxy for socio-economic class, but also because Soweto is primarily residential, and therefore, as we shall see in Chapter 7, different kinds of houses feature in Sowetans' own imagery as markers in their models of class.

The next part of the chapter locates Soweto in its environment, while the section after that emphasises the internal configuration of the place. Here I focus on four areas: migration, of interest because of the previous role of influx control in determining who could live in Soweto; housing, given the township's main use as a residential area; an estimate of the distribution of poverty and wealth in Soweto; and work, although only sketchily in this chapter because it is the meat of Chapter 4. These last two are chosen for their importance in many schemes of class. Other demographics, such as gender and education, are dealt with in Appendix 2. The last section of the chapter assesses housing type as a proxy for stratification.

We shall see that while Soweto now has a distinctly settled population, it also accommodates a significant proportion of new arrivals. We shall also see that Soweto averaged is a 'middling' place (we elaborate on this in Chapter 6) compared to the average situation of black people in the country as a whole, but it is hardly a concentration of the new, black 'middle class'. It is overwhelmingly not rich, but contains pockets of poverty as well as smaller, fewer pockets of well-being. Finally, I show that a number of non-economic factors besides income – particularly age and availability of housing – shape who lives in which house in contemporary Soweto, making this a weak marker of socio-economic class.

Locating Soweto

Soweto remains distinctly a township despite many changes, both subtle and stark. This is evident not only because its 1 101 103 residents, according to the 2001 census, remain overwhelmingly African (99 per cent, compared to 79 per cent for the country as a whole), but also from its location. Former Sowetans and descendants of Sowetans must drive between mine dumps or belts of decaying light industry to get back to their roots on the weekend (see Photograph 3.2 and Map 3.1).

These are lasting reminders that Soweto's geography originated in the dynamic of creating and controlling a workforce through racial logics: apartheid planners intended to keep blacks remote from Johannesburg without removing the workforce impossibly far from work in 'white' areas.[2] We drew on common conceptions in defining the boundaries of Soweto for the survey, explained in Appendix 1.

How does Soweto compare to South Africa as a whole? Sowetans in 2001 came off better on a number of indicators of basic living standards than most black people in their province – Gauteng – and in the country as a whole, which includes the impoverished former Bantustans. Nevertheless, Sowetans as a whole lagged behind whites as a whole on all of these (Table 3.1). Of course, not *all* Sowetans have greater access to piped water, brick houses, TV sets and so on, but a greater *proportion* of Sowetans have access to these things than the proportion of black people in the country as a whole. However, we should remember that the flush toilets to which Sowetans have access are often outside their houses; and the apartheid legacy shows up in Table 3.1 in the high proportion of people who had access to piped water on the property, but not inside their houses. Consequently, many of our respondents considered an indoor bathroom to be a marker of improving one's class. Soweto also has a smaller proportion of freestanding shacks than the rest of the province and a much higher proportion of backyard shacks.

Table 3.2 uses data about household goods that appears in our survey, the 2001 Census and the Statistics South Africa (Stats SA) 2007 Community Survey. This

Table 3.1 Basic living standards in Soweto compared to Gauteng and South Africa (percentages).

Selected indicators of basic living standards	Whole country		Gauteng			Soweto (%)
	Total (%)	Black Africans (%)	Total (%)	Whites (%)	Black Africans (%)	
Piped water inside dwelling	65.9	17.9	47.2	85.8	33.6	27.6
Piped water inside yard	14.6	33.8	36.4	9.7	45.8	60.4
Flush toilet	51.9	42.6	81.7	98.7	75.7	88.4
Brick houses	63.8	55.5	65.6	95.0	55.2	61.2
Freestanding shack	12.3	15.5	16.9	0.3	22.8	9.8
Backyard room or shack	7.8	8.9	14.3	2.7	18.3	9.8
Refrigerator	51.2	39.9	62.1	97.5	49.8	63.5
Television	53.8	44.2	65.7	92.9	56.2	66.0
Computer	8.6	1.8	15.1	50.3	4.0	3.4

Source: Stats SA Census 2001, compiled by the author.

Table 3.2 Household goods ownership in Soweto compared to Johannesburg Metro (percentages).

Percentage who own a working . . .	Black African	White	Whole population
Refrigerator			
Johannesburg 2001	43	97	66
Johannesburg 2007	65	98	74
Soweto 2001	62	86[3]	62
Soweto 2006	80	–	78[4]
Computer			
Johannesburg 2001	7	51	22
Johannesburg 2007	12	71	26
Soweto 2001	3	31	3
Soweto 2006	14	–	14
Cell phone			
Johannesburg 2001	45	75	54
Johannesburg 2007	81	89	82
Soweto 2001	32	64	32
Soweto 2006	77	–	77
Television			
Johannesburg 2001	58	94	73
Johannesburg 2007	71	97	78
Soweto 2001	65	80	65
Soweto 2006	84	–	84
Radio			
Johannesburg 2001	75	94	81
Johannesburg 2007	81	89	82
Soweto 2001	75	86	75
Soweto 2006	84	–	85

Sources: Stats SA Census 2001; Classifying Soweto survey 2006; Stats SA Community Survey 2007.

table allows us to compare the three areas and also shows change over time for Soweto and the Johannesburg Metro. Firstly, it shows that the proportion of Sowetans owning these goods has increased since 2001 by a percentage similar to the increase in the proportion of black people in the metro owning these goods. Secondly, it shows that, when measured against the Johannesburg Metro, of which it is a part, Sowetans are once again better off on average than black people in the metro, with the exception of cell phone ownership and, in 2001, computer ownership, but worse off on average than white people in the metro. Johannesburg Metro contained inner city slums at the time of our survey, and still contains sprawling shack settlements, such as Diepsloot in the north of Johannesburg. People from any other 'race' group living in Soweto are below the average for their counterparts in the metro as a whole (not shown in this table).

According to this sketch of basic living standards (we deal with incomes later in this chapter), black Sowetans are worse off than most whites, but better off than most other black people in the country, except with regard to one or two quirks of the apartheid township legacy. This may well explain why Soweto remains a destination for migrants, as discussed in the next section. However, these are averages that tell us something about Soweto's place in a broader context, but imply a socially flat township, when we know this is not the case. What is the picture when we zoom in still closer to look at the internal configuration of Soweto?

Coming and going: Soweto after influx control

Three large social forces have acted on Soweto since the dying days of apartheid. One is the collapse and eventual abandonment of overt racial controls on where people live (Simon 1989; Bonner and Segal 1998; Crankshaw 2008). This took place in the context of the intensified privatisation of housing provision (Bond 2000; Khan and Pieterse 2006). A second involves the substantial restructuring of racialised labour markets in several ways. New career opportunities began to open up for black people as certain racial barriers in work became inconvenient to business towards the end of apartheid (Crankshaw 1993). At the same time, several waves of retrenchments, plus increased use of casual labour in particular sectors, such as shop workers (see Kenny 2003), replenished the classes of poor and very poor black people. The third is the physical fact of the township inherited from apartheid, such as its location, its housing stock and, indeed, its former 'uses' to the governments that built and administered it. How have these shaped Soweto and the way in which Sowetans live?

This section speaks in particular to the effects of the first two social forces on the social geography of the township. Later sections will address the interaction of the third with the first two. This section addresses Soweto's growth, including who is leaving and who is coming to the township and for what purposes. It is unclear if Soweto's rate of growth is increasing or declining, but clear that the township is expanding. It appears to be becoming denser and more settled, but continues to attract a substantial proportion of migrants.

Growing

Soweto was shaped by influx control and the Group Areas Act. This grandiose attempt to manipulate black labour markets intended that only a few black people should reside in 'white' South Africa while the rest should come and go as they were needed for work (Posel 1991; Bonner and Segal 1998). As influx control and, later, group areas were being relaxed, racial barriers in certain skilled, better-paid work also began to soften (Crankshaw 1993). Together, these changes have enabled a flux into, out of and perhaps past Soweto. It is easier than before to come to Soweto, and it has also become easier to leave it. Additionally, migrants to the city now have options besides the township, such as the inner city or Diepsloot.

One side of this picture – leaving the township – is sketchy in any survey confined to Soweto. Our survey questionnaire had to cover a number of bases and there was no quick, reliable way to establish who had left the township. What do we know about the flux out? Local knowledge and our own observations tell us that at least some Sowetans used their improved spending power to escape the township, at first for nearby Naturena Extension, across the highway from Soweto (Photograph 3.2) and later for the spreading townhouse complexes around Mondeor, east of Soweto, then for the formerly 'white' suburbs (Mbembe, Dlamini and Khunou 2008: 239). The traffic jams leaving Soweto on a Sunday night attest to the existence of those like Milton Nkosi, who 'chickened out of the township but . . . spend much of our time there for weddings, funerals and family gatherings. So we say we sleep in the suburb but we live in Soweto' (*Independent* 2004). This was facilitated as Johannesburg's backyard sprawled south and west to meet Soweto's eastern satellites at a large shopping centre, Southgate, which was opened the year before the Group Areas Act was repealed, with the aim of mopping up some of Soweto's disposable income, thus introducing 'affording' Sowetans to a different mix of people from those they would meet in the township. The southern suburbs were originally white working-class areas, also containing white ethnic congregations, such as a concentration of Portuguese speakers in La Rochelle. These areas do not represent the race distribution of the entire population, but they had desegregated more than the richer northern suburbs by 2001. Crankshaw (2008: 1703) found that Africans already made up 28 per cent of southern suburbs' householders, while 51 per cent remained white. He counted only the householder in the main dwelling, because residents in backyard rooms could have been tenants or domestic workers in the data he used. The remainder of householders were 'coloured' or 'Indian'. The northern suburbs, by contrast, comprised just 16 per cent African householders and 72 per cent white householders in the same year.

On the other side of the picture, there is no doubt that Soweto has expanded physically. During the sampling, when comparing aerial photographs from 2001 with those from 2006 (see Appendix 1), we saw that some small informal settlements had disappeared from Soweto, but much more significant was the expansion of subsidised housing on the north-west edges of the township, around Braamfischerville and Goldev, and of shack settlements within and around Soweto.

Alongside this, our data suggests that there may have been an overall densification of households since 1997. The modal household size was three in the Wits survey (Morris et al. 1999) but four in our survey, where the average household size is 5.0 humans. The Wits figures may not be properly comparable to ours, because the authors stratified their sampling frame according to housing type, which, as we shall see later, interacts with household size in our survey. However, my calculations using the 2001 census data yield an average household size of 3.7, substantially below our finding, implying a trend to densification. By contrast, the corresponding figures for Gauteng, the province in which Soweto is situated, show a mild decline from 3.7 per household in 1996, the year before the Wits survey, to 3.4 for 2001 and 3.2 in 2007 (my calculations from Stats SA 2007: 6). For the country as a whole over the corresponding periods, the figures were 4.4, 3.9 and 3.8. The Johannesburg Metro shows an insignificant increase, from 2001's average household size of 3.1 to 2007's 3.3. Looking at distributions of household size, however, the 2007 Community Survey reports that the province is experiencing a decline in the proportion of one- and two-person households, and an increase in the proportion of households with five or more people, supporting the picture of an overall densification of households in the province. These trends chime with the argument presented in Chapter 4 that proletarian people are forced to band together in the face of a crisis in reproduction. However, Soweto's differences from the metro and the country show that this is not a uniform densification. We may be seeing densification specifically of urban proletarian households in the richer provinces – closer to perceived job opportunities – complicated by the absence of rapidly increasing housing opportunities in those areas in which people's social networks lead them to settle.

We cannot conclude from the available data whether Soweto's population growth has been accelerating or declining. Population estimates are not available from Stats SA at the level of Soweto for the years since 2001. We do know that Soweto's population grew by around 21 per cent between the 1996 Census and the 2001 Census, using the figures quoted in the Wits survey (Morris et al. 1999: 5) and my own calculations from the 2001 Census data. This was close to the rate of change for Gauteng, in which Soweto is situated, while the change for the country as a whole, during this period, was 10 per cent (Stats SA 2007: 6). For the period 2001–07, the estimated population of the province grew by 14 per cent, which was slower than during the 1996–2001 period, and the country as a whole increased by only 8 per cent (Stats SA 2007: 6). I chose the 2007 Community Survey for comparison because it took place only a year after our survey. Because the Community Survey is based on a sample rather than a headcount, this data is also not available at the level of Soweto. If Soweto's population changed at exactly the same rate as the whole of the Johannesburg Metro (Stats SA 2007) – summing deaths, births, in-migration and out-migration – then it would have grown from the 1 101 103 people at the time of the last census by about 200 000 people by the time of our survey, to constitute about half of the black population of the metro. However, population growth over an area as socio-economically varied as the Johannesburg Metro is bound to be uneven and averages do not capture flows between its different parts.

Can we produce a Soweto-specific estimate? Using data from our 2006 Classifying Soweto survey, I arrived at a growth rate of about 24 per cent over the five years before the survey.[5] This is faster than the 20 per cent estimated for the metro as a whole over that period, but comparable to the rate for black people in the metro (23 per cent from my calculations using Stats SA interactive data, the 2007 Community Survey and the 2001 Census). At this rate, Soweto's population could have grown by as much as 350 000 by the time of our survey, totalling around 1 451 000. However, if, for example, children do not migrate at the same rate as adults, then the rate would be lower. At the unlikely extreme of no child migrations in the five years before the survey, for example, Soweto's population would have grown to about only 1 301 000, a growth rate of only 19 per cent. This would still be well above the provincial average and close to the Johannesburg Metro average, but would be a declining growth rate for the township itself compared to the previous five-year period and slower than the rate for black people in the metro.

Arriving and staying

We can be more precise regarding when our respondents arrived in the township. While Soweto is becoming settled, migrancy, especially of young adults, remains a feature of the township.

Around half of the people living in Soweto in 2006 were born there (see Table 3.3, first row). Soweto-born residents make up 60 per cent of Sowetans under the age of 27 years, and only among those 60 and older are those born in Soweto outnumbered in any age group.

The Wits survey shows a substantially lower proportion – 31 per cent – of adults born in Soweto than our survey. One reason for this discrepancy is that the Wits survey is ten years older, meaning that the proportion that had arrived earlier would be greater. Another reason may be that the Wits survey selected 'the individual who led the household's residential movement' (Morris et al. 1999: 71), which would naturally tend to bias the sample towards older people, whereas our respondent could be any person older than fifteen years on the selected stand. Our sampling, therefore, would pick up more of the children born in Soweto to these household-moving individuals.

But migrants remain a substantial part of the population. Close to one-third of Sowetans in 2006 had arrived in the fifteen years prior to the survey (see Table 3.3, first row). Note that the category '2000 and after' covers only six years, while the other categories, chosen to compare with the 1997 Wits survey, cover a decade each. This proportion is a little higher than the proportion in the population as a whole for the previous equivalent period, the five years before the 2001 Census (12 per cent) and among black people (11 per cent) for that period (Stats SA 2006: 8). We did not ask where people came from. In the Wits survey, about 27 per cent of Soweto's adult population were born in a town (excluding those born in Soweto), but many born in rural areas had lived in urban areas for a long time (Morris et al. 1999: 20ff.). For the Johannesburg Metro, of which Soweto is part, 70 per cent of people who had moved in the five years before the 2007 Community Survey had come from elsewhere in Gauteng. At the same level, the 2001 Census shows 58 per cent had moved from within the province, with higher proportions coming from KwaZulu-Natal, Limpopo and the Eastern Cape in this survey than in the 2007 survey.

Table 3.3 Year in which respondents moved to Soweto.

Arrival in Soweto	No. of respondents	Percentage of adult Sowetans
At birth	1 153	53[6]
2000 and after	312	14
1990–99	288	13
1980–89	142	6
1970–79	94	4
1960–69	133	5
1950–59	115	5
Before 1950	36	1
Total	2 273	100

Source: Classifying Soweto survey 2006. Percentages do not add up due to rounding.

Young adults are the backbone of migration. Our survey shows that 64 per cent of residents who were born outside Soweto, but were still living in the township at the time of the survey, came to Soweto after their eighteenth birthday. Of these people who arrived in the township as adults, one quarter arrived by the age of 21 and another quarter between the ages of 22 and 24. Another quarter arrived after they turned 24, but before they turned 31. This age range is consistent with people starting a new life nearer to the city and closer to work, education opportunities, better facilities, and the promise of excitement. Among people who were in their late twenties and early thirties at the time of the survey, the number of remaining migrants nearly equals the number of Soweto-born. This may also represent a spike in the number of young people coming to Soweto soon after the first universal election in 1994.

Work is certainly an issue for the newest arrivals. People who came to the township as adults were more likely to be formally employed (that is, working regularly for someone else for more than 20 hours a week), than others of similar age in each of the age categories, 16–22 years, 23–29 years and 30–38 years. On the other hand, about half of the respondents who were younger than 23 at the time of the survey and who had moved to Soweto as adults were looking for work or reported no economic activity. For comparison purposes, a quarter of that age group as a whole were looking for work or reported no economic activity in our survey. After that age, the difference disappears, perhaps because newcomers who do not find work move elsewhere or return home. Before 1986 that would have been enforced by the influx controls, which made the right to migrate between rural and urban areas dependent on having work (Morris et al. 1999: 18). Currently, availability of accommodation and money are most likely the enforcers.

It is not clear whether the preponderance of young adults among newcomers has been a consistent pattern over the years or a recent phenomenon. Our data is incomplete with respect to such questions, because our sample covers only people who stayed in Soweto, who were still alive at the time of the survey and who were older than fifteen years. Anyone who moved to Soweto at age 50 in 1940 and stayed until their death at age 81 is invisible in our 2006 data, as are those who moved to Soweto at age 50 in 1999 and then left the township in 2005. Anyone who moved to Soweto in 2003 at age ten is also invisible, because they would have been only thirteen years old at the time of our survey.

Figure 3.1 gives a picture of what we do know about the scale and timing of influx. It represents our data as if every Sowetan older than fifteen years were asked to go into one of three rooms, depending on whether they were born in the township, arrived as an adult or arrived as a child. There they line up behind the sign corresponding to the number of years they had lived in Soweto by 2006. We should not be surprised by small distortions near multiples of ten because, especially for more distant years, people may tend to round off the number. Remember also that as we go further back, we encounter more 'missing' data due to old age and death, and recent years truncate births and child influx into the township. Finally, remember that these graphs show only remaining migrants – people who arrived and stayed until the time of our survey.

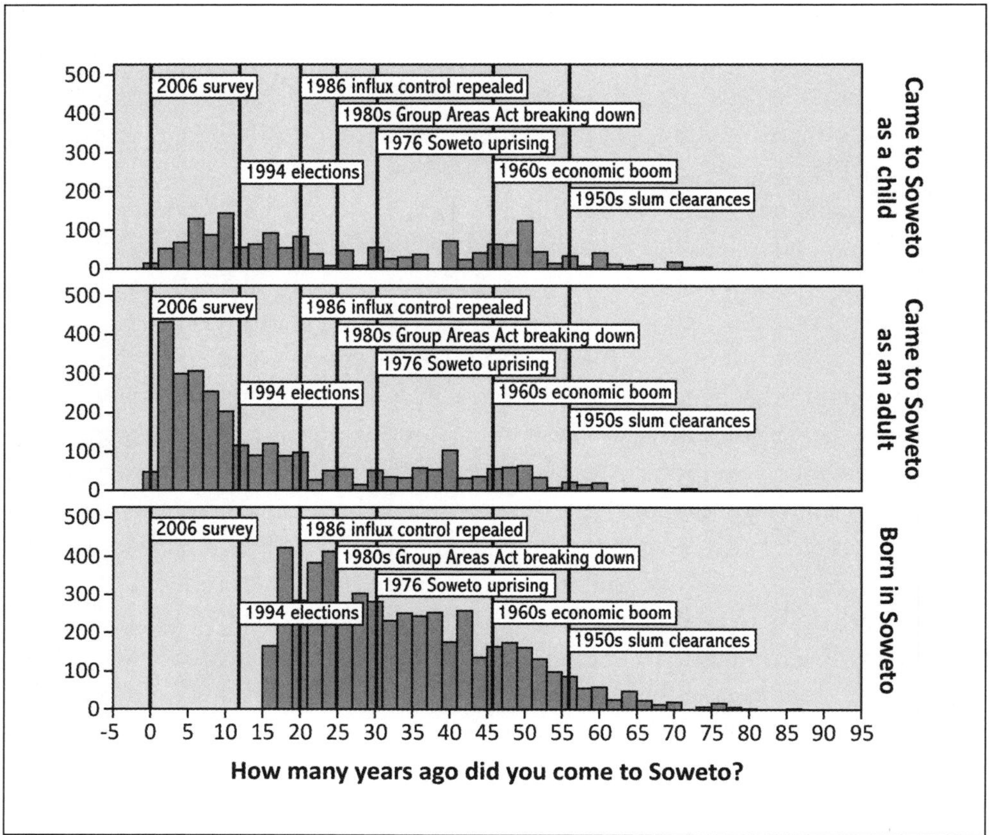

Figure 3.1 Timing of migration or birth among still-resident, still-living Sowetans aged sixteen and over, in two-year increments.

Source: Classifying Soweto survey 2006.

Much about the shape of these graphs can be explained by the history of influx control interacting with fluctuations of the economy and conditions inside the township. The slum clearances in the 1950s forcibly removed people from the city to Soweto, appearing here in several spikes in adult and child migration and steadily rising births in Soweto (remember that much information about migration will be missing in this decade). The economic boom of the 1960s could explain the sudden increase in adult migration 40 years before the survey, as people were drawn to work in the township. There is a dip in adult migration from 1970, 35 years before the survey and six years before the 1976 Soweto uprising. In data not shown here, it is clear that this dip owes most to the absence of remaining *adult* immigrants –

remaining child migrants outnumber remaining young adult migrants to the township in this decade, and in this case it cannot be owing to missing data, as would be the case for earlier and later decades. This may be related to fewer work opportunities and hence fewer rights to enter the township in terms of the influx laws, but also Soweto's housing shortage may have acted against successful migration in that decade, just before the backyard rooms and shacks began to mushroom. It is also possible that the 'missing generation' came to Soweto possibly in defiance of the pass laws, but left soon after, having failed to find jobs and accommodation. Finally, there is the possibility that many of this generation would have been in the prime of their working lives when the Group Areas Act and influx controls were lifted, and therefore well placed to lead an exodus from the township to the suburbs. However, one would have expected this to show up among people born in Soweto, as well as those born outside, unless migrants are more likely to be successful. The number of remaining adult immigrants and remaining Soweto-borns dips from the early 1980s, when the enforcement of the Group Areas Act was breaking down (Beall, Crankshaw and Parnell 2002b: 61), possibly representing already urbanised people moving out of the township to formerly white areas. It rises around the time influx control is lifted in 1986 – which would have allowed greater freedom of movement to the city from outside – and reaches a plateau until a new take-off with the democratic elections (remember that births in the township and child immigration are missing data at this end of the graph).

So the picture that emerges is firstly that migration to Soweto was affected by the removal of racially exclusive legislation; and secondly that, as in the past, Soweto remains an important destination or launching pad for job seekers in post-apartheid South Africa.

Soweto's internal configuration: Living, consuming and working

Earlier I mentioned three large forces that have acted on the internal geography of Soweto. These were the removal of racial barriers on living areas and movement, in the context of the intensified privatisation of housing provision; the restructuring of the labour market; and the physical legacy of the township built by the apartheid state. This section turns to an internal comparison, that is, a comparison of Sowetans with other Sowetans. We see growing visible differentiation of housing stock, persistent poverty, dependence on the service industries for employment and large numbers of people without regular employment.

Living: Houses

At the end of apartheid, a much greater proportion of Sowetans lived in brick houses than was the case for the other main township associated with Johannesburg, Alexandra. In 1998 less than 35 per cent of Alexandrans lived in or behind a brick house (CASE 1998) compared to more than 70 per cent of Sowetans (Morris et al. 1999). However, by the time the Group Areas Act was formally repealed in 1991, Soweto's brick housing – mostly former council stock – was bursting at the seams. Beall, Crankshaw and Parnell (2002a: 6) explain:

> Towards the end of the 1960s, the apartheid government began to channel funds for housing from townships such as Meadowlands to townships in the so-called 'homelands' . . . As early as the late-1970s, this shortage of housing manifested itself as residents were forced to overcrowd their standardised four-roomed houses and to build temporary shacks in their backyards to accommodate their adult offspring . . . Estimates of the shortage of houses in 1979 ranged from 25,000 to 32,000 units.

The pressure on housing has expanded Soweto on all its edges opposite Johannesburg, as well as in all its interstices. Newer housing is mostly of two kinds. Firstly, there is commercially built housing for sale – commonly called bond houses, because they are usually bought with a bond (mortgage) from a bank (see Photograph 3.3). Acres of bond houses have stretched to the south-west corner of Soweto until they are engulfed by a settlement of the second sort of housing, self-built tin shacks (see Photograph 3.4). Bond houses accommodate about 11 per cent of Sowetans (see Table 3.4), a small increase from the 9 per cent in the Wits survey, but remember the caveat that this was sampled according to strata of housing. We do not know how the proportion of bond houses compares to other areas today, because data from Stats SA does not distinguish between different types of brick houses.

Over the past 20 years, self-built tin shacks have mushroomed in all of Soweto's nooks and crannies. Freestanding shacks (also called *mkhukhus* or chicken huts) now accommodate approximately 8 per cent of Sowetans (see Photographs 3.4 and 3.5). Nevertheless, Table 3.4 shows that Soweto's proportion of shacks has been consistently lower than its surroundings. This could be related to the lack of empty space in and around Soweto or to the availability of backyard accommodation, which I will discuss shortly. Shacks in Soweto are frequently built on land considered to be unsuitable for building. Jumbled informal settlements have filled up the floodplains around the stream in Kliptown, ironically within sight of the bomb-

Table 3.4 Dwelling of respondent: Contemporary contextual comparison.

<table>
<tr><th colspan="3">Type of dwelling</th><th colspan="2" rowspan="2">2006 adult Sowetans (%) Johannesburg</th><th rowspan="2">2007 black people in Metro (%)</th><th rowspan="2">2007 all races in Johannesburg Metro (%)</th></tr>
<tr><th colspan="2"></th><th>Detailed description</th></tr>
<tr><td rowspan="5">Brick structures</td><td></td><td>Bond house</td><td>11</td><td rowspan="5">75[7]</td><td rowspan="5">60.6</td><td rowspan="5">69.9</td></tr>
<tr><td></td><td>RDP house</td><td>4</td></tr>
<tr><td rowspan="5">In and among former council stock</td><td>Former council house</td><td>34</td></tr>
<tr><td>Former council house renovated</td><td>20</td></tr>
<tr><td>Former council house major rebuild</td><td>6</td></tr>
<tr><td rowspan="2"></td><td>Backyard room</td><td colspan="2">6</td><td>8.6</td><td>7.4</td></tr>
<tr><td>Backyard shack</td><td colspan="2">7</td><td>11.4</td><td>8.4</td></tr>
<tr><td colspan="2"></td><td>Freestanding shack</td><td colspan="2">8</td><td>14.6</td><td>10.7</td></tr>
<tr><td colspan="2"></td><td>Hostel</td><td colspan="2">3</td><td>4.4</td><td>3.2</td></tr>
<tr><td colspan="2"></td><td>Other</td><td colspan="2">1</td><td>0.3</td><td>0.3</td></tr>
<tr><td colspan="2"></td><td>Total</td><td colspan="2">100</td><td>99.9</td><td>99.9</td></tr>
</table>

Sources: Classifying Soweto survey 2006; author's calculations from interactive online database of Stats SA 2007 Community Survey.

proof concrete monument to the Freedom Charter. Motsoaledi, under the power lines along a river behind the Chris Hani Baragwanath Hospital, has by contrast a more ordered and open grid that leaves space for a few trees. Motsoaledi emerged a little before the first democratic elections and it is possible that people were originally mapping out the kind of suburb they wanted to live in with an eye to the future, expecting formal housing and facilities to follow shortly, once they had done their part (Photographs 3.6 and 3.7). Elsewhere, shacks are built on land originally allocated for something else. South of Soweto, for example, relatively ordered, well-spaced informal settlements took over land earmarked for light industry in Devland. In Protea South, shacks clash with bond houses on land intended for the latter.

Low-cost, government-subsidised housing, called Reconstruction and Development Programme (RDP) houses (Photograph 3.8), have pushed the north-west edge of Soweto towards the rail lines separating the township from the West Rand, and their western edge now connects to Tshepisong, a township outside Krugersdorp, by a foot path. Some of the space beyond Noordgesig in the north-east was also being turned to RDP housing at the time of the survey, and an older, large RDP development is tucked away south of Soweto around Goldev.

The provision of these small houses is partially privatised: they are usually built by private companies on government tender to the value of a small subsidy, then handed over to low-income occupants to complete or extend as they can. Just 4 per cent of Sowetans live in RDP houses, far fewer than in the various kinds of makeshift housing (see Table 3.4). The government claimed in its 2009 electioneering campaign to have delivered 2.6 million low-cost units in the country, but this lags behind its own figures regarding the growth in need. According to the Department of Housing, the new government inherited a backlog of about 2.2 million housing units by 1997, counting all those in informal settlements and backyard shacks. At that time, it expected the need to increase by about 204 000 units a year (Department of Housing 2000). This adds up to about 2.4 million extra units between then and 2009. By 2001 the Department of Housing estimated a slightly higher backlog of 2.8 million (Miraftab 2003: 231), suggesting that new housing was barely keeping pace. In 2008 the backlog remained at 2.1 million (IOL 2008).

As far back as the 1970s, people responded to overflowing former council houses and government indifference by building backyard shacks and rooms (Photographs 3.9 and 3.10). Freestanding shacks were not tolerated then, and privately built houses were only rarely a viable business prospect. By 2006 around 60 per cent of Sowetans lived in a house that started life as a former council house and 13 per cent lived in the backyard rooms and shacks tucked behind and between them (Table 3.4), meaning that a little less than three-quarters of Sowetans live in and among the oldest housing stock.

The proportion of Sowetans living in backyard shacks and rooms is only 13 per cent in our survey (see Table 3.4), but they remain a key form of rental accommodation and a way to accommodate an expanding household. The means plot in Figure 3.2 shows that the average age of people who live in backyard shacks and rooms is substantially younger than those in the main former council houses. This supports the findings of Owen Crankshaw, Alan Gilbert and Alan Morris (2000), who posit that backyard shacks and rooms provide accommodation for the grown children of council house residents who cannot afford to leave Soweto. Additionally, we observed that they may accommodate unemployed relatives partially incorporated into households, for example, where the main household helps with some, but not all of the person's upkeep. Backyard rooms and shacks, as we will demonstrate later, are also the main rental space available to young, single workers and small families, especially those moving in from outside the township. They also provide rental income for poorer households who inherited former council houses when the former council handed over title deeds to residents (Crankshaw, Gilbert and Morris 2000).

Of course, the former council houses are no longer all the same, and this is one of the starker changes in Soweto since the end of apartheid. Elaborate, custom-

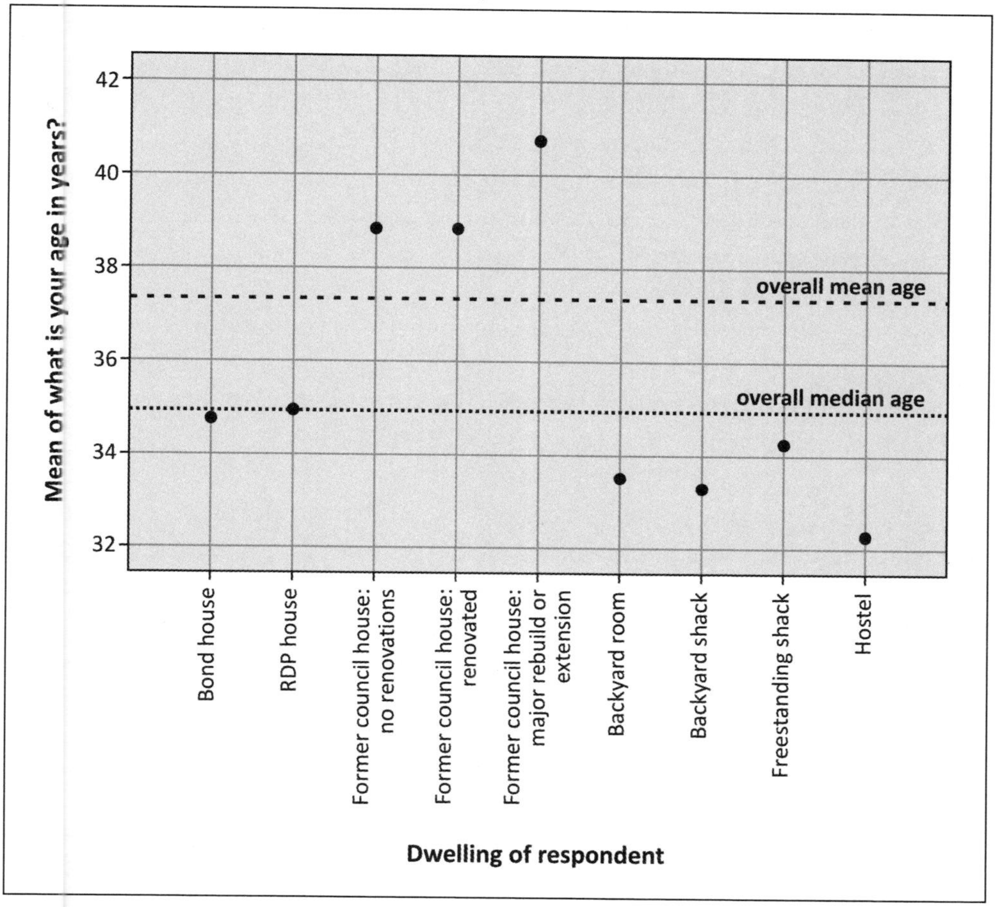

Figure 3.2 Average ages of Sowetans aged sixteen and older in different types of housing.
Source: Classifying Soweto survey 2006.

built, double-storey houses now sit among unreconstructed matchboxes, and some areas have changed more than others in this regard. After the title deeds were handed over, those who could afford to extended, remodelled or renovated their former council houses (Beall, Crankshaw and Parnell 2002b). About 40 per cent of former council houses, equal to 26 per cent of all Soweto housing, have been renovated beyond cosmetic improvements (Table 3.4). In some cases, the house has been completely rebuilt or unrecognisably extended (Photograph 3.11), but simpler renovations may involve choosing a better front door or installing larger windows (Photograph 3.12), adding rooms to expand family accommodation (in our survey, respondents living in renovated and rebuilt former council houses live in households that have, on average, more adults than other Soweto households), adding a garage or building the ultimate luxury in former council houses, a bathroom.

Tiling floors and building a higher perimeter fence (Photograph 3.13) are seen as ways to improve houses, for which the skills seem readily available around Soweto. About 28 per cent of our survey respondents, even in ordinary former council houses, had done the former and 60 per cent the latter. Trevor Ngwane, a Soweto activist, says:

> Building a big house is both a practical thing [to accommodate a growing family], but it's also a status thing, and it's also a form of escape from '*siyafana*' (we are the same) – because remember the matchbox houses are all the same, so you try to distinguish yourself.[8]

Alongside the renovations, some 85 per cent of unrenovated former council houses had no hot running water at the time of our survey and 70 per cent had no kitchen sink. Even renovated former council houses may lack facilities considered basic in houses in former white areas: 64 per cent of Sowetans in such accommodation lack hot water and half still had no kitchen sink. Areas of formal council housing are marked, then, by growing diversity of housing, manifesting some of Soweto's inequality in visual forms.

Finally, around 3 per cent of Sowetans live in hostels (see Photograph 3.14.) Seven single-sex hostels were built in Soweto from the 1960s. They were meant to accommodate migrant workers with temporary urban status, while family accommodation in council houses was reserved for workers with more urban rights. Today, only one hostel is still single-sex (Beall, Crankshaw and Parnell 2002b: 50). Hostel dwellers in our survey were less likely than all other Sowetans put together to own refrigerators, television sets or DVD players, but hostel dwellers appear otherwise no more deprived than the average Sowetan.

Hostels were intended as rental accommodation for workers who were not permanent residents, although one of the attractions of hostels towards the end of apartheid was that rents were seldom actually collected (Beall, Crankshaw and Parnell 2002b: 51). By 2006 hostels made up a tiny proportion of Soweto's limited rental accommodation. Table 3.5 shows that 23 per cent of Sowetans aged sixteen years and older rent the place in which they stay.

Summarising from Table 3.5, we see that the majority of Sowetans, 65 per cent, owned a brick house or lived in a brick house owned by a family member. Council houses and backyard dwellings are the numerical backbone of rental housing, accommodating 16 per cent of Sowetans, while 5 per cent rent hostels and shacks.

Table 3.5 Rental and ownership (percentages of adult Sowetans).

Housing type	Is the place in which you live . . .			Total
	Rented?	Owned by you or a family member?	Don't know	
Bond house	0	10	2	10
RDP house	0	4		4
Former council, any kind	9	51		60
Backyard accommodation	8	6		13
Freestanding shack	3	5		8
Hostel	2	0		3
Other	0	0		1
Total	23	75	2	100

Source: Classifying Soweto survey. Due to rounding, figures do not necessarily add up.

But rental is more pronounced in hostels, shacks and backyard structures when these are considered proportionately. Brick houses of every kind are overwhelmingly owned, not rented. RDP houses and unrenovated, former council houses have the highest proportion of rentals – 14 per cent – among brick houses. By contrast, as much as 60 per cent of all backyard accommodation is rented. Nearly 40 per cent of freestanding shacks are rented. Shack owners own the construction, but not the land on which it sits. The rate of home ownership in Soweto is substantially higher than for black people overall in the Johannesburg Metro, where about 42 per cent of people own formal homes, 33 per cent rent and the remainder occupy their homes rent free. It approaches the rate for whites in the metro – 70 per cent – but the type of house owned will differ radically. The high rate of home ownership in Soweto is primarily the legacy of the handover of title deeds of former council houses.

To conclude, Soweto's housing is increasingly diverse. Old housing has been altered. New forms of housing accommodate about 20 per cent of all Sowetans (RDP houses, bond houses, shacks and rebuilt council houses). Their visual impact in conveying a sense of difference punches above their actual proportion. Chapter 4 deals with households from the point of view of work and mutual support, and household sizes will be discussed later in this chapter.

Getting and spending in Soweto

If we listen to marketers, the main point of Soweto after apartheid was its annual spending power, estimated at R10.4 billion in 2003 for the City of Johannesburg

(Palmer Development Group et al. 2005; Pernegger and Godehart 2007). Most of its disposable portion was then spent outside the township (*Joburg News* 2006). But moves have been made by big retailers to mop up that spending power at source. A drive-by observer might notice that the lonely billboard advertising OMO® washing powder, which stood for years near the Diepkloof hostel, is gone. This approach to Soweto is now marked by a flock of billboards advertising banking, cell phones, lagers and sometimes 'traditional' beers being enjoyed by well-dressed models. In the past, most shopping within Soweto was small scale and often informal. Dobsonville Mall was the only major shopping mall in Soweto until 2005, when the Protea Glen Mall opened. During our fieldwork in 2006, Bara Mall opened near the taxi rank close to Motsoaledi, the big informal settlement, and construction advanced on Jabulani Mall and the swanky Maponya Mall. The latter has some very expensive shops and attracts visitors from outside Soweto. A monumental elephant and fountain guard the parking lot and in the swooping, airy foyer, a statue of Hector Peterson, the iconic victim of the 1976 Soweto uprising, reminds shoppers of the cost of this new price-tagged freedom. Security guards, kitted out in black and grey top hats, are instructed to forbid photographs being taken of this statue.

The shopping malls and billboards add to a barrage of factors that encourage people to place themselves in the new South Africa as consumers. A grittier edition of the post-apartheid consumer grates against this aspirational version. Even before the shopping centres mushroomed, Sowetans were forcibly turned into consumers with regard to basic services such as water and electricity by the framework of central government's Growth, Employment and Redistribution policy. Following government's Masakhane (let us build together) campaign, the corporatised Johannesburg Water, Eskom and City Power launched a cost-recovery campaign. The campaign claimed a post-apartheid legitimacy dividend to reverse the 1980s boycotters' 'culture of non-payment', but cost recovery was backed up by cut-offs and, later, installation of pre-paid meters when people returned to the old tactic of reconnecting themselves. Themes of deprivation and exclusion also emerge in shack-dwellers' protests (see Ballard, Habib and Valodia 2006).

By certain measures, such as the Gini coefficient, inequality has been increasing in South Africa and inequality within race groups has been increasing (Presidency 2007: 22). The most recent UN-HABITAT survey pegs Johannesburg as one of the most unequal cities in the world on income distribution, with a Gini coefficient of 0.71 (UN-HABITAT 2010). How do income distributions in Soweto compare to the rest of the country?

In the 2001 Census, which recorded only formal incomes, Sowetans were concentrated in the annual household income ranges roughly equivalent to R400 to R6 400 a month. Some 67 per cent of Soweto households fell into this range (R4 801 to R76 800 annually in Figure 3.3), with 40 per cent concentrated in the narrower range of R800 to R3 200 per household per month. Soweto is represented by the thick, solid grey line in Figure 3.3, which plots income profiles as a percentage of households in each annual income category, for Soweto and for white and black South Africans, Johannesburgers and Gauteng residents. A further 20 per cent of Sowetan households reported no formal income.

The most striking feature of this graph is the disproportion between black and white incomes, with white incomes concentrated above R6 000 a month per household, and outstripping the proportion of black incomes in all the income categories above that. Soweto's income profile is firmly in the camp of black South Africa, but its proportion of the lowest income categories is below the overall national proportion, and below the proportion for black people nationally. At the other end of the scale, Soweto falls below national proportions for formal incomes

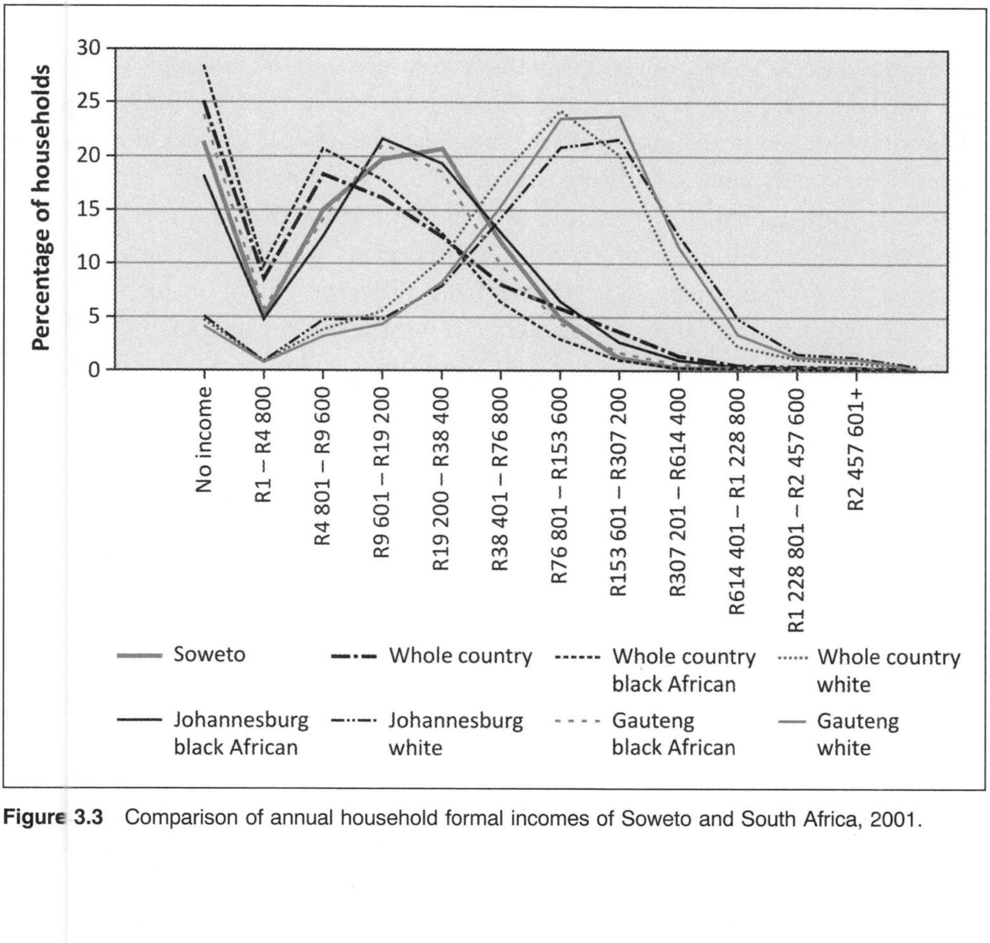

Figure 3.3 Comparison of annual household formal incomes of Soweto and South Africa, 2001.

above R6 400 per month. Soweto's income profile is very similar to that for all black people in Johannesburg and the province, Gauteng, although it lags behind black people in Johannesburg (the city, not the Metro) in higher income categories.

However, we must stress again that this reflects only formal incomes.[9] The figures refract reliance on wages and salaries, without including other complementary or alternate incomes, such as informal incomes, transfers between households, social grants and intra-household transfers, such as discussed further in Chapter 4. A very rough calculation using Census 2001 data for Soweto puts about 24 per cent of households below the rule-of-thumb 'dollar-a-day' poverty line (around R250 a month or R3 000 a year, per head) mentioned by the Presidency (2007) in its poverty headcount. But this figure includes the 20 per cent of Sowetan households controversially reporting no income at all in the census, and therefore should be treated cautiously. Per-capita census data encompasses only employed people and therefore is of little use here.

For our own survey, we decided not to collect information directly about incomes. First, and most importantly, we would be interviewing individuals who were not household heads. Our sample included, for example, schoolchildren who would not have known much about the whole household's income. Collecting data on their individual incomes would have been too limited because individual and household incomes are entwined in complicated ways that are seldom universal. Second, our questionnaire had to cover many bases and its primary concern was with identities. Establishing reliable income data, even from a more informed member of the household, is time consuming, especially when people have informal incomes, irregular incomes and incomes from different sources, which even the respondent may not easily recall. That is further complicated by multiple breadwinners and varied informal and sometimes-irregular arrangements for distribution within and between households.[10]

Instead, we opted to use the Living Standards Measure (LSM) as a pragmatic compromise to establish a relative scale of living standards. The LSM measures the accumulation of goods and services in a household: things a household owns (radios, cars, DVD players, television sets, and so on) and services it accesses (domestic workers, security, water, toilets). These are weighted and combined into a single indicator, which is periodically updated, and organised into 10 categories in 2006, each associated with a particular set of demographics, including the *average* household incomes of people in that category. The LSM is devised by the South African Advertising Research Foundation as a marketing tool, and therefore has certain limitations from a sociological perspective. For example, the index interacts with the age of the household because it measures an accumulation of goods.

However, the data for the index is quick to collect in a questionnaire survey, and it multi-tasks. We used each of the variables collected for the index independently of the index (for example, to consider car ownership or housing type and class identity or religion). The index itself provides both a relative measure of living standards and a very rough proxy of incomes. The reader must remember, however, that the LSM indicator is, for our purposes, a pragmatic compromise when it comes to reporting incomes. It is of more use for comparison than for firmly establishing absolute incomes in Soweto.

Our LSM indicator is even more approximate because two LSM components (the number of radios per household and the number of flush toilets) were lost in shortening the pilot questionnaire. We were able to compensate for the latter by observing that certain housing types in Soweto always have access to a flush toilet, albeit overused, and certain housing types never do. We can also calculate the maximum effect of the radio component. I have therefore represented our income distributions in the discussions to follow with two sets of figures: a maximum which assumes all the flush toilets are working, and a minimum calculated from the maximum assuming that nobody in Soweto has more than one radio, which is of course unlikely. (Elsewhere we have used the base LSM score before adjustments, which is very similar to the maximum score produced by adjusting for toilets.)

With these caveats in mind, what can we say about the income distribution of Sowetans in our data? In Table 3.6 we see that while Gauteng's population, using comparable data, is spread along the top half of the scale, and South Africa's across the bottom half, Soweto's is bunched in the middle. (Note that this does not represent the middle of the range of incomes, but the middle of the LSM income categories, which stretch to a wider range as they get larger.)

Using the LSM extrapolation of household income, between one-tenth and one-quarter of Sowetans older than fifteen years live in households that, on average, brought in less than R2 000 a month (Table 3.6). Remember that this is a percentage of Sowetans over fifteen years, not a percentage of households. For context, a loaf of brown bread in the January following the survey cost R4.44 (R7 = $1) and white bread R4.70 (Tema and Nyhodo 2007). At least half of Sowetans lived in households bringing in R2 680 to R4 400 and at least one-tenth in households bringing in an average of R6 880. Note that these figures cannot be compared directly with the 2001 Census figures reported above. Aside from the issue of formal and informal incomes, our figures count the number of individuals in each type of household, whereas the census figures count households.

Unfortunately, the 2007 Community Survey is not available at the level of Soweto, and we cannot use it to compare Soweto with its surroundings because the

Table 3.6 Income distribution in Soweto compared to South Africa and Gauteng.

Monthly household income estimated from LSM category in rand (R7 = $1 in July 2006)	Percentage of Sowetans living in such households, 2006		Percentage of South Africans living in such households, 2006	Percentage of Gauteng residents living in such households, 2007
	Lowest possible LSM score[11]	Highest possible LSM score		
999 (LSM 1)	1		6	0
1 210 (LSM 2)	3	>1	12	1
1 509 (LSM 3)	5	3	13	3
1 924 (LSM 4)	15	7	15	6
2 680 (LSM5)	26[12]	22	14	13
4 400 (LSM 6)	31	38	14	24
6 880 (LSM 7)	10	15	8	14
9 304 (LSM 8)	5	7	6	11
12 647 (LSM 9)	3	6	7	14
19 974 (LSM 10)	0	2	6	12
Total	100	100		100

Sources: Classifying Soweto survey 2006; AMPS 2006 and AMPS 2007.[13] Due to rounding, figures do not necessarily add up.

Community Survey reports incomes per individual, or incomes per household, rather than numbers of individuals in particular household-income categories. Neither can we directly compare it with the 2001 Census because the *Community Survey* collected comprehensive income information while the Census asked only about formal incomes. However, the different shape of the income data emerging from the Community Survey and the 2001 Census suggests the importance of incomes other than formal incomes in South Africa. The number of households reporting no income at all drops to less than 10 per cent for the country in the Community Survey, and the income profile peaks a few categories beyond the poorest. About 40 per cent of households fall into the range R800 to R3 000 per household per month (R9 600 to R38 400 annually).

What about income per head? The Community Survey shows that 43 per cent of black people in the Johannesburg Metro and 45 per cent in the country report no income (of their own) and a further 30 per cent in the Metro earn less than R1 600 a month. In reality, some of the people without incomes live in households with some of the people who have incomes, so these proportions are misleading as measures of wealth or poverty. In our survey, 30 per cent of respondents report that their main source of income was another person's wage or salary. I used the number of people in each household in our survey to approximate an income per head, including children, shown in Table 3.7.

Table 3.7 Approximate income per head.

Income in rand (R7 = $1, July 2006)	Percentage of Sowetans aged 16 and over	
	Lower LSM adjustment[14]	Higher LSM adjustment
250 and less	7	3
251–430	14	11
431–800	29	25
801–1 600	32	36
1 601–3 200	14	19
3 201–6 400	3	6
6 401 and higher	>1	1
Total	100	100

Source: Classifying Soweto survey 2006. Due to rounding, figures do not necessarily add up.

Table 3.7 suggests that half of Sowetans were living on less than R800 per person per month in 2006. (Remember that our income figures are an approximation.) As many as one-fifth of Sowetans may have been living on or below the poverty line, suggested by the Treasury, of R430 per head per person per month in 2006 (National Treasury 2007; see also Woolard and Leibbrandt 2006), but less than one-tenth were living below the dollar-a-day poverty line mentioned earlier. By this measure, Soweto does not have the same degree of deep poverty as the country as a whole, if we are to believe the estimates of the Presidency (2007) and Van der Berg et al. (2005), who use the All Media Products Survey (AMPS) to suggest that at least 43 per cent of all South Africans lived below the Treasury poverty line in 2006 (Presidency 2007: 22; see also Van der Berg et al. 2005; Meth 2006b).

To conclude, a large gap between the mean and the median of a population indicates inequality. In our survey, the median approximated monthly income per head of Sowetans is R845/R962 (depending on which LSM adjustment I used). Between 63 per cent and 65 per cent of Sowetans live below the mean of our approximated income per head, which is R1 100/R1 370 (depending on which LSM adjustment is used). In the Wits survey, around 58 per cent of Sowetans lived below the mean (Crankshaw, Gilbert and Morris 2000: 10), but we cannot say if this indicates polarisation of Sowetans or a difference between the methods of the two surveys. Inequality among Sowetans seems less pronounced than among black Africans in the country as a whole: The Presidency, using incomes and expenditure data, puts mean incomes for a black Africans in 2005 at R775, and the median at R407, with the median for whites at R5 331 and the mean at R7 645. (Presidency, 2009: 22).

Other measures of consumption are more reliable in our data. Table 3.8 gives a picture of goods and services accumulated by Sowetan households by the time of our survey in 2006, five of which were compared with the rest of the country in the introduction to this section, where we saw that, except for some legacies of the way in which the township was built, Sowetans tend to be better off overall than most blacks, but worse off than most whites (Tables 3.1 and 3.2). Table 3.8, which covers 23 goods or services, does something different: it illustrates aspects of the spread of internal differentiation and some markers of differentiation by charting which of these goods and services are commonplace for Sowetans and which are luxuries.

The goods in the black band in Table 3.8 can be considered basic for Soweto. Almost everyone lives in a household with these goods and the minority without them may be considered deprived in the Soweto context. There is a substantial gap to the next band: fewer than half of Sowetans live in households with the small durables such as hi-fis and DVD players listed in the dark grey band. The goods and services in the light-grey and white bands may be considered luxuries. The 14 per cent of Sowetans who do not have basics, such as an electric stove, are concentrated in squatter areas like Kliptown, where an electric stove is owned by fewer than 9 per cent because electricity itself is a luxury. By contrast, in newer 'middle-class' areas like Protea North, a quarter of households employ a domestic worker. Of course, a certain amount of differentiation results from the structural inheritance of the township. For instance, in newer areas like Protea Glen, up to 80 per cent of people had hot running water, enjoyed by only a third of people in Soweto overall.

Relative poverty is reflected again in food consumption. Maize-meal porridge – known locally as *pap* – remains a staple for Sowetans in many income brackets, but eating it night after night was frequently mentioned by Sowetans we talked to as one of the frustrations of perceived poverty. On the night before the survey, 60 per cent of all Sowetans had eaten *pap* for supper. While half of the respondents in rebuilt former council houses had eaten *pap* for dinner, 67 per cent of those in freestanding shacks had eaten *pap* for dinner the night before the survey.

Sizeable portions of Sowetans are also deprived in terms of 'cultural' consumption: 44 per cent of Sowetans had never watched a movie in a cinema and a further 30 per cent had last been to a movie more than a year before the survey. Fifty-five per cent had never bought a book that was not a schoolbook or a magazine, and only 20 per cent had bought such a book within the year before the survey. Forty-two per cent had never been to a restaurant.

Table 3.8 Distribution of selected household goods and services among Sowetans aged sixteen years and over.

Does your household have the following items in working order?		**Yes**	
		No. of respondents	**Percentage of Sowetans aged 16 and over**
Most adult Sowetans live in a household with . . .	An electric stove	1 968	86
	A radio	1 982	84
	A TV set	1 949	84
	A fridge/freezer	1 887	80
	A cell phone	1 756	77
Fewer than half, but more than one quarter live in a household with . . .	A DVD player	1 123	49
	A microwave oven	1 095	44
	A hi-fi or music centre	1 019	42
	A built-in kitchen sink	974	38
	VCR (video machine)	789	32
	A Telkom telephone (landline)	712	29
	Hot running water	727	28
	A washing machine	653	26
Fewer than a quarter live in a household with . . .	A deep freeze	570	24
	A running motor vehicle	538	22
	A sewing machine	371	16
	A computer	335	14
	A tumble dryer	281	12
Fewer than 1 in 10 live in a household with . . .	A vacuum cleaner or floor polisher	252	10
	An employed domestic worker	184	7
	Cable TV	124	5
	A dishwashing machine	54	3
	A home security service (such as Chubb or ADT)	57	2

Source: Classifying Soweto survey 2006.

Work

Soweto remains an important pool of labour, and this is evident in the busy minibus taxi rank at Baragwanath, from which taxis ferry people between Soweto and Johannesburg. However, the streets of Soweto remain busy during the day because the majority of adult Sowetans do not work for wages. Soweto, like the rest of the country, was affected by the wave of retrenchments that hit South Africa in the 1990s. The activity on Soweto's daytime streets includes people making work for themselves in home industry (Photograph 3.15) and roadside selling.

In 2006 the township's unemployment rate (calculated using the official definition detailed in Chapter 4) was 32 per cent, well above the national level of

Table 3.9 Soweto compared to Gauteng and South Africa: Employment status as a proportion of the population aged 16–65 years, 2001 and 2006 (percentages).

	Employed, official definition (includes survivalist activity)	**Unemployed, official definition (excludes discouraged workseekers)**	**Not economically active (includes discouraged workseekers)**	***Sources***
2001				
% whole country	45.1	16.2	38.7	*Labour Force Survey*, March 2001; author's calculations from online data
% black Africans in whole country	40.8	18.4	40.8	
% whole Gauteng Province	52.0	27.4	20.5	
% black Africans in Gauteng	48.3	24.5	27.2	
% Sowetans	*Comparable data not available*[15]			
2006				
% whole country	43.1	14.8	42.0	*Labour Force Survey*, March 2006; author's calculations from online data
% black Africans in whole country	38.4	17.0	44.6	
% whole Gauteng Province	52.2	15.8	32.0	
% black Africans in Gauteng	48.3	19.0	32.7	
% Sowetans	40.0[16]	21.0	39.0	Classifying Soweto survey 2006

25 per cent. Table 3.9 shows employment status as a *proportion* of the working age population (usually 15–64 years, but in this table, people aged 16–65 years, for comparability with our data) for 2001 and 2006. The Stats SA definitions used here distinguish between the officially unemployed, who had looked for work in the past seven days, and 'discouraged workseekers', who had not done so.

Table 3.9 shows a generalised decline, particularly pronounced in Gauteng, in the proportion of workseekers, accompanied by an increase in the proportion of economically inactive rather than an increase in the proportion of economically active people. Much of this increase represents unemployed people who have given up looking for work. Ten per cent of black people in Gauteng, for example, moved from the economically inactive group to the unemployed group if discouraged workseekers are counted as unemployed. However, the decline in active workseekers is much less pronounced for black people in Gauteng, suggesting that job hunting is an important motivator, or perhaps a consequence, of migration to Gauteng by black people. Finally, our data about Soweto suggests a lower proportion of employed, a slightly higher proportion of workseekers and a markedly higher proportion of economically inactive people than in the province as a whole. This supports the picture of Soweto as both a destination for job hunters and, increasingly, a reserve for unwanted labour. These arguments will be developed later in this and the following chapter.

Waged work of Sowetans is dominated by service industries, such as retail and government. Industry is not easily accessible from Soweto. Semi-skilled workers such as machine operators form fewer than 10 per cent of the Sowetans employed by others in our survey, partly the result of a generalised decline in manufacturing on the Witwatersrand (Barchiesi and Kenny 2002: 36). Our survey shows that government, notably the Department of Education and the South African Police Service, are the main employers of employed Sowetans, followed by large retailers such as Pick n Pay, Shoprite and Edgars. Less than 10 per cent of working Sowetans are domestic workers, around 20 per cent are in routine white-collar work – cashiers, bank tellers and the like – and about 15 per cent are in menial jobs such as cleaning. Table 3.10 shows the occupations of Sowetans who worked for a company or an individual for wages or salaries in 2006, as a percentage of all Sowetans and as a percentage of waged/salaried Sowetans. The figures include the occupations of irregularly and regularly employed people.

When considered as a proportion of all Sowetans older than fifteen years, including people older than 65, no more than 25 per cent of Sowetans were regularly waged/salaried in our 2006 survey (Table 3.11). Another quarter reported no economic activity, but they were neither pensioners nor students. Close to one-quarter were pensioners, disabled, receiving government grants, still at school or post-school students. Only 6 per cent were successfully self-employed or employers. The remaining fifth were in makeshift work, such as survivalist vending, irregular employment and economic pursuits somewhere between the two, such as scrap collecting (who would have been employed according to the official definition). We will elaborate on and discuss these categories in Chapters 4 and 5.

A gender breakdown of employment and unemployment, not shown here, reveals that women are more likely than men to be unemployed and less likely to be employed.

Summary: Differentiated living, earning and working

The preceding section considered three types of internal differentiation in Soweto. Differentiation is increasingly visible in the diversification of housing in past years, both in terms of changes to existing housing stock and in the development of new

Table 3.10 Occupations of Sowetans aged sixteen years and older.

Occupation	No. of respondents	Percentage of Sowetans aged 16 and over	Percentage of waged/ salaried Sowetans aged 16 and over
White-collar routine (such as bank tellers)	145	6	17
Menial (such as waiters, cleaners)	144	6	18
Domestic workers	73	3	9
Semi-skilled manual (such as machine operators)	64	3	9
Drivers and security guards	63	3	8
Skilled manual	47	2	7
Teachers and nurses	45	1	4
Managers and supervisors	34	2	4
Cashiers	33	2	4
Organising other people's lives (personal assistants, administrators)	33	1	4
Labourers	32	1	4
Sales representatives and merchandisers	26	1	3
Technicians	19	1	3
Police and South African National Defence Force	18	1	2
Home help, but not a domestic worker (e.g., volunteer health worker, unskilled crèche worker)	18	1	2
Professionals and consultants	16	1	2
Total waged/salaried	810	34	100
Unemployed, self-employed, students, pensioners, survivalists, etc.	1 743	66	–
Total population older than 15 years	2 553[17]	100	–

Source: Classifying Soweto survey 2006. Percentages do not add up due to rounding.

Table 3.11 Forms of work and worklessness in Soweto.

Work status as a proportion of Sowetans aged 16 and over	No. of respondents	Percentage of Sowetans
Regularly waged or salaried	606	24[18]
Irregular wages or survivalist self-employment	476	22
Unemployed with no alternative activity	535	24
Successfully self-employed or business owner	133	6
Student or at school	261	12
Others not in the labour force (incl. pensioners, disabled, looking after home/children)	309	12
Total	2 320	100

Source: Classifying Soweto survey 2006.

Photograph 3.1. Aerial view of Diepkloof. Diepkloof Extension, in the bottom right corner, is visibly different from the rest of the township.

Source: Google Earth

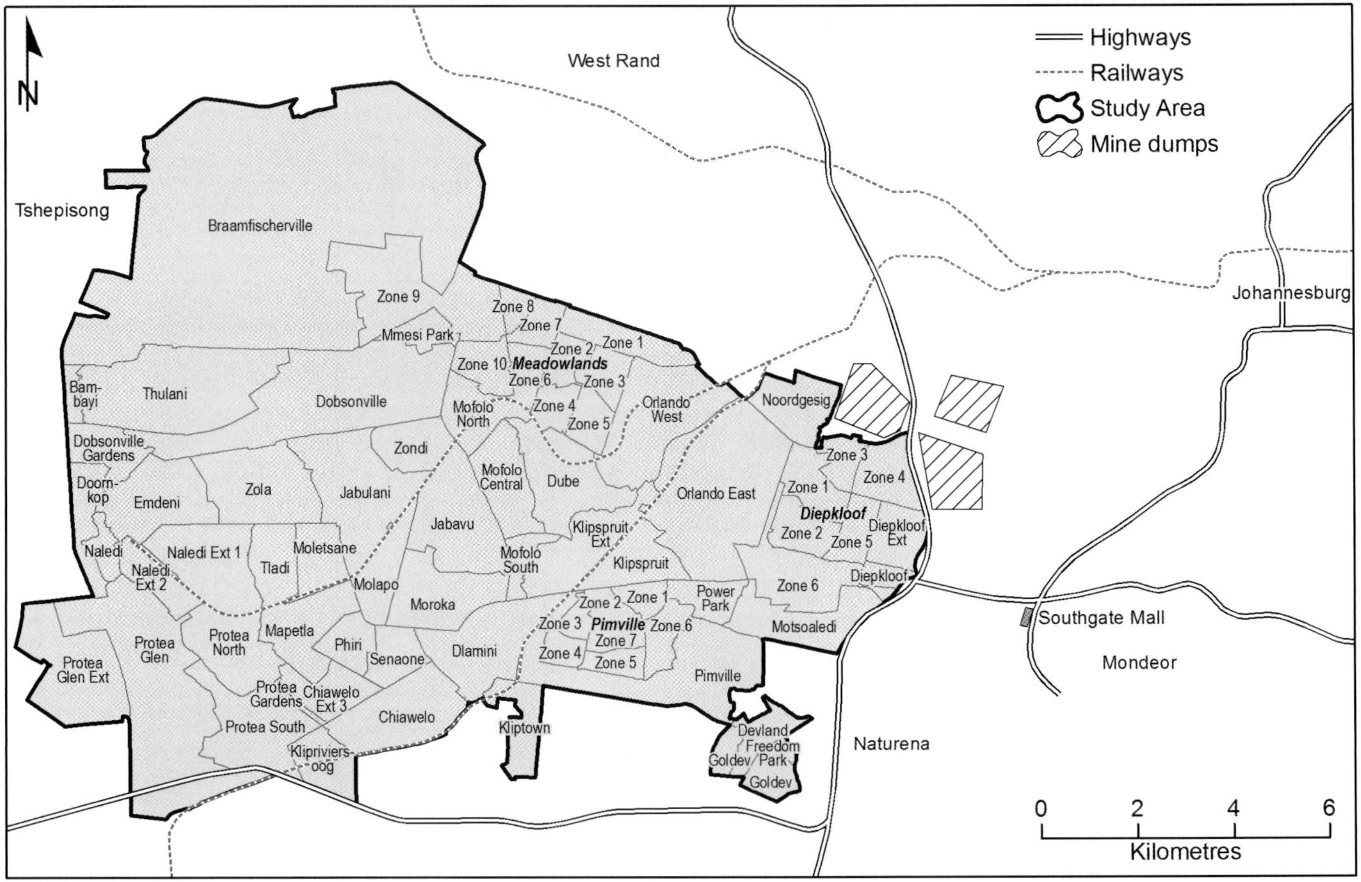

Map 3.1. Place names and surroundings of Soweto. The outlines on this map should be imagined superimposed on the Google Earth image in Photograph 3.2.

Source: Frank Sokolic and Statistics SA

Photograph 3.2. Aerial view of Soweto and its immediate surroundings. Johannesburg city is in the top right corner. The white trapezoids are mildly toxic mine waste dumps. The richer northern suburbs are beyond the top of this picture. The southern suburbs, once white working-class areas, spill from south of the city towards Soweto's eastern edge (right in the picture).

Source: Google Earth

Photograph 3.3. A bond house in Protea South.

Source: Claire Ceruti

Photograph 3.4. Freestanding shack settlement in Protea South.

Source: Claire Ceruti

Photograph 3.5. Pre-fabricated sections of tin housing for sale on the roadside near Orlando station. The sign on the tree lists prices for one, two and three rooms.

Source: Claire Ceruti

Photograph 3.6. Aerial view of Kliptown shack settlement. The settlement is on the floodplain of the stream on the left. Former council houses are adjacent.

Source: Google Earth

Photograph 3.7. Aerial view of Motsoaledi informal settlement. This is tucked behind Chris Hani Baragwanath Hospital (just visible in the top right corner). The settlement is laid out on an ordered grid with wide streets.

Source: Google Earth

Photograph 3.8. Government-subsidised RDP house in Protea South.

Source: Claire Ceruti

Photograph 3.9. Various backyard structures among former council houses (pitched roofs) in Jabavu.

Source: Claire Ceruti

Photograph 3.10. The former council house in the middle is obscured by add-ons and backyard shacks.

Source: Claire Ceruti

Photograph 3.15. A home industry in Soweto. The seats on the pavement are for a mini-bus taxi, the most common means of transport for Soweto and its surroundings.

Source: Claire Ceruti

Photograph 9.1. Cars at Anglican Church, Emdeni, Soweto

Source: Gugu Kubali

Photograph 9.2. Youth-led activity at the Methodist Church.

Source: Gugu Kubali

Photograph 9.3. Shembe churchgoers, Orlando West.

Source: Gugu Kubali

Photograph 9.4. Men in uniform at the Church of Zion.

Source: Gugu Kubali

Photograph 9.5. Women in uniform at the Church of Zion.

Source: Gugu Kubali

Photograph A1.1. A fieldworker updates our Small Area Layer (SAL) map. The shaded SALS were selected for our survey.

Source: Claire Ceruti

areas. There are high levels of poverty in the township alongside visible improvement for some. A small majority of adult Sowetans work, but regular waged employment is a minority experience for adult Sowetans.

In the following section, we consider the extent to which types of housing reflect class stratification.

Stratification in housing

Housing type has been used as a proxy for income and other kinds of socio-economic stratification in Soweto. Beall, Crankshaw and Parnell (2002a: 4) argue that '[b]y the 1990s, state reforms that privatised the provision of housing meant that Sowetans lived under increasingly differentiated housing conditions'. They say:

> Social differentiation in Meadowlands, as in Greater Soweto more generally, is characterised not only by the differential access of individuals to employment and income but also by differential access to housing and basic services, such as water supply and sanitation, refuse removal and electricity . . . we trace social differentiation along the axis of different housing-types: homeowners, tenants in backyard shacks and hostel dwellers. Social relations based on income (the proxy for which is housing type) are an important part of our analysis (Beall, Crankshaw and Parnell 2002a: 2).

Such stratification was used as a proxy for class in the Wits survey (Morris et al. 1999), and elsewhere Beall, Crankshaw and Parnell (2002a: 59) state that 'the emergence of . . . differentiated forms of housing in Alexandra and Soweto reinforced class divisions in the African population', while I have already mentioned that Sowetans are conscious of housing differentiation and take housing as a marker of class. Given the differentiation outlined in the previous section, Sowetans are recognising something real, but what is the nature of the stratification of housing? Chapter 4 considers whether the stratification we see in Soweto is indeed class stratification. Here I limit the discussion to outlining some patterns regarding a range of fairly mundane indicators, such as income associate with different housing, but show that there is a wide variation *within* a housing type, particularly with regard to former council stock. Moreover, although housing type is associated with indicators such as income, it is also associated with non-economic indicators such as age and availability. Therefore, I argue, housing type is – or has become – a weak marker of economic stratification.

Household size

The single most common household arrangement for Sowetans is four people, including children, and the modal number of adults per household is two. Here and elsewhere, when household structure is discussed, adult means eighteen years and older. However, living in a nuclear family is a minority experience for Sowetans (see Appendix 2). Just less than half of adult Sowetans live in households with more than five adults. The average number of adults in a household is 3.6 and the average household size is 5.0. Compared to Johannesburg as a whole, it appears that a higher proportion of Sowetans live in households with a total of seven or more members (Table 3.12).

Table 3.12 Distribution of Sowetans aged sixteen and over according to household size.

No. of people in household	No. of respondents in CS survey 2006	Percentage of Sowetans aged 16 and over, 2006	Percentage of Johannesburg residents aged 16 and over, 2007
1	184	6	6
2	326	11	14
3 or 4	797	30	36
5 or 6	587	26	25
7 to 9	292	17	14
10 or more	105	9	5
Total	2 291	100	100

Sources: Classifying Soweto survey 2006; Stats SA Community Survey 2007. Due to rounding percentages do not necessarily add up.

In our Soweto data, former council houses had the widest range of household sizes and the biggest households overall, and leant towards households with more adults (Figure 3.4). This fits the pattern of generation after generation continuing to live in a family house, where inherited houses become assets. To explain how to read Figure 3.4, which is a box plot, let us consider the category 'former council house no renovations'. The graph shows the median, the distribution and the range of household sizes. The thick black line across the box is the median. In this case, the median is four adults. Half of respondents in unrenovated, former council houses have more adults than this, and half have four or fewer. The ends of the box represent the 25 per cent and 75 per cent marks, respectively. Hence, a quarter of respondents in former council houses lived in households that had one or two adults, a quarter in households with three or four adults, a quarter in households with five adults, and a quarter in households with more than five adults. The whiskers extend from

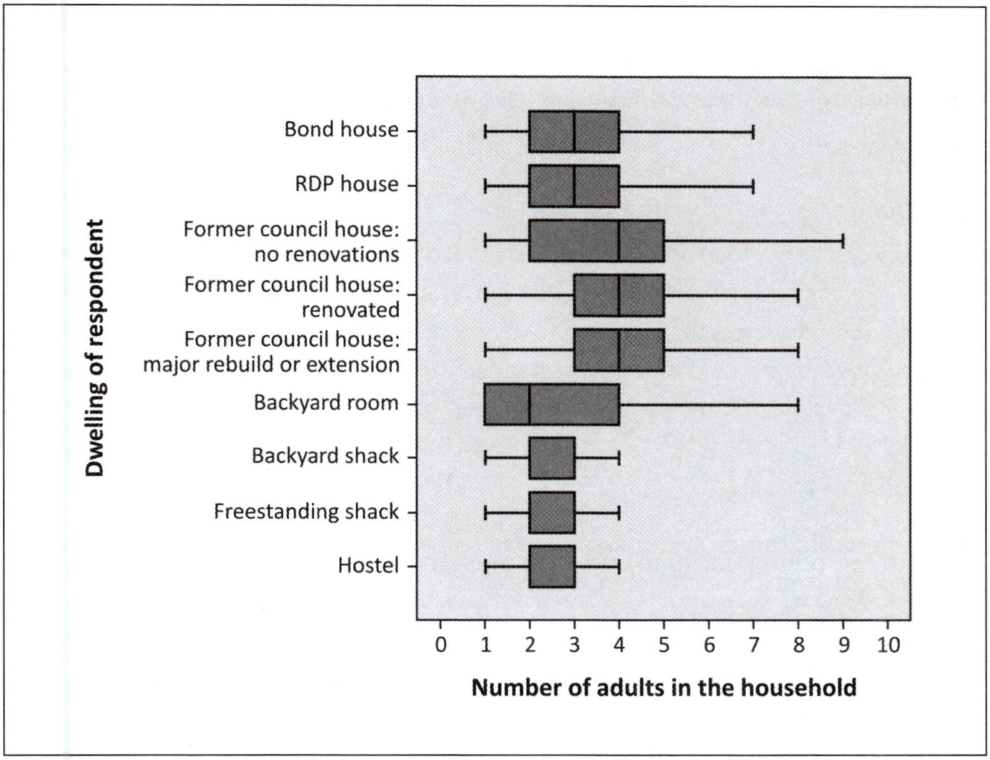

Figure 3.4 Range and median number of adults per household in different types of housing.
Source: Classifying Soweto survey 2006.

each end of the box to the high and low points, respectively, indicating the full range – in this case a low of one adult and a high of nine adults.

Bond houses and RDP houses – at opposite ends of the income scale – have remarkably similar ranges and medians of adults. This fits with their status as newer households that may have split away from older, larger households in response to pressure on accommodation. The small size of RDP houses may also contribute to the lower household size. Freestanding shacks, backyard rooms and hostels, as one would expect, given the size of the accommodations, have the smallest range of adult numbers and the lowest median numbers of adults. But when children are included (not shown here), the median for backyard shacks leans to larger households. We might speculate that this type of accommodation is used particularly by single mothers, for whom a backyard shack might feel like a safer option than living alone in a shack settlement.

Household size, then, is associated with dwelling type in a purely practical and somewhat historic way. Older housing stock has accumulated (and can accommodate) larger households, while newer stock accommodates spreading households.

Occupations, work status and incomes

Respondents in backyard rooms and backyard shacks had the highest proportion of regularly employed people (Figure 3.5). This makes sense, because these are often rented, thus requiring some form of income. Bond houses, which would involve repayments or cash outlay, had the next highest proportion of regularly employed people. Counter-intuitively, perhaps, freestanding shacks have proportions of regularly waged comparable to former council housing, alongside a proportion of unemployed comparable to RDP houses and hostels. This may reflect that informal settlements in a squeezed housing market exist not only because people are searching for comparatively cheap housing, but also because of proximity to work and work opportunities. By contrast, RDP houses have the lowest proportion of regularly waged. Clearly, this is partly because of the conditions for qualifying for this form of housing, but it may also reflect the distance of the RDP areas in our study from work opportunities and the easing of pressures to hustle for income. It is not surprising that pensioners are concentrated in former council houses, given that these are the oldest housing stock.

When considering the occupations of waged and salaried Sowetans, our data shows a concentration of teachers and nurses in renovated, former council houses and bond houses. There is a concentration of routine white-collar workers, such as cashiers and shop assistants, in backyard housing. This completes a picture of backyards as accommodation for younger workers and young families just starting out, given that people with these sorts of occupations are, on average, younger. The picture is supported by the fact that people in this kind of accommodation also have substantially more shop accounts. Former council houses have a spread of occupations, but unrenovated, former council houses accommodate, in particular, people in occupations that are less well rewarded. As might be expected, the cheapest forms of housing – freestanding shacks, RDP houses, hostels and backyard shacks – have a noticeable ratio of menial and domestic workers, although both occupations are present in all types of housing. One element stratifying housing types, then, appears to relate to the ability to afford a certain kind of house *interacting* with the limited availability of certain kinds of housing, thus making housing an unreliable proxy even of 'consumption' class.

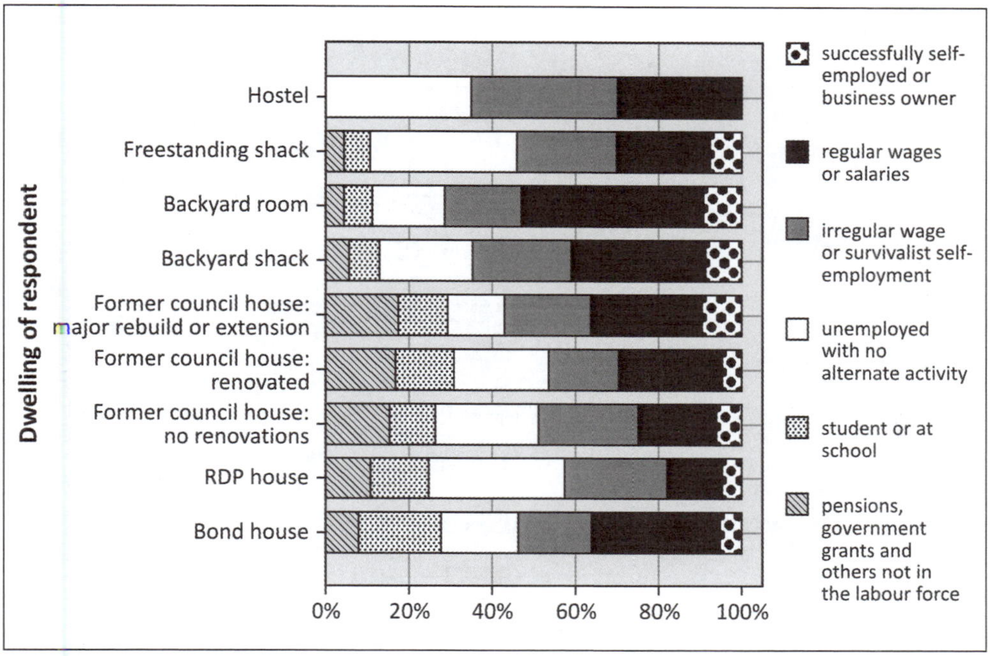

Figure 3.5 Work status in different kinds of housing.
Source: Classifying Soweto survey 2006.

Our proxy of earnings produces a predictable picture (Figure 3.6). As explained earlier, the LSM score is a composite measure of household goods and services – essentially a measure of how much stuff the household has – which can be used to approximate household income. (Of course, the results can be misleading in individual cases – for example, an older household that has been slowly and painstakingly accumulating things, such as toasters, would fall into the same category as a younger, upwardly mobile household with high income that gets a TV, computer and car all at once. Similarly, a household that has recently lost all sources of income might briefly appear better off than it is, until the gadgets begin to break.) By this measure, shacks and hostels accommodate the poorest; bond houses are for the best off; former council houses accommodate people in the middle; renovated, former council houses house the better off; and people in rebuilt, former council houses are almost as wealthy as those in bond houses. In Figure 3.6, the dwelling types are arranged in descending order according to mean LSM score. The housing types therefore read in order from richest to poorest means.

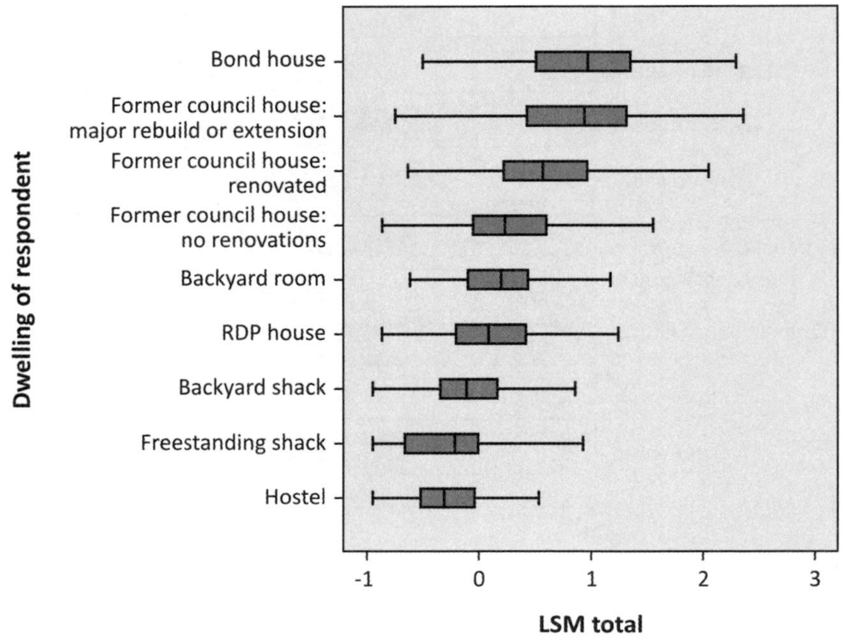

Figure 3.6 Accumulation of household goods and services (LSM) by housing type.
Source: Classifying Soweto survey 2006.

However, this does not take into account the size of the household. Using income per head, a more complex picture emerges in Figure 3.7. Again, the type of housing is arranged in descending order of mean income per head. Those in bond houses remain the wealthiest, but they are hardly rich. A quarter of these inhabitants are no better off than the median for renovated, former council houses, and half of the inhabitants of bond houses fall within the same range as RDP houses. The difference between freestanding shacks and unrenovated, former council houses and RDP houses becomes much less pronounced, and people in renovated, former council houses appear to be not much better off than people in backyard rooms (although the latter could be more likely to be sending remittances to other households). Income (and therefore to some degree occupation) is working as a filter for certain kinds of housing, excluding the lowest incomes from the most expensive housing (bond houses and renovations, followed by backyard rentals). However, the income

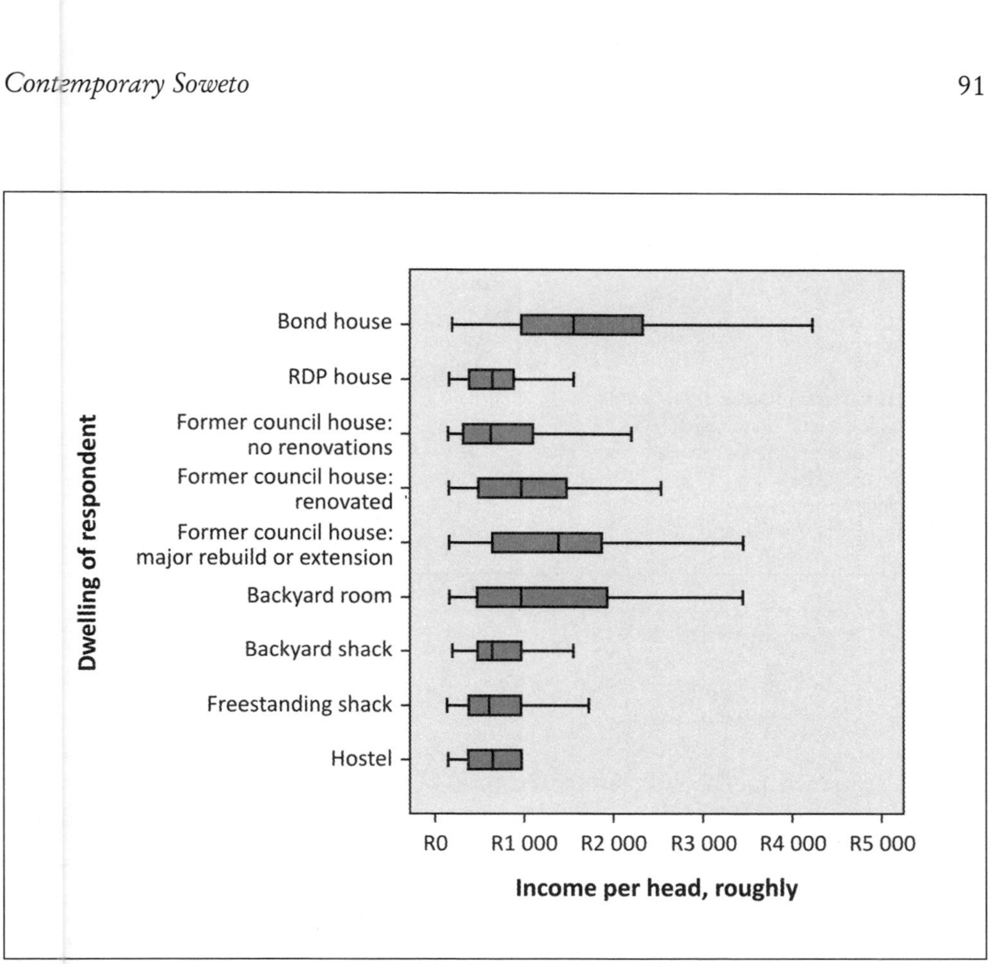

Figure 3.7 Income per month (in rand) per head in different types of housing.
Source: Classifying Soweto survey 2006.

profile of the rest of the housing stock seems more uniform than it appeared initially, suggesting that with all these other forms of housing, inheritance – related partly to the length of time you or your family have stayed in Soweto – may be the bigger segregator of former council houses from shacks and RDPs. Mean values cluster into four groups: the mean for bond houses stands alone, as is also true for rebuilt council houses. Backyard rooms cluster with renovated, former council houses and all the rest make a fourth cluster.

Migration and housing type

It is not surprising that time of migration affects the kind of housing inhabited. About 60 per cent of residents of any kind of former council house were born in Soweto (Table 3.13). People in former council houses seem to be the most settled: 70 per cent of Sowetans who were born in Soweto are currently living in some

Table 3.13 Migrancy and housing type of Sowetans aged sixteen years and older.

Housing type	Born in Soweto	Came to Soweto aged under 18 years	Came to Soweto aged 18 years or older
Bond house	55	22	23
RDP house	35	19	46
Former council house: no renovations	61	16	22
Former council: renovated	62	20	18
Former council: major rebuild or extension	59	15	26
Backyard shack	40	11	49
Backyard room	54	9	38
Other shack/*mkhukhu*	21	23	56
Hostel	6	14	79
Total	53	17	30

Source: Classifying Soweto survey 2006.

kind of former council house, compared to 45 per cent who arrived in the township as adults. Before 1986 access to council housing was linked to having certain 'insider' rights in terms of influx control, sometimes conferring the right to bring the spouse and children to the township.

Backyard rooms and shacks, on the other hand, accommodate a much greater proportion of people who were born outside the township, particularly recent arrivals. Backyard shacks lean more to accommodating newcomers, whereas backyard rooms are split between Soweto-borns and new arrivals, given that they are often used to accommodate grown children of people in former council houses.

In our survey, every kind of housing accommodates recent arrivals, but freestanding shacks and hostels have a significantly greater proportion of recent arrivals than other kinds of housing. About a third of people in backyard rooms arrived in the township in the fifteen years before the survey.

Age also plays a role here: backyard shacks were a little more likely to accommodate new arrivals for the age groups lying between 22 and 47 years (effect strength: 0.109). We have said already that people who were born in the township are significantly more likely to now live in unrenovated, former council houses, although the correlation is weak (effect strength: 0.122), with 39 per cent of today's former council houses' residents born outside the township. When we break the population down into age groups, the correlation is stronger for younger people, reaching a peak for people aged 30 to 33 years. It disappears altogether for people older than 42 years. Renovated and rebuilt, former council houses show no effective difference. This supports the notion that one mechanism that stratifies housing in interaction with income is sheer availability, which in turn necessarily interacts with the age of the individual and migration.

Complexities of housing stratification

We have seen, then, that certain housing types are more or less available to people with particular incomes or work status, but that there is also a wide range of variation beyond the averages. Moreover, income and occupation are not the only stratifiers of housing type. At least three other factors are also connected with housing type: age, length of stay in Soweto and the availability of different types of housing stock. It is therefore difficult to read class from housing type, even if class is defined by socio-economic stratifications such as income. Areas with former council houses, in particular, are very mixed. It is harder to discern the extent to which new areas – RDP settlements, shack settlements and the areas made up exclusively of bond housing – are consolidating income- and occupation-based stratification. Chapter 4 touches on this.

Conclusion: Soweto after the Group Areas Act

The preceding description aimed to create a sense of the socio-economic conditions that shape Sowetans' sense of place, including things that may be invisible or obscured to residents themselves.

Firstly, we saw that Soweto averaged somewhere in the middle when compared to the whole country, but contains internal distinctions. On the whole, the township is far from rich: it is differentiated, but accommodates very few of the 'toppest of the top' mentioned by one Sowetan in a discussion about class. However, Soweto is big enough that, while the diversity forced on it by the Group Areas Act is at an end, it remains possible to live in the township without directly enduring the ghetto conditions of its poorest areas, and therefore, for the moment, it retains a spread of people. While housing type is no longer connected tightly with income or occupation, especially in the older areas of Soweto, the new areas of shack settlements, RDP houses and private housing are facilitating area-based, internal differentiation along socio-economic lines.

Secondly, we saw that Soweto's physical legacy as a township (a racially exclusive dormitory town) has shaped its contemporary purposes for the people who 'use' it today. In several ways, it remains above all residential. It is located within reach of employment and the city, but is somewhat distant from both. This makes it attractive to migrants, but inconvenient for anyone who can afford better (Beall, Crankshaw and Parnell 2002b: 59).

Finally, Soweto's proximity to the city means that there is job-hunting migration combined with a significant proportion of people who are unemployed or who make their own work in the township. With the end of the Group Areas Act, Soweto's old use by the apartheid system as a dormitory town for active labour may be transforming into something more like a reserve, or even a dumping site for inactive potential labour. In Chapter 4 we develop this idea by considering Soweto as an overwhelmingly proletarian township.

Notes

1. Even Mike Davis (2006) made this mistake when he included Soweto's whole population in his calculation of the total of slum dwellers in his influential book, *Planet of Slums*. See Zeilig and Ceruti (2007).
2. See, for example, Wolpe (1972); Legassick and Wolpe (1976); Bonner and Segal (1998); Crankshaw (2008).
3. There is a nearly invisible number of whites living in Soweto – 384 in the 2001 Census, none of whom our survey picked up – who have occasionally been profiled in the media (see, for example, Maphumlo 2002). 'Soweto's whites face uneasy times'. *IOL news*. Available at: http://www.iol.co.za/news/south-africa/soweto-s-whites-face-uneasy-times-1.97537#.T9h17lLWkwc (accessed 13 June 2012). Such profiles suggest that whites move to Soweto for at least two reasons – marriage, or by accident when falling on hard times – and then stay on. I have included the data in this table for what it illustrates about the crosscutting of class, race and geography.
4. Precision: ±1 per cent. Precision is calculated at a 95 per cent level of probability. This means that if we drew our sample over and over again and administered the questionnaire on each new sample, we could expect 95 out of 100 samples to produce results within the range given by the confidence interval (double the figure behind the ± sign).
5. Firstly, I had to adjust for children. Our survey sampled only people above the age of sixteen years, while the 2007 Community Survey and census data include everyone. However, because we recorded the ages of every member of the respondents' households, we can estimate the number of children from the ratio of adults to children under sixteen in the households of our respondents. This works out at 0.4 children to every adult, a little higher than the 2001 Census figure of 0.3 children to every adult. I used the 2001 Census figures to estimate the proportion of children in each decade. Finally, I assumed a similar rate of migration for children and adults to arrive at a new figure for the five years before the survey. I used these estimates in the following calculations. Population growth rate = final population divided by original population, where final population = sample population plus 0.4 times sample population (to include children), and original population = final population minus new arrivals. Where new arrivals = number of respondents who arrived in the five years before the survey,

plus one-third of estimated children (the proportion of children under five years from 2001 Census) plus 0.4 times the number of respondents who arrived in the five years before the survey (assuming in-migration of children).

6. Precision: ±2 per cent.
7. Precision: ±1 per cent.
8. Audio recording of an interview with Trevor Ngwane at the Careers Centre, Soweto, conducted by C. Ceruti in English, 12 August 2005. *Note:* While every attempt has been made throughout this book to provide comprehensive information regarding interviews, the same level of information was not recorded on each occasion, so there will be discrepancies regarding the extent of the documentation provided.
9. The 2001 Census disclaimer reads: 'Please note: Users are warned to use this variable with caution and to be aware of its limitations. Census 2001 collected income information from one question on individual income without probing about informal income, enterprise profits or income in kind. As a result, the census income is understated for most of the population. Further direct comparisons with other data sets cannot be made . . .'
10. See, for example, Muthwa (1994), who finds resource sharing between neighbouring households with irregular incomes, which are discussed in Chapter 4.
11. As discussed in the text, I have represented our income distributions to show two adjustments for missing indicators in our LSM score. The higher score assumes all flush toilets are working and the lower assumes that nobody in Soweto has more than one radio, which is unlikely. The distribution is somewhere between these two.
12. Precision: ±2 per cent.
13. Use of AMPs figures has been controversial in attempts to estimate poverty. See Meth (2006a); Seekings (2007b) and Meth (2010). For our purposes these concerns are less important because the intention here is comparison of similar indicators across different geographic scales.
14. See note 11 above
15. The employment categories are calculated differently in the 2001 Census and in the *Labour Force Surveys*, producing a substantial discrepancy between national and provincial figures calculated from each. Our survey included a section following Labour Force Survey convention.
16. Precision: ±2 per cent.
17. The desired sample size was 2 550. This differs from the actual sample size in our tables here and elsewhere in the book because three records had fictitious cluster numbers resembling more than one of our real cluster numbers on the original questionnaires. These individuals fell outside the adjustment for overcounting in certain small-area layers.
18. Precision: ±2 per cent.

4

A proletarian township

Work, home and class

Claire Ceruti

This chapter considers the economic class structure of Soweto as a backdrop to the interrogation of classed practices and subjectivities in later chapters. Jeremy Seekings and Nicoli Nattrass (2005) set out to quantify the class structure of South Africa using a model that starts with what people do – their occupation and their place in the labour market. These authors develop a framework inspired largely by John Goldthorpe's schemes (see Goldthorpe and Marshall 1992), but with important adaptions.[1] The original schemes, they point out, are inadequate for the global South, where unemployment and 'informal' work are widespread. Large proportions of people cannot, therefore, be 'classed' by occupation. Using extensive data about South Africa, they find an unemployed (but not lumpen) underclass.

This chapter uses data from our Soweto survey to theorise similar observations, but from an angle that problematises the use of occupation as a proxy for class. Our exploration of what Sowetans 'do' illuminates much about the contemporary labour market in South Africa, but despite appearances, it is not a labour market model of class. For a start, it does not understand class to be the micro-stratification of life chances. We seek to root class, rather, in the organisation of society for exploitation.[2]

I consider a class structure of Soweto built around how our respondents dispose of their own and other people's labour power. This assumes that people without a conventional occupation can nevertheless be 'classed' according to what they are actually doing and not doing with their own labour power, and what they are likely to be able to do with it. Further, the earnings, opportunities and life chances of other people in their households directly shape the life chances and living standards of an unemployed person or student. However, the opposite is also true: the life chances and living standards of people with an occupation are shaped by the locations of people they share their lives with. This makes occupation a weak marker of class even if you take class to be merely about income, living standards and status. Most importantly, the class scheme developed here is not content with simply carving up data, but tries to understand people's social locations as locations within a moving system, which includes developing a picture of how Sowetans are affected by changing opportunities for disposing of labour power.

Our data about occupations, work histories and households suggests that Soweto's proletariat is a differentiated unity. I use 'proletariat' here in a slightly broader sense than Hal Draper (1978: 33–5), although not as broadly as earlier meanings of the term that encompassed all the poor and non-bourgeois (Draper 1977: 131ff.). Draper limits the proletariat to workers in waged employment who, collectively, contribute to producing surplus value. I extend the concept beyond waged people to mean that group of people who have access to only one main means of production – their own ability to work – and whose opportunities for exploiting this ability are therefore circumscribed by the availability of employment. I will describe a group of people who share an abstractly similar relation to production in that they lack viable alternatives to employment. This aspect of their lives is jointly, but unevenly conditioned by a labour market in which exploitative production has no need to match the expansion or contraction of the economy with the number of pairs of hands available in society. It has only to match sufficient numbers of hands with opportunities for producing profit, thus making endemic the continual re-creation – and recently, over-inflation – of a 'surplus population'.

This is not a purely academic exercise: Erik Olin Wright (2005: 14) writes: 'Marxist class analysis is ultimately about the conditions and processes of social change.' Work restructuring in South Africa, leading to high unemployment and a growth in insecure work, has implications for class formation – the process by which people constitute themselves as a collective subject. How is the growth in unemployment and 'informal' work affecting both class structure and formation?[3] Why have 'new social movements' such as the Anti-Privatisation Forum, which tend to organise unemployed people and pensioners (see McKinley and Naidoo 2004; Ballard, Habib and Valodia 2006) remained separate not only from the Congress of South African Trade Unions (COSATU), but also largely from waged workers of any kind? Hawkers do not organise within trade unions as 'displaced workers' (despite COSATU's attempts to organise them), but in traders' associations (which have on occasion become organisations of competition for one set of hawkers against another). My aim is to investigate how work restructuring might contribute to a divided township, but also to point out obscured commonalities among its different sections – the possibilities of bridges between, for example, the steadily waged and those on the margins and in the interstices of the mainstream economy.

In an era characterised by crisis capitalism, people who share a general relation to production find themselves in a variety of concrete situations, which depend partly on their suitability for a tight job market, and the income associated with the jobs they are suited for. This creates both divisions and dependencies. This chapter will show that mixing and similarity are evident in our data in that individuals from different concrete positions combine in households in a variety of ways. Moreover, proletarian individuals move across different kinds of jobs over their lifetimes. On the other hand, the proletariat as a group is stratified by virtue of the way the labour market develops, and I will show that this very stratification is among the levers that facilitate the ceaseless restructuring of the labour market as the economy lurches from one configuration to another. It is precisely the stratifications of the labour market that bind different sorts of proletarians into an 'actual community of fate',[4] to borrow a phrase from Margaret Levi and David Olson (2000). The paradox here is that what *binds* this community to a shared fate is exactly what *blinds* people in different strata of the community to their commonality.

The next section evaluates the difficulties of getting at class through occupation, as work restructuring restructures the proletariat.

Work polarisation, unemployment and informalisation

The polarisation of work in South Africa is well documented. Restructuring has created a 'de facto two-tier labour market', where, according to Devan Pillay (2008: 51), casual workers comprise at least 20 per cent of all workers in the retail sector and 60–80 per cent of all labour in construction. Simultaneously, unemployment and makeshift self-employment have become increasingly obvious (Horn 2005; Webster 2005, 2006; Barchiesi 2010).

The majority of South Africans cannot readily be classified by standard occupational categories. By 1993, in the whole of South Africa, 'about 34 per cent of households [had] nobody in [any kind of] employment' (Seekings and Nattrass 2005: 244). Karl von Holdt and Edward Webster (2005: 6) contend that, among people of working age, there are more people unemployed or selling on the street than are employed in this country, and one-third of the employed are in precarious work.[5] These authors use a figurative onion to represent 'new worlds of work' (see Figure 4.1), following concepts developed by various authors, including Moody

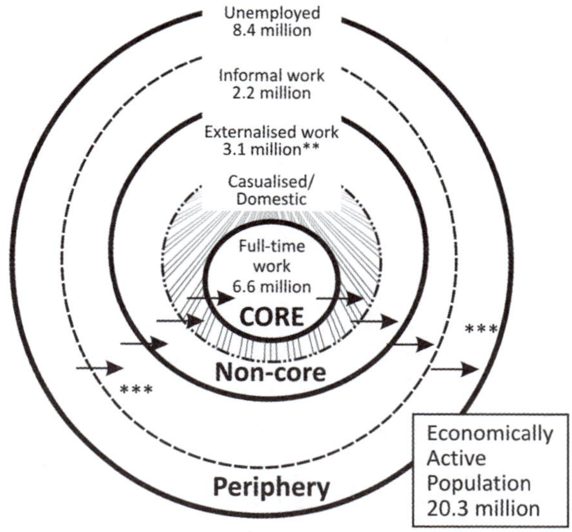

Figure 4.1 Von Holdts and Webster's worlds of work onion.

Source: Von Holdt and Webster (2005: 22). Permanent, stable workers are in the core; then precarious, low-wage workers with few rights in the non-core; and on the outside there is a periphery of unemployment and informal subsistence activities.

(1997), Tilly and Tilly (1998), Standing (1999) and Munck (1999). The onion implies a privileged core and a marginalised periphery.

What are the implications for class? Guy Standing (2011) makes the case for a new class – which he calls 'the precariat' – that corresponds roughly to the non-core zone of the onion. Jeremy Seekings and Nicoli Nattrass (2005: 254) conceive of the overall class structure of society as a pyramid rather than an onion. Here, differences such as those across the zones of the onion constitute class divisions, demonstrated by 'observable relations between class and other variables', such as income.[6] They group occupations with similar economic security, career prospects and autonomy into five broad categories: a core working class (semi-skilled and unskilled workers); a marginal working class (domestic and farm workers); an intermediate class of skilled, white-collar or supervisory workers; a semi-professional class that includes teachers and nurses; and an upper class of managers and professionals (Seekings and Nattrass 2005: 247–60). The self-employed and unemployed are accommodated mostly in two adaptions. Firstly, some are assigned 'mediated' class positions or locations, which Wright (2005: 18) explains in the following way:

> People are linked to class relations not simply through their own direct involvement in the control and use of productive resources, but through various other kinds of social relations, especially those of family and kinship . . . Mediated locations are especially important for understanding the class locations of children, of retired people, of housewives, and of people in two earner households.[7]

Seekings and Nattrass (2005: 247ff.) generally assign the entire household to the class of its highest-classed member, but this is sometimes modified for households where incomes from 'wealth and entrepreneurship' activities – self-employment, share income and the like – exceed the value of an old age pension (Seekings and Nattrass 2005: 251), which was R613 in 2006. Secondly, many of those who are covered by neither occupation nor mediation are allocated to three wealth and entrepreneurial classes, two in the higher echelons of society and the third among the poor, again in relation to the value of an old age pension (Seekings and Nattrass 2005: 251). The remainder are allocated to a residual class, which is later divided into a totally unemployed 'underclass' (unemployed plus poorer survivalists) and households entirely outside the labour force (Seekings and Nattrass 2005: 289).

Considering households, not just individuals, is a crucial adaption. We are, after all, dealing here with whole humans who enter work contracts as individuals, but seldom live completely alone, and for whom privilege or marginalisation at work is also felt outside the workplace. Several authors note how work restructuring has negatively affected reproduction, which is that area of life concerned with the work of maintaining life; it is generally organised via the household in our case. Sarah Mosoetsa (2003) proposes that 'managers may be solving the crisis of the post-apartheid workplace order by displacing confrontation, antagonism and disorder into the family, the household and the community' (see Von Holdt and Webster 2005: 31). Mosoetsa (2011), Andries Bezuidenhout and Khaayat Fakir (2006) and Ben Scully (2011) point out that work at home is subsidising low wages, while Rosa Dalla Costa noted in the 1970s how thrifty housewives 'can absorb a fall in the price of labour power' (Dalla Costa 1971: 17).

But to what extent does polarisation in the workplace also polarise reproduction? Von Holdt and Webster (2005: 30) understand the 'growing fragmentation of the world of work' to be 'deepening poverty both in the non-core and peripheral zones' of their onion (see Figure 4.1). But they do not go on to grapple with the effects on the households of those employed in the core zone. Bridget Kenny, in her study of a major retailer, notes in passing that 'in the majority of casuals' households there are other contributors [to earnings]. It is when casuals are the only income earners, 32 per cent of them [in Kenny's case], that access to resources is reduced' (Kenny 2003: 178). The converse of this insight is that other wage earners are subsidising non-core employment. A full-time wage is less of a privilege in a household with many unemployed members. We need to know more about the patterns of how different kinds of employment, unemployment and informal work cluster in households to fully grasp what work restructuring has meant for class in South Africa. This also urges a rethink of how to mediate class locations. Mediation may be better conceived as a centre of gravity, pulling different members of a household towards one another's standards of living and life chances, rather than as a water level that floats all members of a household to the level of the highest classed individual, as in Seekings and Nattrass's (2005) operationalisation of mediation.

The worlds of work are not strictly separated at a household level. Previously, Haroon Bhorat and Murray Leibbrandt (1996: 155–6) had argued that wage earners are not a labour aristocracy, by looking at the 1993 distribution of unemployed people in households categorised by the number of wage earners.[8] These households were drawn from across the country. The authors showed that 70 per cent of unemployed people depend on wages, either directly or through remittances from one household to another. However, we should be wary of homogenising. As Leibbrandt, Bhorat and Ingrid Woolard (2001: 78) point out: '[T]he role of wage income [in inequality] is significantly influenced both by the fact that many households have no access to wage income and by the fact that wage income is very unequally distributed across those households that do have access to it.' Scully achieves a finer picture. Crucially, he shows that 'amidst the decline of wage labour, South Africans are relying on multiple social forms of livelihood for their income' (Scully 2011: 10). Wages make up at least one-fifth of incomes in all but the poorest decile of households, but only in the highest two deciles do wages provide more than half the household's incomes. In all others, wages are supplemented by government grants in particular, by remittances from other households, and by earnings from survivalist self-employment.

But what should we make of the 30 per cent of unemployed people with no connection to wage income in Bhorat and Leibbrant's (1996) analysis? Scully (2011) analyses the sources of livelihoods of households and therefore he need not confront the particular issue of unemployed in households where everyone is unemployed. For labour market models of class, this is more of an issue. Seekings and Nattrass

(2005) conceive of the unemployed in households where no-one is employed as an underclass whose members have separate interests to the working classes, because they have different access to labour markets. They write critically:

> In Marxist terms, the [South African] growth path had the consequence of putting the unemployed, most of whom were unskilled and inexperienced, in an objectively different relation to productive forces than the employed; and the relations of production served to reinforce and reproduce such divisions (Seekings and Nattrass 2005: 294).

Here they have overlooked how restructuring was driven by an attempt to restore the rate of profit by increasing exploitation. There is evidence of an increase in exploitation in South Africa in the documented transfer of wealth from labour to capital:

> The share of national income going to profit earners picked up to 38 percent in 1990, reaching a high of 45 percent in 2002, and falling slightly to 42.5 percent [in 2004]. The wage share, on the other hand, fell from 51 percent to 45 percent over the same period (Malikane 2010: 89).

How has this been achieved in South Africa, given that average real wages have risen (see Meth 2006a)? Exploitation can be increased by having the same amount of work done by fewer workers through increased productivity. Another means is to reduce the overall wage bill through 'flexibilisation'. It goes without saying that such tendencies do not affect every household uniformly, purely because such restructuring is an anarchic process. One household might enter the ranks of the totally workless, while another finds its income unchanged and its relative standing in society increased.

Valuably, Seekings and Nattrass (2005) highlight how geography (physical distance from labour markets) and networks (social distance) affect people's chances of unemployment in the modern era. They are correct that 'displaced workers' is an inadequate term to describe the life experience of people who are unemployed for a long time. But it is equally inadequate to substitute for class analysis a description of how the finest income variations are disproportionately consequential near the bottom of society. Elsewhere, Seekings (2003a: 23) observes that 'working people are certainly privileged relative to the unemployed in terms of income. Their superior quality of life is reflected in their living conditions also.' He writes of the overall class scheme, in keeping with the pyramid conception of society:

'[B]oth mean and median household incomes descend steadily as one moves from [the] Wealth and Entrepreneurship Class . . . to the Upper Class . . . to the Marginal Working Class and finally to the [Unemployed Underclass]' (Seekings 2003b: 42).

Such comparisons drag the scheme towards a gradational approach (where class is a series of ranked divisions) and away from the relational view of class they aspire to. They certainly show that *employment* is consequential to quality of life – reflected also in our Soweto data and in Leibbrandt, Bhorat and Woolard's (2001) discussion of wage income as a driver of inequality. But one can also find a great consequentiality in Seekings and Nattrass's results if one groups together their 'Wealth and Entrepreneurial Classes 1 and 2' with their 'Upper Class', then compare them to all the other classes together. I refer to their table, 'Selected social and economic indicators, selected classes (South Africa, 1993)' (Seekings and Nattrass 2005: 290). Let's call the first group 'Top Class' and the others 'Everyone Else'. There are theoretical and empirical grounds for this classification, and it shows a high empirical consequentiality in South Africa. In the 'Top Class', more than two out of three people say they are satisfied or very satisfied with life. Only two in five of the highest among 'Everyone Else' are satisfied, and around one in five of the lowest among 'Everyone Else'. More than 70 per cent of the 'Top Class' have piped water and toilets in their homes, but less than half of the rest. Then one might conclude as follows: 'Top Class is certainly privileged relative to Everyone Else in terms of income. Their superior quality of life is also reflected in their living conditions.'

Using the classic Marxist phrase, what the long-term unemployed share with workers is not *whether* they have sold their labour power or *on what terms*, but that *they have nothing else to sell*, regardless of their distance from labour markets and of how appropriately embellished their labour power may be. The fate of people in long-term unemployment cannot be reduced to contrasting the individualised characteristics of households. A common *general* relation to exploitation is obscured by its *concrete* expression when the labour market is shrinking and work, therefore, appears as a scarce resource rather than the natural power of any human. Of course, individual characteristics probably matter more than ever to the micro-outcomes of a very tight labour market. But no amount of personal employability alters the number or quality of jobs available. Seekings and Nattrass (2005) make no attempt to uncover the obscured mechanisms by which the different parts of the labour market hang together, and thus class in their scheme is limited to the superficial and readily observable. What is missing from the impressive detail of their analysis is a real sense of how 'actors are linked *behind their backs* by systemic processes' (Silver 2003: 27; my emphasis).

In summary, then, understanding class in Soweto in an era of work restructuring requires primarily a consideration of how the worlds of work are mixed at the level of the household. Secondly, movements between the worlds of the 'work onion' need to be better understood over the lifetime of individuals, as well as the effect of such movements on households' fates, to grasp the extent to which these may represent class boundaries. Finally, class structure cannot be understood as a snapshot, but must be understood in the context of a moving system, which, to complicate matters, obscures many of its relations. My aim in the following discussion is not to refine, elaborate or improve on occupational schemas of class, either Goldthorpian or Wrightist, but to outline and refine an alternate conception of class as a dynamic system of social relations.

The remainder of the chapter addresses these issues in four sections. Firstly, it considers Sowetans' reliance on employment and the alternatives; secondly, how households are constituted; and thirdly, movement between the worlds of work. Here I am trying to tease out both polarisation and new dependencies, and the *mechanisms* driving both. Finally, I situate these observations in a systemic understanding of class, where most Sowetans are linked together, such that the fate of people with steady work remains bound to that of people who are socially distant from mainstream labour markets.

Employment and its alternatives around Soweto

Of necessity, Sowetans' work takes a variety of forms beyond paid employment. Both narrow (official) and broad (expanded) unemployment rates are substantially higher for Soweto than the average for the country. By March 2006, the year of our survey, the official narrow unemployment rate[9] (which excludes discouraged job seekers) was 25.6 per cent nationally for all 'races' (Stats SA 2006: iii) and 23 per cent in Gauteng. Table 4.1 defines various measures of the labour market used by Statistics South Africa (Stats SA) and compares their figures with our survey, which included three questions based directly on the Labour Force Survey (LFS). Note that these ratios are calculated from the number of people considered unemployed and employed,[10] and therefore differ from the figures in the previous chapter, which give the employed and unemployed as a percentage of the total population. Also note that the technical definitions of unemployed and employed here differ from our use of the term later in Table 4.2.

Work remains central to many Sowetans' sense of self-respect. During our survey, we briefly employed an otherwise-unemployed local activist. Whenever we met someone she knew who asked 'How are you?' she replied, '*sisebenza*' (we are working). Trevor Ngwane, a Sowetan social movement activist, explains:

Table 4.1 Various measures of the labour market for Soweto and South Africa, 2006.

Labour market measure[11]	Sowetans, July 2006[12]	National, March 2006	National, Sep. 2006
Narrow unemployment rate: unemployed as % of employed + unemployed (i.e., actively seeking work)	32%[13]	26%	23%
Broad unemployment rate: unemployed + discouraged workseekers as % of employed + unemployed + discouraged workseekers	51%[14]	30%	35%
Labour absorption rate: % of working-age population who are employed	41%[15]	41%	45%
Labour force participation rate: labour force (employed plus narrow unemployed) as % of working-age population	60%[16]	56%	58%

Sources: Classifying Soweto survey 2006; Stats SA Labour Force Survey 2006.

> In the township these days, when your child or you get a job, when you greet each other that's the first thing you say . . . And then when you talk about someone else, you'll say, 'oh but he lost his job' so he's now a different person.[17]

However, employment is a mixed blessing – employees frequently dream of retiring to a small business, while vendors dream of a fixed income. Nelson, a welder for a big company, who calls himself a worker and a 'poor somebody', described himself in three words: 'wants more money', adding 'to start a small business'.[18] But most vendors, even when they refer to their activities as businesses, nevertheless hang their aspirations on employment. Mamsie is 28 years old with two young children. She trained in security and gets a day's work here and there, but 'usually they prefer men . . . so I decided to start this business'.[19] For about four years she has been selling facecloths and basins near Orlando Station. She takes home between R10 ($1.5 when the interview was done) and R80 on a rare day – 'washcloths and basins take a long time to wear out'. Her whole family sells: her father sells cow heads and her mother sells chicken feet. The children's father used to do piece jobs,[20] laying paving in places like Sandton (a rich area north of Johannesburg) and Roodepoort (a formerly white town west of Soweto), but started selling ice cream about seven years ago when the piece jobs slowed. When asked, 'If you could change one thing in your life, what would it be?' Mamsie answered: 'Good shelter

. . . or, wait, the better thing – I want a job especially.' Even Sam, a roadside haircutter with a wheelbarrow of capital such as a car battery, who wishes for formal premises, ended our interview like this: *Interviewer:* 'Is there anything else you would like to say to us?' *Sam:* 'You must find me a real job.'[21]

Soweto's pavements are busy during the day with people like Mamsie making a plan in the absence of employment. Roadside traders sell live chickens, vegetables and car oil. Signs on houses advertise tuck-shops, upholsterers and taverns. Less visible are home-based dressmakers, hairdressers, bakers, caterers, plumbers, bricklayers and people who leave the township to search for a day's work here and there. Official statistics count all these people as employed when calculating the unemployment rate: the LFS in use at the time of our survey included as employed all those 'aged 15–65 who did any work or who did not work but had a job or business in the seven days prior to the survey interview' (Stats SA 2006: ii). This is frequently contrary to the participants' own interpretation of their activities. We heard people call the activities described in the preceding paragraph, *bayaphanda* in isiZulu, translated as 'making a plan', but meaning literally 'they are scratching' (like a chicken). Undoubtedly, many of these traders and home manufacturers are galvanised by entrepreneurialism, such as Mpho, a former McDonald's employee, who imagines he will franchise the delicious T-bone steaks he barbecues outside the shipping container from which he and his family run a make-shift restaurant. Far more typical, however, is Jabu, a 21-year-old selling *kotas* (stuffed bread) with a family friend: 'We have seen no progress.'[22] Barbara Piazza-Georgi found in 2000 that 'the majority of self-employed persons in Soweto are not primarily motivated by entrepreneurial aspirations: 74 per cent report having started in business . . . as a result of unemployment' (Piazza-Georgi 2000: 10) and '[i]t appears that 49 per cent . . . consider that they are just able to make a living'. Even those who call their activities work may not feel they are viable for the future. A woman vendor from Diepkloof said:

> I consider myself as a worker because I get money with which I can do something for my household. [But] it is not work as such . . . If I could get employed, I could let go of this activity . . . I am looking for work.[23]

The implication is that she is filling in as she waits for something more formal.

Such descriptions alerted us to the fact that Soweto's working life cannot be accurately described using an employed/unemployed binary such as assumed by the LFS. This problem is laid out well by Peter Alexander and Kim Wale in Chapter 5. Even a three-way categorisation of employed, unemployed and self-employed proves insufficient; the categories described in Table 4.2 emphasise this. We allowed

Table 4.2 The structure of employment and unemployment in Soweto (all Sowetans aged sixteen years and over).[24]

Employment categories	No. of respondents (unweighted count)	Estimated percentage of Sowetans (weighted)
Capitalists	3	0
Managers	24	1[25]
Regularly employed workers	582	24[26]
Partial workers	251	11[27]
Unemployed (our definition)	535	24[28]
Survivalist self-employed	225	10[29]
Petty bourgeoisie	129	6[30]
Students	261	12[31]
Pensioners and others not in the labour force	309	12[21]
Total	2 319	100

Source: Classifying Soweto survey 2006.

these categories to grow iteratively from the data, drawing on key Marxist class concepts such as capitalists and petty bourgeoisie, but not confining ourselves to these. The core of these concepts is exploitation – who appropriates surplus and how – which in turn hinges on how people dispose of their own and other people's labour power. We also kept in mind Sowetans' own descriptions of their activities, beyond simple labour market categories such as employed and unemployed. Our survey used a range of questions to get at the nature of the respondent's activity rather than simply asking for an occupation. We began with the subjective question 'do you work?' followed by a series of 50 variables that progressively unpacked the nature of the respondents' economic activities. We also recorded every member of the respondents' household, their age and their labour market status. Another fifteen questions sketched sources of income and support.

The first column of figures in Table 4.2 shows the actual number of respondents in each category. The pie graph in Figure 4.2 is a visual representation of the percentages in the next column in Table 4.2. I have applied the weight explained in Appendix 1 to extrapolate to the whole of Soweto and am referring to weighted figures whenever I talk about 'Sowetans' in the survey data. The reader should remember that weighting is a scientific approximation, but nevertheless an approximation. Note that the terms 'employed' and 'unemployed' here should not be confused with the technical definitions used to calculate the unemployment rate, discussed at the beginning of this section. We found official definitions unsatisfactory for capturing what we observed. Our definitions are explained below.

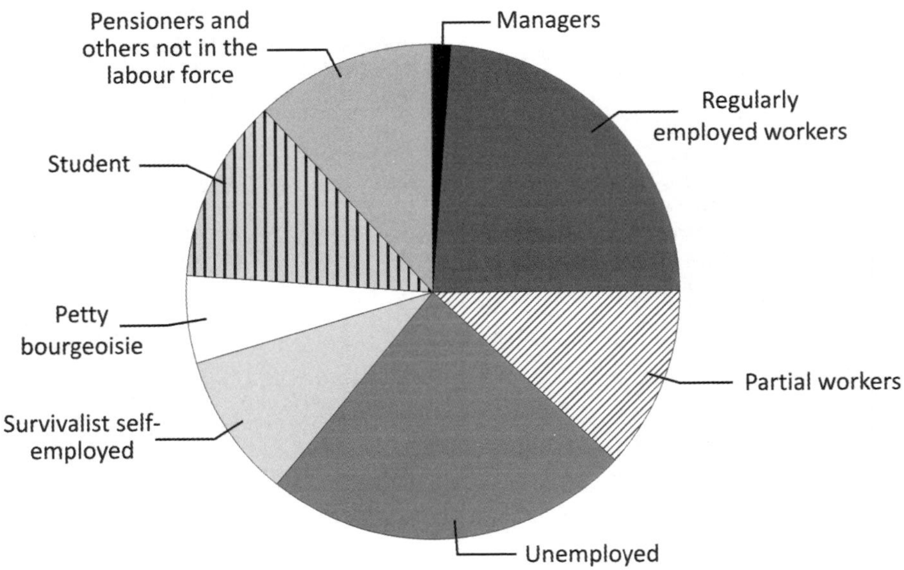

Figure 4.2 The structure of employment and unemployment in Soweto.
Source: Classifying Soweto survey 2006.

We found only three people whom we classified as 'capitalists' (business owners), that is, who employed others. We called 'petty bourgeoisie' the 6 per cent who worked for themselves and in many cases hired one or two others in small shops, family businesses, more successful vending and contracting businesses. We also included doctors and lawyers, because they employed people in their practices/firms. Although the petty bourgeoisie sometimes hire others, as do capitalists, they are different from the capitalists in that an element of self-exploitation is implied in the small numbers of people hired and in the fact that these are often irregularly hired. We did not distinguish between formal and informal business here, but took into account accumulations of equipment related to the business. The majority of people we classified this way – 85 per cent – were not available for employment and had not looked for work in the past seven days.

Approximately a quarter of all Sowetans older than fifteen years work for someone else regularly. We separated out as 'managers' the one per cent who are employed in managerial or supervisory roles. Service industries, such as retail, public service and cleaning, dominate Sowetan's employment (as seen in Chapter 3). We grouped teachers and nurses who were not also managers into the regularly employed. This category also includes part-time workers who regularly worked more than half a day for the same employer, and may include people on short-term contracts and 'casual' contracts, who work for the same employer regularly. It does not include seasonal workers, who we included in the category of partial workers, as explained below.

Twelve per cent are students, of whom 70 per cent are still at school. Some 13 per cent of all students worked while they studied and 66 per cent were available for work. They are most often part-time workers. We did not reclassify these people as employed because this is not a labour force survey, and they stated their main activity as being students.

About 12 per cent of Sowetans are otherwise 'not in the labour force'. Approximately 70 per cent of these declared themselves old age pensioners, and 18 per cent of these (2 per cent of the total population) said they looked after the house, family or children. The remainder were on disability grants or received child support grants. We did not define 'pensioner' in terms of age per se, but in terms of a person's main economic activity. Somebody could be under 65 and still be a pensioner, or they could be over 65 and specify a job or business as more important than being a pensioner. Approximately 80 per cent of old age pensioners were 'surplus population' in the sense that they were previously employed, and about 17 per cent of old age pensioners remained available for work.

About a quarter of Sowetans are outright unemployed, with no alternative activity. When asked, 'do you work?' they replied, 'no'. When asked, 'what do you do?' they answered, 'nothing', 'sit at home' or 'looking for a job'. They report no other activities like piece work or occasional selling; they do not say they are looking after children or households (although undoubtedly women especially are expected to fill their days like this); they are not drawing a grant or pension; and they generally report that they are available for work, even when they are not actively seeking work. Only 42 per cent had looked for work in the past seven days, but 86 per cent were available for work.

Then, there were people who would not fit comfortably into any of the above categories. There were two such groupings. The 'survivalist self-employed' fall somewhere between the unemployed and the petty bourgeoisie. Our survey indicates that about 9 per cent of Soweto's population above the age of fifteen years may be engaged in such 'fill-in' activities, labelled 'survivalist self-employed' in Table 4.2. Their availability for employment is the main distinction between them and those we dubbed the petty bourgeoisie. The survivalist self-employed's own assessment of what they do suggests their activities are less an alternative to employment than an alternative to unemployment. They maintain themselves at their own expense while remaining available for work. Although outside formal industry, they are not necessarily outside of the circuits of capitalist production and distribution. They tend to plug pinholes in production and circulation – increasing the reach of products at little extra cost to the manufacturers, like the people who sell cell phone chargers at road intersections or sweets on street corners; as a self-exploited service class, providing plumbing, tiling or unique clothing within the budget of the more ordinarily exploited; and in awkward niches of raw material production, such as scrap collecting and recycling.

Finally, there were those whom we defined as 'partial workers' who were either employed irregularly or were employed regularly but for fewer than the 20 hours a week, which would have classified them as regularly employed. These included people with 'piece work/jobs' in our survey. By this, Sowetans mean working for different employers, usually on a day-by-day basis when called in for gardening, labouring and domestic work. Well-established slang words for this kind of work remind us that unprotected work is hardly new. *Togo* – we think this derives, via Sesotho, from the Afrikaans word *tog* meaning 'journey', implying that you move from place to place for work – is sometimes rendered as *amatogonyana*, 'little piece jobs', in isiZulu. *Iskorobo* was probably derived from 'scrub' (as in washing) and subsequently generalised beyond domestic work. The Diepkloof vendor describes such employment:

> In this area . . . those who do not work are looking for work like I do. A lot of people I know do not work. They just have temporary jobs for one day. From there, they just sit with us here. If there is someone who says go and hunt somewhere, we go and hunt. If we are unsuccessful, we come back and just sit.

'Piece work' was also used to describe irregular seasonal work. Dry cleaners commonly have people who are called in only during busy times, and large retailers use agency workers over Christmas. We called all these 'partial workers'. This category is not synonymous with workers on casual contracts. Only some casuals are partial workers. Like the survivalist self-employed, partial workers maintain themselves largely at their own expense, often by providing services to individual households in niches too small and unprofitable for most companies. In this role, they cheapen the cost of reproduction, increasing the reach of wages of more regular employees. Elsewhere, they minimise the wage bill of small building contractors or facilitate seasonal expansion and contraction for more formal companies.

In conclusion, our employment categories are neither an occupation-based class categorisation nor classes. However, they take us beyond crude categories oriented to labour market statistics to a more refined picture of how Sowetans join, are excluded from or try to side-step the labour market (the buying and selling of labour power). They also sketch one element of a Marxist scheme of class – how individuals dispose of their own and other people's ability to work. (Other aspects would include access to productive assets and, flowing from these, power, including control or autonomy at work, as well as the ability to organise; classed practices; and interests.)

How do these categories stand up theoretically? The employment categories revolve around two closely related planes in the disposal of labour power. The obvious one is who exploits whose labour power: whether you are exploiting, being exploited, self-exploited, or not exploited at all, and related to this is whether you are extracting surplus value (profit) or merely subsisting. The other, subtler plane is the form in which you realise the value of your labour power (and hence the way in which you realise your subsistence): these range from not realising it at all (unemployed) to the wage form (workers), through market exchange (street vendor or scrap collector) and interpersonal transfers (unpaid work around the home) to any number of hybrid and other forms. These forms represent, to some extent, people's differential places in the labour market, but not exactly. To purveyors of occupational or labour-market models of class, the 'regular workers' category would seem ridiculously broad in that it lumps together teachers with metalworkers, service contracts with casual workers. These different kinds of workers are not exploited in exactly the same way. Teachers, for example, contribute only indirectly to surplus value, insofar as they contribute to skilled labour power, which may or may not be exploited in the future. A worker in a crèche contributes to surplus value by freeing up another worker for exploitation, but unpaid housework may similarly contribute to surplus value by cheapening the socially acceptable wage. However, what all the workers share, and what differentiates the crèche worker from the homemaker, is that they sell their labour power to someone else. Among other things, the form in which subsistence is realised shapes how exploitation is concretised and the forms that struggles over exploitation may take. (For example a worker – even a teacher – may blame low levels of subsistence on an employer, and understand the wage level as a tussle between subsistence and surplus value,[33] whereas the survivalist vendor experiences low levels of subsistence as the consequence of far more amorphous market forces, easily personified only as customers or fellow vendors, although the forces shaping the customers and fellow vendors are also beyond their control.) Certainly, the finer differences among those realising their subsistence through the wage form can be important, too, when it comes to concrete experiences of exploitation. However our employment categories were not developed with the primary aim of segmenting Sowetans. Rather they were a means of grasping those forms of realising subsistence that we observed in Soweto, which are 'non-standard' to most occupational class schemes and also under-theorised in Marxism. We did this, not to extend occupational class schemes, but to understand where these categories fitted in approximating a delineation of the contemporary proletariat and other classes in Soweto.

The picture that emerges is that the majority of Sowetans are similar in that they are employed or available for employment even when engaged in other activities, and that many of the activities that are counted as employed in official statistics are stopgaps in the absence of either employment or more promising alternatives to employment.

Movement between the worlds of work

Industrial restructuring constantly restructures the workforce, and as a result, individuals may move between different worlds of work over the course of their lifetime. Some, like the partial workers described above, dip in and out of work. Others move between fill-in activities and employment, like Mamsie, who takes security work whenever she can. Partial work and certain kinds of self-employment may lead to more regular employment. Ngcaba, a petrol-pump attendant, moved from unemployment to poorly protected work. He and his eldest brother pool their wages with their parents' pensions to support his younger sister, his dead brother's eight children and his dead sister's six children. He told us: 'My brother fixes TVs. I think he's permanent now. Before, he was doing the same work for himself.'[34]

A work trajectory that appeared frequently in interviews before and after the survey involved moving from school through unemployment, to a period of intermittent casual work, and then, for some, on to permanent work. A worker at the retail chain Pick n Pay, whose dream was 'just to have an ordinary house where I can have a bath', had worked seven years there, first as a casual and then as a permanent. Before that she had not worked for 'five or six years'. She was the only one working in a household comprising herself and her mother, aunt, child and sister. Her mother previously worked at Pick n Pay. The aunt had not worked for 25 years. The sister used to work in a hair salon, but had not worked 'for a long time'.[35]

Such trajectories were reflected in our survey data. The mean age of respondents who worked fewer than 20 hours a week was 32 years, while that of other working respondents was between 35 and 36 years. The blot-plot in Figure 4.3 further

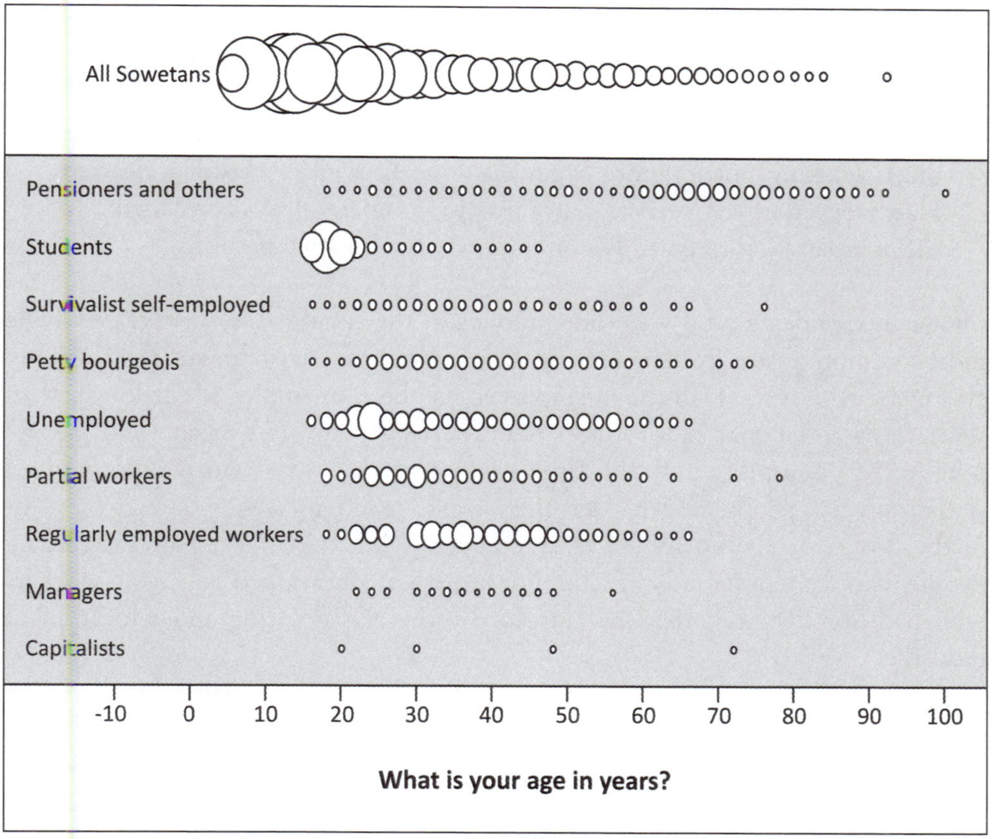

Figure 4.3 How age structures the labour market in Soweto.
Source: Classifying Soweto survey 2006.

illustrates how Soweto's labour market is structured by age. To understand this, imagine you are looking down into a room in which we have asked our respondents to queue up behind our labour market categories according to their age.

Unemployed people cluster around the age of 25, while the employment queue is thickest around 35 years, and partial workers concentrate at ages between these two. A form of extended childhood results in proletarian households carrying the cost of maintaining a substantial part of the potential labour force while they gain work experience.

We also saw clear evidence of the 'dumping' of workers who were no longer suited for the needs of new industries or simply surplus to requirements, or who no longer had access to the industries that would want them. A cohort of Sowetans around 40 or 50 years of age reported losing steady work over the previous decade-and-a-half and held little hope of ever getting it again, such as Francinah:

> I am unemployed. We are five: my mother, me, my kids, my sister. Not one is working, not anymore. We make some piece jobs – washing, cleaning. I last worked fifteen years ago, in a plastics company. I was permanent, but the company left to go to Benoni [a town east of Johannesburg].[36]

Of our respondents who were unemployed at the time of the survey, the single most common reason given for leaving their last job was retrenchment, the company closing or relocating. Half the unemployed had been unemployed for longer than seven years and a quarter for longer than fourteen years. The mean age of people who were unemployed at the time of our survey was significantly higher, statistically, for people who had left their previous activity owing to retrenchment or the closure of a company (46 years, compared to 37 years), even after excluding people who were previously at school or in higher education. These were workers who had literally been rendered surplus by the restructuring and relocation of industry.

I suggest that, within these partly generational movements, labour is also being retooled – not only with skills suited to new and expanding service industries, but also to accept unprotected, casualised and subcontracted work as inevitable, despite long workplace struggles for job security during the apartheid era. The evidence here is not conclusive, as our survey did not clearly distinguish between casual and permanent workers, but cashiers and merchandisers in retail – occupations known to be heavily casualised and subcontracted – tend to be younger than respondents in other kinds of occupations. Moreover, union members in these latter occupations were, on average, older than non-union members, although there was no significant difference in the age of union and non-union members in the sample as a whole. It is, of course, easier for permanent workers to unionise.

So our study gives some substance to the contention in the 'work onion' model about how people move between different zones of work. However, age, which is not considered in the work onion model, is important in the contemporary reformation of the labour force in Soweto.

Movement between the worlds of work is felt not only by individuals, but by entire households. It seems that Seekings and Natrass (2005) underestimate how perilously close 'core' working-class households may be to their 'underclass' in the current labour market. Here again, trajectory is important in understanding polarisation. One respondent, Sello, described households that lose earners slowly spiralling into the 'lower class', a trajectory that is reversed by finding a job.[37] I interviewed Tebza in 2005 when he was 32 years old and had recently got his first regular job, a learnership. When he added his income to his brother's public sector wage it meant that '[w]e have better food and more food, and we bought a VCR'.[38] But no one had worked in his family from 1991, when his mother, a textile worker, was retrenched, until 2001, when his brother found work.

We still do not know whether workless households in urban settings will become permanently separated from the labour market if their unemployment continues for a very long time. This question cannot be answered in advance. Whether the unemployed ever find work again depends largely on whether the economy expands or contracts, in what sectors and which regions this occurs, and on which skills (or lack of skills) are required. For the moment, urban households remain in a work-mixed environment and may rely on solidarities from there. Both Tebza and Sello describe workless households that remained embedded in working-class areas despite a certain degree of social isolation. Tebza described how a workless household continued to attend church as before and received donations from there. Workless households do seem to concentrate in places such as Kliptown, a large shack settlement, but these areas retain mixed households.

Households pushed together and pulled apart

As Mosoetsa (2011: 58–78) points out, the household is a first line of defence in the face of job losses and work insecurity. If the worlds of work are an onion, at the township and household level the onion is chopped and diced.

Survey-based models of class that assign any member of a household to the class of its main breadwinner are unsatisfactory in the case of Soweto, where multiple breadwinners are common and where breadwinners' life chances are shaped by levels of unemployment in the household. Lawrence, whose work is to crush glass – collected by informal collectors – at a recycling depot for scrap, is aged 22 and the 'only one that carries that responsibility' in his family of nine. He described his lot as 'a pity life'.[39] ZT, a salesman who, together with his brother, supports their respective wives and one unemployed cousin, could see himself as reasonably well off, 'though not able to afford luxuries'.[40]

Table 4.3 shows the distribution of household arrangements across Soweto. We recorded the work status of every other member of a respondent's household. We had, of course, not yet developed the categories described earlier in this chapter. We offered a number of cruder occupational categories, which included employed, unemployed, contractor, vendor, small business and formal business owner, piece jobs, student (that is, post-school), scholar (that is, school student), pensioner, child category includes self-employed contractors, vendors, pensioners, piece workers and students. We came up with the six household constellations given in the second column of Table 4.3. The first column groups households by combinations of employment and unemployment. The last column shows the percentage of households in each of these six categories.

Table 4.3 shows that 34 per cent of Sowetans lived in households containing no regularly employed member – the bottom three household categories. Their income came from businesses large or small, government grants and pensions, or other households. Equally important, however, was the fact that two-thirds of respondents lived in households with at least one employed member, and the single biggest group – 41 per cent of all respondents – lived in households that pool resources among the employed, the unemployed and others. Not shown in Table 4.3, more than half of our employed respondents lived in a household with some unemployed adults and six out of ten unemployed respondents lived in households with someone employed. Another two out of ten employed people pool resources with pensioners and/or self-employed people and/or partial workers.

Some 5 per cent of respondents reported that everyone in their household was unemployed. How did they survive? A third of respondents in such households reported child support grants or other government grants as their main source of income, while approximately 40 per cent depended primarily on another person's salary or wage. Not a single respondent mentioned government unemployment insurance as being either a primary or secondary source of income. This figure suggests the inadequacy of the existing unemployment insurance system, which pays out only to people who have worked for a maximum of six months.

Table 4.4 shows more about different constellations of mutual support. It shows each of the six categories of household against the number of adults in the household. The last row tells us that roughly one in ten respondents is the only adult in their household, a quarter of households have two adults, and two-thirds have three or more. Each cell in the rows above is a percentage of all Sowetans. The table adds to the information contained in Table 4.3 that one-third of Sowetans live in mixed households with three or more adults. At the other extreme, we also see that most respondents who live in fully employed households live without another adult. This supports the contention that people in Soweto are banding together in the face of the crisis.

The data in Table 4.4 does not tell us much about the type of employment in these households. For example, it does not distinguish between permanent and contract workers. Qualitative interviews following the survey suggest that low-quality work clusters in certain households – piece workers, vendors and casual or

Table 4.3 Constellations of forms of work and unemployment in Sowetans' households.

Household composition: • **employed = waged/salaried** • **others = vendors, piece workers, pensioners, students and other self-employed** • **unemployed = no other activity**		**No. of respondents (unweighted counts)**	**Percentage of Sowetans 16 years and older (weighted)**
No one unemployed	All employed	239	9[41]
	Employed and others	431	17[42]
Mixed	Employed with unemployed, may include others	806	41[43]
No one employed	Unemployed and others	378	18[44]
	All unemployed[45]	141	5[46]
Neither	Only others	297	11[47]
Total		2 292	101

Source: Classifying Soweto survey 2006.

Table 4.4 Distribution of Sowetans by household composition and number of adults (aged eighteen years and over).

Household composition: • **employed = waged/salaried** • **other = vendors, piece workers, pensioners, students and other self-employed** • **unemployed = no other activity**		**Percentage of *all* respondents, extrapolated to Soweto (weighted)**			**No. of respondents (unweighted counts)**
		1 adult in household	**2 adults in household**	**3 or more adults in household**	
No one unemployed	All employed	4	3	2	239
	Employed and others	–	5	11	431
Mixed	Employed with unemployed, may include others	–	7	34	806
No one employed	Unemployed and others	–	5	13	378
	All unemployed	2	2	2	141
Neither	Only others	5	3	2	297
Total		11	25	64	2 292 (= 100%)

Source: Classifying Soweto survey 2006.

not at school and the like. We cannot, therefore, distinguish all partial workers and survivalist self-employed with these categories, for example. We grouped households according to three crude categories of its members – employed (paid by someone else), unemployed (no alternate activity to employment) and others. This last contract employees often lived together, although we do not know the extent of this. Several mechanisms could drive this kind of clustering. Seekings and Natrass (2005), we have seen, posit networks. However, it is equally possible that the whip of deprivation drives acceptance of lower-quality jobs, and this is demonstrated by the fact that partial workers in our survey tend to come from households with higher unemployment, fewer regular jobs and lower living standards. The last point is clearly illustrated in the means plot in Chapter 5, which shows that, on average, partial workers tend to live in the poorest households.

However, the importance of wages in supporting other kinds of work and unemployment is illustrated when we look at living standards in the different constellations of households from Table 4.2. By comparing the means of the Living Standards Measure for our categories of households we found, as one might expect, that people living in households where all the adults were unemployed were the poorest and that partial workers were more likely to live in poorer mixed households than people in other employment categories. But the survivalist self-employed and pensioners who share a household with employed people are better off than the average for mixed households and better off than the average for employed people living in mixed households. The employed and unemployed from mixed households have similar average living standards.

Qualitative data fleshes out this picture. We met a driver, who introduced himself as Mr Khumalo, at a march against job losses organised by COSATU. Mr Khumalo was previously a teacher. He lived with his wife, a nurse, and three children, one of whom was at university. He also supported his brother and his sister. His brother had been unemployed for two years (the factory where he had worked as a labourer had closed). His sister had been unemployed for a long time owing to sickness. He said: 'We don't have enough money to eat what we like at the time we are hungry for it.'[48]

A textile machinist from Zondi lived on the same stand with her brother, who stayed in a converted garage. Her daughter and sister's child stayed in outside rooms. Her daughter was a data capturer, on contract with agents; her brother worked as a driver; her sister's child was not working. Her son was working at Mr Price as a contract worker. 'But now he's no more working. He was a tiler too [piece jobbing]. They don't pool their money, but they are buying clothes and maintaining the boys. Sometimes I do help my sister [who lives elsewhere], because she is not working too.' Her sister had not worked since 1984. She was working at the factory, in the 'financial section. Sometimes she gets some temporary work in Sandton. Only a week, then for three weeks she's at home. I want my son to get a job, and also my sister to get a permanent job so she can maintain her children.'[49]

A municipal worker who lived with his wife and three children also helped his mother and father, who were former farmworkers on state pensions. He supported his two sisters, who were both in their thirties and had not worked 'since their birth'.[50] Another labourer reported:

> We are plus/minus nine. Only three are working. Two are pensioners. Others are grandchildren of my mother. Then there are two other adults. One is a taxi driver. The other finished his matric in 2000 and since then he couldn't find a job, so now he is selling on the streets.[51]

Nelson, a welder in a big company, supported four children, a nephew and his wife. Only he and his first-born (a daughter) were working. She had got a job as a cleaner the previous year 'and she gets [paid] nothing!' She was 34 years old and it was her first job.

These stories show that labour market polarisation does not always privilege people with core employment in the sphere of reproduction; instead, a sizeable number experience increased demands on their wages. However, labour market polarisation does emphasise the relative well-being of the minority who escape extra demands and the severe deprivation of households without access to wage earners.

Taking on extra members often increases friction in households, spreading limited resources thinner (Mosoetsa 2011). But there are also echoes of what Fantasia (1998) calls 'cultures of solidarity'. The textile machinist from Zondi told me: 'Those who are not working, they don't have food to eat. Sometimes they come to me, I give them something. Some of them are short of many things in the house, no one is working, they are suffering. I have to help them.' Nelson, the welder, said: 'I can see other classes because they are not working; they are staying at home. I must give them food to help them. But even I don't have money to give them.' These impulses to solidarity demonstrate a sense of identity across the worlds of work.

Conclusion: A differentiated unity as a lever of accumulation

Most Sowetans, then, share a dependence on availing themselves for exploitation. When opportunities to do so are absent, their dependence is often manifested in deprivation. This commonality is further supported by the fact that people from the different worlds of work are frequently pushed together at the household level and by the fact that individuals' work trajectories frequently cross the worlds of work. However, these commonalities are crosscut by three broad areas of differentiation. The first is the labour market itself. While neither the employed nor the unemployed have viable alternatives to employment, their common dependence on employment may set the unemployed into perceived conflict with workers. Secondly, people are pushed together at the level of the household, but these forced dependencies are fraught with tensions. Thirdly, at the level of the township, the number and quality of jobs in a household draw a fine line in terms of its living standards.

Processes of assortive living and playing are therefore at work.[52] For example, 36 per cent of unemployed people lived in freestanding shacks in our survey, well above the 10 per cent of the population as a whole who lived in such shacks, while the requirements of getting a bank loan excluded households without steady income from the bond housing in Protea Glen on the western edge of Soweto. Tebza described another driver of assorting:

> You find they [workless households] don't have people who hang out with them. They become quite isolated . . . Also, probably because for them this has gone on so long that they are just demoralised. People don't like to associate with them. If you go out you need money to go out.[53]

Similarly, Swazi, a cleaner who moved onto a better job in the municipality in which he works, described difficulties in socialising with old friends as disposable incomes diverged.[54]

It is difficult for Sowetans to see markedly different kinds of people as belonging to the same class, as Chapter 6 will show. However, there is a *systemic* link among these different groups that begins from their common general relation to production, but concretely stratifies the proletariat. Marx's discussion of surplus population and the labour reserve, although it cannot simply be transplanted to the present, is a useful starting point:

> . . . if a surplus population of workers is a necessary product of accumulation or of the development of wealth on a capitalist basis, this surplus population also becomes, conversely, the lever of capitalist accumulation, indeed it becomes a condition for existence of the capitalist mode of production. It forms a disposable industrial reserve army, which belongs to capital just as absolutely as if the latter had bred it at its own cost. Independently of the limits of the actual increase of production, it creates a mass of human material always ready for exploitation by capital in the interests of capital's own changing valorisation requirements (Marx 1976: 784).

For Marx, a 'surplus population' – that is, surplus to the requirements of industry – is an inevitable although anarchic (that is, unplanned) by-product of continual industrial restructuring. It is simultaneously the detritus of the labour market – people rendered redundant, briefly or permanently – and it is elastic: 'Modern industry's whole form of motion depends on the constant transformation of a part of the working population into unemployed or semi-employed hands' (Marx 1976: 786). Because capitalist industry does not develop smoothly, but in fits and starts, accumulation would be hampered during a growth spurt if the number of people available for employment did not outnumber employment opportunities. Marx (1976: 796) recognises several sections of the labour reserve: some who flow in and out of work; others thrown out of 'decaying branches of industry' who stagnate in 'extremely irregular employment', whose 'conditions of life sink below the average normal level of the working class', making them 'a broad foundation for special branches of capitalist exploitation'. Others in Marx's (1976: 797) description will *never* work because they are 'mutilated . . . sickly', unable to adapt to the current requirements of industry, or have lived 'beyond a worker's natural life span'. If their subsistence cannot be 'transferred onto the shoulders' of the working class and petty bourgeoisie or, in the contemporary world, transferred to state welfare, they fall to the lowest kind of work.[55]

This last-mentioned group is particularly relevant for contemporary analysis, where proletarianisation (the process of separating people from other ways of making a living than selling their ability to work) has advanced far enough that the surplus population may grow far beyond the size of a practical labour reserve. Particularly in a recession, such high levels of long-term unemployment may become increasingly *dys*functional to capital, creating various forms of social instability.

In Marx's exposition, it is not only the existence of a surplus population, but the differentiation within it that works as a 'lever of accumulation'. It therefore becomes a means to 'retool' labour as mechanisation, new work techniques and the reorganisation of work also come into play. People are discarded and replaced with workers better suited to new requirements. Manufacture replaces handcraft in Marx's description; work insecurity is normalised in our day.

David Byrne (2006: 43) points out that the existence of the surplus population not only disciplines wages, but is also 'crucial to processes of restructuring when capitalism is in crisis'. We have seen already that partial workers are concentrated in the poorest households and I suggested that people from the most deprived households are most likely to accept poor-quality employment. Household ties, then, may be working as a lever for restructuring, helping to downgrade job quality.

This may also work beyond the deprived household itself. Sowetans are keenly aware of fine differences in living standards, and the threat of sliding into the lower classes may, therefore, discipline the most secure workers.

Questions remain in terms of broader geographic assorting. It is unclear if Soweto's 2006 population has stabilised or whether we have captured it during a process in which the best-off workers and the middle classes are gradually drifting out of the township, leaving behind only the 'lower classes', making Soweto a surplus population 'dump' as much as a labour reserve. Class matrices of the sort drawn up by Seekings and Nattrass (2005) are inadequate for grasping these subtle and systemic senses of 'class interest'.

What of our original question about the process of class *formation*? In those moments when class goes beyond a social location and becomes a collectivity, people's concrete positions may expose different issues and articulate conflict differently, and they may therefore gain different insights out of the experience. Electricity cut-offs in Soweto, for example, affected pensioner–unemployed households especially severely. Power may appear differently: a service delivery protest focused on a councillor wields voting as a bargaining chip; catering workers contemplating a strike may, however, observe that wealth is produced 'by our hands'. Alexander and Peter Pfaffe (2011) distinguished 'the unemployed' from the 'youth' in the township they researched. The former, who wore overalls and worked piece jobs, generally eschewed politics – possibly because their role as wage earners constrained their ability to act according to their individual beliefs. The latter, who tended to be younger and were active in the local uprisings, also had responsibilities (children, for example), but no way of meeting those responsibilities except through placing demands on the state.

Nevertheless, in the case of Soweto, many unemployed and informal workers rub shoulders with the employed in former council housing. Out of all the categories of waged employees, only teachers and nurses were completely absent from shack settlements. Trade union members were present both in squatter settlements and in areas dominated by people with steady jobs. Any of these individuals could form a node in a network to link one world of work with another. The possibilities of bridging these divides emerges, firstly, in the mutual recognition described above by many workers of the unemployed and destitute; and, secondly, through the physical proximity that still obtains in many areas of Soweto between those in different worlds of work. Finally, however, while the peculiarities of class structure may go part way to explain the divide in the working-class movement, the influence of ideology and organisation in building particular ways of seeing and organising in the world cannot be ignored.

In summary, this chapter has outlined the commonality of Sowetans with regard to dependence on employment and the mixing of worlds of work at the household level and over the lifetime of an individual. However, in the end, unity may depend less on living the same kind of life and more on whether organisations exist that scratch the surface appearance to expose the fourth area of commonality outlined above, the hidden dynamic of how the fates of the employed and the unemployed are bound together.

Notes

1. See also Goldthorpe (2000), which incorporates different kinds of employment contracts.
2. 'Exploitation' here refers to the appropriation of surplus value. Surplus value is the value created by people's work over and above their own subsistence.
3. Informal work is a somewhat slippery concept. See, for example, the discussion by Lindell (2010: 5ff.), which points out that the general definition of 'informal' as being economic activity beyond the sphere of state regulation lumps together dissimilar pursuits, including 'non-poor' activities (see also Barchiesi 2010: 77). I reproduce the phrase here as a shorthand for its use in the literature under discussion.
4. Their community of fate is delineated by understanding harm to another outside of one's own sector or geographical space as harm to oneself. I employ the phrase at a less subjective level to mean a group whose fate (the things that happen to us that are beyond our control) is mutually interdependent and mutually constituted, in which harm to another *is* harm to oneself, regardless of their understanding.
5. See also Webster (2005: 66).
6. But as we shall see shortly, in the final stages of constructing their model they use income from non-occupational activities as one of the criteria for classing some 26 per cent of households with income from 'entrepreneurship or wealth' (Seekings and Nattrass 2005: 251ff.), which slightly weakens their claim that income demonstrates the consequentiality of their class categories.
7. Wright's is a multifaceted concept, not merely a means to operationalise a variable.
8. A more political/organisational explanation for polarisation appears in work by Buhlungu (2006a: 14), Lehulere (2005) and Seekings (2004), while for Pillay (2006: 189) union members, in particular, are coming to 'resemble an incorporated labour aristocracy surrounded by a sea of poverty'. However, I will not deal with these arguments directly here, because other elements enter the picture, in particular the question of political alliances. I tackle this argument elsewhere (Ceruti 2008).
9. The narrow rate is calculated as the number of unemployed divided by the labour force, which is the number of unemployed plus the number of employed. The broad rate includes 'discouraged workseekers' among the unemployed.

10. '*Unemployed*: persons aged 15–65 years who did not have a job or business in the seven days prior to the survey interview, but had looked for work or taken steps to start a business in the four weeks prior to the interview and were able to take up work within two weeks of the interview' (Stats SA 2006: ii). 'The *employed* are those who performed work for pay profit or family gain in the seven days prior to the survey interview for at least one hour or who were absent from work during these seven days but did have some form of work to which to return' (Stats SA 2006: ii). Note that our survey sampled people of sixteen years and older. In the equivalent calculations for our survey we use the population aged 16–65 years.
11. Stats SA counted all persons 15–65 years in the working-age population, while our survey included all persons aged 16–65 years.
12. That is, weighted figures.
13. Precision: ±2 per cent (at 95 per cent level of confidence; see Chapter 3, note 3).
14. Precision: ±2 per cent.
15. Precision: ±2 per cent.
16. Precision: ±2 per cent.
17. Audio recording of an interview with Trevor Ngwane at the Careers Centre, Soweto, conducted by C. Ceruti in English, 12 August 2005.
18. Audio recording of an interview with Nelson at an ANC rally at Orlando Stadium, Soweto, conducted by C. Ceruti in English, 24 February 2006.
19. Audio recording of an interview with Mamsie at her 'business' near Orlando Station, Soweto, conducted by C. Ceruti in English, 16 January 2006.
20. Piece jobs involve working for different people on a piece-by-piece (job-by-job) basis.
21. Audio recording of an interview with Sam at his place of work by the roadside, conducted by C. Ceruti in English, 2006.
22. Transcript of an interview with Jabu at her 'business' in Zondi, conducted by K. Khumalo in isiZulu and translated by the interviewer, November 2008.
23. Transcript of an interview with a woman vendor at her 'business' in Diepkloof, conducted by R. Mudau and translated by the interviewer, November 2006. Original recording not available.
24. It is a truism that unemployment affects men and women differently. Additionally, our survey under sampled men. Women are more likely than men to be pensioners or unemployed, and less likely to be students, petty bourgeoisie or employed.
25. Precision: ±0.04 per cent.
26. Precision: ±2 per cent.
27. Precision: ±1 per cent.
28. Precision: ±2 per cent.
29. Precision: ±1 per cent.
30. Precision: ±1 per cent.
31. Precision: ±1 per cent.
32. Precision: ±1 per cent.

33. For the state-employed teacher, the concrete form of the tussle is between the wage bill and state spending, hence indirectly levels of taxation and corporate surplus value.
34. Audio recording of an interview with Ngcaba at his workplace, on Old Potchefstroom Road, Soweto, conducted by C. Ceruti and R. Mudau in English and isiZulu, 17 January 2006.
35. Audio recording of an interview with a Pick n Pay worker conducted during a COSATU march for jobs in central Johannesburg by C. Ceruti in English, 18 May 2006.
36. Audio recording of an interview with Francinah conducted at a Soweto Electricity Crisis Committee march in Soweto by C. Ceruti in English, 10 June 2005.
37. Handwritten detailed notes of an interview with Sello in Soweto, conducted by C. Ceruti in English, June 2005.
38. Handwritten detailed notes of an interview with Tebza, conducted at the interviewer's home by C. Ceruti in English, 2005.
39. Audio recording of an interview with Lawrence at his workplace, conducted by C. Ceruti in English, 12 December 2005.
40. Audio recording of an interview with ZT, a salesman, at Jabulani Mall, Soweto, conducted by C. Ceruti in English, 12 February 2006.
41. Precision: ± 1 per cent.
42. Precision: ± 1 per cent.
43. Precision: ± 2 per cent.
44. Precision: ± 1 per cent.
45. This should not be mistaken for Seekings' and Nattrass's (2005) underclass. Their underclass is derived, as explained earlier, by splitting up a residual category of households where no one is employed and income from assets and self-employment is less than the value of an old age pension. They split that group into households where no one is available for work – a 'not in the labour force category' – and the remaining underclass. Their underclass would, therefore, include many of our survivalist self-employed and exclude pension-dependent households and households containing partial workers, both of which fall into the 'other' category in our table. Respondents in households in their underclass would, therefore, be more than the 'all unemployed' category and fewer than the three categories where no one is employed, but probably no more than 15 per cent if we remove those respondents living in households with at least one partial worker. (Note that this is not a percentage of households but of individuals living in such households.) We cannot be more exact because we collected different data and our sampling unit differed. For example, our income data does not analyse the share of income coming from different sources in a household. More importantly, the difference in how we manipulated the data reflects a theoretical difference, where I conceive of pensioners and partial workers in Soweto as mostly part of the 'surplus population' and to some extent the labour reserve, as elaborated elsewhere in this chapter.
46. Precision: ± 1 per cent.

47. Precision: ± 1 per cent.
48. Audio recording with Mr Khumalo conducted during a COSATU march for jobs in central Johannesburg by C. Ceruti in English, 18 May 2006.
49. Audio recording of an interview with a textile machinist from Zondi at a COSATU shop stewards' meeting in central Johannesburg, conducted by C. Ceruti in English, 24 November 2005.
50. Audio recording of an interview with a municipal worker at Jabulani Mall, Soweto, conducted by C. Ceruti in English, 2006.
51. Audio recording of an interview with a labourer conducted at an ANC rally at Orlando Stadium, Soweto, by C. Ceruti in English, 24 February 2006.
52. 'Assortive' usually refers to the tendency of people to marry people of the same socio-economic class. Here I use it more generally.
53. Handwritten detailed notes of an interview with Tebza conducted at the interviewer's home by C. Ceruti in English, 2005.
54. Audio recording of an interview with Swazi at Maponya Mall, Soweto, conducted in English by C. Ceruti, 7 May 2009.
55. See Ceruti (2008) for a fuller exposition of Marx's analysis.

5

Underemployment

Too poor to be unemployed

Peter Alexander and Kim Wale

> 'Employment' as interpreted in industrial countries is not the appropriate concept. The ILO [International Labour Organisation] employment missions discovered or rediscovered this, and they also discovered that, to afford to be unemployed, a worker has to be fairly well off. To survive, an unemployed person must have an income from another source. The root problem is poverty, or low-productive employment, not unemployment. Indeed, the very poor are not unemployed but work very hard and long hours in unremunerative, unproductive forms of activity.

In the quote above, Paul Streeten (1981: 13) turns the equation of poverty with unemployment on its head, exposing the inappropriateness of the 'employment' concept as a measure of well-being. This insight comes strongly to bear on our own attempts to understand various forms of precarious and low-productivity work reported by many of the respondents who participated in our qualitative interviews and quantitative survey. In Soweto, however, underemployment took the form of casual jobs, where the hours were few, as well as the kind of unproductive labour mentioned by Streeten. To grapple with these forms of work requires that we rethink the privileging of employment as a route out of poverty and hardship. Perhaps the point is most strongly made by drawing attention to the description of Lawrence, one of our qualitative interview participants, of his experience of work as a scrap collector in the context of the daily financial struggles faced by him and his family:

> At home no one works. Even my older brother does the same job as I do. My mother sometimes gets piece jobs [casual employment] of doing people's laundry in the township. In the whole week she might get a call to do the laundry maybe two or three times only. My father passed away a long time ago. My two younger brothers are still at school. The money that I get from selling these scrap metals, I use it to buy food. Just like today I got R80, I am going to buy food. My brother can also bring home some money, and then we can pool it and get some food. My mother also does the same. Everyone in the house has a responsibility to make things happen. There is nowhere else we get money from except from these activities. We have no relative or friend who sometimes helps us. We have no one to turn to for help.[1]

Based on the internationally recognised definitions followed by Statistics South African (Stats SA) in its Labour Force Surveys, Lawrence, the young man quoted above, would be classified as 'employed'. This category, however, fails to recognise the experience of extreme hardship and poverty contained beneath the label. In our survey, many participants responded to questions on work and employment in ways that mirrored the kind of underemployment reflected by Lawrence. Further analysis of our data demonstrated that, in terms of the Living Standards Measure (LSM), a proxy for household income, the underemployed are generally worse off than the unemployed. In light of these findings, it becomes clear that the dichotomous measures of employment and unemployment obscure more than they reveal. The broader aim of this chapter is to disrupt the hegemony of this binary by locating it historically and with respect to criticisms raised by other writers. We begin with the big picture and then narrow down to consider our survey research.

Conceptualising and measuring underemployment

The employment/unemployment binary

Unemployment emerged as a concept in Britain in the second half of the nineteenth century, although the reality was much older (Boyer 2004; Dooley and Prause 2004). However, the depression of the 1930s brought urgency to debate about ways of understanding, defining and measuring the problem. The notion of 'labour force', which contained the binary as we know it today, emerged as a critical term. The working-age population was divided into two distinct categories: those who were 'economically active', that is, the labour force, and those who were 'economically inactive'. The former included the unemployed 'who were involuntarily out of work but were actively seeking a job' and the employed 'who did work for pay and profit'. The latter consisted of 'persons who, of their own accord, did not work for pay or profit and hence did not directly contribute to the formal economic product' (Clogg 1979: 1).

The dominance of the labour force concept and the employment/unemployment binary within it continues into the present. The ILO's (2007: 4) definition of employment, which is accepted internationally, includes 'all persons above a specific age who during a specified period, either one week or one day, were in . . . paid employment . . . [or] self employment'. The employed include those who have a job or run an enterprise, even if they performed no work in the specified period, as well as those who were actually at work. The qualification for being 'at work' is having 'performed some work for wage or salary, in cash or in kind'. Furthermore, 'for operational purposes, the notion of "some work" may be interpreted as work for at least one hour' (ILO 2007: 4). Therefore, for a person to be considered employed, they have to work for only one hour within the specified time period. According to the ILO, one of the reasons for including such low levels of working time in the definition of employment was to satisfy the desire for this definition to remain mutually exclusive from the definition of unemployment. This desire was driven by a concern for the quantity of labour that goes into production rather than the quality and variety of different forms of labour (ILO 2007: 2).

Critiquing the binary

As early as 1936, Joan Robinson criticised the employment/unemployment binary for its inability to represent all forms of employment hardship. She proposed the idea of 'disguised unemployment' to describe forms of inferior 'hand to mouth' occupations such as 'selling matchboxes in the Strand [in London], cutting brushwood in the jungle, [and] digging potatoes on allotments' (Robinson 1936: 230). Robinson's criticism highlights a key problem when applying the labour force concept even within Western industrialised nations, that is, that it glosses over significant qualitative differences occurring across a variety of different forms of employment, resulting in an unquestioned inclusion of badly paid, insecure, informal work in the same category as well-paid, regulated formal employment.

A further set of challenges came out of attempts to export the binary to developing countries, where mere subsistence was generally more important than 'pay and profit' (see Moore 1953; Myrdal 1968; Turnham 1971). Gustavo Esteva (1992: 8–10) and Arturo Escobar (1997: 86) locate attempts at universal applicability within the post-Second World War development project, which assumed that

Western industrialised nations represented the pinnacle of progress, towards which the recently decolonised nations would inevitably advance. Wage labour came to represent both modernisation and emancipation from backwardness, poverty and social exclusion (Barchiesi 2005: 36; Du Toit 2004; Du Toit and Neves 2007). Reality contradicted the paradigm, but despite this, the paradigm promoted measures of employment as measures of success.

The International Conference of Labour Statisticians (ICLS) had discussed the problem of 'underemployment' as early as 1925, but it agreed a statistical definition only in 1957 (Laurie 1968). In 1966 the ICLS resolved that both visible underemployment (involuntary short duration of work) and its invisible form (low economic returns and under-utilisation of skills) should be measured (Clogg 1979). The term was subsequently theorised using the Labour Utilisation Framework, first advanced by Philip Hauser (1974) and later developed by Clifford Clogg (1979: 2–4). According to this model, inadequate utilisation included unemployment, working few hours, working for low pay and under-utilisation of skills (Jensen and Slack 2003: 23–4). The last three of these were regarded as forms of underemployment. In 1998 the ICLS recommended measurements limited to time-related underemployment, but contemporary ILO thinking recognises the importance of quantifying the other two forms as well (Hussmanns 2007: 18; ILO 2010). The term 'inadequate employment situations', which refers to the desire to change one's work because it limits 'capacities and well-being', includes low pay, under-utilisation of skills and, in addition, working excessive hours. The ILO accepts that calculations for this category must include workers' own assessments of their potential for increased 'productivity and quality of work', and also that legal definitions should be taken into account (ILO 2010). Given this subjectivity and national specificity, international comparability is necessarily conditional (Hussmanns 2007). Recently, Ralf Hussmanns (2007: 17) from the ILO's Bureau of Statistics recognised that the 'relevance for industrialised countries' of measuring underemployment is 'increasingly felt'. And this was before the 2008 credit crunch and subsequent expansion of the problem (ILO 2012a).

Despite important advances, problems with the ILO's approach remain. Firstly, it continues to be flavoured by Northern developmentalist concerns of progress through economic productivity. By framing the issue of underemployment in terms of adequate or inadequate utilisation, the hand-to-mouth nature of much underemployment experienced in the global South becomes hidden beneath a metaphor of economic development. Secondly, and related to this, underemployment is still treated as a sub-category of employment. Thus, while the binary has been challenged by reality and ongoing debate, officially it is retained.

This has implications for the lack of attention given to 'underemployment' in the collection of national statistics, and for its absence from public discourse and the making of policy. Thirdly, while the ILO recognised the significance of 'underemployment' more than 60 years ago, it still fails to reinforce its concern with the compilation of internationally comparative statistics (perhaps because only a few countries collect the required data) (ILO 2010).

Underemployment in the current historical moment

While the binary retains its dominant position, it does so in the face of assessments that echo Streeten's argument quoted above. For instance, the ILO (2007: 3) states:

> In the absence of social safety nets and unemployment insurance, a total lack of work is only an option for those who are not poor and are themselves financially viable (or have access to family resources, for example). The open unemployment figure, therefore, tends to measure those who are economically better off.

This recognition that the underemployed are often worse off than the unemployed gets to the heart of the survivalist experience of underemployment in the global South, where, to quote Jan Breman (2003: 195), unemployment becomes a 'luxury poor people cannot afford'.

In conceptualising the realities of underemployment in poorer contexts, we have found that the notion of the 'labouring poor', which Breman (2003) developed in relation to India, contains particularly useful insights. The labouring poor include the 'unregulated and complex community' at the bottom of the informal sector, as well as informal, flexible forms of casual, day labour in the formal sector (Breman 2003: 195). Such people continually rotate among different forms of work in a context of sometimes-intermittent work and sometimes a sustained shortage of work. Breman (2003: 226) explains:

> It is this lack of job security that is responsible for the pattern of rotation between different locations (places of work), economic sectors (the retail trade, building, small-scale industry), and modes of employment (self-employed, casual day labour, member of a gang led by a jobber).

Breman's approach leads on to the recognition that the terms 'employment' and 'unemployment' as they are conceptualised in dominant labour history and development discourse obscure the situation in India, where only a small minority engage in the 'norm' of secure, formal wage work (see also Behal and Van der Linden 2007).

Significantly, this kind of sociological insight is implicit in India's official statistics, which recognise the importance of underemployment and its often seasonal character. Arguments regarding the inadequacy of Western labour concepts holds lessons for other developing countries, even if the nature of variation from 'international norms' differs from country to country.

Measuring unemployment and underemployment in South Africa

The history of conceptualising and recording unemployment and underemployment in South Africa is enmeshed within the history of colonialism, segregation and apartheid. The historical formation of the black working class within an engineered and institutionalised system of white capitalist supremacy has had a marked impact on unemployment and its measurement.[2] Through the system of migrant labour and pass laws, unemployment and underemployment were displaced from urban centres to rural homelands (Aliber 2003: 474; Iliffe 1987: 260). Because Africans were generally only allowed to be in urban areas when they were employed, the assessment of unemployment was completely distorted (Maree 1975: 71).

Prior to 1976, the government made no attempt to quantify joblessness among the African population. However, growing unemployment among urban Africans and unofficial measurement by academics led to a change in policy (SAIRR 1976: 282; SAIRR1977: 213–19). The Current Population Survey (CPS) was introduced as an attempt to measure the number of unemployed Africans. The first CPS results, published in November 1977, estimated that these totalled 11.4 per cent of economically active Africans, which was approximately half the figure calculated by Charles Simkins, the pioneer researcher in this field (SAIRR 1977: 215; SAIRR 1978: 170; Simkins 2004).[3] In criticisms echoed in recent debate, the South African Institute for Race Relations complained that the strict definition of employment used by the CPS excluded those people who had become despondent and given up looking for work (now usually referred to as 'discouraged workseekers'). It also noted that it 'ignores the underemployed, that is, people who work a few hours a week to eke out an existence, and who form a large percentage of the economically active population' (SAIRR 1978: 170). Partly because of poor sampling methods, the CPS lacked credibility and eventually, in 1990, it was suspended (CSS 1993: 1; see also Simkins 2004).

With the end of the apartheid in sight and lessons learned from the CPS in mind, there was a new attempt to measure unemployment. This was contained in the October Household Survey (OHS), first conducted for the whole of South

Africa in 1994. The new expanded definition of an unemployed person marked an important change in thinking, as it now included discouraged workseekers as unemployed. Initially, the OHS also provided a definition of the underemployed, which included '[w]orkers . . . who involuntarily worked less than 35 hours during the reference week and who were seeking or had the desire for full-time or additional work'. It later transpired that the data required to calculate this indicator was collected, but not published (Stats SA 2008d: 13). The OHS also introduced the category 'invisible underemployed', which consisted of 'workers who are "overqualified" for their occupations and those making inefficient work procedures', but this variable was never measured (Stats SA 1996: 9).

As early as the 1996 OHS, the expanded definition lost its official status, and Stats SA reverted to the strict definition of the apartheid era (Stats SA 1999). In 2000 the OHS was replaced by the LFS, but there was no change in the essence of the official definition. Eventually, from 2005, Stats SA stopped publishing the expanded rate of unemployment altogether (although it could still be deduced using figures for discouraged workseekers) (see Figure 5.1). Rather than utilise a conception of unemployment more suitable for South African conditions, where very high unemployment discourages many people who are jobless from seeking work, the

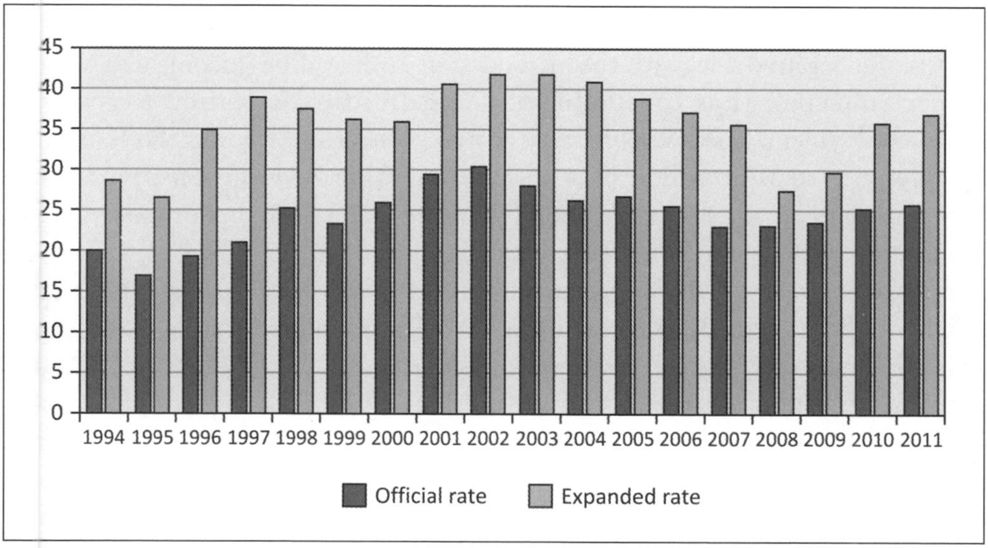

Figure 5.1 Official and expanded rates of unemployment, South Africa, 1994–2011.

Sources: Stats SA October Household Survey; Stats SA Labour Force Survey (September); Stats SA Quarterly Labour Force Survey (Quarter 2).

government preferred to follow a model based on European conditions. At the same time, official interest in underemployment disappeared altogether. This shift demonstrated South Africa's reluctance to consider a model for understanding itself in socio-economic terms as something different from the West.

We agree with the view that 'the non-searching unemployed [the discouraged] are no less part of the labour force than the searching unemployed and their joblessness is no less associated with hardship' (Kingdom and Knight 2000: 3). However, our own interest extends beyond this debate to a concern that various forms of underemployment are included under the homogenising category of 'employment'. In keeping with ILO policy, the qualification for being counted as 'employed' is minimal and includes all those 'who performed work for pay, profit or family gain in the seven days prior to the survey interview for at least one hour'. Thus, somebody who works for as little as 60 minutes would be included as employed. The category also includes some people earning nothing at all, perhaps because they were working in a family business. Indeed, the September 2007 LFS recorded 318 000 employed people who received no monetary reward whatsoever (Stats SA 2008a: 18).

In 2008 the LFS was replaced by the Quarterly Labour Force Survey (QLFS). Significantly, this followed a report by the International Monetary Fund, with subsequent 're-engineering' undertaken by a team of experts. There is no indication that local conditions and popular conceptions were studied as part of the review (Stats SA 2008d: 2).

On the negative side, with the introduction of the QLFS, income data was no longer collected, thus precluding the possibility of assessing pay-related underemployment. However, there were two positive innovations, both justified by reference to ILO policy (but with no mention of local sensitivities and experiences) (Stats SA 2008b; see also Hussmanns 2007). The first of these was the publication of data on 'time-related underemployment', defined as 'employed persons who were willing and available to work additional hours, whose total number of hours actually worked during the reference period was below 35 hours per week' (Stats SA 2008c: xi). For the second quarter of 2008, these totalled 2 095 000 people, constituting 6.8 per cent of the working-age population (Stats SA 2008c: Table 3.9). A new notion of 'under-utilised labour' combined the time-related underemployed, the unemployed and discouraged workseekers. However, as Stats SA (2008c: xi) noted at the time, 'at this juncture, no attempt is made to measure other forms of underemployment such as occupation or income related underemployment, as a result, the . . . [total figure for] underutilised labour is perhaps underestimated'.

The second improvement was the measurement of 'informal employment'. The intention here was to gauge 'precarious employment', with the indicator including all those who were working in the informal sector; plus those helping unpaid in their household or business; plus those employed in the formal sector or in a private household, if they did not receive either a contribution to medical aid or a pension, or did not have a contract of employment (Stats SA 2008c: viii). For the first quarter of 2008, 4 651 000 people were engaged in informal employment, and four years later, in the first quarter of 2012, the number was 3 841 000; a decline from 33.8 per cent to 28.6 per cent of all those employed.[4] Informal employment cannot be equated with underemployment, now rather neatly defined by the ILO (2010) as 'all those who worked or had a job during the reference week but were willing and available to work "more adequately"'. For instance, it is reasonable to assume that some of the 151 000 managers and professionals who were recorded as informally employed in the first quarter of 2012 were not 'underemployed'. On the other hand, there must be many people in formal employment who are underemployed.

The data on informal employment provide a reminder that many jobs in South Africa are badly regulated, as well as poorly remunerated. They also show that the profile of the formally and informally employed is quite different. In the first quarter of 2012, 61.4 per cent of the former had completed their secondary education, but this was true for only 24.0 per cent of the latter. Further, as with the distinction between official and extended rates of unemployment, the division between formal and informal employment assists us in challenging the unemployment/employment binary. Figure 5.2, using 2012 data, expands our perspective. It provides a breakdown of the working age population, which numbered 32 786 000 people (Stats SA 2012a: vi): 45.3 per cent was 'not economically active', but some of these, 7.1 per cent of the total, were counted as discouraged workseekers and have been included with the rest of the unemployed. Nearly half those in the reduced 'not economically active' segment were students (18.8 per cent of the pie). Only 41 per cent of the working age population was employed. This so called 'labour absorption rate' is considerably lower than that for any comparable country (India's rate, for instance, is about 55 per cent, and the numbers for Russia, Brazil and China are higher still) (Stats SA 2012a: vi; CDE 2011: 10). Just 27.4 per cent of the working age population was formally employed. These figures are emblematic of the South African crisis. However, our data from Soweto provide access to another level of complexity, revealing further deprivation. They show that many of those who have jobs are actually worse off than the unemployed.

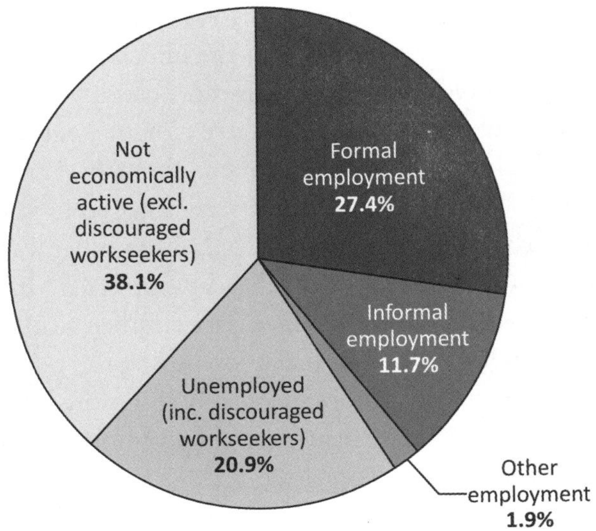

Figure 5.2 Forms of employment and non-employment in South Africa, 2012, as a percentage of the working age population (15–64 years).

Source: Stats SA Quarterly Labour Force Survey 2012 (Quarter 1).

Findings on underemployment in Soweto

Initial qualitative expressions of underemployment

During the initial qualitative phase of our research, we found that many expressions of work and employment could not comfortably be captured by the employment versus unemployment distinction. Lawrence, whom we quoted earlier, provided one example, and others are to be found in Chapter 4. 'Work', even when it is paid, was generally associated with regular employment and excluded 'piece jobs'. The following quote from a person who fits our definition of a partial worker underlines this point:

> I once worked, but now I am not employed. I lost my job in 1982. I have not been working since 1982. I only work piece jobs. Just as you can see, I am wearing these overalls – I paint so that I can get something for a living. I consider myself a worker, although it's not the type of work that you could expect to sustain you. I am looking for employment.

Such formulations echo Breman's (2003) discussion of the labouring poor in India, for whom extreme poverty precludes the possibility of remaining unemployed and leads to work that is too insecure, irregular and intermittent to be considered employment. While the labouring poor represent the majority of workers in India, the underemployed are still a minority in South Africa, thus indicating significant differences between these two Third World contexts. However, there are also important similarities in the sociological quality of these experiences. For instance, the underemployed in Soweto, like the labouring poor in India, exist in a space that escapes the assumptions in terms of which the categories of employment and unemployment make sense.

Quantitative research on underemployment

Our basic research questions were not aimed at testing hypotheses about employment categories as such or about counting numbers of people that conformed to each definition. Our reading of relevant debates on 'underemployment' was a consequence of ideas that emerged from analysis of our data, and our understanding of the concept emerged without any a priori assumptions. A bonus of this approach was that our conceptualisation grew out of South African conditions rather than theorisation based on experience elsewhere. We hope that the ensuing dialogue between international conceptualisation and our own thinking will prove fruitful.

In the analysis that follows, we investigate the association between employment category (EC) and household income. We developed nine ECs, and our 'underemployed' category combined two of these: 'partial workers' and 'survivalist self-employed'. Our justification for the nine categories lies principally in the main questions we were asking, and our rules for distributing individuals between these categories are explained elsewhere in this book. Income level was operationalised using LSMs.

Partial workers engage in 'piece work', by which Sowetans mean working for different employers for short amounts of time, usually on a day-to-day basis. This is often irregular employment, although it could be regular, but for only a few hours a month (see Chapter 4). A partial worker respondent from Diepkloof described his experience of piece work as follows:

> A lot of people I know do not work. They just have temporary jobs for one day. From there, they just sit with us here. If there is someone who says 'go and hunt somewhere', we go and hunt [that is, for work]. If we are unsuccessful, we come back and just sit.

Our survey showed that the most common piece jobs involved domestic duties (such as cleaning floors, washing and ironing clothes, caring for children and cutting grass), construction (for instance, tiling, painting and laying bricks) and retail work (mostly cashiers and shelf stackers). Next came work in the hospitality sector (such as waiters), packing (in various industries), stock taking, marketing and assorted clerical activities. The range of work was wide, with particular individuals employed as an exam assistant, an events' organiser, a voting assistant, a caddy, a cinema observer and a singer. For the most part, these were inherently short-term jobs, and partial workers can be seen as the quintessential 'reserve army'.

The term 'survivalist self-employed' refers to people working on their own account. A majority were petty traders. They survived by 'selling'. They sold food, clothes, cigarettes, sweets, perfume, airtime and so on. Again, there were people with construction skills, although this time they had their own hand tools. The group also included hairdressers, and people who did sewing, baking, catering, laundry and electrical work. There were also a couple of traditional healers, a deejay and an artist. Unlike the partials, they required access to some capital (albeit minimal), in the form of goods to sell or simple equipment. So, while the survivalist self-employed could also engage in piece work, it would be more difficult for a partial worker to join the survivalist self-employed. While partial workers are dependent on somebody providing a job, survivalist self-employment can be conceptualised as a form of more active underemployment. On the surface, the survivalist self-employed might appear similar to our petty bourgeoisie category – a poorer form of the same species, perhaps – but in practice they were easily distinguished. The main difference was one of availability for employment. The survivalist self-employed wanted a proper job, and we sometimes referred to them as 'fill-ins'. For the fill-ins, self-employment was regarded as an alternative to unemployment or even an aspect of unemployment, not the first stage of developing a small business. For instance, a woman from Dube told a fieldworker: 'I am just selling things because I do not work anymore.' What was pushing people into the two underemployed categories was the same – they were too poor to be unemployed.

Our partials and many of our survivalist self-employed would fit the Stats SA definition of the time-related underemployed, but this category, with its 35-hour dividing line, would also include very many people we included as (fully) employed workers. The ILO's definition of the underemployed – that is, those working, but 'willing and available to work more adequately' – includes everybody in our two underemployed categories, as well as many of our (fully) employed workers. Thus, our approach, which draws on local experience, actually provides a lower figure for underemployment than one based on an updated labour utilisation model.

Findings and analysis

Table 5.1 shows, firstly, the proportion of Soweto's adult population falling within each of our nine ECs, and, secondly, the average LSM score of people within each of these categories. Definitions of the categories and calculations of LSMs are discussed elsewhere, and a graph illustrating data presented in Table 5.1 is presented in Chapter 4. Unsurprisingly, the better-off groups included capitalists, managers and petty bourgeoisie. The average student also came from a relatively better-off household. Employed workers ranked in the middle. Pensioners and others not in the labour force, the two underemployed categories and the unemployed are at the bottom. Such people are found within the poorest households.

Table 5.1 Percentage of adult population and mean LSM score for households associated with each occupational category.

Occupational category	Percentage of adult population (weighted)	Mean LSM score
Capitalists	0	1.788
Managers	1	0.895
Students	12	0.657
Petty bourgeoisie	6	0.511
Regularly employed workers	24	0.417
Pensioners and others not in the labour force	12	0.318
Survivalist self-employed	10	0.311
Unemployed	24	0.249
Partial workers	11	0.150

Source: Classifying Soweto survey 2006.

Partial workers, who comprise approximately 11 per cent of Soweto's population, had the lowest mean LSM score at 0.150. The unemployed, who represent 24 per cent of Sowetans, had the second-lowest LSM score at 0.249. The survivalist self-employed, 10 per cent of the population, were slightly better off, with a mean score of 0.31. The differing LSM scores for the partial and survivalist self-employed categories make sense, given that the latter require some start-up funds, which may come from household support. The mean score for the two underemployed categories combined was lower than that of the unemployed.

The next step was to test the significance of the differences between household income levels as reflected in LSM scores. Here we were interested mainly in a comparison between the unemployed and the two groups of the underemployed. For this purpose, the Dunnett T3 test was chosen to conduct a multiple comparisons test for the analysis of variance between each of the mean LSM scores. The results for this test are shown in Table 5.2.

Table 5.2 Results of Dunnett T3 test for significance of difference in mean LSM score, comparing the unemployed with all other occupational categories.

Occupational category	Difference in mean LSM	Standard error	Significance	95% confidence interval	
Capitalists	-1.5394*	0.1465	.000	-2.177	-0.902
Managers	-0.6454*	0.0666	.000	-0.862	-0.428
Students	-0.4076*	0.0226	.000	-0.480	-0.335
Petty bourgeoisie	-0.2614*	0.0302	.000	-0.358	-0.165
Regularly employed workers	-0.1680*	0.0185	.000	-0.227	-0.109
Pensioners and others not in the labour force	-0.0686	0.0219	.060	-0.138	+0.001
Survivalist self-employed	-0.0617	0.0231	.243	-0.136	+0.012
Partial workers	+0.0995*	0.0210	.000	+0.032	+0.167

* Indicates that the difference between mean LSM scores is significant at the 0.05 level.

Source: Classifying Soweto survey 2006.

In Table 5.2, the important columns are 'difference in mean LSM' and 'significance'. The others have been included for readers interested in the finer details of the analysis. The only ECs that are not starred are 'survivalist self-employed' and 'pensioners and others not in the labour force', indicating that there is no significant difference between the mean LSM of these groupings and the mean LSM of the unemployed (although in the case of pensioners, etc. the difference is close to being significant). This conclusion is reflected in the figures in the 'significance' column. In the case of five ECs, the LSM figures are significantly higher than those for the unemployed. For partial workers, it is significantly lower. So, in material terms, while the households of the survivalist self-employed are not significantly better off than those of the unemployed, those of partial workers are significantly worse off. At least in Soweto, there are clearly forms of work and employment that do not afford people a living standard any better than those of the unemployed. Thus, our evidence contradicts the assumption that unemployment data can be used as a measure of well-being.

Conclusion

We have sought to destabilise the employment/unemployment binary by asking the reader to consider underemployment as a distinct category, rather than a sub-category of employment. Our data tend to confirm the assessment that the underemployed are often worse off than the unemployed. Moreover, one cannot defend a definition of 'employment' that includes somebody who has worked only one hour, unpaid, in the whole of the previous week. Further, we are critical of basing labour statistics on the paradigm of modernity and the model of labour utilisation. These reify market relations at the expense of a perspective that takes people's poverty, insecurity and self-respect as its point of departure. While it is valid to argue for data that permit comparability over time and between countries, there is a danger of our statistics becoming disconnected from social reality. Yet, even now, South Africa's official figures point to the relatively tiny number of workers who sustain the South African economy. Underemployment makes the picture grimmer still. The official rate of unemployment – one of South Africa's six 'key indicators' – cannot begin to convey the full extent of the county's socio-economic malaise or quantify the misery that people experience.

Notes

1. Audio recording of an interview with Lawrence at his workplace, conducted by C. Ceruti in English, 12 December 2005.
2. For more on this history, see Bundy (1979) and Terreblanche (2002).
3. Seekings and Nattrass (2005: 167) make the point that much of the difference was accounted for by the use of different definitions of unemployment, with Simkins conceptualising the problem as one of 'underutilisation of labour'. For a valuable outline of the history of unemployment in the last decades of apartheid see Chapter 5 in their book (Seekings and Nattrass 2005).
4. Data for formal and informal employment have not appeared in the published version of the QLFS since the second quarter of 2009, but they are available on request. Thanks to Jeremy Seekings for drawing this to our attention and to Malerato Mosiane of Stats SA for providing assistance.

6

Models, labels and affordability

Mosa Phadi and Claire Ceruti

What does class mean to people in Soweto? In this chapter we describe Sowetans' class models and identities. We shall see that they are aware of class and it matters to their self-view. In interviews, Sowetans displayed a rich imagery and language of stratification, elaborated in Chapter 8, which was used even by people who did not recognise the word 'class', although most did. For instance, there was the 'cheese boy', the child whose lunchbox is superior to that of his classmates at the township school because his mother can afford an individually wrapped wedge of processed cheese. We asked Ngcaba, a petrol pump attendant, about his class and he replied: '*Eish*! I don't know what you're talking about.'[1] A minute later we asked if he had a collective name for the residents of Diepkloof Extension, the distinctly richer 'suburb' on the edge of Soweto (see Chapter 3). Without missing a beat, he laughed and said: 'oh, *ama-bourgeois*!'[2] Mamsie, a facecloth vendor, interpreted class to mean her type of business and insisted that everyone was the same in Soweto. But when asked about Diepkloof Extension, she compared her own miserable existence as one of the *sisiwana* (literally 'orphans', but translated by her as 'poor') with *labofuma* (the rich, literally 'ones with fat to smear on their bodies'). She offered this picture: '[Rich] children get money to go to school, but us, as a poor person . . . our children, when school closes they arrive here [at the market to help sell facecloths].'[3]

This chapter discusses what Sowetans mean by class, how many classes they see and how they class themselves, concentrating here on their explicit class definitions and descriptions. It explores empirically Sowetans' views rather than trying to force their perceptions into a preconceived sociological theoretical frame. This approach alerted us to the fact that Sowetans may have more than one class identity at the same time. Therefore, unlike other sociological investigations into class,[4] our survey allowed respondents to choose more than one class identity.

Chapter 7 builds on this discussion by focusing on perceptions of class mobility and the worldviews implied in respondents' constructions of class. We will see that the concept of class starts from the process of socio-economic stratification. The key concept used by respondents in describing their views of class was 'affordability', which might seem like poor grammar, but encapsulates the ability to consume and maintain a certain lifestyle. It therefore links consumption to income, and hence to work and class,[5] and contributes to other themes, such as self-sufficiency, which emerged in Sowetans' description of their class identities. Finally, we conceptualise four popular class types and consider the extent to which people's self-descriptions match their socio-economic circumstances. Here we see that there was a high correlation between the general description, the self-description and actual circumstances for people who called themselves lower class and working class, but the term 'middle class' operates differently on each of these levels.

We investigated Sowetans' perceptions of class through two rounds of interviews and the survey, all detailed in Appendix 1. The first round of informal interviews was exploratory and these interviews often developed into conversations. They usually started with the questions: 'What class are you? How do you know?' In order to get people to talk about class without predetermining a definition of class, we avoided replying to the response: 'What do you mean by class?' The survey used eight class labels, which emerged from these conversations, to get at how people classed themselves. People could choose all eight or none of the class labels from the survey. All the class labels were asked in English to avoid problems with translations, as explained in Chapter 8. The semi-structured follow-up interviews, which were more formal than those in the exploratory research, probed people's notions of class. Where we have quoted from this second round, this is indicated with the words 'interview' or 'interviewee'.

What do Sowetans mean by class and how many classes are there?

There was a keen eye for material differentiation around Soweto, and most people's descriptions of class hinged on this. For instance: 'One determines class through affordability [explained above] and what a person has.' Overall, Sowetans were aware of class, with less than 10 per cent rejecting any class identity. Workers and street vendors in our conversations commonly unpacked this very concretely, using variables such as where you live; the state of your house; whether you have a car or appliances; and the quality of your furniture, clothes and food. Additionally, in conversations, professionals, middle managers and young people, who classed themselves as 'middle', accepted that 'the size of your pocket' determines lifestyle, but included where you socialised and the make of car, brand of beer or label of clothing you displayed as part of their definition. For instance, in terms of type of beer consumed, one of the young male respondents disparagingly pointed out: 'Even Heineken® is not drunk by everyone; only some can afford it. But if you go to the informal settlers, now you'll find him there with . . . his Black Label®.' These young people included aspirations ('it's what you want to study') and attitudes, such as confidence, when describing class. Workers and vendors also described behaviours (walking in a certain way, greeting on the street, talking with a particular accent) or even facial expressions. These performative dimensions of class are explored further in Chapter 7.

Class was defined largely in terms of consumption, but also generally by comparison. A person who described himself as middle class explained: 'There are poor people who can't afford maybe even to feed their families. There are those who can afford everything and those who have nothing, nothing.' Lawrence, a 22-year-old supporting nine family members, described himself in the following terms: 'Some of them are . . . cheese boys. Their mothers are working, taking responsibility for them. I am not that.'[6] Classes were often described from the perspective of one's own experience, such as the young man trying to get some money by directing cars to parking at the Soweto Beer Festival, who described a middle-class house by reference to the household possessions that he lacked: 'He has computer, DVD – you see, that person can feed himself! Maybe a car. You can't buy a car when there's no pots and pans in the house.'[7]

Mostly, we asked people to consider class in Soweto, that is, in a residential context. It is possible that the consumption models that respondents draw on may be modified in other contexts, for example in a workplace environment, enabling people to adopt a double or multiple class identity. In our conversations, a shop steward working in retail consciously described herself as both middle class and working class – the former in relation to her consumption; the latter in relation to her means of making an income. And other elements, such as control, entered another shop steward's definition of his class at work. 'Working class', he said, was 'someone who knows their rights at work and helps others', while 'inequality' was associated with 'the capitalist who gets directly from his house into a car to come to work, but scolds the employee using public transport for being five minutes late'.

Interestingly, race did not feature in Sowetans' conception of their class identity when speaking about class in the township, but Manda (2009) found that when people are asked about class in their workplace, race enters into their definition of class identities. In some of the follow-up interviews, race featured when people spoke about greater Johannesburg, the city to which Soweto is attached.

A general three-class model grew readily from Sowetans' tendency to picture class through a comparison of consumption ability. Both poverty and upward mobility have become more visible in and around Soweto since the end of apartheid (see Chapters 3 and 4). Sowetans were aware of the richest and poorest people in their midst, and most respondents interviewed used the yardstick of what they understood to be rich, poor or neither to locate themselves in class terms. In our conversation, Sello explained a fairly typical class scheme:

> I know of the low class and the middle class. I am low class, because I grew up in an informal settlement where there is no life . . . The middle class is neither rich nor poor. It is just in the middle. These people can afford . . . There is also a high class – those who live in suburbs [historically white residential areas]. They can afford anything they want in life.[8]

In the Classifying Soweto survey, we asked people how many classes there were in, firstly, in Soweto and, secondly, in Johannesburg. The results, presented in Table 6.1, show that a three-class model predominated; it is ordered from the most popular class model to the least popular.

Table 6.1 Number of perceived classes.

How many classes are there . . .	. . . in Soweto? (% of Sowetans)	. . . in Johannesburg (% of Sowetans)
3 classes	41	34
2 classes	14	12
4 classes	12	15
5 classes	6	7
6 or more classes	5	7
1 class	4	3
None	3	4
Did not know; would not answer	15	18
Total	100	100

Source: Classifying Soweto survey 2006.

At least 40 per cent of Sowetans thought there were three classes in Soweto and 53 per cent of these had a model unmistakeably comprising some version of bottom, middle and top. (The remainder were scattered among other variations, or the third of their three classes was uncoded, or they said there were three classes, but named four or two or ten.) Respondents tended to view Johannesburg as more complicated than Soweto,[9] evidenced by the fact that two-class models were the next most popular for Soweto, but four-class models were the second most popular for Johannesburg as a whole.

Of people who said there were two classes in Soweto, 43 per cent mentioned a scheme of extremes: poor/lower and rich/top/tycoon/upper. A further 20 per cent, however, had a two-class scheme comprising a 'middle' class and a class either above or below middle. These models were possibly three-class models, where classes that appear only outside of Soweto filled the gap on one or the other side of 'middle'. On the one hand, many considered life in Soweto to be better than life in a small town or rural squatter camp. On the other hand, however, there was a persistent belief that there was no upper class in Soweto. South African Communist Party member, Jack Shilowa, concurred with the latter position: 'If you have so much money, you then start thinking that you belong somewhere else.'[10] Several of the managers and professionals we met at the Soweto Wine Festival, an annual event promoting wine drinking, had roots in Soweto, but now live in formerly white suburbs, where services and schools are generally better. Trevor Ngwane, a Sowetan activist, contended: 'The black middle class, as soon as they get enough money, they leave the township. There is a real sense that we are here under sufferance.'[11] Those who identified an upper class in Soweto often defined it very modestly, with teachers included, but a man running a *spaza*[12] added a new category when asked about class beyond Soweto: 'You're talking of the big guns there – something bigger than affording.' Among people who said there were four classes in Soweto, there was considerable variation. The largest category among these extended the upper class in a basic three-class lower/middle/upper scheme by adding a grouping such as 'stinking rich' to upper.

Difference was not the only story of class in Soweto. A minority said there were no classes or just one class in Soweto, both in conversations and the survey. In discussions, one form of *siyafana* (isiZulu for 'we are the same') proceeded from recognising material differentiation, but rejected the idea that richer people are better people, like the cleaner who said 'we all go to the toilet the same way'. From a different position in life, *siyafana* also expressed the mild embarrassment of the 'progressed' at moving beyond their roots. The owner of a smart Soweto pub, who grew up in a worker's household in Soweto, but who now lives outside the township, declared that he 'didn't like the idea of class' because he found it 'a bit elitist'. The third form of *siyafana* asserted that the differences within Soweto are minor compared with the differences beyond. Of those people who said there was only one class in Soweto, 39 per cent defined this class as 'poor' and a further 10 per cent said it was lower class. Finally, 23 per cent of those who believed there was only one class named it as middle class. This may be related to a comparison between Soweto and rural areas.

Sowetans modelled their class world, then, around consumption and comparison. The next section will consider how and why Sowetans position themselves within these class models.

How do Sowetans class themselves?

Where do Sowetans place themselves within these class models, and why? Our survey asked respondents which class or classes they identified with, using a list of labels drawn up from exploratory conversations. Respondents could accept or reject any of the eight identities most commonly mentioned in the interviews. The exact words used in the survey were, 'would you call yourself . . .?' (placed here in the same order as the questionnaire): poor, middle class, working class, third class, second class, upper class/top class, a tycoon, lower class. They were able to accept more than one of these or reject all of them.

Table 6.2 shows that 'middle class' was the most common identity. Two-thirds of Sowetans responded 'yes' to the question in our survey: 'Would you call yourself middle class?' 'Working class' was the next most popular label, which was particularly interesting because people seldom volunteered the term in conversations, but then often used it in a literal sense to describe people with wage employment. This made it interchangeable with categories like 'affordable', because employment confers an income. In the survey, poverty featured high in people's self-identities, with the labels 'poor', 'third class' and 'lower class' each being accepted by more than a third of Sowetans.[13]

Table 6.2 How respondents identified their own class.

Would you call yourself . . .[14]	Yes (% of Sowetans)
. . . middle class?[15]	66
. . . working class?[16]	43
. . . second class?[17]	40
. . . poor?[18]	39
. . . lower class?[19]	38
. . . third class?[20]	33
. . . upper class, top class?[21]	13
. . . a tycoon?[22]	3
. . . none of the above?	7

Source: Classifying Soweto survey 2006. These questions were asked in English. The questionnaire had a strict instruction not to probe respondents in this case and to use the English terms.

In order to gain a better sense of how people were linking identities, we conducted further analysis on the data. This also assisted in developing the ideal types discussed later in this chapter. We began by combining those identities, such as 'poor' and 'lower', which tend to operate as synonyms. These combinations, with one exception, were based on factor analysis backed up by evidence from exploratory interviews, where words like 'poor' and 'lower' were described very similarly. Although there was a strong correlation between middle class and working class, we decided to keep these distinct, because the interviews had suggested that these were parallel and associated identities rather than synonymous. This was our exception. Subsequent research showed that we were correct to handle middle class and working class separately. This process of combination left us with four broad identities: the lower, middle, upper and working classes. We distinguish among the initial eight identities, which we have called *raw*, and the four produced through combination, which we refer to as *broad*. The broad lower class included the raw poor, lower and third classes;[23] the broad middle class included the raw middle and second classes;[24] the broad upper class comprised the upper class/top class and tycoon;[25] and the working class was people who chose working class only and no other identity.

We then developed combinations of broad identities, but reflected the raw identities that respondents provided. If they offered raw identities that fell within a single broad identity, there was no need to combine, and these were referred to as *singular* identities. Where they had two or more identities that fell outside a single broad identity, these produced a *multiple* identity. Two examples will help to illustrate this. If somebody said they were lower class and poor they were listed as 'singular lower class', but if they said they were lower class and middle class, they were recorded as 'multiple lower and middle classes'. So, except where respondents rejected all class labels, they either had a singular or a multiple identity. The results of these two processes are reflected in Table 6.3.

Table 6.3 indicates that only 38 per cent of Sowetans had a singular identity. In keeping with the raw identities, the most common was the singular middle-class identity, at 21 per cent, while 13 per cent were recorded as singular lower class, which was considerably more than the singular upper, at 1 per cent. Importantly, whereas 43 per cent of Sowetans identified themselves as working class (raw identity), only 3 per cent were singular working class. In other words, overwhelmingly, people who considered themselves working class combined this identity with something else. It is necessarily the case that singular identities include fewer people than the raw identities with the same name; they are, one might say, more refined. For example, 66 per cent of the population regarded themselves as middle class,

Table 6.3 Singular and multiple class identities.[26]

Identity	Percentage of Sowetans
Singular middle class	*21*
Multiple lower and middle classes	15
Singular lower class	*13*
Multiple working and middle classes	13
Multiple working, lower and middle classes	10
No class identity	*7*
Multiple working and lower classes	5
Multiple working, middle and upper classes	4
Singular working class	*3*
All identities	3
Multiple middle and upper classes	2
Multiple working and upper classes	1
Singular upper class	*1*
Multiple working, middle and upper classes	1
Multiple working, lower and upper classes	1
Total	100

Source: Classifying Soweto survey 2006.

that is, had a raw middle-class identity, but only 21 per cent could be regarded as singular middle class. What do class identities mean to people? The next section unpacks both their explicit and hidden dimensions.

Four popular class types

In this section, we construct four ideal types from Sowetans' qualitative imagery and quantitative associations. These include the three that fit the dominant three-class model – the lower, middle and upper classes – plus the working class. The 'working class' category was added because, although it existed beyond the model, it was a widely held identity (with more people specifying it as a raw identity than any other, except middle class). For quantitative assessments of the lower, middle and upper classes, we focused on singular identities, but also included raw identities where this helped flesh out the picture. For quantitative assessments of the working class, we also drew on the multiple working and middle classes, because this was the main form taken by those with a raw working-class identity. We refer to such people as 'working middles'. They have similar attributes to the singular working class, except with more disposable income. In the discussion that follows, we consider the middle-class identity after the lower-class and upper-class identities, because middle class is widely defined in relation to the two extremes. Then we look at the working class.

In this section, we look at three dimensions. Firstly, we consider how Sowetans described each of these classes when they were talking about a general class model. This we refer to as the *general view*. Secondly, we look at how these class identities were described by those who accepted the labels. We refer to this as *view of self*. The general view and view of self are summaries extracted from qualitative interviews. Lastly, we compare how the identities shape up with regard to questions in our survey, which tease out a range of material factors and opinions. We call this the *actual in the survey*. Table 6.4 summarises our findings.

Table 6.4 Four principal class types.

Class	General view	View of self	Actual in the survey
Lower class	Deprived; not coping; struggling	Deprived; struggling; lacking many things	Deprived of a range of services, durables and activities, and with lower levels of education
Upper class	Those who have everything	*No interviewees admitted to being part of this class*	Aspirational and optimistic
Middle class	Neither rich nor poor; normal; just okay; ordinary; those who can afford	Differed from person to person; included affordability, self-sufficiency, supported by others (if young), better off than the neighbours, young and aspirational	Wide range of people; no clear correlations
Working class	Steady work	Steady work	Steady work; the working 'middles' have more disposable income

Source: Classifying Soweto survey 2006.

We will elaborate on Table 6.4 shortly. Key insights that emerge from it are that, for the lower and working classes, there was a high degree of agreement among the general view, the self-view and responses to the survey questions. However, Sowetans viewed the upper class, when described in the third person, as having everything, but in the survey this identity, as a self-description, related to being aspirational and optimistic rather than to ownership of consumer goods. Middle-class identity was the most divergent in material terms, with a standard general meaning, but various personal meanings attached to the self-view and few patterns of association in the survey. Below we elaborate on how the four ideal types were represented in our exploratory conversations, in the formal interviews and in the survey.

Lower class

> I am low class. There are a lot of things I would like to have, but I can't afford (self-identified 'lower class' in exploratory discussions).

Deprivation was the defining feature of the lower class and poor. For instance, a self-identified middle-class man at the Soweto Wine Festival described the lower class as submissive and linked this to poverty: 'They are more humble, and don't stand up for themselves. If you have money you have power. They don't think they have the right to live over others.' The words 'suffering', 'struggling' and 'not coping' were often heard in descriptions of this class, as in the following examples: 'The people in my class lack what is necessary to earn a living. We are just struggling' (a woman who described herself as down); 'It's a person who's short of food . . . those classes have to wait [for payday] to buy the food they want' (a woman at the Soweto Wine Festival); 'Some people sit on tins [instead of chairs or sofas] in their houses. Then you can see they are struggling' (a man at the Soweto Wine Festival); 'You'll just see, a person's face tells a lot of stories . . . when you look . . . this person doesn't have a smile; the face is always showing that age, showing I slept on an empty stomach' (a worker). A street vendor in our conversation described visiting a lower-class house: 'You notice that . . . there are a number of things missing that are supposed to be in a house.'[27]

These descriptions are supported in the survey. People who were part of the singular lower class were more likely than the rest of the sample to agree with the statement: 'We are suffering.' People with raw poor and raw lower-class identities were more likely than others to have no floors at all, and less likely to have tiled floors, good paint inside their house, an armchair and sofa, net curtains, ceilings or electricity. Respondents with any form of raw lower or raw poor identity were more likely to live in informal settlements than other respondents. People who called themselves poor in the survey were, additionally, more likely to live in hostels and less likely to live in mortgaged houses than those who rejected this identity. However, they were not necessarily destitute – for example, a majority of raw poor and raw lower-class respondents lived in a household with a fridge (68 per cent), but this was lower than the proportion in the general population. They were also less likely than the population as a whole to have a string of other durables and services, including hot running water, a microwave, a vacuum cleaner, a washing machine, an electric stove, a radio, a tumble dyer, a television, a running motor vehicle or a domestic worker, and the list goes on.[28]

People who called themselves lower class in conversation mentioned their main problems to be unemployment, proper shelter and lack of education due to financial limitations. Others also associated this class with unemployment. However, people who described themselves as lower class also included street vendors, informal workers and piece workers, as well as some formal workers and pensioners who were supporting many unemployed people. Employed respondents were more likely to be part of the singular lower class if they lived in a household in which more than a quarter of adults were not working. Singular lower-class people were more likely to have irregular hours, less likely to be employed and less likely to be students than the rest of the sample. They were also less likely to identify their main means of support as their own salary. The raw poor and raw lower class were less likely to agree with the statement 'social grants encourage laziness' than was true of the general population, which may have reflected their own experiences.[29]

Critically, those who described themselves as poor or lower class in the survey were less likely to have any kind of post-school qualification and more likely to have only primary school education than the population as a whole. In all, 39 per cent of the singular lower class had not been to secondary school. The 62 per cent who did have some high school education should be compared with 75 per cent for all other singular and multiple identities. Of course, we do not know whether poor education was a cause or a consequence of being lower class – and probably it was both. The point here is that education marked the poor and lower class off from people with other class identities.

A shop steward who classed himself as poor in our conversation said he recognised his class, because 'when you need help you can't get it'. In the survey, people who accepted lower class and raw poor identities were more likely than others to describe themselves as 'discouraged' and less likely to call themselves 'happy' or 'fortunate'. Those who called themselves poor, specifically, were less likely than the rest of the sample to call themselves 'free' and more likely than the rest of the sample to agree with the statement 'things were better under apartheid', suggesting that this was a layer for whom little had changed.

The raw poor and raw lower class respondents were less likely to have ever had a braai (barbeque) or bought a present for an adult than people with other identities. They were less likely to have savings accounts or investments than those who rejected these identities. Additionally, these respondents were less likely than others to feel close to businesspeople, close to people who drive Mitsubishi Pajeros, or close to people who can go to a movie or a restaurant in the middle of the week.

So the singular lower class and the raw lower class and poor showed a close connection with deprived lifestyles, which is consistent with the general descriptions of this class and with the self-description.

The upper class

> They've got cars; they've got everything they want. The house is well furnished, well painted, plastered, even the security (self-identified 'middle class' in exploratory discussions).

Around Soweto, the so-called 'upper class' was also referred to as 'high class', 'tycoons', '*ama-bourgeois*', 'rich', 'first class' and 'elites'. The main word associated with this class was 'everything' (as in, 'you'll go to their house and you'll be surprised, they have cars, DVDs . . . everything!') (a man at the Soweto Wine Festival). In an interview, Pamela described an upper-class house: 'There are paintings on the walls.'[30] Upper-class people were understood to wear expensive clothes and drive 'a Porsche, Mercedes-Benz, Volvo. You'll just admire.' A young shop worker identified the tycoon as 'the one with car keys in hand, who comes out pushing a trolley with R1 000 groceries, while everyone else is carrying two grocery bags'. Several working people noted the ability to buy at any time of the month. A worker stated: 'The rich, you can see – they can get whatever they want at anytime they want. They've got a luxury life.' Having 'everything' was understood to affect one's behaviour. A cashier at the Soweto Wine Festival, who claimed to be middle class, said she recognised upper-class people from 'the way they talk. Their English comes from the nose. And the way they hold themselves.' Another person defined 'upper class' as people who 'don't want to mix with a low-class person'.

There were some disagreements over where the upper class lived, as discussed previously. Jack Shilowa explained: 'Those who are wealthy [haves] do not want to associate themselves with those who are poor [have nots].' But a vendor respondent insisted: 'In the township, not everyone is poor. We've got people who can compare them with the Sol Kerzners.'[31]

No one we interviewed identified themselves as upper class, although a handful of people in the survey accepted this label. There was a contrast between the general view of the upper class and the 'actual in the survey'. Indeed, in the latter, members of the singular upper class were not discernibly richer than other respondents, except that they lived in households more likely to own a vacuum cleaner. However, members of the raw upper class were more likely to describe themselves as happy and professional, and more likely to feel close to businesspeople. This suggests that the adoption of 'upper class' labels in the survey was related to aspiration and self-worth rather than imagining oneself to be part of the class that has everything.

The upper class, then, appears in the general imagination as the class that has everything, often living outside of Soweto, but in the personal imagination seen as being characterised by a feeling of self-esteem.

Middle class

> 'Middle class . . . means we can afford stuff. We can afford to go to a movie or a restaurant in the middle of the week' (two self-identified middle-class young men in exploratory discussions).[32]
>
> I am working and I can get all the basics of life – I can manage. I'm not earning that much, but can get the basics. The middle class to me is everyone who is working (sales worker in exploratory discussions).[33]

In terms of a middle-class identity, there was a pronounced divergence between the general view, the self-view and the actual in the survey. From the survey, the 66 per cent of Sowetans who identified with this class were not marked out significantly by particular socio-economic characteristics or opinions. However, in our post-survey interviews, key terms such as 'affordability', 'normal', and 'neither rich nor poor' were widely and consistently used by respondents when describing the middle class.

There was no association between the label 'middle class' (either raw or singular) and any of those occupations previously understood to be middle class in Soweto, such as teaching and nursing. This was also in contrast to much sociological thinking, which defines class in occupational terms (including Mills 1953; Abercrombie and Urry 1983; Bourdieu 1986; Nzimande 1986; Gerth and Mills 1991; Wright 2002). Education is used as a principal marker of being middle class in several sociological studies (see Schlemmer 2005), but our raw middle-class people were no more likely to have a post-school education than others. They were more likely than most others to have completed high school, but the differences were small (with the exception of the raw poor and raw lower class).

Those accepting a middle-class label were not marked out greatly by their living standards. The raw middle class were a little more likely to have tiled floors[34] and good paint[35] inside their houses, but other differences were minor. They were slightly more likely to have certain consumer goods and housing conditions, which are in any case very common in Soweto, such as hot running water, a fridge/freezer, a microwave oven, a VCR, a washing machine, a DVD player, a hi-fi and/or a built-in kitchen sink. But still, for example, 31 per cent of the raw middle class did not have a DVD player. Thus, consumer goods do not clearly distinguish those who identified themselves as middle class from other Sowetans. Their attitudes were, however, more positive. For example, they were less likely than the sample to agree with the statement 'we are suffering'[36] or to describe themselves as 'discouraged', and more likely to describe themselves as 'happy',[37] 'free',[38] 'inspirational',[39] 'professional'[40] and 'fortunate'[41] than the rest of the sample. Compared to the rest of the sample, the singular middle class were less likely to have worked in the last seven days, less likely to have full-time employment, more likely to have irregular hours and less likely to have their own income as their means of support. All these associations begin to hang together when age was considered. The category 'singular middle class' was associated with people in the age bracket 16–25 years, and 38 per cent of people in this age bracket identified themselves as middle class, compared to 28 per cent who did not accept this class identity.

Overall, the survey data supported the contention that a broad range of people called themselves middle class, substantiated by the fact that the kind of people who thought of themselves as 'middle' ranged from people who lived in shack settlements to a successful businesswoman.

In the follow-up semi-structured interviews and in the interviews we conducted for the documentary film we made, both of which explored the middle-class identity in greater detail, the notion that middle class meant 'neither rich nor poor' was commonplace, but there was little agreement on what this meant in practice. Six broad themes emerged in the self-descriptions: affordability, self-sufficiency, support, comparison, youth culture and language. Finally, context tied the whole story together. People compared themselves to their neighbours and their contexts as a way of locating themselves in class terms. However, they revealed their concrete social position in the way they described their middle class location (see Phadi 2010a; Phadi and Ceruti forthcoming)

We already mentioned the word 'affordability'. To remind the reader, 'affordability' encapsulates both the ability to consume and maintain a lifestyle, as well as the actual material goods that can be afforded. Some respondents mentioned the ability to 'afford basic commodities' and to 'sleep at night fed'[42] as central to their middle-class identity. However, while many of our respondents referred to the ability to afford food, for others it meant the ability to afford imported furniture and top-of-the-range cars.

Work was central to the understanding of 'affordability', because it brought in an income. Vusi, a male interviewee, regarded himself as middle class because work provided the ability to afford basic commodities: 'Going to school, working and being sure that you have certain money at the end of the month, and you are able to meet basic needs, food and clothes.'[43] At the same time, downward mobility occurs when a person loses work. Ntombifuthi, a female interviewee, said losing her job meant that she could not 'afford' the material goods that she once could.[44] A filmed male interviewee, Sabelo, linked his understanding of 'middle class' – ability to afford 'basic commodities' – to his past. He found work and moved from the squatter camps to a Reconstruction and Development Programme (RDP) house, and derived his middle-class identity from this upward mobility.[45]

The ability to manage wages was important to some who accepted a middle-class identity and were employed full-time. Jerry, a middle-aged clerk, said: 'I am in the middle class (*phakathi*). I think I am able to control my salary. To say that with the money I am earning, I am going to do this and this . . . I do not overspend and I do not create for myself many credits. I check my budget; I handle that nicely.'[46] For Hilda, a filmed interviewee and businesswoman, the concept played out very differently: being middle class means 'I can afford anything that I want. I have sufficient money to afford anything that I want, no debts. Everything of mine is cash!'[47]

Affordability was linked to self-sufficiency, especially, it seemed, among those who had irregular work and those who were unemployed. For Gugu, a female interviewee who worked part-time at a major insurance company, middle-class (*phakathi*) identity was associated with independence, dignity and self-respect.[48] Being able to wash and feed oneself with what little one had gave some self-identified middle-class people the sense that they were indeed middle class. They were aware that they could not 'afford' material goods, but they had pride and were self-sufficient. Charles, a filmed interviewee and a survivalist refrigerator repairer, defined his middle-class identity in terms of independence and self-respect. The fact that he had never begged in his life and that he was not the type to bother his neighbours by begging was a source of self-esteem. In addition, he was able to manage his money – he would wait until he had enough money to buy whatever he wished. Middle class to him was related to the autonomy he had in his life:[49]

> I have been [middle class] for a long time, from birth because I cannot recall begging in my entire life . . . going around asking for handouts, money and mielie-meal. Even my neighbours can tell you I am not a needy person that bothers others . . . I can do things for myself. If I want something, I can devise a plan to get it and if I do not have money, I can save up until I have enough money to buy it.[50]

Unemployed young people who identified themselves as 'middle', on the other hand, felt middle class precisely because they were being supported. Johanna (interviewee) was unemployed except for occasional piece work. She lived with her father who works: 'No, I wouldn't say I am poor, because I have bread that I am able to eat . . . I am still being supported.'[51] Papo, a 24-year-old male law student interviewee, also mentioned support: 'I am probably middle class and this is because of the opportunities I have been given which some people never get . . . I wanted to go to school and I am doing exactly that – my parents paid for me.'[52]

For young people, their friendships may open doors to a middle-class lifestyle that those who had not 'achieved' would nevertheless perform/act out. Disebo, a young woman interviewee who had found full-time work, lived in two worlds: 'Just because I work I am not going to stop hanging out with [my township friends]. Then at work I have white and coloured friends . . . [who will say] let's go to News Café at Maponya's.'[53] (News Café is a chain of coffee shop/bars associated with middle-class youth. Maponya Mall is the upmarket mall built in the heart of Soweto.) Louis, an unemployed interviewee, created and performed his middle-class identity through his friends: 'I go to News Café – friends who can afford to fit the bill, friends who have made it in life, those who have achieved everything they want in life, pay for our bill.'[54]

Comparison was central to an identity understood as 'neither rich nor poor'. Abu (male interviewee), for example, compared himself to his neighbours, explaining as follows:

> There are those who have money, who live a nice life . . . and then there are those who have nothing and those who are just people; others do not have houses and they are those who have absolutely nothing . . . I am middle class (*phakathi*) . . . there are things I have that others do not have . . . I studied until matric [Grade 12] . . . I know of others who only studied until Standard 8 and they wish to continue, but could not . . . unlike them, I have matric.[55]

Andronica lived in a one-room shack in an informal settlement, but understood herself to be middle class by comparing herself with those around her. She explained: 'Others are looking for work and cannot find it; others are educated and not finding work . . . so I am better off; at least as I can go to bed fed; others cannot feed themselves.'[56]

Mother-tongue concepts influenced people's interpretation and representation of class concepts. Chapter 8 explains how people frequently used the word *phakathi* when talking about 'middle class' in isiZulu; or *mahareng/magareng* in Sesotho or Setswana. In his study, Mayer found Sowetans used *abantu abaphakathi* in the 1970s. Chapters 2 and 8 explore his work and the use of his concept. These terms mean, literally, 'in the middle' and can be used spatially to mean 'inside' or 'between' in English. However, *phakathi* can also be used to denote social standing: a person is in the middle if they are neither a leader nor a drunkard. A family is *magareng* if they are respectable. We found that people interchanged the term 'middle class' with the words *phakati/mahareng/magereng* as they slipped from mother tongue into English. Sowetans' descriptions of middle class, then, may be laced with these older senses of 'middle' even when using decidedly more modern concepts like 'affordability'.

Context was crucial to understanding the meanings people gave to their identity. What became materially important to individuals depended on where they were positioned in society. For Andronica – whose informal settlement was infused with high unemployment and poverty, and who hardly travelled outside her community – eating daily and having a generator shaped her middle-class identity. Her social and physical context determined her sense of self and in her tiny community she identified herself as 'middle' through her ability to go to bed every night having eaten. In contrast, Hilda, the businesswoman, associated with those in business. Her environment was about distinguishing and comparing herself to other businesspeople. Hence, Richard Maponya, who owns the shopping mall named after him, was used as a marker in her location as a middle-class person: 'Maponya is higher than me'.[57] Also, she had travelled a lot, permitting a global comparison. Hilda was able to buy a Mercedes-Benz car for cash, but for her she was just middle class compared to Maponya, who owned a whole mall. Both these women's perceptions of what it meant to be rich, poor or middle class were shaped by their respective environments.

In summary, people used a middle-class identity to position themselves in their context, and in doing so they revealed the scope and range of their social world. The meanings and definitions people gave to their middle-class identity said much about their actual social positions.

Working class

The survey data confirms that the working-class identity is primarily about being employed. Fifty-eight per cent of people who self-identified as working class had steady employment, compared to 27 per cent of those who did not call themselves working class. Eighty-five per cent of the working class received a salary or a wage, compared to 67 per cent who did not call themselves working class. People who were raw working class were more likely than the rest of the sample to have worked in the past seven days and less likely to be unemployed without other activities. Compared to those who rejected the identity, they were moderately more likely to be in full-time work, strongly less likely to have irregular hours and more likely to have their own income as their main means of support. They were also more likely to have savings accounts and the kind of debt that is possible only with a regular salary: insurance, loans, hire purchase agreements, bonds, shop accounts and credit cards.

Working-class identity was also connected with organisations: 40 per cent of those who called themselves working class felt close[58] to trade union members, compared to 27 per cent of those who did not call themselves working class. Furthermore, 27 per cent of those who called themselves working class had been on strike,[59] compared to 17 per cent of those who rejected the label.

The working 'middles' shared all the attributes of the people who identified as working class only, except that they were less likely to agree with the statement 'we are suffering' and more likely to have the string of durables and services associated, albeit weakly, with a middle-class identity. However, they were distinct among those with a middle-class identity because they were more likely to have engaged in activities that display moderate spending power, such as hosting a braai (barbeque) at home. Their houses were more likely to be in good shape than the population as a whole (including those who described themselves only as middle class). They were less likely to rely on government pensions and more likely to have heard about their jobs through an agency. While the 'working middles' were indebted, like the rest of the self-identified working class, they were more likely than others to have investments (such as unit trusts and fixed-term deposits).

Essentially, the 'working onlys' and the 'working middles' have jobs with incomes that confer greater ability to consume than is the case with most other Sowetans, that is, 'affordability' is more extensive.

Conclusion: Class identity as a marker of social position?

We have shown that people are aware of class in Soweto and that class matters, defining in material terms where they stand in relation to others. Class identity in Soweto today is based strongly on comparison of the ability to consume. We saw that the working-class identity operates in parallel with more directly consumption-based identities, but is linked to these via the 'affordability' conferred by having an income. A key argument of this chapter is that, through affordability, identities are explicitly connected to income, and therefore to having good work or having some other means of generating an income. Other chapters nuance this finding. This chapter has also highlighted the significance of generational difference. The middle-class identity is especially popular among younger people, who construct it differently to older Sowetans, emphasising 'being supported' rather than supporting oneself (and maybe others). As we show elsewhere in this book, the link between affordability and identity is also modified by other factors, such as household composition (Chapter 4) and, as we will see in Chapter 7, whether people are looking 'up' or 'down'.

We also saw that Sowetans' class identities can sometimes reveal a good deal about their actual social position. A lower-class identity proved a reasonable marker of deprivation, while people who said they were working class generally had a job. By contrast, simply adopting the middle-class identity tells us little of a person's social location, because diverse people accept the label. What matters here are the meanings people attach to the identity, which expose their understanding of their real social position relative to others.

We have noted repeatedly that popular notions of class are developed contextually, and therefore in conclusion, we want to problematise our own findings. As an insight into particular ways of constructing class, such notions offer much. But as an overall study of how people's ideas about class develop, our survey is limited by the fact that we interviewed people as individuals in their homes and around the township. A series of township protests over services, which spread across South Africa from 2004, drew powerfully on discourses of deprivation, while a strike wave beginning around the same time highlighted inequality in the workplace. If people's class models are contextual, then we may expect these conflictual contexts to bring new meanings of class to the fore or to modify the class identities discussed above.

In Chapter 7 we expand on these findings by looking more specifically at respondents' perceptions of class mobility and how these feed into their worldviews.

Notes

1. Audio recording of an interview with Ngcaba at his workplace, old Potchefstroom road, Soweto, conducted by C. Ceruti and R. Mudau in English and isiZulu, 17 January 2006. The original interview is missing; we had access to only the transcripts translated in English.
2. '*Ama-bourgeois*' was originally borrowed from class terminology to describe a youth subculture of snappy dressers, also called 'Ivies', but has now been borrowed back into class terminology.
3. Audio recording of an interview with Mamsie at her 'business' near Orlando Station, Soweto, conducted by C. Ceruti in English, 16 January 2006.
4. That is, in the English-language literature that we have encountered.
5. Later in this chapter and in other chapters it is shown that household composition and age also shape class identity. For example, being young in a family that supports one encourages a middle-class identity. Those who have work and who live in households in which the majority of their household members are unemployed accept a lower-class identity.
6. Audio recording of an interview with Lawrence at his workplace, conducted by C. Ceruti in English, 12 December 2005.

7. Some of these arguments appear in Phadi and Ceruti. (2011).
8. Handwritten detailed notes of an interview with Sello in Soweto, conducted by C. Ceruti in English, June 2005.
9. This might be because, when people think of Johannesburg, they compare to white and black South Africa, whereas Soweto, which is essentially black, seems less complex. This is speculative and requires further research. It may be related more simply to the fact that Soweto has neither many very poor people, nor many rich people as outlined in Chapter 3.
10. Audio recording of an interview with South African Communist Party member, Jack Shilowa, conducted by C. Ceruti in English, 2005.
11. Audio recording of an interview with Trevor Ngwane at the Careers Centre, Soweto, conducted by C. Ceruti in English, 12 August 2005.
12. A *spaza* is a small, informal shop, usually run from a person's house.
13. In the semi-structured interviews, we interviewed two individuals from each household (see Appendix 1). Interestingly, there were cases where one individual from a household identified themselves as, for example, middle class, while the other identified themselves as poor. This suggests an individualised notion of class.
14. The identities are arranged from the most popular identity to the least popular.
15. Precision: ±2 per cent. For an explanation of precision, see Chapter 3, note 4.
16. Precision: ±2 per cent.
17. Precision: ±2 per cent.
18. Precision: ±2 per cent.
19. Precision: ±2 per cent.
20. Precision: ±2 per cent.
21. Precision: ±1 per cent.
22. Precision: ±1 per cent.
23. The effect strength for lower and poor was very strong, 0.5. The association between third and poor/lower was weak, 0.2.
24. Effect strength moderate, 0.3.
25. Effect strength weak, 0.2.
26. The composite identities are arranged from the most popular identity to the least popular.
27. Transcript of an interview with a vendor at her 'business' in Diepkloof, conducted by R. Mudau and translated by the interviewer, 2006.
28. We tested for associations between class identities and almost every other variable in our questionnaire, not only the obvious ones. For example, we tested for associations between each class identity and the respondents' mother tongue, how many spoons of sugar the respondent takes in tea, frequency of attendance at funerals, and so on. In general, we have not reported on variables that did not correlate with class labels except when the lack of correlation was particularly interesting, as in the case of middle-class identity.
29. The effect was statistically weak in all cases.

30. Audio recording of an interview with Pamela conducted by S. Mazibuko. Her exact word is '*siyahlupheka*'.
31. Kerzner is a white, self-made multi-millionaire who built hotels and casinos in the Bantustans during apartheid.
32. The interview was conducted in English.
33. The interview was conducted in English.
34. All variables had less than 0.5 p-value, which indicates that there is a relation between variables.
35. Effect strength 0.12.
36. Effect strength 0.18.
37. Effect strength 0.13.
38. Effect strength 0.10.
39. Effect strength 0.10.
40. Effect strength 0.12.
41. Effect strength 0.11.
42. All these interviews were conducted in English.
43. Audio recording of an interview with Vusi. He spoke IsiZulu and used the word middle class to identify himself. His exact words were: '*ukuya esikoleni, ukusebenza ubenesiqiniseko sokuthi unemali uma kuphela inyanga futhi uyakwazi nokufeza izidingo njengokudla nezingubo.*'
44. Audio recording of an interview with Ntombifuthi conducted by S. Mazibuko. She used the word *phakathi* to describe herself.
45. Recording of a filmed interview with Sabelo in Pimville Extension 9, conducted by M. Phadi, 2008. The interview was conducted in English and he used the word middle class.
46. Audio recording of an interview with Jerry conducted by S. Mazibuko, 2008. The interview was in IsiZulu and the interviewee's exact words were: '*Ngiphakathi. Ngicabanga ukuthi ngiyakwazi ukuphatha kahle umholo wami. Kuso ukuthi ngiyakwazi ukuthi ngalemali engiyiholayo ngizokwenza ukuthi nokuthi . . . angiyisebenzisi mawal imali ngizenzele izikolodo. Ngibheka i-budhet yami, ngiyiphathe kahle.*' Jerry used the word *phakathi* while the fieldworker used the term middle class.
47. Recording of a filmed interview with Hilda in Diepkloof Extension conducted by M. Phadi, 2008. The interview was conducted in English and she used the word middle class.
48. Audio recording of an interview with Gugu conducted by K. Khumalo, 2008. The word *phakathi* was used.
49. Charles as well as other respondents in the film mentioned their favourite music. Jazz was Charles's favourite type of music. (The choice of music does not necessarily indicate being cosmopolitan but is, rather, a generational gap. Young respondents indicated a love for RnB while the older generation loved Jazz, gospel and Motown music.)
50. Recording of a filmed interview with Charles in Orlando conducted by M. Phadi, 2008. Charles used the word middle class throughout the interview. His exact words

for the quote above were: '*Ke kgale ke le middle class . . . Ho tloha popelong wa mme waka . . . ha ke hopole ke kopa mobophelong ba ka kaofela . . . ke tsamaya ke ntse ke kopa eng kashota (shota is slang for short) eng ntlatse eng hakena phofo. Le di*neighbours *(slang appropriated for neighbour) tsaka kaofela di ya tseba . . . le ha ka ba botsa batla hojwetsa hore motho o ha a hlophe . . . gore motho o wa kopa eng . . . ha ke sena hona, hakena sona . . . ke ya amohela ke kamong modimo a rateleng ka teng.*'

51. Johanna used the word 'poor' to refer to others and middle class to describe herself, even through the interview was conducted in IsiZulu. Her exact words were: '*Cha angeke ngithi ngipoor ngoba nginesinkwa futhi ngiyakwazi ukudla . . . ngiyanakekelwa.*'
52. Audio recording of an interview with Papo conducted by K. Phokane, 2008. Papo used the word middle class even though he spoke in Sesotho during the interview. His exact words were: '*Ke kgolwa hore ke middle class, ka baka la hore hona le menyetla e ke e fiiloeng e batho babang ba sa e tholeng. Ne ke batla hoya skolong, ke moo, ke kgonne ho ya – batswadi baka bang patalletse.*'
53. Audio recording of an interview with Disebo conducted by K. Phokane, 2008. She used the word 'in the middle'. The interview was conducted in Sesotho, and her precise words were: '*Ha ho bolelle hobaneng fela ke sebetsa ha ke sa hlola ke chomana le dichomi tsaka ba lekeisheneng. Le mosebetsing ke na le dichomi ya makgowa le ba ma coloured ba tla teng, ha re ye News Cafe ya Maponya.*'
54. Audio recording of an interview with Louis conducted by S. Mazibuko, 2008. Louis used the word middle class even through the interview was conducted in IsiZulu. His exact words were: '*Ngiya e-New Café – abangani abokhonayo ukusikhokhela i-bill abangani abesephumelele empilweni abesevune konke bebakufuna empilweni, bayasikhokhela.*'
55. Audio recording of an interview with Abu conducted by K. Khumalo, 2008. Abu used the word *phakathi*. The exact words used were: '*Laba abanemali banempilo emnandi . . . bese kukhona laba abangenalutho, abantu nje; abanye abanazindleko labo ke abanalutho . . . mina* phakathi *nendawo . . . kunezinto enginazo abanye abangenazo . . . nginomatric, ukhona engibaziyo abano-standard 8 ababenesifiso sokuqhubeka kodwa bengakwazi . . . bayi njengabo nginomatric.*'
56. Recording of a filmed interview with Andronica in an informal settlement in Klipspruit conducted by M. Phadi, 2008. In the first part of the interview she used the word middle class and then later she started using the word *mahareng*. Her words were: '*Ba bangata ba batla mosebetsi ha ba thole. Ba bang ba rutehile empa mosebetsi ha ba thole.*' So that's way (using English) '*ke re ke betere Ke kgotsofalla hore ke robala ke jele . . . Ba bang ba ba kgone . . .*'
57. Recording of a filmed interview with Hilda in Diepkloof Extension conducted by M. Phadi, 2008. The interview was conducted in English and she used the word middle class as self class identity.
58. This variable was recoded. Question 'close and very close' to trade union we combined and coded as close to trade unions.
59. The percentage is based on those who answered 'yes' to having been on strike.

7

Perceptions of class mobility

Kim Wale

While Chapter 6 drew on qualitative and quantitative data to show how people construct class in Soweto and how they locate themselves within a broader class schema, this chapter expands on the analysis of the qualitative interviews, and particularly on the key finding that 'affordability' is the pivotal concept in people's construction of class identities. Here, this concept has been used analytically as an organising principle that forges a connection between the economic circumstances (work and income) and cultural expressions (consumption and lifestyle maintenance) of class. In a review of debates on class, Rosemary Crompton (2008) argues that these two legs of class analysis tend to separate class theorists into those who emphasise the economic or material aspect of the concept and those who emphasise its cultural aspects. The key contribution of the concept of 'affordability' is that it represents the connection between economic and cultural capital in respondents' understandings of class.

This chapter probes 'affordability' further by focusing on perceptions of class mobility that appeared throughout the interview transcripts and attempts to show how the concept is taken up in the different worldviews expressed by respondents. It begins with a discussion on the direction of their perception, demonstrating how the emphasis on the economic or cultural referents changes depending on whether respondents are looking up or down the metaphorical class ladder. If respondents focus their attention on the lived experience of the lower rungs of this ladder, the lack of income and work is emphasised. However, when their focus is on the upper rungs, the cultural component of the 'affordability' relationship comes to the fore. This chapter demonstrates how this shift in focus is exemplified in two contradictory worldviews occurring in respondents' discussions of class mobility and captured by the phrases 'upgrade your life' and 'no money, no life'. In each case, the implications for imagining the possibility of class mobility and social change are very different. Findings demonstrate that through the 'upgrade' perspective – popular among younger respondents – the cultural component is emphasised and a just society is imagined that places the onus of responsibility for change on the individual. However, when respondents focus their attention on the lived experience and witnessing of poverty, they emphasise the economic component and place responsibility on unjust structural constraints. This contradictory class consciousness, which moves between a just and an unjust view of the class system in South Africa, is further reproduced and discussed in respondents' considerations of race in relation to class in post-apartheid South Africa.

Methodology

The arguments presented in this chapter are based on a qualitative analysis of the interview texts. As discussed in Appendix 1, the third stage of the research generated data through a semi-structured, qualitative questionnaire that focused discussion on work-life histories, work relations within households and conceptions of class. The analysis developed here emerged from a close re-reading of the transcribed data generated from the section of the interview that dealt with conceptions of class. This section was further divided into questions that focused on the way in which respondents construct class, on whether and how respondents think it is possible for people to change their class position, and on the relative significance of race versus class in post-apartheid South Africa.

The method of analysis was based on Miles and Huberman's (1994) approach to the grounded theory method, which is both inductive and deductive. It was guided by the broader aim of identifying respondents' perceptions of class in Soweto, and codes were developed through an iterative process of reading through all the interviews, allowing preliminary codes to emerge and then refining these in constant conversation with the data until a set of representative codes emerged. A running record of the meaning of codes was kept and a final step in the analysis consisted of looking at the relationship among the codes to develop higher-order categories and themes. While this process was based on my reading of the transcribed interviews as a whole, I have chosen key quotes to represent the general picture that emerged. Respondents were interviewed in their own language and translated into English by interviewees. In most cases I have been able to provide the original language quote in a footnote, but there are a few instances where interviews or parts of interviews were inaccessible.[1] Data was coded in terms of the construction of class difference, the direction of perception and the possibility of class mobility. The breakdown and meaning of the codes were as follows:

1. Constructions of class differentiation: concepts used by respondents to describe the difference between classes.
   1.1. Affordability: being able to afford certain consumables that are seen to represent class positions.
   1.2. Income and work: the means through which people can afford these consumables.
   1.3. Consumption: the accumulation and performance of things deemed to represent class position.
      1.3.1. Presentation of self: consumption to express style through adornment and performance.
      1.3.2. Maintenance of self: basic survival consumption and the satisfaction of basic needs.

2. Direction of perception: in terms of the class model of relative stratification occurring in the interviews, this code refers to whether respondents are looking towards the higher or lower strata of this model.
   2.1. Looking up: respondents are talking about the higher strata in a popular class model and use terms such as the 'upper', 'higher' or 'top' classes to label this group.
   2.2. Looking down: respondents are talking about the lower strata and use terms such as the 'lower', 'poor' or 'down' classes to label this group.

3. Responsibility for class mobility: where respondents locate responsibility for changing one's class position.
   3.1. Individualist: responsibility placed on individual; hopeful view; imagines society as open and presenting possibilities for social advancement.
   3.2. Higher power: responsibility placed on a higher power, such as God or the forces of luck; emphasises the acceptance of class position and the handing over of power to a supernatural force.
   3.3. Structural: presents a view of the oppressive nature of poverty and the hopelessness of living in a situation with no work and no money; the structures of inequality that prevent individuals from moving out of poverty are emphasised.

The first argument presented in this chapter comes out of the interaction between the first and second groups of codes to demonstrate how emphasis shifts in the relationship between consumption (both cultural and embodied) and income through the concept of 'affordability', depending on the direction of perspective.

The second argument layers in the third set of codes dealing with the concept of responsibility for class mobility and looks at the relationship among all three levels of codes. It is argued that, depending on the direction of their perspective, respondents put the mediating concept of affordability to work in ways that connect two contradictory worldviews on class and social change.

Class distinctions and the direction of perception

In his theory of class distinction, Pierre Bourdieu (1984) emphasises the importance of taste as a form of cultural capital that constitutes different class positions. Taste refers to learned cultural codes for consumption. Bourdieu (1984: 1) demonstrates how, in the France he writes about, a social hierarchy of consumer taste functions to reproduce and legitimise social difference in terms of perceived cultural capital. He discovers a two-way relationship between the subject and object of taste: 'taste classifies and it classifies the classifier' (Bourdieu 1984: 6). Not only are objects of consumption classified by learned cultural codes of taste, but people are classified in terms of the kinds of taste preferences they express. Moreover, in his development of the concept of cultural capital, Bourdieu recognises the importance of the embodied dimension of class, captured in the concept of embodied cultural capital in terms of bodily hexis, which refers to the appearance and presentation of the body to others and can include accent, posture and demeanour (Bennet et al. 2009). As Bourdieu (1990: 128) asserts, 'social distances are written into bodies'.

While cultural capital was emphasised in respondents' discussions of class distinction, it was firmly rooted in access to economic capital rather than in different taste. The relationship between the cultural and economic is crucial to this section and has been underlined by researchers and theorists focusing on material culture and consumption in South Africa. Deborah Posel (2010: 161) defines consumption as the 'the acquisition of durable and nondurable goods, along with the cultural, political and psychological antecedents and effects thereof'. Goods, therefore, are consumed within a broader system of meaning and are a vital part of the presentation of self within this system of meaning. By turning their focus to the practices of consumption, these writers emphasise the subjective dimension of class, as well as the importance of understanding how socio-cultural factors interact with economic concerns (Narunsky-Laden 2010: 4). This section focuses on two forms of embodied cultural capital occurring in the interviews. The first is self-presentation, and represents the consumption and display of goods and styles that indicate class position. The second is self-maintenance, and represents the ability to satisfy one's basic bodily needs of food, clothing and health. It is argued that when looking upward towards the 'higher classes', class distinction is constructed in terms of self-presentation through consumption. When looking downward, it is constructed in terms of bodily maintenance.

Looking upward: The 'higher classes'

In constructing class distinction, respondents compared the three different levels of class to one another through the concept of affordability. The following picture emerges: while the 'lowers' can afford barely anything, the 'middles' can afford more than the 'lowers' and the 'uppers' can afford whatever they like. The constitution of class difference through 'affordability' was summarised by Wilheminah in her description of why she is middle class: 'It's probably because there is a lot I can't afford and a lot I can afford.'[2] Building on this common line of argument, Emily specified what it is that she can and cannot afford as a person in the 'middle' class: 'I cannot say I am rich. I can afford, but there are things that I want and cannot get. I cannot say I am very poor, because I go to bed with a full stomach.'[3] As a person in the middle, Emily could not afford everything she wants, but could afford to go to bed with a full stomach.

When distinguishing between what it means to be in a 'middle' position and what it means to be in an 'upper' position, respondents talked about the ability to afford and display particular kinds of expensive consumables, such as cars, accessories and clothes. For example, self-identified middle-class Respondent 1 argued that in comparison to the lower classes, the 'middles' could afford some expensive consumables, but the rich, who 'wear expensive clothes, carry expensive things and drive expensive cars' could consume whatever they wanted: 'If you are rich you will always get the rich stuff . . . If you are middle you would like to wear those things but you have to count your money because you are not rich.'[4]

The construction of the upper classes in terms of being able to afford to 'wear' the 'rich' consumables that the 'middle' people cannot afford emphasises the self-presentation element of the construction of class through affordability. It is not only that the 'uppers' can afford rich tastes, but that they display them. In talking about class difference, participants often discussed dress as being a key signifier of class position. This emerged most strongly in the distinction made between the 'lower' and the 'middle'. Respondent 2, who identified himself as middle class, described the way middle-class people dress: 'You must dress so that you look good in the eyes of the community.'[5] This assertion demonstrates that class position is not just about what you have, but about how your community perceives the way you present yourself through dress. However, for other self-identified lower-class people, the link between class and dress means that by shopping for bargains they can present themselves in ways that make them look 'nice' and of a higher class position. For example, Anne told us: 'You must try to put your things together. Right now things are much better because you can buy clothes on the streets and fix yourself nicely [so] that you look like other people.'[6]

The above respondents all point to the importance of the presentation of self so that you can appear to inhabit a certain kind of class position in the 'eyes of the community'. For these respondents, there is a link between affordability and self-presentation, because class is distinguished by your ability to afford to dress in a neat and respectable way. You may pass as belonging to a higher-class if you are able to present yourself as if you could afford the consumption habits of that class. The importance of dressing the part of a particular class is emphasised by Raymond in the quote below. Furthermore he concludes by asserting that class is a combination of what you have (economic capital) and the kind of styles you have (cultural capital):

> If you have personally defined yourself as a particular class, then you will try to dress the part, because you know that how you dress tells a lot about you, it tells people about the kind of person you are . . . Basically, I think class is not just about what you have, but about the kind of styles you have.[7]

Respondent 1 further highlighted the ability to 'pass' by demonstrating the expensive consumption habits of the higher classes when he asserted that 'I sometimes go to top class [when] I wear expensive clothes and carry expensive stuff'.

In addition to cars, accessories and clothes, respondents emphasised the presentation of 'high-class houses'. In the following quote, Respondent 3, who is 18 years old, emphasised that you could immediately tell when a house belongs to 'the rich' – 'everything' about that house will be 'huge' with 'big lights' and 'bling': 'You can see from the front as you enter the gate that here are the rich. They can afford big gates and walls, huge houses with double storeys; everything and then you can see that these are the rich.'[8]

Similarly, Margarette, a woman in her sixties, argued: 'The houses of upper-class people are also upper class themselves and you can see from outside that this house is filled with glistening things inside.'[9] The key thing distinguishing people in the upper class is that they can afford everything they want, as Wilheminah emphasised: 'People in the high class, their houses are big and they have everything they want.'[10] In the case of Bourdieu's study of France, he argues that class is constituted through different cultural taste. Cultural capital is an important constituter of class for these Sowetans, who construct the 'uppers' in terms of their ability to afford glistening, stylish and expensive consumables. However, these different levels of cultural capital are constituted through different levels of economic capital (affordability) rather than through differently learned cultural codes (taste). Therefore, while culture is indeed the emphasised referent when respondents look towards the higher classes, through the concept of 'affordability' respondents assert that different forms of cultural consumption indicate different levels of economic capital rather than different aesthetic preference.

Looking down: The lower classes

When talking about relatively higher-class positions, the distinction between 'middle' and 'upper' or 'lower' and 'middle' is constructed in terms of the ability to afford certain forms of self-presentation. However, when respondents discuss what constitutes a lower position, they emphasise the way in which class impacts on the body. This is demonstrated by the respondents of Julian May's (1998) study on the experiences and perceptions of poverty in South Africa, where poverty is painted in terms of continuous ill-health, bodily vulnerability, stress and disease. In talking about what it means to be lower class, our respondents moved from talking about the ability to afford consumption styles to talking about the ability to afford life's basic bodily necessities.

While some of the self-identified 'lower' respondents talked about the ability to dress in a way that you do not present yourself as lower class, for other respondents this was not an option. Phindile (1), who identified herself as lower class, reminded us that your ability to present yourself with dignity and beauty is dependent on what you can afford. She told us that 'the clothes I wear are only that I should not go naked; these are just clothes so I can go outdoors and not be naked'.[11] This respondent cannot afford to dress in respectable and neat ways, as the only function of the clothes she manages to find are to cover her nakedness. Another respondent by the same name, Phindile (2), described the experience of being 'at the bottom':

> I am at the bottom, because I cannot reach my needs; what I need, I cannot get it . . . When you are employed, it is easy to get what you want. You buy for yourself instead of begging. Begging is tiring. At times you ask [for] food from next door; it is not good . . . when a person starts to work, even the body changes, indicating satisfaction . . . [Being low class] causes high blood pressure because you think too much; at times you are not able to give a child what he wants – maybe at school they want something, maybe his friend is wearing something nice, and as a parent you do not have the money to buy it for your son. You see, it affects your life in that way.[12]

The experience of being lower class is expressed as one where you are not able to afford the basic needs of life, which is surrounded in the shame of having to beg others for food and not being able to provide for your children. Poverty is linked to health problems, and changes in financial status are described through bodily changes. Phindile (2), whose only form of income comes from what Chapter 4 termed 'survivalist self-employment', barely survived on less than R500 per month through selling sweets and biscuits, and she longed for decent employment. Sam, who was a 'partial worker', provided a similar description of what it means to be 'down level' and how this is linked to the survivalist, hand-to-mouth nature of the work he engaged in: 'I am in a class of down level. In the way I live I understand I am down level and in the manner I do piece jobs so I can get money to buy food for three days but it gets finished in two days and I go back to work without food.'[13]

Following Chapter 5, these respondents would both be classified as 'underemployed'. Furthermore, their lower-class position is constructed in terms of the lived experience of the structural oppression of being underemployed. Strong emphasis is placed on the economic and structural determinant of class position, especially in terms of the nature of employment.

In discussing what differentiates the middle class from the lower class, many respondents argued that it is the ability to earn enough money to satisfy your own basic needs without asking anyone else for help. Respondent 4 described a middle person as: 'Anyone who is able to go to work and realise his needs, even if he can't satisfy them all . . . is able to meet his basic needs, food and clothes.'[14] Similarly, Mantu defined an average person (often associated with being middle class) as follows: 'A person who is not in need of anything . . . he is in need of a better life, but for other things, no, he's okay. For me, that is an average person, someone who wants a better life.'[15]

A key phrase occurring throughout interviews, when describing a middle-class person in relation to a lower-class one, is their ability to 'maintain themselves'. For example, Sibongile described herself as middle-class because 'I am able to live, I can maintain myself and do things for myself'.[16] What is important in the behavioural distinction between 'lower' and 'middle' is that 'middles' can act independently to satisfy their own basic needs without having to ask others for help. By contrast, 'lowers' cannot fulfil their needs and have to resort to the shame of asking others for food. This reference to class in terms of the ability to maintain oneself is another expression of embodied cultural capital, but unlike the cultural capital expressed in the construction of the upper classes, the emphasis is placed firmly on economic capital and employment when distinguishing the lower classes. Class distinction in this instance is defined in terms of an individual's relation to his/her bodily maintenance, which is mediated through access to decent employment and money. The implications of the shift in emphasis are demonstrated in the next section as the mediating concept of affordability is drawn into two contradictory worldviews.

Competing worldviews

Jenny Stuber (2006) differentiates three different modalities of class talk: class awareness, class consciousness and cultural constructions of social class. She defines class awareness in terms of the recognition of class divisions in society, class consciousness in terms of the ideological understanding of whether and how class difference matters in society, and cultural constructions of social class in terms of the symbolic boundaries constructed around social class. In this section I look more closely at what Stuber calls 'class consciousness'. While this was not a specific question posed to respondents, it can be gleaned through their discussion of class difference and class mobility. The analysis of respondents' discussions of class mobility led to the development of three codes to classify different kinds of responses. 'Individualist' refers to points of view that emphasise the responsibility of the individual to move up the class ladder; 'higher power' indicates responses that locate the responsibility for change in class position in a higher force, such as God or luck; and 'structural' responses emphasise the structural constraints to class mobility, such as finding decent work or having access to financial resources.

The question of class consciousness, or how class matters in society, was addressed through an analysis of the 'worldviews' underpinning respondents' discussions of class mobility. A worldview is a set of beliefs or an interpretive framework that provides an understanding of the nature of reality (Miller and West 1993; Koltko-Rivera 2004: 3). In particular, Melvin Lerner's (1980) formulation of the 'just world hypothesis' and Adrian Furnham and Edward Procter's (1989) expansion on this formulation provide an interpretation of the worldviews/class consciousness underpinning talk on class mobility in Soweto. Social psychologists have used the concept of a 'just world hypothesis' to refer to the way in which people often make sense of their social world through theorising it as a just place where people get what they deserve (Lerner and Miller 1978; Lerner 1980; Furnham 1988). Furnham and Procter (1989) add to this recognition by demonstrating how the 'just world hypothesis' is one option within a larger dimension that also includes an 'unjust world hypothesis' and a 'random world hypothesis', and that these options are related to different spheres of control and responsibility. A number of psychological studies have researched popular explanations of poverty, indicating that people (and especially wealthy people) tend to explain poverty in individualistic ('blame the poor') terms (Feagin 1972; Harper et al. 1990; Wright 1995). The tendency to blame individuals rather than social structures for poverty is an example of the operation of a just world hypothesis, because it is imagined that the world is a just place in which individuals are responsible for their relative positions within it. On the other hand, we may think of explanations that emphasise the structural conditions in explaining poverty and hardship as an unjust world hypothesis. While the former hypothesis emphasises the personal realm of control, the latter emphasises the political realm and therefore has different implications for imagining social change.

While individualistic explanations for class mobility represent a just worldview of South African society, structural explanations emphasise the unjust nature of society, while the higher power view could represent both at the same time. While not considered in depth in this chapter, when articulating the higher power view, respondents would discuss class mobility in terms of God's plan and emphasise the importance of accepting your lot in life, even if that lot seemed unfair. Some respondents said they were 'happy' with God's plan for them, while others accepted their lot in life, but were unhappy with it. While the higher power view represents one of the three ways in which interviewees responded to questions of class mobility, this section focuses the discussion on the other two perceptions of class mobility: the individualist and structural views. Furthermore, it demonstrates how these two views correspond to the way in which class distinction is constructed in Soweto. The two understandings of class as constructed in terms of the ability to afford certain styles of life, on the one hand, and the inability to afford life itself, on the other hand, wrap themselves into two different stories of class mobility. In unfolding these competing understandings of 'upgrade your life' and 'no money, no life', it is argued that each implies a different expression of affordability, representing different worldviews with different political implications. I also demonstrate how the 'upgrade' view filters down to popular discourse from the 'official' line on the nature of South African society from above, and how this is both reproduced and contested in discussions of race in relation to class in the post-apartheid context.

Upgrade your style, upgrade your life

In answering the question about class mobility, many younger respondents emphasised the importance of having a positive mindset, confidence and a strong work ethic to pursue the opportunities available.[17] The assumption underpinning this view is that the opportunities of a better life are there for the taking.

Responsibility is placed on the individual to make the most of the 'New South Africa' and claim his/her better life. This view was demonstrated by many of the youth interviewed who, like Simelo, argued that: 'It depends on the determination of an individual to change class or he will stay that way.'[18] Similarly, in the quote from Raymond, a young self-identified 'middle', he explains that it is the responsibility of the individual to 'manoeuvre around challenges' and take the opportunities available to them:

> For me, it's about when you look at your life as a whole. Do you think you have achieved all that you wanted to achieve or are you in a process of achieving what you wanted to achieve? . . . If you have the opportunities to make them true, then I can call myself middle class. I can't say that I really struggle – okay there are some challenges, but you get ways to manoeuvre around those challenges. Personally, for me, if there is something that I want to do, with the opportunities that I have right now, then I do it.[19]

Similarly, Respondent 3 said she was critical of 'township people' who do not take the opportunities available to climb the class ladder:

> Township people undermine themselves and they have the power to change that. We have so many opportunities that we must take . . . I dream of getting the best education I can to move up the ladder as quickly as possible and open my own business to get rich too.

This idea of class upward mobility being the responsibility of individuals to grab hold of the opportunities available and upgrade their position is often linked to the expression of class through consumption. These youth express a view that if you want to live the high life, you have to combine your hard work and striving with the right self-confident thoughts and consume the desired styles. The importance of consumption and style in 'upgrading' your class position finds its most vibrant and extravagant form in the consumer culture expressed in many of the interviews with younger respondents. By wearing the right brand names, so these younger respondents argue, one's perceived class position can shoot from lower to upper class. The value of wearing the right brand names in terms of how others perceive your financial status is seen in the quote below from Mbulelo:

> If you are neat and take care of yourself, then the person who sees you won't see you as low class, but they will see you as high class. The person will be looking at you from his own situation, which might be different from mine. He will see how neat you are, wearing designer jeans and Carvela shoes and he will see that, *Iya!* (wow), the brother has money.[20]

While the price of the clothes is important, they need to bear the right brand name for you to attain top-class status. Echoing the brand names mentioned above, Siyabonga (1), an 18-year-old, self-identified middle-class respondent, asserted that he 'tops the lower classes by far!' when he wears his 'grand things, brand names . . . Levis, Carvela, Nike, Addidas' and when he goes to the places rich people go: 'Maponya Mall, News Café, Jabulane Mall'.[21] Echoing the findings of the 'looking up' section on the construction of the 'higher classes', for these young stylish consumers, class is very much about how others perceive you, and if you are wearing the expensive brand names and are seen in the stylish, rich hang-outs, then you are seen to be top class. These examples further emphasise the privileging of cultural capital in the perceptions of upward class mobility. The assumption underpinning these quotes is that instead of economic resources determining class position through limiting possibilities of consumption, here consumption can be in a sense 'faked' in order to appear to achieve a class position that is above your economic means. However, while dimmed down, the economic component is still present in the idea of 'passing', because it rests on relatively 'affordable' cultural markers and implicitly recognises economic constraints as a key factor determining the expression of style.

In discussing the possibility of moving up the class ladder through determination and dreams, in another part of the interview Mbulelo used a popular marketing and consumption term, 'upgrade', to describe this process:

> Yes, it is possible [to change class], because in life you have to upgrade. You can't live in a shack for the rest of your life; you have dreams and you tell yourself that 'this is what I want to achieve with my life'. You have to say to yourself 'I want to get out of this shack and live in a big house', but in order for you to do that, you have to work hard. You have to get a job and whatever, then you will upgrade. You will move from low class, then go to middle class, then if you succeed strongly you will move to high class, depending on your determination, on how determined you are to move from low class, then you can change. Depending on determination, the job you work in and the salary you earn.[22]

Mbulelo emphasises determination and aspiration as the qualities one needs for upward class mobility. Although he recognises that work and salary are important to moving up the ladder, he believes that it is determination that gets one into the top jobs. In these quotes, notions of class are linked to an aspirational class identity. Posel (2010) argues that consumerism in South Africa includes these aspirations to consume. Even among South Africans 'who are not economically well-off, the aspiration to wealth through displaying desirable things (cell phones, cars, etc.) is celebrated as a sign of "joyous emancipation"' (Posel 2010: 159). An emancipated South African citizen is, therefore, imagined in terms of an aspiration to consume. Research into youth culture in South Africa similarly demonstrates how new identities are constructed and reconstructed through the lens of taste, culture and aspiration (see Dolby 2001; Nkuna 2007; Nuttall 2004).

The views expressed by these respondents are very similar to the kinds of interpretations found in the ideological media and government discourses that define the terrain in which the 'New South Africa', nationhood and development are imagined. Williams (2006), Narunsky-Laden (2008) and Posel (2010) demonstrate how government, media and commercial discourses intersect to paint a picture of South African citizenship as one ripe with possibilities of success through consumption. Williams (2006) argues that South African newspapers contribute to celebrating the market as a panacea for socio-economic problems and to denying the necessity for broader structural changes in addressing continued inequality in South Africa. Through the media, the message is passed down to South Africans that even without structural transformation, the African National Congress's electoral promise of 'a better life for all' is possible and that this will happen through the free market. Combined with this message, nation making is achieved through commercial discourses of conspicuous consumption. Narunsky-Laden (2008) points to the role that consumer culture plays in constructing South African national identity; similarly, Posel (2010) demonstrates that with the rise of the new black elite, conspicuous consumption is often embraced by black South Africans as a symbol of deracialisation and freedom.

In the quotes on class mobility in Soweto, we see this kind of understanding of South Africa filter down to everyday understandings of the possibility of class mobility. The link between broader discourses of citizenship and local expressions of material culture are similarly demonstrated in a description of the cultures of commodification in Soweto discussed by Grace Khunou (in Mbembe, Dlamini and Khunou 2008: 243–4). In a reflection on marketing advertisements in Soweto, she asserts:

> Some adverts seem to suggest that if you can have it in Sandton, then you can have it in Soweto too . . . So adverts are playing on the elements of desirability, accessibility, and opportunity. Everywhere you go in Soweto, for example, you will meet adverts for MTN and Vodacom cell phones, not to mention beauty products. They all sell a lifestyle, and in many ways, the youth are buying into it. Through acquiring these products, the youth want to be seen as connected and as beautiful.

Khunou argues that marketing discourse in Soweto draws on discourses of South African citizenship and identity, to symbolically construct success in the 'New South Africa' as linked to consumption and style. Furthermore, the youth of Soweto, as argued by Khunou and demonstrated in this section, are buying into this notion that the opportunities in the 'New South Africa' are open to those who consume the right kind of styles. In another of Khunou's quotes, she further links consumption in Soweto with resistance and challenge to apartheid: 'A man with a car is the man . . . But not just any car: VW Golfs and BMWs used to be linked to being fast, having money and challenging the apartheid system' (Mbembe, Dlamini and Khunou 2008: 244). This quote connects with Posel's (2010) argument that discourses of consumption are linked to discourses of racial emancipation in post-apartheid South Africa. For many Sowetans, class is therefore connected to a sense of being included in a contemporary citizenship that is imagined and enacted through consumption.

When talking about the upper classes and upper-class mobility, these Sowetan respondents buy into the official line that a better life is possible for all South Africans and believe that they can achieve that better life through upgrading their styles. These 'upgrade' understandings of class mobility highlight the cultural element of affordability through emphasising the importance of consumption as a means through which to tap into new South African citizenship. A 'just worldview' underpins this understanding, as responsibility for 'upgrading' is placed firmly on the shoulders of the individual who must be positive, work hard and consume correctly in order to grab the opportunities available to improve his/her lot in life. Opportunities for 'upgrading' are constructed in the quotes above in terms of 'getting the best education' in order to 'open my own business and get rich', or in terms of finding well-paid work. However, in order to step into these imagined opportunities, respondents believe the mechanism to be a combination of an aspiring and confident mindset coupled with consuming the right styles. The following section demonstrates a very different worldview that appears alongside this 'upgrade' view.

No money, no life!

In the conclusion of her article on youth culture in Johannesburg, Sarah Nuttall (2004: 251) poses the question of the gap between aspirational identity and social conditions. The tension held in this gap emerged similarly in these interviews. Despite expressing a sense of belonging to the 'New South Africa' through an aspiration to consume, many respondents held this dream alongside an expression of a severe, embodied and hopeless experiences of continued poverty. In the 'looking down' section, respondents emphasised the difficult experience of not being able to maintain oneself, of having to ask others for help and how being lower class impacts on one's life and body. Furthermore, the inability to maintain oneself was firmly connected to decent work and money. While the idea of 'upgrading' locates responsibility at the level of the individual and emphasises the cultural component of the affordability equation, when respondents focused on the 'lowers', they emphasised the material component of income, stressing the idea of 'no money, no life'. This key phrase was captured in Siyabonga (2)'s expression of what it means to be 'last class'/'third class':

> I am last class, which is third class, because the things I need in life, I am not able to afford you see. You know that when you have money, you can afford anything you can fit to any class you want . . . it affects me psychologically, mental wise and physically. You know life is all about money . . . No money, no life.[23]

When directing attention to the lower classes, access to economic capital plays a key role in explaining class position and class mobility, and the locus of responsibility changes from the individual to the structural. This worldview was emphasised by Rose who, at 79 years old, painted a sombre picture of what she saw as dream versus reality:

> There are times when you dream of doing something, but you realise that you cannot and that you were just dreaming. You cannot because you do not have money to do so . . . I don't have the power to turn my dreams into reality, and you know that you only get power from money. My pension money is not enough, as it is spent on electricity and rent, while whatever is left from it goes to buying food.[24]

In Rose's account of class mobility, she strongly asserted that aspiration is not enough. In contrast to the perception that opportunities are ripe for the taking, she asserted that without money you have no power.

Linked to the power of money, employment becomes central to moving out of the lower class. To reiterate the point made by Phindile (2): 'To change class is to be employed.' While employment is highlighted as the important factor in moving out of poverty, the 'looking down' section of this chapter further emphasises the problems of underemployment for the lower classes. The realities that many remain 'poor while working' were stressed by Anne, who worked at a dry cleaners and argued that to change your class you have to find a 'job that pays well', as many of the forms of work 'lowers' are engaged in do not offer enough economic capital.

The phrase 'no money, no life' sums up the weight of poverty in a world that denies life to those without the money to afford it. Along a similar vein, Ndofaya and Sakile described a middle-class person as someone who 'can afford life'.[25] When respondents refer to 'life', they are not talking about living the high life, but rather about being able to satisfy their basic needs. Unlike the discourse of the 'upgrades', respondents do not locate the responsibility for change within the individual. Instead of blaming the victims for their poverty, many of the self-identified middle-class respondents recognise that the lower classes would act independently if they could afford it. The problem, then, is not about the cultural values of the 'lowers', but rather their lack of money and decent employment, which prevents dignified behaviours of self-maintenance and necessitates the embarrassing behaviour of begging. One of the reasons for this empathetic lack of judgement is that many of the respondents who call themselves middle class nevertheless feel close to the plight of the 'lowers' and can recall a time in their own lives when they were in a similar position.

In her interview, Respondent 3 demonstrated the way in which the shift in perception happens as respondents move from talking about opportunities to move up the ladder to a sobering empathy for the lived experience of what it means to be poor. While from her position in the 'upgrade' section Respondent 3 appeared critical of the 'township people' who do not take the opportunities available to them, in the quote below she remembers what it was like to be poor and the fear that she could be 'lower' again comes through in her wish not to return to this class position. Instead of the blame being placed on the individual, there is a personal understanding of the lived experience of the lower classes and recognition of how difficult it is to move out of these classes and stay out of conditions of poverty.

> I could say I am middle class; I'm not poor because I work and can afford to take care of myself. There are people who go today without eating . . . that is poor for me . . . I don't wish to be lower at this point, and it is based on my own experience. I know what it is to be poor . . . [I remember when]

> my mom and dad got divorced and my mother was doing a job that didn't earn her that much . . . and there were days when there were school trips we wanted to go on, but couldn't afford it. I remember . . . a point where there was no food and we had to go and pick in the bins to get food. That is poor for me.[26]

Respondent 3 discusses the same points of class differentiation as other respondents (the lack of independence, the bodily experience of not having food, the shame of having to look for food in rubbish bins). While she is now a self-identified 'middle', she nevertheless feels close to the experience of the lower class, as it is an experience she has felt before. The issue for her is no longer one of a lack of determination and striving, but rather an inability to change one's class position, linked to the conditions enforced by lack of work and income. Similarly, when Sibongile describes the difference between her ordinary position and the poor, she ends by saying that she has not reached that point. This statement indicates that this is a point that she could reach, that perhaps she has come close to it, but has luckily not yet reached that point:

> I see myself as ordinary, because I am able to do for myself. I am able to maintain myself . . . there is no day I go without food. People who are suffering or poor may ask for food. I personally do not do that. I have not reached that point.

In both the middle-class respondents discussed above, there is a sense of close proximity to being lower class. We see that these boundaries between 'middle' and 'lower' are not strongly entrenched. While class distinction between these two groups exists in Soweto, it is predominantly constructed in terms of economic capital and decent employment, but has not settled into strong cultural distinctions. It is the ability to afford rather than a different set of cultural values that is emphasised in the explanation of 'lowers' in relations to 'middles'. The closeness that these 'middle'-identified Sowetans feel to the poor is further demonstrated in the survey data, where 89 per cent of Sowetans said they felt close to the unemployed. It appears that a high majority of Sowetans are connected to the lived experience of poverty, whether they have felt it for themselves or witnessed the unemployment and poverty of those closely connected to them. As much as respondents look towards the bright lights of a better life for all and believe in the power of consumption to open up the world of class to them, there is also a strong awareness of the lived experience of poverty in Soweto and a recognition that the possibilities of consuming your way to the top are not available to many Sowetans.

These interviews hold this tension between a hope for a better life for all, contradicted by a lived experience of a lifeless life for most. This tension between imagining post-apartheid South Africa as a just place in which the individual is responsible for his/her future versus South Africa as an unjust place, which unfairly denies its fruits to some and privileges others, is reproduced in respondents' constructions of race.

Class versus race in post-apartheid South Africa

When asked which was more important in the new South Africa, race or class, those who said class greatly outnumbered those who said race. In the instances where respondents demonstrated confidence in answering this question and provided reasons for their responses, some interesting findings and interpretations emerged that are worth discussing, as these reflect the contradictions in worldview seen in discussions of class mobility. These responses not only highlighted the 'upgrade' understanding of class, but also demonstrated that, when respondents were prodded, it was often held alongside a structural interpretation of continued racial oppression.

Respondents often justified their choice by arguing that legal racial segregation is no longer enforced as it was during apartheid, and that black South Africans are no longer restricted from climbing the class ladder through making money and exercising their right to consume. South Africa's history of racial oppression is a particularly brutal one, with black South Africans being systematically disenfranchised and dispossessed. The shift to a democratic South Africa and the lifting of racial barriers to equal citizenship will be a key influence on the response to this question and the way in which respondents paint class difference in a more positive light in relation to the racism of apartheid. Furthermore, the connection between racial liberation and consumption makes sense in a context in which oppression was tied to the inhibition of consumption in townships (Posel 2010). A history of legally enforced restrictions on consumption, combined with the way in which the media and marketing industry expresses the 'New South Africa' discourse through a lens of consumption, means that the ability to consume becomes a powerful (if problematic) marker of liberation in Sowetans' discussions of class. We see this logic unfold in the quotes from Simelo and Sakile, respectively, below:

> Concerning the olden days, I would say 'race'. The old [system] was divided into two races: the blacks and the whites. The main focus was race. Whether you were black and have no food or black and rich, race was the number one thing in the olden days, which was explicit . . . now we can no longer focus on race; class is the one. The kind of car you drive, the phone you have, the things you have make it class [rather] than race.[27]

> Class is playing a more prominent role. However, I can't talk about race, because I was young during apartheid, I wasn't there during racism, but class is becoming a more permanent thing in that the people are also moving up and they are also directors of companies . . . Class has become more important.[28]

These respondents argue that the focus is no longer on race, now what is important is class in the form of consumption and upward mobility (the type of car you drive, the phone you have and 'moving up'). Furthermore, while the racial segregation of the past is seen as a negative thing, class in the form of consumption is seen as a positive thing in that it is evidence of the new possibilities open for black South Africans.

In the quotes above there is a sense that after the end of the system of racial oppression, a new process of class upliftment through consumption developed. This notion ties into the discourse of hope, aspiration and consumption, discussed as part of the discourse of the 'upgrade', and reinforces the analytical argument about the just worldview underpinning respondents' discussions on class. Through discussions of class mobility and race versus class, we see that most of these Sowetan respondents do not see class as an oppressive system of power, but rather as presenting the possibility of an opening up of a better life for all to be seized through consumption. Similarly, reflecting on race, Respondent 1 asserted that 'we no longer have these negative things' and then moved on to associate class in the new South Africa with dreams for a better future: 'So we are in class because we always thinking about the future, because everybody has a future and we all have dreams.' Similarly, Jabu associated class and the new South Africa with striving for 'the high life' and 'expensive things'.[29]

Although respondents asserted that race is no longer important in South Africa, some of their quotes nevertheless reflected the continued significance of race. This can be glimpsed on subtle and overt levels. Beginning with the subtle, there are moments in these interviews when a deeply taken-for-granted connection between race and class is asserted. Despite the arguments that race is no longer important, these statements indicate that racial differences continue to be so significant that they are normalised. For example, respondents do not think twice about racialising class in their assumptions that there are two different kinds of high class that depend on the racial make-up of the group. For example, Tshehla described whiteness as a separate class and put forward a view that to be white is to be upper class: 'White people . . . they are high class . . . most of the time they have everything they need, they have everything they want.'[30] On the flipside, Respondent 5 claimed that the 'upper classes' are 'the BEE' (Black Economic Empowerment), which means the people who have made money through BEE.[31] This refers to wealthy black South Africans. Thus, even though South Africans may belong to the same class (upper class), they continue to be distinguished by race. A picture is painted that looks like this: all whites are upper class and then there is the other upper class, the BEE upper class. These subtle assumptions about racial belonging are further evidenced in our quantitative findings, with 96 per cent of Sowetans reporting that they feel close to people of the same race group, thus indicating the continued significance of race in South Africa.

The separation between the upper classes according to race is further demonstrated in the following quote, in which the respondent discusses the continued residential racial segregation in South Africa and demonstrates the more overt forms of racism that continue to pervade South African society. Curiously, his expression of the significance of race comes straight after an assertion that race no longer matters in South Africa. This kind of contradiction between official narratives of the 'New South Africa' and the lived experience from below reproduces itself throughout the interviews. In this case, it partly stems from an emphasis on the legal racial barriers that were indeed lifted when apartheid was demolished. However, quotes signify that racial segregation is still a characteristic of South African society and that white South Africans continue to hold various forms of racial privilege over black South Africans. For example, Tshehla began by asserting that race no longer matters because all South Africans are equal and allowed to live side by side. However, towards the end of the quote, he reflected on the unfortunate South African reality that as black people move into previous 'whites-only' suburbs, white people move out. This is evidence of the continued white racism towards black South Africans, despite the legal changes:

> Class is more important, because even white people are poor. In apartheid South Africa, you would never find a white person who was poor, but now we are all equal . . . it doesn't matter if you are white or what, even your neighbour can be white, which would have never been allowed in apartheid before . . . now a lot of [black] people have moved to town and there is really nothing white people can do. There is no more apartheid and black people are now showing what they are capable of . . . before you would find only one black person among many white people in the suburbs, but now things have changed, you now have more black people living in the suburbs than white people, because many white people have moved to other areas.

In a similar vein, Mbulelo began by asserting that race is no longer important in South Africa because we judge people's success irrespective of their race, but then moved on to show how this colour-blind approach is, in fact, racist in its ignorance of racial differences in accumulated wealth and privilege. He reported that the privileged position of young white South Africans, who have the accumulated wealth of a racist past supporting them, means that they do not need to work very hard to be successful in life. Furthermore, their black counterparts, whose families have been historically prevented from accumulating wealth and assets, have to struggle from nothing and work much harder to become successful:

> We look at class more than race as race doesn't matter anymore, you check. People and how big they have made it irrespective of whether the person is black or white; actually, we so know that white people don't have to do much . . . They don't do much, like for example, the mother is working and already successful and if there is a child, the child won't work as hard as we have to. Whatever we have, we have worked hard for, unlike white people – from the age of 18 years a [white] person already has a car and they get everything from their families.[32]

Mirroring the contradictory consciousness expressed in views of class mobility, we see how respondents hold together a just and unjust worldview of post-apartheid South Africa. While there is an official line about the 'New South Africa' – that race is no longer an issue and a better life for all is possible – respondents' experiences nevertheless constantly contradict this line and demonstrate that the power structures in place continue to prevent many South Africans – and especially black South Africans – from claiming a better life.

Conclusion

This chapter aimed to show how the concept of affordability links the cultural to the economic in constructing class difference and to argue that as a mediating concept it can go in either direction, with different political implications for imagining class mobility. Because of its connection to the economic, it holds the potential to recognise and challenge the unjust structures of class inequality in South Africa. However, in its connection to individual cultural expression, it can sometimes veer towards placing the responsibility for change on the individual in what is imagined as an otherwise-just system. These different potentials inhabiting the affordability concept are demonstrated through two different perspectives that emerge from the interviews, which represent two different worldviews operating in both discussions of class mobility and race versus class in contemporary South Africa.

In considering the relationship between these components of analysis, a deeper reflection on the class ladder metaphor is possible. If we take, on the one hand, the class ladder and imagine a sliding 'affordability' dial on the sides of the ladder that represent a continuum, with the economic component at the bottom of the ladder and the cultural component at the top, both sides of these components are present at any point, but to differing degrees and with different worldview implications. As the direction of perception moves towards the upper rungs of the class ladder, the affordability dial slides towards the cultural component, which becomes highlighted as the economic component dims. When the direction of perception is towards the upper classes, the affordability dial emphasises individual drive and cultural consumption, and can be mobilised by a depoliticised worldview that imagines a just society, as we saw in the 'upgrade' perspective and official discourses of nationhood. When the focus is on the lower classes, the affordability dial slides towards an emphasis on the economic and feeds into a worldview that emphasises the injustice of structural constraints in terms of employment and income for the lower classes, as in the 'no money, no life' perspective. Therefore, because affordability is the mediating factor, its implication for politics can go in either direction, and this is dependent on where respondents focus their attention.

Economic inequality and racial privilege persist in post-apartheid South Africa, and many Sowetans are located in a disadvantaged position in terms of both race and class. We see the push and pull between a view of South Africa from above and a view from below. On a broader level, this provides insights into the politics of Sowetans' perceptions of class and whether these work to support or subvert forms of inequality and injustice in South Africa. On the one hand, these respondents draw on a view from above that denies the need to change South African society and therefore subtly supports the current status quo. Alongside this worldview, these respondents also demonstrate a perspective on the lived experience of continued class and race inequality, thereby exposing the unjust nature of South African society, where many individuals are inhibited structurally from satisfying their most basic needs, despite their aspirations and values.

Notes

1. When quotes were checked against statements originally made in vernacular languages, five relevant recordings were found to be damaged and inaudible. However, in other instances the original translations, undertaken by fieldworkers, were good representations of the vernacular, and we have assumed this to be true of the eight quotes drawn from the five damaged tapes. The eight quotes do not affect the general analysis presented here, but they do add interesting detail.
2. Transcript of an interview with Wilheminah at her home in Braamfischerville, conducted by K. Khumalo in Sesotho and translated by the interviewer. *Note:* All interviews were conducted in November 2008. '*Dintho tse ngata ke pallwa ke ho di afforda tse dingke a kgona ho di afoda. hake sokole hakalo, mare tshokolo yona e teng.*'
3. Transcript of an interview with Emily at her home in Orlando East, conducted by T. Matshediso in Setswana and translated by the interviewer. '*No hobane nka se re ke rich kea afforda that, hona le dintho tse ke di batlang tse ke sa kgoneng ho di thola, mare nka se re ke hlopheile hobane ke robala ke jele.*'
4. Transcript of an interview with Respondent 1 at his home in Protea North. Interview conducted in English.
5. Transcript of an interview with Respondent 2 at his home in Diepkloof, conducted by S. Mazibuko in isiZulu and translated by the interviewer. '*Vele umuntu noma egqoka kufanele ubemuhle emphakathini, ebukeke.*'
6. Transcript of an interview with Anne at her home in Zola, conducted by K. Khumalo in isiZulu and translated by the interviewer.
7. Transcript of an interview with Raymond at his home in Dobsonville, conducted by K. Khumalo in Setswana and translated by the interviewer.
8. Transcript of an interview with Respondent 3 at her home in Pimville. 'Rich people stay in huge houses, the big lights, the bling and stuff . . . You can tell from *osa kena ka gate nje hore yah ba* they're rich they can afford whatever amount, *gate eturang, mabota*, you know huge houses double storeys *wabona* you can tell *ukuthi* they're rich.'
9. Transcript of an interview with Magarette at her home in Malapo, conducted in isiZulu. '*Azifani ngoba ezabantu aba amaclass aphakamile ziphakamile nazo nawe ubona ungaphandle ukuthi lendlu ayi, uma ungena ngapha nje phakathi kucwebecwebe.*'
10. '*Ya di different kaore batho ba* high class *ba kgona ho achieva dintho tse di ngata kaore bana le* everything *ka montlong. Ene dintlo tsa bona di kgolo, bana le* everything *ka montlong okile wabona.*'
11. Transcript of an interview with Phindile (1) at her home in Jabulani, conducted by T. Matshediso in Sesotho and translated by the interviewer. '*Le tsona di aparo tse ke di aparang ke gore fela ke seke kea tsamaya ke sa apara, ee fela fela ke tswe le nna ke le . . . keapere ke seke kea tsamaya ketsotse.*'
12. Transcript of an interview with Phindile (2) at her home in Braamfischerville, conducted by S. Mazibuko in Sepedi and translated by the interviewer.
13. Transcript of an interview with Sam at his home in Moletsane Street, Moletsane, conducted by S. Mazibuko in Sesotho and translated by the interviewer. '*Nna ke mo*

classeng e down level, ee keore watseba kehore ke mo down level ke the way ke phelang kateng wautliwisisa, yah . . . ke phela . . . ee keautlwisisa, keore kea kokoretsa kea kgona ke inkele chelete hore keje for three days *ebe ke fetsa* two days *keye hape ke thole mosebetsi ke ntse ke saje? ebe le hona kethola bohobe.*'

14. Transcript of an interview with Respondent 4 at her home in Diepkloof Extension, conducted by S. Mazibuko in isiZulu and translated by the interviewer. '*Noma ubani okwazi ukuya emsebenzini futhi azi izidingo zakhe noma ke engasakwazi ukwezeneza zonke . . . uyakwazi ukufeza ama-basic needs; njengokudla nezimpahla zokugqoka.*'
15. Transcript of an interview with Mantu at his home in Chiawelo. 'From my point of view *umuntu ongafuni niks . . . kodwa ufuna i-life engcono kodwa ngezinye izinto ngoba u-right/u-sharp*. For me *loyomuntu u-average ngoba ufuna i-life engcono.*'
16. Transcript of an interview with Sibongile at her home in Meadowlands, conducted by K. Khumalo in isiZulu and translated by the interviewer. '*Ngiziiphilela kahle nje yah,* it's because *ngiyakhona ukuzi maintaina ngiyakhona ukuzenzela yonke.*'
17. The theme of youth/generation as an important dimension of stratification within Soweto has been flagged in Chapters 1, 3 and 6. It emerges again here as an important factor when considering different worldviews on class mobility, because the 'upgrade' view was particularly popular among the younger respondents. This is perhaps because they see themselves as children of the 'New South Africa', with a life in front of them filled with the imagined new opportunities brought by democracy.
18. Transcript of an interview with Simelo at his home in Orlando West, conducted by T. Matshediso and translated by the interviewer. '*Ee, hoya fela kaore motho oe kemedisitse hakakang bophelong ba hae hore a ka changa class or tlabe antse ale yalo fela.*'
19. 'No I think for me it's a matter of if *wena* in your life when you look at your life as a whole do you think *gore wena,* have achieved what you wanted to achieve in your life or are you in the process of achieving what you wanted to achieve and so personally for me if *ona le di* opportunities *tsa gore etsa ntho tse yalo* and you can make them come true that's why I think I can define myself as middle class cause I can't say *gore* I struggle quite a lot to get what I want. Okay there are some challenges someway somehow but you get ways *gore* to manoeuvre around those challenges for *nna*. So personally for me if *kenna le ntho e ke batlang go etsa* then I try my best *go etsa ntho eo* then I get the opportunity which I have right now then *kea etsa* . . . That's what I think *go re* if you can achieve this then yah.'
20. Transcript of an interview with Mbulelo at his home in Dobsonville, conducted by K. Khumalo in isiZulu and translated by the interviewer. 'Only you know *ukuthi* you're lower class middle class whatever, cause *uma uzophuma ugqoke ube-neat, uyazincanywa uyang'thola? So uma uphuma umuntu angak'boni* as a lower class *uzok'bona ungumuntu o-high class cause uzokubheka from isituation yakhe* which is different from mine *uzokubona u-neat, ugqoke ne-*designer jeans, Carvelas and whatever so *uzothi yah unemali.*'
21. Transcript of an interview with Siyabonga (1) at his home in Jabulani, conducted by K. Khumalo in isiZulu and translated by the interviewer.

22. 'Yah it's possible to change classes, *ngathi* it's possible cause in life *vele kumele u-upgrade neh ngeke uhlale emkhukhwini* for the rest of your life, you have dreams *neh usho'ukuthi* okay *ng'funa uk'phuma emkhukhwini ngihlale kwi*-big house but in order for you to do that you have to work hard *unyangthola? u thole ispani nani nani* then *uzo-upgrada uzo phuma kwi* lower class *o move kwi* middle class then if you succeed strongly then *uzokuba kwi*-high class depending on your determination *ukuthi u-determined kanganani ukuphuma elower* class, then you can change, depending on determination, the job you work in and the salary you earn.'
23. '*Ke* last class, which is third class, *ntho tse ke di batlang mo lifeng ha ke kgone ho di reacha wabona, watseba haona le chelete ho na le dintho tse oka direachang o kgona hoikenya classeng e oe batlang, ngaaffecta* . . . psychologically and mentally wise . . . cause *watseba lewena* life it's all about money.'
24. Transcript of an interview with Rose at her home in Dobsonville, conducted by K. Khumalo and translated by the interviewer. '*Ya ngoba kwesinye isikhathi uphupha ngokwenza okuthize kodwa ubuye ubone ukthi yiphupho ngoba ungeke ukwazi ukulifeza. Uwukwazi ngoba awunamali yokwenza izinto* . . . *Anginamandla okushintsha amaphupho ami abeyi*-reality and you know *amandla uwathola emalini. Imali ye-pension ayanele njengoba isebenza ku-electicity ne-rent bese esele ithenga ukudla.*'
25. Transcript of an interview with Ndofaya at his home; transcript of an interview with Sakile at his home. 'Middle class I think *umuntu o afforda i*-life just put it that way *ya, umuntu uma afuna* something *kuzokhoneka ukuyithola* reasonably.'
26. 'I could say middle class, I'm not poor in a way cause *kea bereka* most of the things *kea kgona godi etsa* you know I can take care of myself and umm what I can say, when you are poor you could go to bed *osaja?* That's poor for me. . . . I think *gore kebe mo keleng* it's because of my experience, uhh I know what poor is to put it that way, like, oh okay just to give you a hint about my life previously. Uhh my mom, my real mom and my dad *baile badivorca* so we had to go stay with my mom, she was like a single parent, she worked but *ona sasebetse mosebetsi* o serious, serious, but she worked, she took care of us. So at times she just made sure *gore* we ate and we're happy and we eat . . . You know such things sometimes *oya skolong* and there's a trip you want to go but you couldn't . . . So ey it wasn't easy cause she wanted to take care of all of us *aetse sure gore raja* and all of that and at times there would be situations *tsaeleng hore hadiyo dijo* at all and therefore you had to go and pick in the bins to get food.'
27. 'Concerning *nako tsa kgale nne nkacho hore ke* race since *vele* democracy *ya kgale ne* I can say *e ne ele* divided into two races; *batho ba batsho le makgoa. hona hore ha o ne o le motho o motsho class ya hao, ona le eng, ha o na eng ene e se ntho e ba ka focusang ho yona, ntho eneng ele* the main focus *ka nako eo ene ele race hore o motho o motsho hao na dijo or o motho o motsho o* rich, race was the number one thing *eleng hore nakong eo banale* straight to the point *ka yona or nkacho hore bana e rata ka nako eo.*'
28. '*i-Class, idlala indima yayo.Kodwa angeke ngikhulume kakhulu nge-race* I was young during apartheid so *nganingekho kodwa i-classsekuyinto e-permanent ngba abantu bayathuthuka, abantu abamnyama nabo ama*-directors of companies . . . *i-class isibalulekile.*'

29. Transcript of an interview with Jabu at her 'business' in Zondi, conducted by K. Khumalo in isiZulu and translated by the interviewer.
30. Transcript of an interview with Tshehla at his home in Mofolo, conducted by T. Matshediso in Sesotho and translated by K. Khumalo.
31. Transcript of an interview with Respondent 5 at his home in Meadowlands, conducted by S. Mazibuko in Sesotho and translated by the interviewer. *'And then di upper-class ke batho baeleng gore ke badi BEE yah ke bona babaleng di upper classes.'*
32. '*Sibheka iclass* more than race *mfethu* race doesn't matter anymore *uyang'thola? i-race ayinandaba* they might be white, black whatever *uyang'thola?, okay ama whites sazi vele wona* they don't do much *uyang'thola,* like for example *umama wakhona usucessful uyaspana unengcosi esakhula lengcosi ngeke isebenze* compared to us *abo-darkie* the way *sisebenza ngakhona into esinayo siyazisebsenzela bona uma-oulady uzomtshela into esoso* from the age of 18 *uyadriva zonke izinto anazo uzithole efemilini,* unlike *thina*.'

8

The language of class

Confusion, complexity and difficult words

Mosa Phadi and Owen Manda

This chapter explores a problem alluded to in the preceding two chapters, that is, how are Sowetans' understandings of class shaped by the terms available to them in their indigenous languages? Raymond Williams (1976), whose views are discussed at some length below, regards the word 'class' as a 'difficult word'. As he shows, its changing meaning was greatly complicated by the intrusion of 'basic relationships' (for example, workers and employers) into a traditional, descriptive model (at its simplest, the distinction among lower, middle and upper classes). Moreover, specialised definitions have been infused by general connotations and vice versa. In Western Europe in the early nineteenth century, when people used the word 'class' in ordinary language, they were both drawing on and contributing to the range of meanings acquired by the word in the course of its varied career in English. Inevitably, both the concept and the word have changed over time. The English language, never singular even in its birthplace, acquired ever-newer avatars as it was borne across the world by imperialism and globalisation, and was – and continues to be – further enriched by the struggles against these forces. Meanwhile, the socio-historical trends that inspired the concept were altered and realigned, not only in its European birthplace, but globally. Thus, ongoing debates about the meaning of 'class' – whether inside or outside the academy – are generally conducted in languages that include the word itself or a similar and easily translatable term.

In South Africa, this complexity is magnified by the interaction of indigenous terminology, originally constructed in particular rural contexts, with an already 'difficult word'. Two empirical issues should be considered. Firstly, there is no general term in indigenous languages that can be equated with 'class' as used in a primarily economic sense (whether basic or descriptive). The nearest counterparts convey implications of standing, status or level, thus having associations with reputation, importance and education. Secondly, and associated with this, while there are no direct equivalents to specific class terms, several words are associated with poverty and a number related to wealth. 'Middle class' poses a particular problem, because the closest translation of related indigenous-language terms means 'in the middle', creating scope for considerable subjectivity and confusion. Further difficulty is posed by the term 'working class', which was used rarely by our respondents in the interviews, as people tended to associate this with being a worker, which limits the potential for developing a class vocabulary that has emancipatory implications. This discussion has a wider significance, because it reveals the inadequacy of imposing an English-language template (with all its 'difficulty') on an African setting, where people are likely to be framing their worldview according to different standards and where a common word – 'middle class', for instance – may have different meanings.

In this chapter, we focus on just two African languages, namely Sesotho and isiZulu. These are the most widely spoken languages in Soweto (see Appendix 2). Moreover, the mother tongue of most other Sowetans is sufficiently similar to one of these two languages to be mutually intelligible. Further, these are the two languages that the authors know best, with Mosa Phadi and Owen Manda being native speakers of, respectively, Sesotho and isiZulu. We have been able to consider these languages together because they both belong to the two dominant, closely related, southern ethnic groups and have developed in similar geographical, economic and political environments. Commonalities have increased in the multilingual setting of the Witwatersrand's black urban areas, where there is considerable mixing of languages, something both authors experienced growing up in townships located close to Soweto.

In the following sections we provides a brief overview of the ideas of some scholars who have influenced our understanding of the relationship between language and class, specifically Williams, and give a brief summary of the research background that provided the context for exploring this relationship. We then provide a brief sketch of the linguistic context that emerged in interviews, and expand on the respondents' words for conveying the English meanings of 'class', 'poor', 'the rich' and 'middle class' in isiZulu and Sesotho. We also report on our field experiences and outline words that were used by respondents to describe 'poor', 'middle class' and 'the rich'. In a brief conclusion we assert that a three-class model is still a dominant class scheme, even though Sowetans used indigenous terms to locate themselves within it.

Some influential views on language and class

Williams, in his seminal work *Keywords* (1976), does not reify the meaning of 'class' as static, but locates it within subjective, lived experience. He explains that when we describe our differences with others in terms of the common phrase 'we just don't speak the same language', we are usually saying:

> . . . that we have different immediate values or that we are aware, often intangibly, of different formations and distributions of energy and interest . . . No single group is 'wrong' by any linguistic criterion, though a temporarily dominant group may try to enforce its own uses as 'correct' (Williams 1976: 10–11).

Since knowledge of lived experiences is 'mingled', 'confused' and 'incomplete', languages develop, he argues, through 'critical encounters, which may be very conscious or may be felt only as a certain strangeness and unease'. This process occurs, he adds:

> . . . when, in certain words, tones and rhythms, meanings are offered, felt for, tested, confirmed, asserted, qualified, changed. In some situations . . . this is a slow process . . . it needs the passage of centuries to show itself actively . . . [and at times it] can be rapid (Williams 1976: 60).

He argues that material conditions, lived experiences, everyday activities and different time and space change the meaning of words. Class as a keyword is 'an obviously difficult word, both in its range of meaning, and in its complexity in that particular meaning where it describes a social division' (Williams 1976: 60).

Williams traces the evolution of the word from a general term denoting a grouping of any kind to a more specific socio-political term associated with relatively fixed names for particular classes (lower class, middle class, upper class, working class and so on). This development occurred essentially in the period between 1770 and 1840, the period of the Industrial Revolution, which decisively reorganised society (Williams 1976: 61). After this transitional period, 'class' became the preferred term to describe social groupings – it was the product of an increasing consciousness that social position is made rather than merely inherited. All the older words used to describe social position, with their essential metaphors of standing, stepping and arranging in rows, belonged to a society in which position was determined by birth. Individual mobility could be seen as movement from one *estate*, *degree*, *order* or *rank* to another. What changed this consciousness was not only increased individual mobility, which could be contained largely within the older terms, but the new sense of a *society* or a particular *social system* that actually created social divisions, including new kinds of divisions (Williams 1976: 61–2).

During this period, 'class' became the dominant term for describing specific social groupings, and it acquired a new vocabulary of its own, with a succession of prefixes such as 'lower', 'lowest', 'middle', 'middling', 'upper', 'higher', 'privileged' and so on. The term 'middle class' was especially popular as a 'self-conscious and self-used' term that, by the 1830s, had turned into a 'swell of self-congratulatory description'. The curious feature in this use, which assumed an implicit hierarchy with classes above and below itself, was the marginalisation of the classes above as a 'residual and respected but essentially displaced aristocracy' (Williams 1976: 62–3).

The next major turning point occurred with the emergence of the use of class to describe structured economic relationships rather than concrete social groups. The process began with the ideologically charged distinction between the 'useful' or 'productive' and, eventually, the 'working' classes, on the one hand, and the 'idle' or 'privileged' classes, on the other hand. The coexistence of divergent yet overlapping usages – the traditional descriptive-social classifications such as 'lower', 'middle' and 'upper', and the newer structural-economic classifications, such as 'working' or 'propertied' – produced a proliferation of terms and made 'class' a permanently polysemic word:

> It is obvious that a terminology of basic economic relationships (as between employers and employed, or propertied and propertyless) will be found too crude and general for the quite different purpose of precise descriptive grouping. Hence the persistent but confused arguments between those who, using class in the sense of basic relationship, propose two or three basic classes, and those who, trying to use it for descriptive grouping, find they have to break these divisions down into smaller and smaller categories. The history of the word carries this essential ambiguity (Williams 1976: 66).

The important point highlighted by Williams's classic semantic-social history is that the usual strategy of segregating the academic-conceptual meanings of a word from its popular use-based meanings is not viable in the case of the word 'class'. This is because social experience – and the self-conscious articulation of this experience – forms an important and indispensable aspect of the theoretical concept of class. The interplay between the objective definition emphasising observable attributes and the subjective definition stressing self-consciousness and collective action has been particularly important in the Marxist tradition, and through it, for the social sciences as a whole. As Williams (1976: 68) puts it:

> This is the distinction between category and formation, but since class is used for both, there has been plenty of ground for confusion. The problem is still critical in that it underlies repeated arguments about the relation of an assumed class-consciousness to an objectively measured class, and about the vagaries of self-description and self-assignation to a class scale.

Thus, academic social science cannot confine itself to its own technical-theoretical definitions of class because the concept itself demands the inclusion of popular conceptions. It is for this reason that we are interested in both (1) the words that ordinary people use to 'translate' or make sense of the academic concept; and (2) the words that they use to describe their own social location, or what from an academic perspective would be called their class position.

Like Williams, Gareth Stedman Jones (1983: 7) argues there is no fixed definition of class and that the term is shaped by context and time; that, therefore, it should be 'embedded in language and should be analysed in its linguistic context'. Stedman Jones (1983: 1–2) further adds that even the notion of 'working class' has come under scrutiny internationally and nationally, hence there is a possibility to 'investigate how [the] historical picture changes', because in most countries the word 'class' has 'acted as a congested point of intersection between many competing, overlapping or simply differing forms of discourse' (Stedman Jones 1983: 6). The emphasis Stedman Jones places on the overlap and subjectivity of definitions of class is illustrated in our study, but we go a step further to show that terms used in Sesotho and isiZulu are based on the intersection between people's sense of their own self-worth or reputation and material stratification.

Sidney Tarrow (2011: 113–14) argues that even the term 'working class' is not 'natural'. The word only became popular through scholarly publications long after the Industrial Revolution. He expands Stedman Jones' notion of subjectivity by arguing that even the word 'occupation' has changed and been reconstructed through people's use of it in daily speech. Tarrow (2011: 6–7) elaborates the mechanisms:

> *First,* words that emerge as symbols of contention are seldom made out of whole cloth: like 'occupation', they have their sources in ordinary speech, or in popular folktales or music, commercial media or huckstering, or previous experiences of war or conflict . . .

> *Second,* over time, the meanings of words change, merge, divide and diversify – nowhere more than in the history of contentious language. Historian Daniel Rogers puts this well when he writes that 'though words constrain their users, hobble political desires, nudge them down socially worn channels, they are in other circumstances radically unstable' (1987: 10). Contentious words are constructed and re-constructed to meet different strategic contingencies. 'Political words take their meaning,' Rogers argues, 'from the tasks to which their users bend them' (1987: 10) . . .
>
> *Third,* some of this construction and re-construction is the work of deliberate symbol-making and symbol-manipulation. But social construction also evolves from the interaction between opposing actors in contingent action situations and from the stock of symbols available to elites and ordinary people . . .
>
> *Fourth,* although we usually think of words only as the expression of something, words themselves can mobilize, unite, divide, and even conquer. 'Words are tools, often weapons', writes Rogers: 'the vocabulary of politics is contested terrain and always has been' (1987: 11) . . .
>
> *Finally,* some words survive and diffuse as symbols of contention while others disappear or are absorbed into ordinary language . . .

In addition to the recognition of the centrality of subjectivity to the meaning of 'class', Frantz Fanon (1965: 1) brings in the crucial role played by power when he posits that power resembles language, especially in colonial and post-colonial countries. Hence the division between 'inferior' blacks and 'superior' whites reproduces an 'assuming of culture . . . bearing the weight of civilization' (Fanon 1965: 2). Fanon (1965: 2–3) therefore recognises the dual place of language as operating in terms of broader relations of power and also as a tool that expresses the world in which people live and their everyday experiences. As a result of lived experiences, language changes and so does the way in which people communicate.

The role of power in language is further examined in the South African context by Neville Alexander (2009), who asserts that the politics of language remain tumultuous, particularly the contestation between English and Afrikaans. On the other hand, Charlyn Dyers (2009: 266) notes that the shifts taking place within language indicate a wider pattern of 'economic dispersion'. This can be seen in South Africa in urban African languages, like *tsotsitaal*, which illustrates a 'creative adaption of new contexts' (Dyers 2009: 263). In Gauteng townships, particularly, there are multilingual contacts, and Stephanie Rudwick (2005: 306) contends that these townships are a 'fertile ground for the emergence of lingua francas'. Hence, mixtures of languages – especially of African languages with English – are dominant features. This mixture of language was demonstrated strongly in our study as respondents frequently used the English word 'affordability', even though our conversations were generally conducted in Sesotho and isiZulu. The significance of the relationship between language and experience is summarised by Harry Garuba (2009: 8) in his claim that 'language does not only order experience, it also creates experience, and in the process sets out what can be experienced and how it can be experienced'. Our study will demonstrate that the word 'class' is subjective and definitions associated with it are based on people's pride and reputations, alongside material stratification. The languages of class used by respondents are thus shaped by both subjective understandings of class and material reality. The following section outlines the research process through which we came to understand the significance of language in relation to the meaning of 'class' in Soweto.

Research background

As is well known, real-life research rarely follows the sequence of events prescribed in textbooks on methodology. This project began with the objective of studying class structure and class identity in Soweto. This was reflected in our exploratory interviews – conducted in a wide range of indigenous languages, as well as English – and in the main survey. The questionnaire was formulated in English, but a professional isiZulu translation was made available to fieldworkers and there were extensive discussions about how best to translate certain terms into different languages so that consistency could be maintained. However, in one critical case, fieldworkers were required to ask the question as stated in the instrument. This was: 'Would you call yourself . . . [followed by a list of eight class identities drawn from the exploratory interviews]?' There were two reasons for this. Firstly, the aim was to test identification with these specified classes, and it was not clear that the nearest indigenous language equivalents were really about 'class' as the term is broadly understood in English. Secondly, from our exploratory research and general knowledge, we were aware that nearly all Sowetans had a basic knowledge of English and would have some sense of what the terms meant. On this second point, the researchers' assessment was vindicated, because the question allowed respondents three choices 'yes', 'no' and 'do not understand the question', and only 7 per cent of the sample opted for the third choice. Results and analysis related to this question were presented in Chapter 6.

Appendix 1 summarises the methodology associated with the main core of our research. As reflected there, the survey threw up new questions that we decided to pursue by means of semi-structured interviews. An exploration of indigenous terms associated with class was still not one of the issues considered. While questions were constructed in a way that allowed people to express and explain what they meant by terms such as 'middle class', at this stage both researchers and fieldworkers did not appreciate the significance of the relationship between language and meaning for class terms. With hindsight, we can speculate that this was a consequence of nearly all the fieldworkers, as well the researchers, having been trained in sociology, and thus they probably shared a common academic understanding of class vocabulary. In addition, as Williams and Jones indicate above, an inherent ambiguity around 'class' as a concept is born out of its dual use as an analytical and descriptive term. Retrospectively, we were clearly naive, but now that we recognise this naivety, we highlight this key issue facing research into class across languages. When looking through the transcripts of the interviews, we were intrigued by the way our fieldworkers – all of whom were mother-tongue speakers of an indigenous language and had at least an honours degree – struggled to find indigenous counterparts for English-language class concepts. This was true across the range of languages used in the interviews, which included Setswana, Sepedi, isiXhosa, isiNdebele, siSwati, Xitsonga and Tshivenda, as well as Sesotho and isiZulu. It was then that we became aware of the problem, although also the potential to better comprehend what Sowetans meant when they identified themselves in class terms. Alongside this research, we were also conducting interviews that fed into our documentary film, *Phakathi* (Phadi 2010b). *Phakathi*, an isiZulu word meaning roughly 'in the middle', was used by many respondents in place of 'middle class', but its meaning is broader and can include people who are very poor (although not the poorest in their communities). This helped us to grasp why such a large number of Sowetans described themselves as 'middle class' and also, perhaps, why respondents saw no contradiction between identifying themselves simultaneously as poor and middle class or as working class and middle class. Transcripts and recordings from the two sets of interviews constitute the main data analysed in this chapter, supplemented by reflections on our own knowledge of Sesotho and isiZulu and by discussions with key informants, colleagues and students familiar with indigenous languages.

Dictionary definitions

As a starting point, we consulted a number of dictionaries for their translations of indigenous terms that came closest to our English target words. We provide a summary of these in Table 8.1. While there is a scholarly, if rather dated, isiZulu dictionary, there is nothing of similar quality for Sesotho, and this unevenness is inevitably reflected in the table.

Table 8.1 IsiZulu and Sesotho approximations for words referring to 'class' and various 'classes'.

English target word	African language		Meanings Approximations	Usage
Class	Sesotho	*Maemo*	Status; standing; standard; situation; position; condition	'Emergency situation'; 'learning context'; 'status bar'; 'assessment standards'
		Seemo	Stature	
	IsiZulu	*Izimo*	Condition; state; status; character; nature; personality	
		Izinga/ amazinga	Ridge grade; level; quality; standard	
		Isigaba	Level; standard	
Poor/ the poor	IsiZulu	*Inhlobo ephansi*[1]	Low species; kind; type; nationality; race; tribe	
		Mpofu[2]	Poor	
		Isopofu	Poor person	
		Abahluphekile	The poor; the sufferers	
	Sesotho	*Futsanehileng*	Poor	
		Sokola	Poor; suffering	
		Hlopehileng	Poor; suffering	
		Tlase	Bottom	
The rich	IsiZulu	*Isicebi*	Rich person	
		Inkensela	Magnate; tycoon	
	Sesotho	*Morui*	Rich person	
		Bahumi	Wealthy person	
Middle class	IsiZulu	*Phakathi*	In the midst; in the middle; inside	'Go inside'; 'in the middle of the house'; 'among us'; 'thou of the inner circle!'; 'in the midst of the people'
			Between	'Between the village and the river'; 'at midnight'
			Centre	'The centre of a circle'
			Assembly of the men of a district; commoners or the common people	'The chief ordered all the common people to come to the royal palace'
			Apex of an arch; the place where the two sides of an arch meet	
	Sesotho	*Mahareng*	Middle	'Middle course'; 'middle child'
			Average	
			Between	
Working class	IsiZulu	*Abasebenzi*	Workers	
	Sesotho	*Basebetsi/ basebeletsi*	Workers	

Sources: Bryant (1905); Colenso (1905); Sharpe (1952); Doke et al. (1990); Dent and Nyembenzi (1995); http://bukantswe.sesotho.org online dictionary; http://isizulu.net/ online dictionary (accessed 3 March 2011).

While these dictionary definitions are helpful, they are insufficient for understanding how the various terms are actually used in Soweto as part of a discourse on class. As with Williams's discussion of the history of the word class, the meanings of many terms in South Africa's indigenous languages are undergoing subtle changes and new words – often Africanised versions of English ones – are being invented. Inevitably, our language follows the reality it is designed to record. Trevor Ngwane (2010) captures this well:

> It seems to me that [in contexts like Soweto] the language is lagging behind class formation and differentiation processes. Hence there is a need to 'invent' terms to describe class categories that did not exist before, and the borrowing of concepts from a pre-capitalist era and their use in the context of a more developed class structure. Here the theory of uneven and combined development is relevant because the combination of the old and the new creates unique forms, words and meanings which 'traditional' class theory and (the English) language cannot grasp or convey. Reference to dictionaries is half useful and half misleading because these are written by scholars who are often divorced from daily social use of words . . .

The evolution of class language through blending the old with the new can be witnessed in the popularity of the key concept of 'affordability' discussed in Chapters 6 and 7. The process that Ngwane outlines will be discussed further as we attempt to advance an understanding of the meaning of mother-tongue terms being used as approximations for English target words associated with class vocabulary. While the meanings given to different class positions reflect the findings of the previous two chapters, in this chapter we attempt to ground these meanings within language, and show how they come out of specific mother-tongue terms across the different language groups interviewed. Furthermore, we shall show terms people used to convey the words 'class', 'poor', 'the rich' and 'middle' in Sesotho and isiZulu, as well as how the term 'working class' has been translated in communist publications and the limitations of those translations.

Experiences in the field

In the following account, whenever we quote our respondents, the particular language spoken, the gender of the speaker and their age are given in italics before the quote. Where quoted discussion was not in English, the original mother-tongue transcript is provided in a footnote. Please note that 'isiZulu' and 'Sesotho' here refer to the language being used, not necessarily to the ethnic identity of the speaker. The following discussion is organised around the class labels used in the questionnaire (see Chapter 6), hence the subheadings use the English terms.

Misunderstandings and ambivalence

One of the biggest problems encountered by fieldworkers when asking the question 'what class are you?' was that respondents often thought about class in a totally different way to the one anticipated or hoped for.[3] The following are some examples:

> *IsiZulu, man, 32*: Which class? The school one?[4]

> *IsiZulu, woman, 45*: I am not familiar with classes, but I am a humble somebody, I respect people . . . I don't classify people . . . I don't classify myself.[5]

> *Sesotho, man, 34*: I don't understand 'class' . . . you mean 'status'?[6]

As fieldworkers realised that some respondents were unsure of what the word 'class' meant, they created words that seemed to be closer to describing class. Words such as *maemo*,[7] *izinga*[8] or *seemo*[9] were used. These words relate to status, stature, position or a person's standing in society. Sowetans in our study used words related to their lived experiences based on material differences and their reputations. When you ask someone about *maemo a hao*, you are referring to a circumstance, status, standing or position in which they find themselves at that time, which has similar meaning to *izimo*.[10] While *izinga* refers to 'ridge', 'levels' or 'grade' and *seemo* means 'stature', both terms explore the grading of the circumstances in which people find themselves. This position can be interpreted in two ways: materially and spiritually. Fieldworkers tried to clarify the questions as follows:

> *Fieldworker*: No, not the school one when talking about the class thing, but the one I mentioned earlier; I think in isiZulu they refer to it as *izimo*.[11]

> *Fieldworker*: There are categories among people . . . when you look at yourself, where do you place your status?[12]

Using isiZulu and/or Sesotho words, fieldworkers gave respondents the opportunity to position themselves. As mentioned before, a three-class model was popular among

Sowetans (see Chapter 6). Respondents compared themselves to other Sowetans. They used stratification to locate themselves, so they were aware of class. When identifying themselves, most respondents either called themselves poor or middle class. They were aware of the rich, but none we interviewed claimed that identity. Sesotho and isiZulu words used to describe the poor were *sokola* and *futsanehileng*. On the other hand, terms for the rich were *topshayela* and *bahumi*. For the rich and poor, regardless of which language one used, these classes were associated with having or not having material possessions. When we went back to the original, untranslated interviews conducted by fieldworkers to investigate the term 'middle', the most frequently used term by isiZulu-speaking respondents was *phakathi*, while for Sesotho speakers the term was *mahareng*. In the next section we assess the meanings of these terms that Sowetans used to describe poor, middle-class and upper-class identities, and end with the problem of the working class.

The poor[13]

As demonstrated in Chapters 6 and 7, the striking finding is that some respondents had a material analysis of their class identity, where money and 'affordability' were the markers of their class position. This was evident particularly when people described their poverty using words such as *sokola, hlopehileng* and *futsanehileng*. *Sokola* is a Sesotho word meaning 'poor', 'struggling' and 'suffering'. *Futsanehileng* is also a Sesotho word referring to 'the poor', 'the destitute' and 'those who have nothing', and *hlopehileng* means 'poor' or 'suffering'. In isiZulu, words such as *abahluphekayo* and *hlupheka* were used. These words have similar meanings, the former connotes 'the poor' or 'those who are suffering' while the latter refers to self, for example, 'I am poor'. These are some examples:

> *Sesotho, male, 33*: *Ke a sokola*;[14] there is a lot of things I want, but cannot afford them.[15]
>
> *Sesotho, female, 38*: *Ba hlopehileng*[16] are those people who live in shacks and have nothing; they can't even feed themselves.[17]
>
> *IsiZulu, female, 55*: *Ngiyahlupheka*. I want a job.[18]
>
> *IsiZulu, man, 45*: I'm down, I know; I work for R410. Some people do not even wake up for that amount . . . I'm down because I was unemployed for a long time. When I did get a job it did not pay.[19]

> *IsiZulu, woman, 28*: I'm low class because I feel low class . . . other families have beautiful houses, earn decent salaries and have a decent job – I do not have.[20]

People who were seen or self-identified themselves as *ba*[21] *hlopehileng or ba sokolang* were indeed living in desperate situations with high unemployment, a lack of education, and a lack of durables and services (see Chapter 6). Those people who regarded themselves as 'down' or *tlase* (meaning 'down' or 'bottom' in Sesotho) or *phansi* (in isiZulu) were the very poor who did survivalist jobs in order to get through a week (see Chapter 5 on the discussion about the unemployed and the underemployed). The self-identified poor were basically those who had nothing and were suffering – in Sesotho, *bafutsana.*

The upper class[22]

Sowetans described the rich as having everything (see Chapter 6), as in the following quote:

> *Sesotho, woman*: They've got cars; they've got everything they want . . . they can afford.[23]

The word used in referring to this class was *bahumi.* This is a Sesotho word meaning 'those with ample wealth'. In isiZulu, a rich person is *isicebi* and a magnate or tycoon is referred to as *inkensela.* Some respondents described the rich as *topshayela* – as being arrogant and being unwilling to associate with them. Here, what is interesting about the respondents' understanding of class is that they used slang. In the township, slang is called *tsotsitaal* (literally the language of gangsters), which is a mixture of various languages, including English, Afrikaans, Sesotho and isiZulu, among others. *Topshayela* is a mixture of English and isiZulu and in *tsotsitaal* means 'top driving'. This is a literal translation, however *topshayela* can be referred to as a 'high flyer'.

> *IsiZulu, woman, 53*: I am paid little money . . . but I must go and work anyway. Someone who is a *topshayela* would not. By now I would long have left, saying 'what can I do with this money?'[24]

Similar to the mixed-language term *topshayela*, Sowetans frequently attributed the term 'affordability', which was used to encapsulate the ability to consume and maintain a lifestyle. In most of the interviews that were conducted in Sesotho or isiZulu, the word was referred to in English, partly, one assumes, because there is no direct translation of 'affordability' in either language. The word 'afford' in Sesotho is almost equivalent to *kgona*. The direct translation of *kgona* is self-sufficiency, which in popular use becomes an indicator of being able to purchase material items. *Kgona* cannot stand alone – a subject before or after it is required to make sense of it. Therefore a person can refer to themselves as *ke a kgona*,[25] and to others as *ba a kgona*.[26] When people use these phrases, they can convey either a sense of self-pride and self-boosting that can be about claiming status or they can imply snobbery – in both cases they are distancing themselves from people who are more or less able to afford than they are. In isiZulu, the word 'afford' in the dictionary is translated as *namandla oku*, meaning 'to be able to bear the cost of'. Other words that have a similar meaning to *kgona*, such as *ukukhona* in isiZulu, could be used, however, neither of these words was used in our interviews. Instead, the English word 'afford', written as *afoda*[27] in isiZulu and as *afodi* in Sesotho, is incorporated into their mother languages. The mixing of languages can mean that some words in African languages cannot articulate the message without having other moral implications, therefore it is easier to use *tsotsitaal*. The following is an illustration of the use of 'afford':

> *IsiZulu, woman, 42*: When I was working at the convention centre, I could afford. There were times when we used to work overtime and it was during those times that we had money . . . Since the money was there . . . I was able to buy myself whatever I wanted.[28]

The middle class[29]

In his study, Mayer (1977: 67) found that Africans tended to use the term 'middle class', not in the Western sense to refer to professional people and business people; but to refer to 'medium people' or people in the middle – '*abantu abaphakathi*'. These people were 'neither well-off nor very poor or dissolute' (Mayer 1977: 67). Similar to Mayer, in our study isiZulu-speaking respondents who identified with the middle class used the word *phakathi*, while Sesotho speakers used the word *mahareng*. *Phakathi* and *mahareng* both literally mean 'in the middle'. Furthermore, our study also revealed that the concept of middle class was far more complicated than just being *mahareng*. As indicated in Chapter 6, a wide range of people identified with this class. *Phakathi* was understood in terms of education, reputation and importance linked to material stratification. At times, *mahereng/phakathi* was translated by our repondents to mean middle class. The fieldworker would use the word 'middle class' in English and the respondent would answer, for example, 'yes, *ke mahareng*' which indicates that some respondents viewed 'middle class' as a direct translation of *mahareng/phakathi*.

IsiZulu, man, 24: I'm average . . . *phakathi nendawo* . . . there are things I have that others don't have. I studied until matric. I know of others who only studied until standard eight and they wished to continue, but could not. Unlike them, I have a matric . . . I live in a four-room house. I think *abahluphekayo*[30] are those who live in squatter camps (*emikhukwini*[31]).[32]

Speaking mostly in English, woman, 36: I'm in between, *ke mo mahareng* – I'm not rich and I'm not poor. I will not say I'm poor, because I go to bed having eaten something, you see; some people go to bed hungry. If you have eaten, say 'thank you' . . . I can wash . . . I want a job, to have a decent income.

Some respondents who self-identified as 'middle' used the word 'affordability' to compare their past and present, and to locate themselves between the two extremes of those who had nothing and those who had everything. Having a full-time job and earning enough to be able to 'afford' things was crucial in shaping class identity. Being *phakathi* for those who were employed full-time meant they could manage on their wage. More importantly, the 'middle' identity amplified the understanding of class that is linked to reputation, importance and respectability. Pride – and with it 'respectability' – became critical in shaping people's understanding of their class identity. Moral judgements were being made, with people who regarded themselves as being able to 'afford' (something) having a measure of self-righteousness. This moral understanding of class was found among self-identified 'in the middle' respondents who had either part-time work or were unemployed. The following respondents demonstrated how behaviour, mannerisms and independence gave them a sense of class identity:

Sesotho, woman, 46: *Ke mahareng* . . . Others are looking for work and cannot find it; others are educated and not finding work . . . so I am better off; at least as I can go to bed fed; others cannot feed themselves.[33]

Sesotho, woman, 40: I'm independent. I take care of my children and myself. I wash myself.[34]

IsiZulu, woman, 38: The way I see myself, I am a person, I am okay,[35] [switching to English] who does everything for herself, looking after her home, her children.

Being able to wash and feed themselves with the little they have gave some respondents a sense that they belonged to a particular class, especially among the self-identified middle class. They were aware that they could not 'afford' many material goods, but they had pride and were self-sufficient. Some respondents used their everyday behaviour and how this was perceived by others to articulate their class identity. The following example of a 24-year-old, Sesotho-speaking male demonstrates this:

> *Speaking in English, man, 24*: I am in a class of quiet people and a bookworm, since they call me a bookworm. Most people do not associate with me, since I am not into things like bashes [parties], drinking and smoking . . . I do not have lots of friends.

Being 'in the middle' should not be equated with being middle class. It could be a physical description – in other words, in the middle of a space. For example, one can be in the middle of a field or in between two people. However 'in the middle' can also designate a social position. For example, in a community, people are in the middle if they are neither leaders nor drinkers. When their family is respectable and dignified, they can say they are 'in the middle'. When a family is referred to as being 'in the middle', it does not necessarily mean it is materially well off, but rather be associated with particular behaviour and mannerisms. For example, Andronica in the research film, who is Sesotho speaking, refers to herself as *mahareng* rather than the English 'middle class', which might explain why she would call herself 'middle'. Thus 'middle class' translated into African languages means 'in the middle', or vice versa, and 'in the middle' can be in the middle of a space or a social position. At the same time, researchers should not assume that all Africans speaking in English have the same meaning for 'middle class'. Overall, the findings on the concept of 'in the middle' indicate the importance of language.

The working class[36]

In conversations, respondents rarely used the term 'working class', instead they tended to use the word 'workers', and they used the term to mean, literally, 'work'. There is no equivalent word in isiZulu and Sesotho that can convey the meaning of 'working class'; usually the few Sowetans who referred to this class used the word *abasebenzi*, which means 'workers'. In several isiZulu translations of the Communist Manifesto, which is called *isibophezelo senhlangano yamakhomanisi*, 'working class' is referred as *isigaba sabesebenzi* – *isigaba* means 'level' or 'standard' and *sabesebenzi* refers to 'workers', therefore *isigaba sabesebenzi* means level of workers;[37] thus the term *isigaba sabesebenzi* refers to a certain layer of workers. It therefore does not situate workers, but it appears to acknowledge a particular section of workers – those who have work. *Isigaba* is based inherently on comparison; hence an assumption can be made that there is a preceding level of workers. For example, *isigaba* can be applied to school grades, because school grades are structured in terms of a continuum that implies progress. The word can also be used to refer to level of income; or the level of a job position, such as junior or senior; or to the level of a driver's licence code. The political implications of 'working class' get lost in this translation. These limitations in vocabulary therefore have the potential to adversely affect the term's emancipatory implications.

Conclusion

As already indicated, the word 'class' in IsiZulu and Sesotho has multiple meanings that range from 'standing' to 'levels'. By unpacking the mother-tongue phrases used by respondents to discuss class, we have drawn on language to add to a general argument, running through this book, that within these various meanings of the term 'class', everyday experiences are combined with economic considerations. In both isiZulu and Sesotho, the term 'class' links the subjective view of reputation and importance to the objective reality of what people have or do not have materially.

The use of the terms *bahumi*, *mahareng* and *ba futsanehileng* illustrates that Sowetans are aware of class and also that they have a conception of a three-class model. Those who identified themselves *ba futsanehileng* perceived themselves as the 'sufferers', and indeed their socio-economically circumstances barely allowed them to cope. Those who identified themselves as *tlase* were the very poor, and they described themselves as being at the bottom of society and having nothing. These descriptions indicate an economic understanding that is associated with reputation and everyday experiences. The term *mahareng* had multiple meanings attached to it that are completely different from the English. 'Middle class' translated into African languages means 'in the middle', which can be in the middle of a space or a social position. Those who were 'in the middle' articulated this social position in terms of moral behaviours by comparing material stratification within their specific context. The comparison was made with an understanding of *bahumi* and *bafutsanehileng*, and they were in the middle of those two classes. 'Middle class' is thus a term that captures a status or position in between other classes, which might seem extreme for those who identified themselves as *mahareng*. *Bahumi* refers to those who have wealth, hence linking economic well-being and status. Even when they used indigenous languages, Sowetans had a sense of both economic differences and a subjective understanding of their circumstances.

Williams (1976) demonstrates that in Western Europe, specifically England, meanings of the word 'class' were contested over specific time and place. Similarly, we have argued that in the contemporary South African context, language is a crucial factor in understanding the shifting meanings of the term 'class'. 'Class' in African languages has some elements of the term as understood in English, but the multiple meanings attached to it ensure that it is even more complex than the English word. To complicate matters further, when better-educated Africans use the word 'class' they may be using it in a more sociological sense. Furthermore, the recognition that language is constantly evolving along with social conditions is shown through the use of the key concept of 'affordability' and the way in which, in some instances, people were mixing English and isiZulu/Sesotho to create the new terms *afoda* and *afodi* in order to express their experience of the relationship encapsulated in this concept.

Notes

1. This is a compound expression (verbatim).
2. *Mpofu* was not used by Sowetans, and some scholars, like Rudwick (2005), make a distinction between urban and rural isiZulu. The word *abahluphekile* can be regarded as urban isiZulu and *mpofu* as rural. IsiZulu words that are more accessible in a multilingual context are more likely to be used and the word has some resemblance to a Sesotho term *ba hlopehileng*, both meaning 'the poor'.
3. When Peter Alexander conducted an hour-long, English-speaking radio phone-in programme about class, many of the callers spoke about 'class' in the sense of 'classy', where people possessed 'class' if they behaved or spoke or dressed in the right way, or were born into a 'good' family.
4. '*Yiphi i-klasi? Usho eyesikolo na?*'
5. '*Angazi kakhulu ngama-klasi kodwa ngingumuntu ozithobile, ngihlonipha abantu . . . angiklasi abantu . . . nami angizi-klasi.*'
6. The respondent spoke in English, while the majority of the interview was conducted in Sesotho. This shows that some respondents were integrating English into their speech.
7. *Maemo* is a Sesotho word meaning 'situation', 'standing', 'condition', 'position', 'standard' or 'status'.
8. *Izinga* means 'levels', 'ridge', 'grade', 'standard' or 'quality' in isiZulu.
9. *Seemo* is a Sesotho word meaning 'stature', 'situation' or 'circumstances'.
10. *Izimo* means 'conditions', 'situation', 'state' or 'status' in isiZulu.

11. The fieldworkers used both English and isiZulu to explain: 'No, not *le yesikolo . . . uma ukhuluma ngalento ye-kilasi le ebesengiyiphawulile*; I think in isiZulu they refer to it as *izimo*.
12. The fieldworker used both Sesotho and English: 'No, I mean *maemo a haho*. You find different people in society *banang le maemo* a different? *Hona le di-categories mo bathong a kere . . . ha o etshebile maemo a haho a ho kae?*'
13. As mentioned previously, 'poor' was one of the class labels used in the questionnaire.
14. A Sesotho word meaning 'poor', 'have nothing'.
15. '*Ke a sokola. Hona le dintho tse ngata tse ke di batlang empa ha ke afodi*' [with the word *afodi* incorporating the English term 'afford' into Sesotho].
16. Sesotho word referring to 'the poor' or 'those who are poor'.
17. '*Ba hlopehileng ke ba dulang mekhukhung, ba se nang letho. Ha ba afodi* [with the word *afodi* incorporating the English term 'afford' into Sesotho] *le ho ifepa*.'
18. '*Ngiyahlupheka. Ngifuna umsebenzi*.'
19. '*Ngiphansi, ngiyazi ngisebenzela i-410 rand. Abanye abantu abayivukeli nje leyomali . . . ngiphansi ngoba bengingasebenzi isikhathi eside. Uma sengiwuthola ke umsebenzi wase ungakhokheli*.'
20. '*Ngiku-klasi ephansi ngoba ngizizwa ngiku-klasi ephansi . . . eminye imindeni inemizi emihle*.'
21. *Ba* is plural for 'those who are poor or suffering'.
22. Upper class was the exact word used in the questionnaire.
23. '*Ba na le dikoloi. Ba na le ntho engwe le engwe e ba e batlang . . . ba afoda*.'
24. '*Mina ngikhokhelwa imali encane . . . kodwa kumele ngihambe ngiyosebenza. Umuntu oyi-topshayela angeke, ngabe manje kudala wawushiya ngelithi ngingenzani ngalemali?*'
25. *Ke a* means 'I can' in Sesotho. A few of our respondents did use the word to indicate that they can afford some material goods.
26. *Ba a* means 'they can' in Sesotho.
27. *Afoda* and *afodi* are written phonetically, that is in the manner in which people pronounced the words in conversation.
28. '*Ngenkathi ngisebenza e-convention centre, ngangi-afoda* [incorporating an English term 'afford' into isiZulu, which becomes *afoda*]. *Kwakunesikhathi la sasisebenza i-over time, futhi kwakuyilezo zikhathi (yinkathi) sasinemali kuzo . . . lapho kwakune* affordability [switching to English] . . . *Njengoba imali yayikhona . . . ngangikwazi ukuzithengela noma yini engangiyifuna*.'
29. Middle class was one of the class labels that people could choose as their class identity in the questionnaire.
30. This is an isiZulu word similar to the Sesotho *futsanehileng*, referring to the poor.
31. This is an isiZulu word meaning an informal settlement made of shacks built from corrugated iron.
32. '*Mina ngi-average, phakathi nendawo . . . kunezinto enginazo abanye abangenazo . . . nginomatric, kukhona engibaziyo abano-standard 8 ababenesifiso sokuqhubeka kodwa*

bengakwazi . . . hayi njengabo nginomatric . . . ngihlala endlini enamakamela afour. Ngicabanga ukuthi abahluphekayo yilabo abahlala emikhukhwini.'

33. '*Ba bangata ba batla mosebetsi ha ba thole. Ba bang ba rutehile empa mosebetsi ha ba thole.* So that's why *ke re ke betere Ke kgotsofalla hore ke robala ke jele . . . Ba bang ha ba kgone . . .*'
34. '*Ke ikemetse. Ke a ihlokomela, le bana baka. Ke a ihlapisa.*'
35. '*Indlela engizibona ngayo mina, ngingumuntu, ngikahle.*'
36. Working class was used in the questionnaire.
37. See http://www.ccs.ukzn.ac.za.

9

Class and religion

Denominations in Soweto

Keke Motseke and Sibongile Mazibuko

From 9h00 until about 20h00 every Sunday, the hustle and bustle of people dressed in their best or various colourful church uniforms, demonstrates the extent to which religion is a critical part of Sowetans' lives. The 2001 Census showed that a large number of South Africans (79.8 per cent) considered themselves to be Christian (Hendriks and Erasmus 2005: 91). In the Classifying Soweto survey, it was found that an even greater proportion of Sowetans (87 per cent) categorised themselves as Christian. While this chapter is also about the meaning and experience of class, it focuses on how class relates to religion and the church, since religion is such a crucial part of Sowetans' lives. It does this by looking at the interaction of religion with various socio-economic variables that coincide with local perceptions of class.

Sean McCloud's (2007: 840) assertion that class plays a role in determining religious preferences, in the sense that certain material circumstances make individuals and groups more or less 'available' to explore different kind of religious options, is explored in this chapter. Richard Niebhur (1929: 21) perceives differentiation and denominationalism as the moral failure of Christianity, with diverse churches conforming to the order of social classes and castes. Denominationalism has become a significant social identifier for many people, particularly in Africa. Niebuhr (1929: 26) also maintains that divisions in Christianity in the form of denominationalism are an indirect or direct result of economic factors. This chapter examines the various ways in which the most popular denominations in Soweto handle class. It poses the argument that people are likely to associate with churches in which they feel comfortable socially. Max Weber's (1967: 40) recognition that churches perpetuate social differences in the way they interpret the Bible, society, economics and politics, which has been supported by many others, including Celia Mariz (1996: 93), Adam Stewart (2008: 36) and Jeremy Ortiz (2009: 184), is further developed in the context of Soweto.

To gather information unique to this chapter, 24 face-to-face, semi-structured interviews with individuals from various congregations were conducted in 2008. Interviewees were obtained from the original Classifying Soweto database, and each interview took between 25 minutes and an hour. In June and July 2011 another 28 interviews were conducted in order to gather more recent information about class and churches in Soweto, as well as to establish how the landscape had changed over the last few years, as several churches had gained more prominence since the first round of fieldwork in 2008. The churches in our study included the Zionist Christian Church (ZCC), the Anglican Church, the Church of Nazareth, the Universal Church of the Kingdom of God (UCKG) and the Grace Bible Church. These were all visible in the quantitative data, except for the Grace Bible Church, which was mentioned often during qualitative interviews. The questions asked covered a range of topics on subjective class identity and the perceived class structure of the churches and their members. Interviews were conducted in the language preferred by the interviewee, and then translated into English. Participant observation was also undertaken in the form of attendance at various church services in Soweto.

One of the findings in the larger Classifying Soweto survey was that Sowetans had varying interpretations of their socio-economic class. These were rarely 'academically correct' in that they constructed their own understanding of their personal class status according to how they positioned themselves in comparison to others and their level of consumption (see Chapter 6). In the interviews about religion, there was much mention of the cars that people drove to church, what language the sermons were conducted in, and the educational qualifications and types of jobs people had in the various churches. These were some of the markers that people used to create a measure of association with the church that they attended and to which they felt a sense of belonging. Along with the original quantitative data about the Living Standard Measures (LSMs), the qualitative interviews helped to clarify the relationship between class and religion in Soweto and how people deal with this relationship.

First, we encapsulate the various denominations and their origins in South Africa, before focusing on the prominent denominations in Soweto. We move on to a deeper engagement with class and its manifestation in the various denominations, through a number of markers of class. We look at denominational breakdowns in terms of age and gender, and then provide subjective accounts about how class plays out inside the church. Finally, we conclude that people ultimately gravitate towards churches that complement their social status.

Churches in Soweto: Past and present

Overview of Christianity in South Africa

It is useful to conceptualise the history of religion in South Africa as occurring in three significant waves. The first wave was made up of the missionary churches that spread to South Africa in the nineteenth century (De Gruchy 1978: 2). The Dutch Reformed Church was the first of these, soon followed by missionaries from the Moravian Church and London Missionary Society. Missionaries established the Wesleyan, Pentecostal, Anglican, Presbyterian and Roman Catholic Churches (Anderson 2000b; Viljoen 1995: 56; Norton 1940: 350). These churches are referred to as 'mainline churches' in this chapter.

The second wave, in the later 1900s, was the African Independent/Indigenous Churches (AICs). The aim of this movement was to establish ecclesiastical and theological autonomy from the white mission churches (Maboea 2002: 7). The AICs were characterised by Ethiopian, Zionist and Apostolic churches (Hastings 1994: 499; Maboea 2002: 8). While the Ethiopian churches were direct offshoots from mission churches and generally maintained the mainline style of worship and organisation, the Zionist and Apostolic AICs assimilated African traditional culture, religion and belief systems that stressed the power of the Holy Spirit and divine healing (Sundkler, 1961; Mbiti 1975; Hastings 1994; Maboea 2002). Walter Makhulu (1998: 15), Elina Hankela (2006: 6) and the Bureau of Democracy, Human Rights and Labour (2008: 1) agree that the AICs are the largest grouping of Christian churches in South Africa, with the ZCC having the most followers.

The third wave was characterised by the emergence of the Pentecostal/Charismatic movement, which began with the founding of the Apostolic Faith Mission Church to South Africa by the Canadian missionary, John G. Lake, in 1908 (Sundkler 1961: 1). This movement gained prominence in the 1990s (Goodhew 2000a: 357). It was fuelled by rapid urbanisation and industrialisation, which left people in South African townships feeling that they lived in an impersonal and insecure world, which resulted in them looking for a sense of belonging (Anderson 2000a: 3). The lively instrumental music, the spiritual high, speaking in tongues, 'New Age' spirituality, and the use of new methods to recruit and maintain church members were decidedly more pronounced in these churches.[1] We shall look at which of the denominations associated with these three waves are most prominent in contemporary Soweto.

Religion in contemporary Soweto

The question from the Classifying Soweto questionnaire used for this chapter – 'What is your religion, faith or belief system?' – had 42 options taken from Census 2001. Jungens Hendriks and Johannes Erasmus (2005: 110) found in their analysis of data on religion from Census 2001, that too many types of churches and church names had to be filled in manually on the census questionnaire. Their suggestion was to create a maximum of 20–30 categories that cater for all the churches in terms of their similarities and characteristics, because many churches functioned in similar ways. Our research faced the same challenge and we merged some small churches with very similar characteristics into a single category (a specific example being 'Pentecostal'). We also lumped churches that, from our survey data, were supported by less than 0.5 per cent of Sowetans into the general category 'smaller Christian churches'. The Grace Bible Church, a Pentecostal church, was referred to frequently in our interviews, but was not listed separately in the census and was, therefore, not mentioned explicitly in our quantitative survey. The growth in support for Grace Bible in Soweto seems to have been rapid, and is probably associated with the opening of its large and prominent 'cathedral' near Maponya Mall, which occurred after the main fieldwork for our project. We refer to the Grace Bible Church in data derived from our qualitative research but, obviously, it does not appear in the quantitative assessments.

In line with the literature and also because it presented an overview of religious affiliations in Soweto, a preliminary step in our analysis involved merging the churches/religions into four main categories. The first category, mainline churches, comprised the more 'conventional', historically white mission churches, such as the Roman Catholic, Anglican, Methodist and Lutheran churches. The second category, AICs, incorporated both the independent and indigenous churches, such as the ZCC, the Apostolate and Shembe churches (West 1975; Bompani 2010; Hope and Young 1983). The third category, Pentecostal churches, consisted of all the Christian charismatic churches, such as the UCKG, Rhema and other Pentecostal congregations. The fourth category comprised all the other religions, and agnostics and atheists, as well as those who responded as having 'no religion'. The largest sub-category in this one consists of those who specified 'Amadlozi/Badimo/ Swikwembu' as their 'religion, faith or belief system'. These terms refer to traditional beliefs (including reverence for ancestors), which play an important part in the daily lives of many people (Mndende 1997: 41). Those who identify with Badimo, etc. often attend church on Sunday, but given the nature of the relevant question, those we included under this heading had given traditional belief systems preference over churches. In Soweto, there is also some support for Islam, Hinduism and Rastafarianism, but all three of these religions added up to only 0.3 per cent.

Figure 9.1 shows the numerical representations of these four main categories. The AICs were the most popular, at 27 per cent.[2] Mainline churches, which represented 26 per cent[3] of Sowetans, still have a good deal of support (Hendriks and Erasmus 2005: 102). Pentecostal churches are gaining ground with support from 12 per cent of the population.[4]

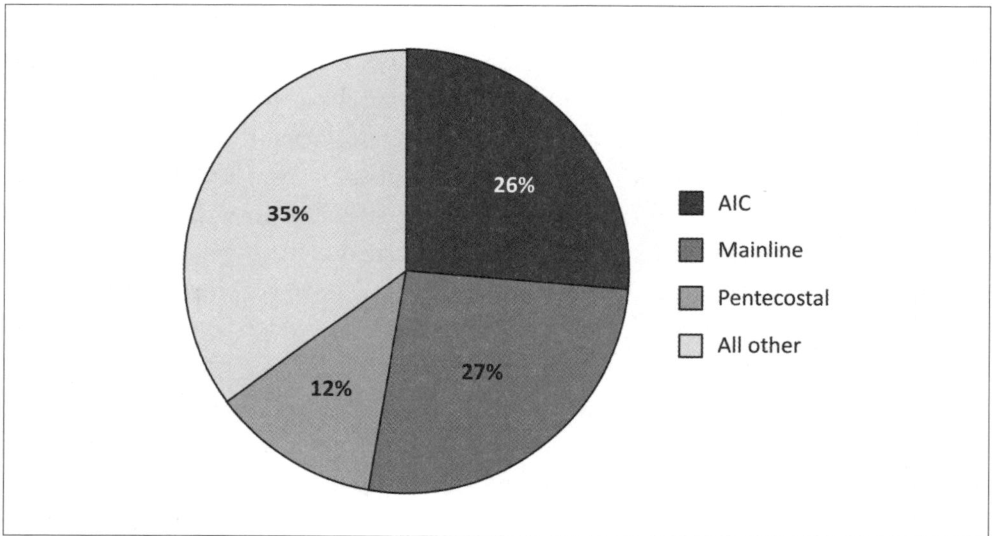

Figure 9.1 Religious affiliation in Soweto.
Source: Classifying Soweto survey 2006.

People who follow the family tradition often attend mainline churches. Rodney Stark (1972: 501) postulates that class is not particularly relevant when it comes to religiosity, but denominational difference is much more important, since 'a man's religious heritage has much more influence on his present religious perspective than do his present economic circumstances'. However, evidence in this chapter and elsewhere suggests that economic circumstances can motivate and sustain church involvement. Mainline churches are associated largely with a middle-class clientele (Nelsen and Potvin 1980: 138), although the scale of general attendance and involvement in these churches has dwindled over recent years (Hendriks and Erasmus 2005: 105).

Bengt Sundkler (1961: 89), Martin West (1975) and Marjorie Hope and James Young (1983) found that large numbers of AIC church leaders are uneducated. Indeed, this as well as other socio-economic circumstances of church leaders and the congregation were often similar (Bompani 2008: 673). Furthermore, in some churches, ministers are not paid and there are no funds to cover the general running costs of the churches (Bompani 2010: 311). This could also be attributed to the generally informal way in which some of the churches are erected, and is observable in that services are often conducted in school classrooms, tents and garages. Only about 5 per cent of AICs are housed in formal church buildings (Bompani 2010: 311).

Pentecostal churches represent at least 10 per cent of the country's population (Garner 2000: 314). Mariz (1996) focuses on the urban poor and lower middle classes of Brazil, where social conditions correspond closely with those of South African townships (Garner 2000: 314). She explores the world of Pentecostalism with positive criticism about what its proponents do to help the poor, thus attracting people with the fewest economic resources and least education. Andre Czegledy (2008: 288) also speaks of how Pentecostalism is seen as a 'band aid' for the poor. On the other side of this coin, however, are to be found the Pentecostal congregations that have greatly benefited financially from their religious activities. Of these, the most discernible in Soweto were the UCKG and the Grace Bible Church. Paul Freston (2005: 40) speaks of the great expansion of the UCKG in South Africa, making it the church's second most successful country after Brazil, where the church originated. In Table 9.1 we pinpoint the specific churches in Soweto that make up the numbers in the four categories. The right-hand column shows religious identification as captured in Census 2001. The figures for certain options are missing because there were some differences in available choices and also in some subsequent combination of categories.

From Table 9.1, it is clear that a few churches dominate church affiliation in Soweto. These more prominent churches have an undeniable social influence on Sowetans, as demonstrated by their popularity and following. However, we attempted to determine the extent to which this impetus spills over or is symbiotically affected by class, and will be further expanding on some of the prominent churches shown above in relation to socio-economic well-being, as indicated by the LSM graph in Figure 9.2.

Class and denomination

Respondents from the three church categories described above (mainline, AIC and Pentecostal) had varying opinions based on their separate experiences of class and

Table 9.1 Support for different denominations in Soweto.[5]

Religion or belief system	Classifying Soweto survey category	Classifying Soweto 2006 (%)	Census 2001 (%)
Other Christian, no specification	Other	15	
ZCC	AIC	12	13.8
Apostle Twelve	AIC	9	
Roman Catholic	Mainline	8	8.9
Agnostic; no religion, but believes in God	Other	7	
Methodist	Mainline	6	9.2
Badimo	Other	6	
Anglican	Mainline	4	4.8
Pentecostal	Pentecostal	4	0.1
Other religions	Other	4	3.8
UCKG	Pentecostal	3	
No religion; atheist; does not believe in God	Other	3	
St John's Apostolic	AIC	3	1.5
Lutheran	Mainline	3	3.2
Dutch Reformed	Mainline	2	9.0
Smaller Christian churches (less than 0.5%)	Mixed	2	
Jehovah's Witnesses	Pentecostal	1	
Seventh Day Adventist	Pentecostal	1	0.6
Presbyterian	Mainline	1	2.3
Assemblies of God	Pentecostal	1[6]	1.2
Faith Mission	Pentecostal	1	0.7
Nazareth	AIC	1	0.7
Shembe	AIC	1	
United Congregational Church	Mainline	1	1.4
Rhema	Pentecostal	1	
Full Gospel Church of God	Pentecostal	1	0.9
Total		100	62.1

Sources: Classifying Soweto survey 2006; Census 2001. Columns do not add up to 100% due to rounding and different categories being used in the 2001 Census.

what it meant, as well as how it was represented in the church. In order to compare these with one another, we examined the popular markers of class that most respondents mentioned during interviews against the options that explained socio-economic status in the quantitative data. In this section, we look at these indicators and compare them with what people had to say about what these represented to them, their churches and their socio-economic status.

LSMs and denomination

Figure 9.2 reveals the mean of LSM total associated with each of the categories listed in Table 9.1. It shows a range from the 'poorest' churches, Nazareth and Shembe, with LSM means of, respectively, -0.11 and -0.06 to the 'rich' churches,

Presbyterian and Rhema, with means of, respectively, 0.67 and 0.75. With the exception of the United Congregational Church (UCC) – which developed out of the London Missionary Society and American Board missionaries (active among migrant mine workers) – the mainline churches all appear in the top half in terms of LSMs. By contrast, all but one of the AICs are located in the bottom half; the exception being Apostle Twelve, which is only marginally above the midpoint. This was what we found in the literature, which shows that the AICs are generally poor (Hope and Young 1983: 191; Bompani 2010: 309). The Pentecostals range across the LSM spectrum from the UCKG, close to the bottom, to the Rhema church at the very top. The 'other' categories were clustered around the middle.

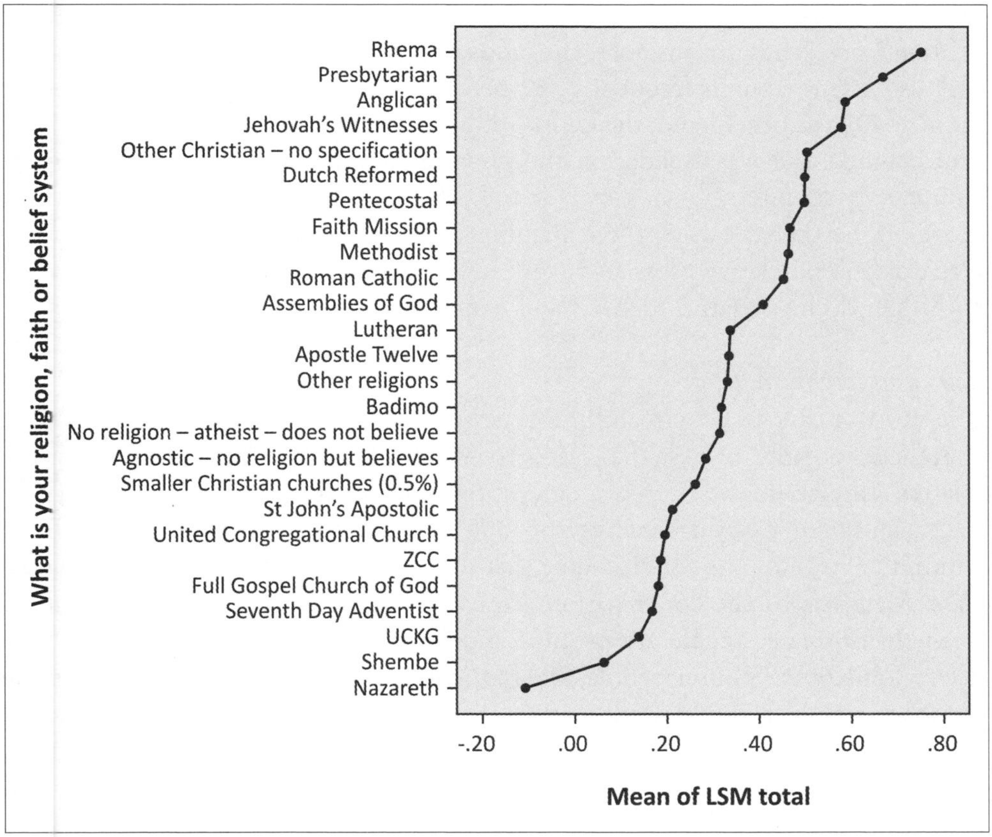

Figure 9.2 Sowetans' denominations and LSM totals.

Source: Classifying Soweto survey 2006.

For further quantitative analysis and interviews we focused on eleven churches. These were selected across the LSM spectrum and included the larger churches, as well as churches that best represented the three categories mentioned earlier – mainline, AIC and Pentecostal. From the AICs we chose: ZCC, Apostle Twelve and Nazareth; from the mainline: Roman Catholic, Anglican, Lutheran and UCC; and from the Pentecostals: UCKG, Jehovah's Witnesses, Assemblies of God and Rhema.

In passing, 57 per cent of Sowetans claimed they attended a religious service in the month before the survey. For our eleven churches, the proportion varied between, on the one hand, 62 per cent for Roman Catholics, 63 per cent for Lutherans and 64 per cent for Anglicans, and, on the hand, 85 per cent for the UCC[7] and 86 per cent for Nazareth.[8] UCC and Nazareth are two of the poorest churches, and Catholics, Lutherans and Anglicans tend to be relatively better off, but it would be wrong to pose a simple association between poverty and frequency of attendance. Thus, for instance, the Jehovah's Witnesses tend to be fairly well off and also attend church frequently (80 per cent having done so in the preceding month). On the other hand, the UCKG adherents tend to be poor, but only 68 per cent claimed to have attended in the previous month.[9] Attendance at mainline churches is definitely lower than for the AICs and Pentecostals, but the UCC, much poorer than the other three mainline churches (and with a different history), is an exception. Relatively low attendance at the mainline churches may be associated with their decline relative to AICs and Pentecostals.

Cars and denomination

The ratio of cars to people and the type of cars in which people arrive at their churches, not only suggest the classes to which they belong, but also reflect the relative affluence of the church congregation. For example, if one were to judge by the various luxury cars driven by the people who attend services at the Grace Bible Church in Soweto, one could assume that this church represents the upper-middle class. Members of the congregation are usually professionals, celebrities and so forth. In this case, people are profiled and classified in relation to the cars they drive. Some of the poorer people, and particularly the younger people, attend the church to associate with this affluence in the hope that they, too, will be successful.

Respondents generally saw the ownership of a car as an important marker of being in a higher class. It was a measure that was immediately visible in the church context, and the types of car gave a further indication (see cars at an Anglican church in Photograph 9.1). The following observations from three of our interviewees are relevant.

> Most people that come to church here were born and baptised here and so on. They have moved out to the suburbs, but they still drive to come to church here; you saw them on Sunday [and] the cars they drive; they are rich. People that come to church here are from [the] upper and middle classes (Father Mcube, Anglican).

> Look, the only way you class people is what you see in terms of materials. You can see the cars that are there. Sometimes the parking lot is too packed, so you can't say someone who is poor or in the lower class have the kinds of cars that are there – or [can] even afford a car, for that matter. That is why I am saying they are middle to high class. You will see the way they dress, you will see the cars, and you can hear the way they talk as well – it will tell you that these people are not in the lower class of society. They are either in the middle or upper class (Milli, Grace Bible Church).

> We don't have cars! All my church members live in shacks (Pastor Khoza, Jerusalem).[10]

People felt strongly that cars in the parking lot of the church were indicative of the class status of that church and the members who attend it. This observation rang true. When we looked at which congregations were more likely to own cars, we found an overlap between the LSM and car ownership. Indeed, the congregations that were generally better off were the ones most likely to have fancy cars and a larger number of cars in their parking lots.

Education

A person's level of education is seen by many as an indicator of class, and those who are educated are more likely to secure better employment, or at least a job. Kgosi from a Pentecostal church, the Zoe Bible Church, which she saw as middle class, made a direct reference to this by saying: 'Most of my church members are educated. I know some of them and I know where they work. Some you can see by the cars they are driving.'

One of the AIC respondents, Baba Khumalo, when asked about his church members' average level of education, said:

> My church members are people who are not educated, because people who are educated don't want to come in churches like mine. They choose other churches with people who are educated, not a poor church like mine. That is what I have noticed. The only people we have in the church are people with matric, not beyond that.

Table 9.2 summarises data on denominations and the level of education of Sowetans identifying with that denomination. There was an inverse relationship between churches that had a high proportion of attendees with post-school education and those with a high proportion who had primary education or less. The pattern was similar to the one for LSMs and cars, with one slight modification: the Lutherans had a higher proportion of supporters with primary or less education than those of the UCC (but they also had a higher proportion with post-school education). That is, mainline churches tend to attract well-educated participants, the AICs tend to attract poorly educated participants and the Pentecostal churches straddle both. The Rhema Church had the highest proportion of post-school educated attendees and the lowest with primary or less education. The Anglicans had the second highest proportion of post-school educated supporters.

Table 9.2 Denomination by education.

	Primary school or less (%)	High school (%)	Post-school (%)
Anglican	14	69	17
Apostle Twelve	24	70	6
Assemblies of God	10	81	10
Jehovah's Witnesses	10	77	13
Nazareth	34	61	5
Rhema	7	71	22
Roman Catholic	9	76	15
UCKG	27	64	9
ZCC	24	72	4
United Congregational Church	15	75	10
Lutheran	19	68	14

Source: Classifying Soweto survey 2006. Some rows do not add up to 100% due to rounding.

Language

Sermons conducted in English are suggestive of a 'middle-class' background. Black people who speak English with their friends are often from former Model C schools or have gone through some form of higher education.[11] In addition, young people increasingly use English with their friends. Although there is no quantitative data measuring this shift, it appears to have been rapid, especially in the period since our survey. Poorer Sowetans may not understand English or may be less confident in the language, and might not comprehend a sermon conducted in English. Some Pentecostal churches have adjusted to this by creating 'African' services, where sermons are conducted in the dominant South African languages, such as IsiZulu and Sesotho. An example of this is the Rhema Church African service in Protea North. Father Timothy Mncube explains the practice in the Anglican Church: 'The services here are mostly conducted in English. Most Anglicans in Soweto sing in English and African local hymns because the youth and the Young Men's Guild like them.' Ntombi Ndlovu adds: 'English is used, but Sesotho, isiZulu and Shangaan are also used, because this is a mostly Shangaan neighbourhood.' In some mainline churches hymns are sung with the traditional tunes but using a variety of languages.

In the survey, we asked: 'What language do you mainly use with your friends?' Appendix 2 reports on the findings, with Figure A2.5 cross-tabulating these with the age and education of the respondent. Among older Sowetans – especially those over 60 – a significant minority of those with post-school education use English with their friends. Among Sowetans without post-school education, the use of English with friends is significantly higher among the age group 25 years and less. Responses to the question of English and the church attended are summarised in Figure 9.4.

The pattern we discerned in relation to LSMs, cars and education is replicated to a considerable extent. The mainline churches tend to attract a higher proportion of adherents who use English with friends and the AICs attract a lower proportion.

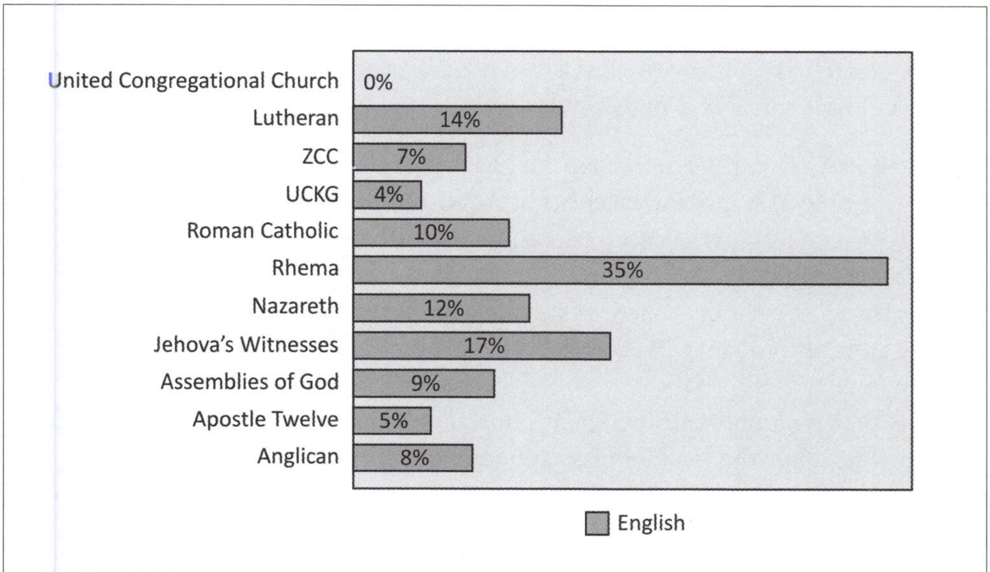

Figure 9.3 Use of English with friends and church attended.

Source: Classifying Soweto survey 2006.

The Rhema Church has, by far, the highest percentage of respondents who speak English, at 35 per cent,[12] followed by Jehovah's Witnesses at 17 per cent.[13] In contrast, the UCC has no members who speak English with their friends. Consistent with other findings used to capture 'class', only 4 per cent of UCKG adherents speak English with friends, the second lowest figure.[14] This reiterates Freston's (2005: 54) observation that the UCKG's clientele is not comparable with the middle-class clientele of churches such as Rhema, as its members are of a lower class and 'raw'. However, there is one notable distortion in the pattern. In terms of adherents speaking English, the otherwise poverty-stricken Nazareth church came fourth. We suggest a possible reason for this below. By contrast, the Anglicans came seventh, with the lowest proportion of English-speakers among the mainline churches.

Qualitative recognition of class difference

So, there was strong evidence of class difference between churches in the survey data. But are these differences recognised by Sowetans? Following the general process of identity construction, many interviewees did, indeed, compare their own church with others in terms of class. Here are three examples:

> Our class is high, boss; you see you first look at the building where we attend the service and look at the Zions; they are attending in the garage or the school or a hall. With us we have a structure where we say 'it's our church' (Sthembiso, Anglican).

> My church is the lowest-class church in comparison with churches like Grace Bible (Sithole, Pentecostal).

> These new churches are too commercialised and it's as if you go there to be with people of status and celebrities. A person like me going to Grace Bible using a taxi – when I arrive there [at a wealthier church] I won't fit in. Maybe I should try churches like Zion or churches that conduct their services in garages or schools where it's my class – we won't discriminate against one another (Gwanta, Apostolic).

It seems that members of prominent churches with better-off members are often comfortable about the issue of class and are, in fact, proud of their churches' class status, as indicated by Sthembiso from the Anglican Church. Milli from the Grace Bible Church said: 'Truthfully? My church is high class. Although there are other people who attend it, it is high class in a sense that most of them are educated people, you know!' However, as we shall see, there can also be a denial of class differences, especially within particular churches.

Gender, age and common ground

Lungi from the Pentecostal church, Unity of Faith, told us: 'The reason that motivates me the most to attend my church is that I am meeting people with common ground between me and them, and when I'm among them I feel more comfortable.' As we have seen, class status was an important aspect of 'common ground', but how about gender and age?

Gender and attendance

David de Vaus and Ian McAllister (1987: 472) showed that women tend to be more religious than men. This is a widely held view so it was necessary to establish the interaction of gender with church attendance in Soweto. Overall 32 per cent of the male respondents in the Classifying Soweto survey claimed to have participated in a religious service in the month before the survey, compared with 68 per cent of females.

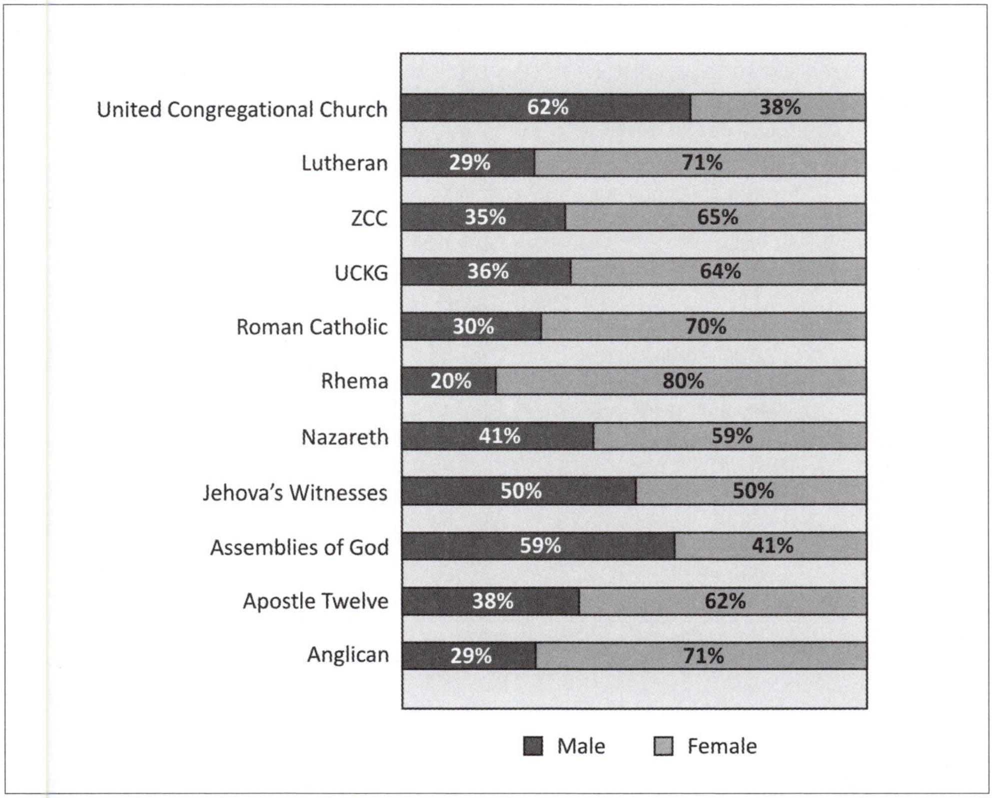

Figure 9.4 Denomination by gender.

Source: Classifying Soweto survey.

When considering the figures presented in Figure 9.4, one should bear in mind that 59 per cent of respondents in the survey were women (see Appendix 1). Support for the different churches varied greatly in terms of gender. The three larger mainline churches were dominated by women (70–71 per cent); Rhema, the wealthiest of the churches, even more so, with 80 per cent. On the other hand, there were churches where most adherents are men. These included the UCC (62 per cent male), Assemblies of God (59 per cent) and Jehovah's Witnesses (50 per cent). UCC, it will be recalled, has a history of recruiting migrant workers. Beyond our eleven churches, Grace Bible Church had a 'Line Crossers Foundation', aimed at attracting men. The association between class and gender is, at most, weak.

Age and attendance

Chapter 4 showed how Soweto's labour market was structured by age, with higher levels of unemployment and partial work among young Sowetans. Does this bear any relationship to the churches people attend? Table 9.3 presents our findings on age and denomination. As with all data from the Classifying Soweto survey, one needs to keep in mind that the population includes Sowetans over the age of sixteen, so the figures exclude activities involving children (see Photograph 9.2 for a Methodist example).[15]

Table 9.3 Denomination by age.

	16–34 years (%)	35–64 years (%)	65 years and older (%)
Anglican	46	43	12
Apostle Twelve	50	40	10
Assemblies of God	60	35	6
Jehovah's Witnesses	40	45	15
Nazareth	67	31	2
Rhema	48	37	15
Roman Catholic	49	41	10
UCKG	54	45	2
ZCC	52	41	7
Lutheran	38	49	13
United Congregational Church	56	26	18

Source: Classifying Soweto Study 2006. Some rows do not add up to 100% due to rounding.

Here there are similarities with our class patterns. If we put the Assemblies of God to one side, and divide the other ten churches between five wealthier denominations (Rhema, Anglican, Jehovah's Witness, Roman Catholic and Lutheran) and five poorer denominations (Nazareth, UCKG, ZCC, UCC and Apostle Twelve), the wealthier denominations are considerably older than the poorer ones. While more than half of all the richer churches comprise people aged 35 and older, more than half of all the poorer churches attract people under 35. It is possible that the larger mainline churches are not as successful at attracting young people as the others, but it is noticeable that Rhema and the Jehovah's Witnesses are also older churches, despite being Pentecostal. Of course, the data cannot tell us whether the poorer churches are attracting young people because young people tend to be poorer, or the involvement of young people, who tend to be poorer, reinforces the poverty of the poor churches. A bit of both one assumes. But this is not a chicken and egg situation – the history of Christianity in South Africa shows that AICs tend to be less 'respectable' than the mainline churches (see Chapter 1). This continues to be the case, with generational implications.

However, it appears that each of the different churches has a different socio-demographic. Significantly, Nazareth is a young persons' church, and this probably goes a long way to explain the high proportion of its adherents who use English when speaking with friends. Let us define the churches using three basic characteristics – economics, gender and age – each with three divisions, respectively: better off/middling/poor, male-dominated/mixed/female-dominated, and young/average/old. Better-off people are catered for by the Rhema Church (older females), Anglican and Roman Catholic churches (average females) and Jehovah's Witnesses (older men). The middling group are associated with UCC (older men), Assemblies of God (young mixed) and Lutheran churches (older females). The poor attend Nazareth (young mixed), ZCC and UCKG (young females) and Apostle Twelve (average females). This is one way of capturing a core socio-demographic component associated with each of the churches. One should not lose sight of the reality that 12 per cent of Sowetans are aligned to the ZCC and less than one per cent to Rhema.

Class inside the church

So far, we have compared one church with another. Now we take a look at evidence of class subjectivities within churches. Here there are both denials and manifestations of the significance of class.

Neutralising class through the 'silent rule'

Karl Marx and subsequently Stark (1972), Mariz (1992), William Swatos (2001) and others have pointed out that the struggle for survival is the principal concern of the poor person. Religion can provide a form of escapism (a place to seek refuge), but it can also provide relief, healing, support and comfort. It can neutralise the feelings of frustration that arise from the lived experience of poverty and struggle of the lower classes. By attending church, the anger, despondency and angst of being poor and being in the lower classes of society are reduced. The church makes the issue of class a non-issue by effectively covering it over. It also fosters an acceptance of one's circumstances, rather than promotes a challenge to injustice and inequality. Class is further neutralised by church leaders promoting the view that it is wrong to 'class' one another in the eyes of God. People are, therefore, encouraged not to be aware of class in the church. Father Mncube of the Anglican Church emphasised this by stating:

> The body of Christ is irrespective of whether one is educated or not, but the church must play a major role. For an example, by using centrifugal methods, we as priests must go out and reach people; we cannot expect people just to come to the church . . . these are people who need talking to.

The argument here is for bringing people together in a unified community. Former President Nelson Mandela, in his address to churches in Soweto 1997, stated: 'We need religious institutions to continue to be the conscience of society, a moral custodian and fearless champion for the interests of the weak and the downtrodden' (Bompani 2006: 1144). Notwithstanding the radical possibilities of this kind of proposition, the solution to the problems of the downtrodden is vested in a moral crusade rather than class struggle. In the Middle Ages, the poor became instrumental to the salvation of the middle class, whose members gave alms to the poor in the hope of securing their own salvation (Bloomquist 2001: 95). Later, Lenin wrote:

> Those who live by the labour of others are taught by religion to practice charity while on earth, thus offering them a very cheap way of justifying their entire existence as exploiters and selling them at a moderate price ticket to well-being in heaven (cited in McLellan 1987: 96).

Mariz (1996) affirms this – charitable help or efforts often display dynamics of class, with the strong benevolent giver helping the weak recipient rather than forming effective, empowering partnerships with persons living in poverty. Members of the congregation are encouraged to be less aware of the class differences in their church and more involved in helping the poor. This affects both the poor and the better off in church. The poor feel appreciated and looked after, while those who are able to assist, are buoyed by the feeling of giving in the eyes of God.

As a consequence, differences in class interests are muted. Elizabeth from the Methodist Church in Dlamini had this to say when asked about the class status of the members of her church:

> Our leaders preach about the word of God and His teachings. We don't look at how the person is living and what they have in their pockets. If you want to share with others, you are more than welcome. But whenever you are in God's presence, you only focus on Him, not the other person and what he or she can afford.

Similarly, according to Bloomquist (2001: 93):

> . . . usually we do not think – much less talk with one another – about how the dynamics of class operate in . . . our congregation or denomination. To do so, particularly when employed by the church, is to risk losing our chance for upward mobility therein. Silence about class is the rule.

This silence about issues of class in the church is also pointed out by one interviewee, Bekwa: 'The minute you mention class the church breaks . . . the aim of going to church is to praise God.' In the same light, Simelane, a youth from the Roman Catholic Church says on the subject of class in the church: 'We talk about class amongst ourselves, not with the priests; we can see that there are top people by looking at their cars and attires.' Mangobeni, from World of Life, another Pentecostal church, said:

> We are not rich in the physical way in my church; we are rich in a spiritual way. We are still struggling as a church; we don't see richer or poorer people; we all work together for the church. But anyway, God doesn't want us to be in a lower class. He wants us all to be in the higher class – you can't be a servant of God and not have food. Our pastor encourages us to make a plan, not to sit and fold our arms – you must do something to sleep and eat well.

This implicit recognition of the importance of class, and of desires to be members of a higher class, is also reflected in this comment by Anna of the UCKG: 'I would say my church motivates everybody to work hard towards being rich and stuff like that. But they don't really judge according to your class – whether you are rich or whether you are poor. You are [all] welcome.'

The formal position of most churches is to recognise the significance of poverty but not class. The wealthy should help the poor by means of charity, thus providing a material basis for a united church community. The practical and ideological implications of church-facilitated solidarity for poor people should not be underestimated. However, class differences and associated identities persist within church life.

Visualising social differences

Despite the attempts to cover over or silence issues of class in the church, further analysis demonstrates that these are often contradicted by the effective visibility of class difference. Various respondents agreed that class expresses itself in the church in a number of ways. Clothes, cars, mannerisms, seating arrangements, language, and financial contributions all reflected class differences in a church.

CLOTHES AND UNIFORM

Most of the poorer churches attempt to mitigate class differences among followers by insisting that members wear a uniform, at least on Sundays. This is general with the AICs and sometimes practised by mainline churches. According to Hennie Pretorius and Lizo Jafta (1993: 223), the well-known khaki uniform of ZCC men is symbolic of human mortality in that all people are made of dust and will return to dust. Other Apostolic uniforms boasting bright blues, greens and whites symbolise the colours of the fields, the sky and water, purity and trust (Bompani 2010: 312). These uniforms and types of clothes that church members wear reflect their image and, therefore, have implications for their class status. For members of AICs, uniforms serve as a form of protection against class profiling:

> We are all the same in that church; there is no such a thing as a poor person or a rich person, whereas in other churches there are times when you can see class by the clothes they wear and you are even scared to go there . . . there is no such a thing here; the only thing that is important is men they must wear a shirt and tie and women must wear a skirt and cover their heads (Salume, Modise Church, AIC).
>
> We are one if we come in church in uniform; you won't tell that I'm a new person and *ey* man! I'm wearing a Gucci. All of us are in that old cloth and jacket bought in the same place. It [a uniform] evens out everything – that is what people in these Charismatic churches don't understand (Bekwa, AIC).

Uniforms are attractive to poorer people, but they appeal far less to better-off people. The effect is twofold. Firstly, uniforms reinforce the separation of the AICs, in particular, from 'respectable' society. Secondly, within the non-uniform churches, class differences are reflected in the kinds of clothes people wear. Respondents who considered themselves poor often referred to the types of clothes worn by the people who attended churches such as Rhema and the Grace Bible Church. The above quote from Bekwa is an example of this. Wearing a uniform was recurrently seen as a concealer of class. Most respondents interviewed from the AICs felt that it was part of what motivated them to attend their churches, because they could not be categorised socially due to the homogeneity created by wearing a uniform. Photographs 9.3 to 9.5 provide examples of some of the uniforms worn by members of the Shembe Church and the ZCC.

THE 'WALK' AND SEATING ARRANGEMENTS

People who are rich or belong in the upper class generally follow certain observed etiquette and mannerisms. Mosote, a respondent from the Methodist Church, alluded to the mannerisms of the rich and middle class in comparison with the poor and working class: 'The rich and the middle classes have a power walk and their mannerisms are different to those of the poor classes in the church. When they walk they exude confidence and assertiveness that the poor do not have.' In observing her own ministry, Bloomquist (2001: 93) asserts that those of a lower class, if they come to church at all, are likely to sit in the back rows of a predominantly middle-class congregation. Mashinini affirmed this view by stating that in his church, '[p]oor people sit right at the back because they don't trust themselves'. When asked where the rich and middle class sit in his church, he stated that 'those who are rich sit at the front so that they can be seen'. This illuminates the level of confidence of the person who is better off in comparison to the one who is poorer. Poorer people would thus not want to be seen, and as a result would try to be as inconspicuous as possible if they felt uncomfortable or ashamed of their shoes or clothes.

LEADERSHIP

Better-off parishioners are more likely to be educated, as illustrated in the previous section. This is a large part of the reason why they usually take on leadership positions in the church. For instance:

> People who are educated like to control and are also power hungry, and then there are those who are uneducated who feel [left] out and they end up

> attending churches like Zion because there class won't show that you are not educated (Father Mncube, Anglican).
>
> High class dominates, because whatever may be happening in the church, they are there. In every decision that is taken from the church, they are there. We do have people who are poor, but also give things to the church, but those who make things happen in the church are from higher classes (Sthembiso, Anglican).

Such perceptions also tie in with feelings of being confident enough to be in leadership positions. In churches that are more varied in terms of their social status, the poorer are likely also to opt for invisibility when it comes to leadership positions. Davidson in Tamney (1991: 20) notes that social elites are over-represented on church councils, boards and commissions, and these elites encourage church activities that do not threaten the social order, such as spiritual growth programmes, pietism and pastoral counselling.

CONTRIBUTIONS (*NHLEKO*) AND TITHING (*VUKHUME*)

Dr Mathole, a resident pastor at the Grace Bible Church in Soweto, defined the church as a community of Christian people who are committed to serving the church. This includes financial support. Bloomquist (2001: 93) also described the church as an earthly institution that requires financial support and members. The payment of tithes is often inconspicuous. According to Mncube (Anglican): 'Tithing is a private thing only the finance committee knows. In this typical English church, one goes to the office and they put you in a system where they will know if you are up to date or not.' However, in mainline churches, the ticket system furthers perceptions of class, as those who have money will pay their contributions and tithes consistently every month. According to Mavundla, a Methodist:

> Classism does affect the church, for example, firstly, the church can be run by high-class people who don't identify with others who don't have money and pressure them to contribute; secondly, when something happens in the families of the less-prominent people, for example, a funeral, wedding, etc., fewer people attend, but the upper class people have higher attendance from church members at their functions. As a result, the lower class feel alienated and end up not attending church . . . and lastly, monthly contributions also create class in the church, especially with the ticket system. When death strikes, the finance committee opens the books to see if the person is up to

> date with payments and if not they don't bury those people in the church [that is, hold a service in church], they then conduct a home service instead.

Here Mavundla explains how those who tithe more because they can afford to do so, are more popular in the church, and the support they receive from the church is more readily available. This discriminates against those who cannot afford to keep up payment of their tithes. Hilma, a female archbishop from the Twelve Apostles, one of the AICs, is against tithing for this reason:

> I think what holds this church together is that there is this tithing thing in the other churches. The poor churches don't stick to tithes. We don't do that because most of the people here are not working and come from poor backgrounds. We don't ask them for tithes [and] we also wear uniform so you will not see if someone is rich or poor because we all look the same. It brings the people together, so you will not say 'I don't have something new to wear' or 'I don't have a fancy hairstyle'.

The purpose of tithing is to aid the poor in the church, and if there is a surplus it is used to assist surrounding poor communities. But there are many problems with the tithing system; for instance, in many churches the proceeds from tithing are used to renovate and extend churches into huge buildings and to fund the opulent lifestyles of the pastors. The UCKG is one of the churches that has been ostracised by the media due to the size of the church and the pastors' wealth in relation to the poverty of congregation members. One former congregant recalled:

> I have been to the Universal Church. If you need help, you have to pay, you have to contribute – if you have more money, you will be helped faster. There are people who contribute half of their wages [in] envelopes. You that have contributed less will be given a little water and small oil for healing. You also get separate days of prayer. Those who have businesses will have a separate day to those who are employed. Those with businesses pray to prosper while the employed pray to keep their employment (Gwanta, Apostolic).

Thus, even when classes, or at least their significance, are denied, the reality forces its way back into the experiences of church members. This happens through cars, clothes, seating arrangements, leadership and the contributions one can afford to make for the upkeep of the church and support for the poor.

Conclusion

It is indisputable that religion is still a very significant part of Sowetans' lives, with 87 per cent of survey respondents stating that they are Christian. One of the biggest challenges in attempting to ascertain the relationship between class and religion for the purposes of this chapter was that of moving past the offence that people felt when one mentioned class in the same sentence as religion. This was more obvious in some churches than others. As the study progressed, differences in reactions to the issue of class in the church began to show further differences within denominations regarding class. McCloud's (2007) assertion, therefore, that people's material conditions affect their religious options, applies in Soweto. Although there is an anxious and ambivalent attitude towards class in the church, there is adequate evidence to suggest that specific salient features do indeed contribute to the presence of class in churches. Also, despite the animosity associated with linking class and the church, class awareness definitely exists and this is expressed through people's observations of factors such as material possessions and language.

The approach to class as a concept and its impact on the church varies in the different church types. It was noted that in the poorer AIC congregations, class is played down more than in other churches. Churches that are struggling were more vocal about helping the poor, hiding the appearance of poverty in the church by covering over the significance of class inequality, or by emphasising the importance of being spiritually rich, when asked about class. In this way, class is neutralised, and food for the soul and community assistance are promoted.

In the churches where the clientele was better off in terms of finances and class position, respondents found it easier to speak about class and the class differences in church. Younger, more upwardly mobile people are more interested in attending a church where they feel inspired by seeing the fancy cars in the parking lot and the expensive attire worn by the pastors and other church members. Examples of this are the mainline Anglican Church and the Grace Bible Church. Certain variations were also found within Pentecostal churches, where some would be quite poor and others rather affluent. Issues such as the language spoken in the church and the types of cars used by the congregation are important markers of socio-economic status that draw people to the churches they feel they are most suited for in terms of how they perceive their own social standing. This is a case in point of how the different churches feed the needs and aspirations of the people who attend them, thus encouraging people to continue to attend their church and allowing them to feel socially accepted.

In general, the churches to which people belong, and their level of participation within these churches, reflect people's class status to a considerable degree. Therefore, although to a greater or lesser extent, churches provide material support for poorer members and repudiate the importance of class differences; in practice they reinforce the importance of class identities. Our research strongly suggests that Sowetans are able to distinguish different denominations and describe different church practices through the language of class.

Notes

1. Grace Bible Church uses person-to-person witnessing workshops, street ministry and mass evangelism (open-air outreaches) to 'turn irreligious people into fully devoted followers of Christ' (Sono 2011). The UCKG has gained most of its members through promises of healing (Freston 2005: 51).
2. Precision: ±2 per cent.
3. Precision: ±2 per cent.
4. Precision: ±1 per cent.
5. Precision of all data: ±1 per cent.
6. 0.9–0.6 per cent; precision of all data: ±1 per cent.
7. Precision: ±1 per cent.
8. Precision: ±1 per cent.
9. Attendance figures for the other four of our selected eleven denominations were: Assemblies of God – 78 per cent; ZCC – 74 per cent; Apostle Twelve – 71 per cent; Rhema – 71 per cent.
10. A small AIC, not in quantitative data but in qualitative interviews.
11. Model C schools in the apartheid era were better-off government schools, mainly for whites. They were located outside the townships. In colloquial usage, the term is sometimes extended to include private schools.
12. Precision: ±2 per cent.
13. Precision: ±2 per cent.
14. Precision: ±1 per cent.
15. According to Mosote from the Methodist Church: 'Older people contribute better than the young ones. The young one is still going to buy a trouser with his/her money, while the older one is just awaiting his/her time of death.' Generational differences can play out in other ways. In McIver and Curow's (2001: 1) study of a congregation in Australia, it was shown that people under 50 years were less likely to tithe than those above the age of 50.

10

Conclusion

Peter Alexander

We opened by asking about the possible class basis of divisions between trade unions and social movements. Since starting the project, my own concerns have broadened into issues associated with the contrasting mobilisations of workers' strikes and the rebellion of the poor. In the first part of this conclusion I summarise key findings from preceding chapters and then, in the second part, link this with analysis emerging from the newer research, thus adding another dimension to the argument. At the outset, our leading question was framed by a hope that we might contribute to wider, international discussion of class, and in the third part of this conclusion we offer some pointers in that direction.

Soweto: A differentiated proletarian unity

Our exploration was based on quantitative and qualitative research undertaken in Soweto, South Africa's largest black township. This included a large representative survey conducted in 2006. It transpired that, compared to black South Africans as a whole, Sowetans were mildly better off in terms of possessions, but experienced higher unemployment. However, the average Sowetan was not even close to being as well off as the average white person. Widespread poverty was highlighted in the percentage of the township's population associated with each of our employment categories (ECs). Less than 0.1 per cent of the population could be regarded as capitalists, only 1 per cent as managers and supervisors, and 6 per cent as petty bourgeois (included self-employed workers). Twenty-four per cent were regularly employed workers, 12 per cent were students and 12 per cent were pensioners (and others not in the labour force); 24 per cent were unemployed and a further 21 per cent were underemployed (engaged in survivalist self-employment or partial work).

Since the end of apartheid, income and class differences among black South Africans have expanded rapidly. In geographical terms this is associated with better-off people leaving townships and moving to formerly white suburbs, something that has happened with Soweto, although the scale of the process, and its implication for 'class' are still unclear. With regard to Soweto, I follow Claire Ceruti in characterising the township as a 'differentiated proletarian unity'.[1] By 'proletarian' we wish to convey important social ties linking employed workers with the unemployed, underemployed, pensioners and most students. 'Differentiation' occurs along various axes. These include variation in employment status; the households of workers, for instance, being better off materially than those of partial workers and the unemployed; quality of housing, education and lifestyle; class identity; and capacity to mobilise for change. Gender and age are also important – in relation to family conflicts, as well as to popular culture and political activity. However, there are also important commonalities. Critically, a person's EC did not impact greatly on the kind of house in which they lived. Thus, many workers who received a regular income were living in shacks, while many unemployed people lived in better quality, brick-built housing. Moreover, a large majority of Sowetans, 67 per cent, lived in a household in which at least one adult aged eighteen or over was employed; a further 29 per cent were in households with somebody who was not unemployed (for example, pensioners, underemployed and students); and only 5 per cent lived in households in which all adults were fully unemployed. Most people in the last grouping were dependent on child support grants and/or the salary of somebody outside the household. Further, although there was some cultural separation between those with a salary and those without, church attendance, funerals and family rituals contributed to social cohesion. As Keke Motseke and Sibongile Mazibuko showed, there is some association between church denominations and Living Standards Measure (LSM) scores, but no sharp divisions.

We also investigated class identity. Ninety-three per cent of Sowetans recognised the existence of two or more classes. The dominant model consisted of some kind of lower, middle and upper class, so it was similar to the pattern found in most of the South African ethnographic literature. But a separate working class also exists in the minds of many Sowetans. We provided a choice of more than one identity, and 56 per cent of Sowetans claimed to be middle class, 43 per cent working class, 38 per cent lower class and 13 per cent upper (or top) class. Factor analysis showed that lower class was almost synonymous with 'poor', a class identity offered in the survey. There was a close association between the 'working class' label and working (in the sense of having a job); and most regularly employed workers considered themselves to be working class. People who claimed to be lower class and/or poor, tended to be more deprived than other Sowetans (in terms of EC, household possessions, education and recreational activity). The 'upper class' was understood to be 'those who have everything', although people who claimed this identity were not significantly better off than other Sowetans.

As self-identity, 'middle class' was ubiquitous, with two-thirds of Sowetans describing themselves as such. This was higher than we had anticipated, and reveals a very different notion of middle class to those available in academic literature (Ceruti 2011: 97). Having asked our question about class self-identity in English, we were able to discover that one reason for the high figure was 'mistranslation' from respondents' mother tongue. As Mosa Phadi and Owen Manda show, specific class concepts used in English do not exist in indigenous South African languages, and people were translating words that mean something approximating 'in the middle' into the English 'middle class'. That is, when people described themselves as 'middle class' they were conceiving themselves as living somewhere between those who were 'suffering' and those who had 'everything', so it is hardly surprising that so many people described themselves as 'middle class'. There were also other reasons for accepting a 'middle-class' label. It was defined in relation to peers, so even well-off people could consider themselves middle class; it was linked to self-respect, to upward mobility and aspirations (especially among young respondents); and it was regarded as normal, thus neither 'above' nor 'below' other people.

It was also revealed that the ways people practise class and talk about it in cultural terms is linked to economic well-being through 'affordability'. Kim Wale showed that when Sowetans look 'upwards' they tend to emphasis cultural and individual characteristics, and when they look 'down' they tend to stress economic considerations, such as unemployment. Linked with this, 'class' can be seen as something positive, because unlike 'race' it permits upward mobility. On the other hand, when poverty stunts mobility, class is connected with injustice, providing a basis for protest action.

However, our account is limited in place and time, so some caution is necessary. Moreover, our research has revealed three areas that would benefit from further empirical research. Firstly, the implication of the exodus to the suburbs is unclear. It is certainly possible that this leads to family and social separation that marks a new form of class division, but it might also be associated with new work-based solidarities. Secondly, if, as claimed, house prices and rentals are rising rapidly in Soweto, this could have a significant impact on social dynamics. Thirdly, households redistribute resources, but they are also a site of struggle over that redistribution, and it would be helpful to know how this works out in more detail.[2]

So, Soweto is a largely proletarian township, albeit one that is cut through by much variation. People with jobs are better off than those without, but there is a spectrum, and what one can afford is affected by a number of factors, including the ratio of income earners to non-income earners. Our research highlighted widespread awareness of class, and it is possible to make a distinction between the working class and lower class based on EC and deprivation. Yet, at the same time, most people regard themselves as middle class, and there is minimal stigmatisation of people regarded as poor.

Relationships to the means and ends of protest

But how does our account of a 'differentiated proletarian unity' square up with the realities of struggle in South Africa today? This is an especially important question given that our opening problem was about the class basis of divisions between unions and social movements/urban revolt. From the outset we should note that there is a clear divide between strikes and what has been termed the 'rebellion of the poor'.[3] Rather obviously, strikes involve regularly employed workers, and other township residents are excluded. By contrast, workers are marginal to the 'community protests' that are at the heart of the rebellion. Available evidence shows that people whom we would have categorised as unemployed, underemployed or pensioners undertake most of the organisation, but one also comes across teachers, pastors, the petty bourgeois and students. The fighting involves mostly young people, particularly unemployed youth, although school students often participate as well. As the historian and Western Cape activist, Martin Legassick, observed: 'There is a disjuncture between protests by employed workers and protests in the townships (by mainly casually employed workers and unemployed).' 'All are part of the working class', he says, adding that 'those in the township protests however tend to identify themselves as "the poorest of the poor"'. Elsewhere, people just talk about 'the poor'. This rift does not run along a fault line marked by the existence of a labour aristocracy or a minority underclass, but can be understood in terms of the kind of distinctions we have made in this book.

The contrast between workers and the poor is particularly significant because the level of strike action and community unrest is extremely high. Since 2005, South Africa may have lost more workdays through strike action per capita than any other country; certainly it is close to the top of that league. The South African economist, Mike Schussler (quoted in Vollgraaff 2011) put South Africa in first place for the years 2005–09, but he did not include Argentina, which the International Labour Organisation (2012a) positioned higher for 2006–08. In 2007, South Africa experienced its greatest number of strike days ever, and this figure was surpassed in 2010; with the fourth most in 2011 (Kelly 2012). Meanwhile, it is possible that South Africa has the highest level of ongoing urban revolt in the world.[4] The country's police recorded an average of two 'unrest-related gatherings' per day in the five years from 1 April 2004 to 31 March 2009, and 2.9 per day for the period from then until 5 March 2012 (Alexander 2012). In the six months to the end of June 2012, there were more protests than in any previous year.[5] Protests have occurred all over the country (including many in Soweto and neighbouring areas), with informal settlements particularly prominent. Using the erection and defence of barricades as an indicator, many of these protests amount to local insurrections, but action ranges from peaceful marches through to blockades of major highways and the torching of municipal buildings.

The distinction between workers and the poor can be amplified. When workers protest they strike against a boss (usually a capitalist) and demand something that she/he can deliver, often a pay increase, but when the poor protest it is usually against local municipalities, and they make different kinds of demands, mainly about the delivery of basic services (such as housing, water, electricity, toilets and roads).[6] Workers have built national unions. These have numerous organisers paid from subscriptions, they participate in time-consuming negotiations and legally protected strikes, and they often have substantial investments. Mass mobilisations of the poor have been uncoordinated and local, mostly ad hoc, and sometimes spontaneous. Organisers are few, and are either unpaid or funded by foreign donors; action is determined with little or no formality, enacted without delay and frequently illegal. The power of workers derives from their capacity to disrupt productive work. Extremely poor youth, in particular, have other sources of strength, including time to organise, the legitimacy to mobilise in the name of a community, the capacity to win backing from workers, the ability to destabilise local party politics and to mount dramatic protests that threaten the rule of the state. Further, immediate interests, narrowly conceived, may be different, so workers may resent expectations that they join a community protest by observing a stayaway strike that leads to loss of pay, or unemployed youth may demand that they, as locals, should be given jobs in preference to workers from another area.

This fissure has its own South African character, but it is not exceptional. For instance, Ira Katznelson (1982: 19), commenting on US history, distinguished between 'work and community based conflicts', concluding that 'the links between [them] . . . have been unusually tenuous'. He continued: 'Each kind of conflict has had its own separate vocabulary and set of institutions . . . Class, in short, has been lived and fought as a series of partial relationships.' In similar vein, Manuel Castells (1983: 268), writing about the massive urban movement that rocked Spain in the 1970s, distinguished between the labour movement and neighbourhood associations, demonstrating that the two 'fought separate battles, even if they often clashed with the same police and exchanged messages of solidarity'. Katznelson and Castells both highlight the different dynamics that separate work/labour from community/neighbourhood movements, and their model can be applied to South Africa. The social composition of community/neighbourhood/township movements is particularly varied, and what divides them from workers' movements is less the specificities of class and more the domain of contestation. This is not to say that class characteristics are inconsequential. Thus, the Madrid citizen movement, described by Castells (1983: 266), stretched across the city, incorporating people from different backgrounds, yet the 'working-class neighbourhoods' were the best organised and most-militant.

Frances Fox Piven and Richard Cloward (1979) were alive to the significance of domain *and* 'class' in their study of poor people's movements in the United States of America, providing an account that is particularly germane to our own analysis. They argue that 'it is the daily experience of people that shapes their grievances, establishes the measure of their demands, and points to the targets of their anger'. In contrast to workers, the unemployed, they say, 'do not and cannot strike, even when they perceive that those who own the factories and businesses are to blame for their troubles. Instead, they riot in the streets where they are forced to linger . . . and it is difficult to imagine them doing otherwise' (Piven and Cloward 1979: 23). Elsewhere, I have attempted to generalise this sentiment in a way that is pertinent to contemporary South Africa, proposing that what separates workers and the poor is *different relationships to the means and ends of protest* (Alexander and Pfaffe 2012). The implication is that the division is not about 'class' in any fundamental or antagonistic sense, but about capacities for action and achievement.

How well does the worker/poor dichotomy described above map onto the divisions of employment and identity we found in Soweto? It appears to be more like the representations of politics and relief found in Abraham Ortelius's maps from the sixteenth century than the latest Google satellite images. There is a lack of detail, proportions are wrong and the names are sometimes different, but the continents are recognisable and approximately in the correct relationship to one another. *The workers* are our 'regularly employed workers' and, from the perspective of people in Soweto, the regularly employed workers are the major component of the 'working class'. *The poor* are more of a mixed bag, and there can be a mismatch between ECs and the community domain (a problem that does not exist with worker and workplace).[7] 'The poor' includes the unemployed, the underemployed (although some may obtain an income outside the township, complicating their relationship with the community as a realm of struggle), students attending township schools, nearly all those defined as pensioners and others not in the labour force.

There is a considerable overlap between 'workers' and 'working class', but the fit is looser between 'the poor' and people whom Sowetans regard as 'lower class'. In part this contrast arises from 'working class' being widely defined by 'employment', which has fairly sharp edges, whereas 'lower class' is associated with concepts such as 'suffering', which are imprecise and subjective. In addition, workers are far more likely to have been involved in collective action as 'workers' than the poor are as 'the poor', which is rarely the banner under which protests are mobilised.[8] Further, in contrast to 'working class', which has more claimants than those we included as regularly employed workers, the 'lower class' is smaller than those we are calling 'the poor'. At a basic level, we can assume that some people are describing themselves as working class on the grounds that they 'work', rather than because they are regularly employed as workers, while some of 'the poor' regard themselves as 'middle class', for reasons suggested earlier. More significantly, the worker/poor distinction is doing a different job to 'working class'/'lower class'. The first is an attempt to depict particular struggles in a way that creates possibilities for comparative analysis. The second is derived directly from popular distinctions. We can aim to achieve more than Ortelius, but we neither hope for nor desire a satellite image.

While one side of our Soweto analysis is about discrete ECs and distinct identities, the other emphasises commonalities (the 'proletarian unity'). To what extent is this second dimension present at the level of struggle? The occurrence of work 'stayaways' linked to protests is largely unreported, but probably common.[9] However, in the cases we know about, the communities initiated the action, rather than workers. When we investigated a 2009 insurrection in detail, we interviewed workers who were highly critical of the youths (referred to as 'comrades') who attempted to stop them from going to work (Alexander and Pfaffe 2012). Workers complained that if they were absent they would lose pay, and possibly their job. We also came across another response. As a municipal worker put it: 'We are members of the community, so of course we support the demands.' The overall effect was one of half-hearted solidarity. However, in a nearby town we came across a community march to a workers' picket line, and workers' solidarity with a community protest (Alexander 2010b: 36). Moreover, in a recent 'workers' household survey' it was found that nearly 25 per cent of the members of the Congress of South African Trade Unions (COSATU) had participated in a service delivery protest in the four years prior to the survey (COSATU 2012: 55). While the picture is somewhat mixed, one should add that, in terms of collective mobilisation, open conflict between workers and the poor is exceptional.

Flipping back to the months after the Soweto uprising in 1976, and to the 1980s, we see similar processes, with workers sometimes reluctant to back community protests, though oftentimes joining huge stayaways (Hirson 1979; Seekings 2000). From 1984 worker militants began taking the lead in initiating solidarity action, sometimes organising strikes with the support of 'comrades'. There were also examples of community boycotts in support of workers' strikes. Eventually, in 1988, COSATU joined with the township-based United Democratic Front in establishing the Mass Democratic Movement, which forced the regime to engage in negotiations for a new South Africa. An important dynamic in 1976 and the 1980s, as today, is that workers were often a generation removed from the unemployed youth activists who spearheaded township resistance. They were separate from, yet sympathised, with their 'children'.

The example of the 1980s remains relevant today, not only because it is sometimes evoked by militants, but also because of what it represents theoretically and politically. We wrote earlier about domains of struggle, and of differences in relationships to the means and ends or protest. The 1980s highlight ways in which the domains begin to overlap and even, momentarily, coincide; a situation in which the *'ends' coalesce and the 'means' turn from being divided action into a division of labour in a common struggle.* Glimpses of this phenomenon exist in the present, not only in the examples given, but also in the reality that when protests succeed in improving services or removing corrupt officials, the whole community benefits, and when strikes lead to higher pay for workers, it is to the advantage of their families and to others around them (through small purchases, partial employment, donations, and so forth). To borrow Wright's (1978: 88) distinction, workers and the poor are separated by immediate not fundamental 'class interests'.

Some theoretical pointers

Any researcher interested in class as a socio-economic phenomenon has to grapple with the problem of categorisation. Their choice will be determined by the purpose of their enquiry (that is, theoretical predisposition) and the time and place they want to understand (in other words, context). Our major concern was with ending poverty, inequality and oppression through the creation of a new society based on democratic control over the economy, in short socialism, and we have tried to make sense of a context, South Africa in the early twenty-first century, that is characterised by historically high levels of socio-economic inequality, very high unemployment and considerable labour and urban unrest.

The two scholars whose concerns come closest to our own are Erik Olin Wright (especially in his 1978 book), on grounds of predisposition, and Jeremy Seekings (especially in his 2005 book with Nicoli Nattrass), because of context. Attuned to the problems of class in late capitalism, Wright's addition of 'control' to the matrix of class analysis was important. He was making sense of the United States, where the middle class was very substantial and posed theoretical problems, and not unreasonably he retained a focus on direct relations of production. But how should one deal with people whose relationship to production is indirect? Concerned with fundamental class interests, he adopted various strategies (Wright 1978; see also Wright 2000): linking dependents to the main breadwinner in a household (that is, 'mediation'); classifying the temporarily unemployed, pensioners and students according to 'trajectory'; and including the long-term unemployed as a separate 'underclass'. But this approach was not designed to cope with a context such as the one considered in this book, where unemployment and poverty, rather than the middle class, pose the major theoretical challenge. Concerned mainly with labour market disadvantage, and influenced by John Goldthorpe as well as Wright, Seekings and Nattrass extended the principle of mediation to include all members of a household, doing this on the basis of 'dominance'. They, too, were left with an underclass – this time defined as people living in households in which nobody was employed and where income from other sources was negligible.[10]

Our own approach was different to both of these. Our emphasis on socialism as self-emancipation meant that we required categories that allowed us to investigate relationships between an objective marker rooted in production and aspects of both reproduction and subjectivity. We did this using a marker, our ECs, that included categories with indirect as well as direct relationships to production. Given that only about 27 per cent of South Africa's working-age population has a formal job, and workers engage in struggles separately from 'the poor', this was important. Individuals could be used as a unit of analysis, and everybody could be treated equally, rather than including some as an appendage (integrated through 'mediation' or 'trajectory'). This suited our orientation. The categories grew out of the data but they also had a theoretical basis, with this derived mainly from Wright (hence Marx). The distinction between the two groupings outside the labour force (students and pensioners, etc.) was partly about 'trajectory' (preparing for exploitation versus no longer available for exploitation), although also about income and capacity to mobilise. The partial workers and subsistence self-employed were our own invention. A significant implication of our approach is that there was no theoretical imperative to have an 'underclass', so we could investigate whether, empirically, such a category was meaningful. From our own research, Wright's distinction between long-term and temporary unemployment held little relevance, and, significantly, it was not utilised by Seekings and Nattrass. Equally, though, we found Seekings and Nattrass' argument about social capital unconvincing. In practice, the distinction that mattered to people – particularly in terms of identity and mobilisation – was one between 'the working class' and 'the poor'. This approach to class categorisation is our first contribution.

Our second innovation was to assume that individuals' might have more than one class identity, and in practice this proved correct. In part, this situation arises from the reality that 'class' names two distinct experiences: hierarchies around income and neighbourhood (commonly three classes) and work relationships (mostly dichotomous). The hierarchical model is more widely held in Soweto, and while 'working class' was the second most popular identity, it was a single identity for only 3 per cent of Sowetans. More broadly, about 38 per cent of the population claimed one class label, 36 per cent went for two, and 19 per cent selected three or more. The existence of dual, indeed multiple, class identities, may go some way to explaining the kind of 'class ambivalence' that, reportedly, exists in the United Kingdom and the United States. Moreover, the meanings attached to class identity varies according to setting, with, as we have seen, a shift from cultural to economic dimensions as one moves from 'looking up' to 'looking down'. This finding adds weight to the possibility – discerned in some British literature – that the way class is defined and practised is determined, in part, by class location, with the higher middle class becoming cultural omnivores and the lower working class emphasising economic disadvantage.

A further advance was to theorise the popular term 'afford', probably the most important concept that people deployed in distinguishing between the lower, middle and upper classes. It is not, though, a crude materialist term, and equivalent indigenous words also refer to being able to look after oneself, thus independent, and with this comes self-respect and pride. However, the significance of affordability is that it provides a bridge between important cultural aspects of class – including food, clothes, education and recreational activity – and the capacity to pay for such things. 'Capacity to pay' is, in turn, affected by a number of factors, including the ratio of income earners to non-income earners in a household and the cost of housing. But it is determined, in particular, by the kinds of jobs people do, and thus, ultimately, by relationships to production. Differences in class identity, income and employment category – all associated with 'affordability' – underline the significance of 'differentiation' in Soweto. However, there is still fluidity among what we have termed the proletariat, and, as with Bennett et al.'s study of Britain, it would be a mistake to talk of homologies in the strong way in which Bourdieu uses the term.

A parallel distinction exists at the level of action, where there is separation between workers' strikes and the rebellions of the poor. There are similar divisions between labour and community struggles in other countries, and one can explain the phenomenon in terms of 'different relationships to the means and ends of protest'. These differences reflect the fact that workers and the poor can have different short-term goals. However, the evidence presented throughout this book shows that there are also many commonalities, and the longer-term interests of workers and the poor are the same. This unity of interests is sometimes manifested in united action, although at present this is the exception rather than the rule.

This study was framed by questions that were cast within a Marxist paradigm, and our conclusions connect with two elements of Marxism. The first of these concerns the importance of 'reproduction', by which I mean consumption, and the dynamics of family life, and interventions of the state in the realm of welfare payments, basic services, schools, health care and so forth. For people without regular work – that is, the majority of adults in South Africa – the household plays a major role in survival (accompanied sometimes by contestation over who gets the spoils). Reproduction also entered our account through the significance of education, housing and consumer durables as markers of class; migration in and out of Soweto; lack of segregation of housing by employment category; and networks of support associated with extended families, neighbours and churches. Further, community protests are mostly about 'reproduction' issues: shelter; water that is free and clean; provision of sewage, drainage and refuse removal so that people do not fall needlessly ill; and about electricity that keeps people warm, prevents their food from rotting in hot weather, allows children to study at night, and reduces boredom by providing power for television sets. In general, our argument that both workers and the poor are part of the proletariat would be very much weaker if reproduction had not been firmly located within our terms of reference.

Karl Marx and Frederick Engels recognised the importance of reproduction for a materialist understanding of history (although it received limited attention, understandably given their political and intellectual priorities). However, Engels, in one particularly important intervention in *The Housing Question*, reached the conclusion that housing problems were a product of the capitalist mode of production and that they could be resolved only through its abolition.[11] David Harvey (2012: 18) points to the contemporary relevance of this pamphlet, using it to emphasise the importance of urban resistance in class struggles against capitalism. Our book highlights the way in which 'affordability' provides a link between class identity, reproduction and class structure, and community protests draw attention to growing inequality matched by pro-capitalist economic policy. My assessment, then, is that if one's analysis of class is anchored in emancipation it is necessary to grapple with reproduction as well as relationships to production.

The second element of Marxism on which I wish to comment is Marx's (1867) description of the 'surplus population' in *Capital, Volume 1*. This has a remarkably strong resonance in contemporary South Africa. Firstly, when there is some expansion in the formal capitalist economy, workers are recruited from the surplus population (from the ranks of the unemployed and underemployed). We found this occurring in highly localised upturns, when a business requires a workforce at short-notice (for example, for construction or a catering contract). Secondly, impoverished people from the rural areas (sometimes outside South Africa's border) migrate into the cities where, initially, they swell the ranks of the reserve army (those without any work). Thirdly, when an employer no longer requires workers, their survival becomes the responsibility of family members – they are thrown onto the shoulders 'of the working-class and lower middle class' (Marx 1954: 603). Fourthly, for Marx (1954: 602–3), there was the 'lowest sediment' – which included old people, the disabled, orphans, etc. – which 'dwells in the sphere of pauperism', and thus had the potential to access 'poor relief'. While, the vocabulary, intentions and details are different, the old-age pension, disability allowance and child benefit play a similar role in today's South Africa. Fifthly, it is clear that South Africa's huge surplus population places pressures on employed workers who are poorly skilled and/or unorganised, pushing them to toe the line and accept lower wages. Yet there are differences. I have not been able to track down figures for late nineteenth-century Britain, but it is unlikely that the surplus population reached the proportion that now exists in South Africa, where, in Soweto, 56 per cent of the adult population consisted of people who were unemployed, underemployed or pensioners.

Marx's (1954: 592–3) description was bedded into a theory that concluded:

> . . . [T]he surplus population becomes . . . a lever of capitalistic accumulation, nay, a condition of existence of the capitalist mode of production . . . it creates a mass of human material always ready for exploitation . . . The whole form of movement of modern industry depends . . . upon the constant transformation of a part of the labouring population into unemployed or half-employed hands.

These formulations could be read as evidence that the surplus population was functional for capitalism, and, indeed this was true to a degree. But Marx's account was rooted in the contradiction that, alongside the development of capitalism, the number of people unemployed would increase relative to the number of those who were employed.[12] Dead labour (in the form of machines) replaces living labour! Workers lives became more 'precarious' (Marx's 1954: 599), increasing the importance of organising against the capitalists. There is a useful parallel here. As we have seen, a generation of Marxists regarded 'race' as functional to the needs of capitalism. But there was always a contradiction, and apartheid became increasingly dysfunctional. The ability of rural production to sustain the capitalist workforce declined; workers came under pressure to improve wages to support their families (many unemployed); black people began to unite against a system that oppressed them all (on the basis of race); and, eventually, apartheid was dismantled.

The present moment not only bares similarities to this history, it is also, in some respects, its extension. If there is a limitation in Marx's account it is that he did not anticipate that the poor might develop their own collective agency. But this does not challenge the fundamentals of Marx's diagnosis or his prescription. He argued that workers and the surplus population were part of the same class and advocated united organisation. Thus, as he put it, 'overwork of the employed *part of the working-class* swells the ranks of the reserve'. Then, a few pages later, he advocates 'regular co-operation between employed and unemployed', through '[t]rades Unions, etc. . . . in order to destroy or to weaken the ruinous effects of [capitalist production] on *their class*' (Marx 1954: 599; my emphasis).

So, then, capitalism involves the development of different relationships to production and a tendency for the surplus population to grow. This produces a differentiated proletarian unity, that is, a set of different experiences combined with common interests that have the potential to unite workers and the poor. There is ample evidence for this in our Soweto findings. The way these differences and commonalities come together in households and communities assists us to comprehend actual class identities. On the one hand, class identifications involve a mingling of practices rooted in production and reproduction, with multiple class identities common and working-class identity existing alongside the dominant three-class model. Notions of affordability tie identity to disposable income and relationships to production. On the other hand, the size of the unemployed population (and of the surplus population more broadly) and the wretchedness of its existence and low expectations of obtaining a job, contribute to the mobilisation of the poor, independently of the working class. That is, the growth of the surplus population has been a major factor leading to massive urban unrest. Despite this expansion and the emergence of the rebellion, the unemployed and the employed are no less part of the same class. The former are still largely dependent on the latter, although now the actions of the former may bring benefits to the latter (improved services in particular). Similarly, successful mobilisation by workers can bring advantages to the poor.

Implications

But how does this relate to our opening concern with inequality in the global arena? The possibility that the reserve army could expand more rapidly than the active army of labour would have seemed remote until recently. The ability to plunder colonies, the expansion of overseas markets, the emigration of part of the surplus population, the importation of cheap labour from rural areas (often across borders), the physical destruction of competitors' means of production and massive state intervention have all, in their different ways, transferred the problem. Development has been uneven, but it has allowed the more dynamic sectors of the world economy to expand the system as a whole. However, as 2012 draws to an end, it is far from certain that this process will continue. A crisis has engulfed the Eurozone, the world's largest economy, and for the moment political leaders seem to have no way out. With rates of unemployment topping 20 per cent in some European countries, South Africa's experience becomes commensurately more important.

In South Africa there are now clear signs of popular disillusionment with and within the ruling bloc. This is reflected in protests and strikes, in discontent with corruption, and in splits within the ANC. In other countries, too, one discerns a rising level of anger about austerity measures, which impoverish the proletariat while retaining capitalism intact. However, there is nothing pre-ordained about the employed and unemployed engaging in common struggle. This is dependent on a range of subjective factors, not least the emergence of alternative politics. Nevertheless, Marx's conclusion remains valid. Workers and the poor would benefit from 'regular co-operation in order to destroy or to weaken the ruinous effects of [capitalist production]'.

Notes

1. Our use of the term 'proletarian' rather than 'working class' is tactical and semantic. As we have seen, in popular South African usage, the term 'working class' is associated with doing paid work, and we wanted a word that conveyed something broader; that is, to use the old Marxist formulation, those 'who have nothing to sell but their labour power'. An alternative approach would be to contest the meaning of the concept 'working class'. See Chapter 4.
2. In a recent study of family life in two KwaZulu-Natal townships, Sarah Mosoetsa (2011: 59) argued that 'there is more conflict than co-operation in poor households', and she showed that households can expand or decline in relation to available resources, with, for instance, destitute members of an extended family attaching themselves to a

household with a stable income (Mosoetsa 2011: 26). Similarly, Jeremy Seekings (2008b) showed that many South African households are 'fluid' (in that individuals move between households), and also that some are 'porous' (in that individuals may be members of more than one 'household' at the same time).

3. Unless stated otherwise, this section draws on material available in Alexander (2010); Alexander and Pfaffe (2012); Runciman, Ngwane and Alexander (2012); and Alexander (forthcoming). There is a growing body of literature on the rebellion. Important contributions include Booysen (2011); Ngwane (2011); Pfaffe (2011); Von Holdt et al. (2011); Booysen (2012); Dawson (2012); and Langa and Von Holdt (forthcoming).
4. China has also experienced a high level of localised protest in recent years, but my reading of literature available in English showed that, on a per capita basis, there were more protests in South Africa (Alexander 2012). The size and intensity of mobilisation in the Middle East has been greater, but the spread and number of insurrectionary protests in South Africa is almost certainly higher.
5. This statement is based on data from the South African Local Government Research Centre, South African Broadcasting Corporation's News Research, Municipal IQ and SA Media. I am grateful to researchers from the first two organisations for making their detailed data available. Information from Municipal IQ is available on that organisation's website.
6. There have also been demands for jobs to be provided by mines (and additionally by municipalities). However, it is difficult to mount a fight over employment at a local level, and the importance of unemployment as a factor propelling the movement is inadequately reflected in the issues being raised.
7. We are not defining 'the poor' in relation to a particular income (that is, poverty per se).
8. See Hirschsohn (2011: 17). The level of participation in strikes will have increased since our survey and since the one analysed by Hirschsohn (conducted in 2008/9). Community protests vary in size from under 100 to more than 10 000 people (Alexander forthcoming), but most are at the lower end of the range. When organisations of the poor give themselves a name, it normally includes a geographical referent (for example, Soweto) and identities such as 'residents', 'crisis [committee]', 'civic', 'youth', 'unemployed people' and 'landless people', rather than 'poor'.
9. In a survey of protest leaders conducted at the 'Academics and activists workshop on the rebellion of the poor' held at the University of Johannesburg on 18 June 2011, out of 22 protests 10 included a stayaway and 12 did not.
10. See Chapters 1 and 3 for less simplified renditions of the approaches offered by Wright, and Seekings and Nattrass.
11. The substance of the pamphlet is a series of articles published in 1872 and 1873, but the preface to the second edition, published in 1887, is particularly interesting.
12. Ceruti (2011) examines the dialectical nature of Marx's theory, placing it in the context of our Soweto research.

Appendix 1

Methodology

Peter Alexander and Claire Ceruti

There were three basic phases to the core research. The centrepiece was a large quantitative survey. This was preceded and followed by qualitative research.

Preliminary qualitative research

The main component of the first phase was 51 informal, exploratory interviews (referred to as discussions in the book) with different people around the township. These provided insights and indicative quotes that we have drawn on in various parts of the book. However, our main aim was to discover how people verbalise 'class' and, in particular, learn the terms they use to define specific class-related categories. More broadly, we were trying to work out how we might best organise our questionnaire and how we should formulate the questions.

Respondents were not selected through a predetermined, systematic procedure. Rather, we combined convenience sampling with the selection of different social contexts that would afford the opportunity to witness and hear different meanings of 'class'. We began at the Soweto Wine Festival, which was marketed explicitly as a middle-class affair, and then moved to the Soweto Beer Festival, which provided a down-to-earth foil. A demonstration about water cut-offs, a march against unemployment organised by the unions, an African National Congress (ANC) election rally and a shop stewards' meeting all offered environments influenced by organisation and politics. Each drew together different socio-economic layers of Sowetans and different combinations of such layers – unemployed people and pensioners at the first, employed people at the union events, and a mixture of the two at the election rally. We stationed ourselves outside a mid-range shopping centre (where consumption might be uppermost in people's minds) and also talked to people selling things on the roadside, to volunteer road workers and to a couple petrol pump attendants at their places of work. We interviewed a few old women at their homes, which was useful for historical knowledge. Our dragnet also captured five workers who came from the East Rand, whose views, interestingly, were similar to those expressed by Sowetans.

These discussions usually started with two questions: 'What class are you? How do you know?' They developed conversationally from there, with respondents allowed to influence the subsequent direction of the interview. If respondents asked what we meant by the word 'class' we spent some time exploring what the word meant to them. The shortest interview was about five minutes, more than half were between 20 and 40 minutes, and several lasted an hour or more. The interviews were conducted by one black man and one white woman; the former in a range of languages and the latter in English. Both researchers received similar responses, including minimal reference to 'race' – something that surprised us.

The first phase also included familiarisation with the many areas of Soweto, each of which developed in a different period and had different kinds of shelter (including hostels, shacks and various kinds of houses), different degrees of socio-economic well-being, and a predominance of different languages (although a form of township isiZulu is now the lingua franca). We photographed buildings and people (including respondents, where possible), so that we could further consider connections between class identity, visible markers of 'taste', such as clothing and disposition, and social context. We used these photographs, and others from the wine and beer festivals, in a group discussion with ten people, who comprised a mixture of men and women who were in their twenties and early thirties. A lively three-hour debate highlighted strong interest in 'class' and sharpened our understanding of many subtleties of class distinction that had emerged in interviews.

Early on, we interviewed two key informants, both of whom were trained sociologists, as well as activists with considerable experience of articulating 'class' in a variety of media, languages and contexts. One was Blade Nzimande, general secretary of the South African Communist Party and now also Minister of Higher Education, and the other was Trevor Ngwane, chair of the Soweto Electricity Crisis Committee (SECC), one of the country's most influential social movements.

Quantitative research

Our survey had three aims, which could not have been accomplished through pure qualitative work. Firstly, we wanted to establish a picture of Soweto's class structure – that is, those aspects of class that are not necessarily conscious or subjective – in a manner that allowed comparison with similar studies, but without binding ourselves to predetermined definitions of class. Secondly, we sought to establish a picture of class identities, whether expressed in terms of named categories or practised as culture or reflected in opinions. Finally, we intended to establish the extent to which class identity mapped onto class structure.

Population

The survey covered a coherent geographical space that most locals call 'Soweto'. It included the following census-defined units: Soweto, Diepkloof and Meadowlands, which are regarded as 'main places', and Noordgesig, a 'sub-place' within the Johannesburg main place. Under apartheid, the first three of these were designated as black residential areas. Noordgesig is a small, formerly 'coloured' area that adjoins Soweto on its northern boundary. In addition, we included new areas that abut these units, but which did not exist at the time of the 2001 Census, the most significant being Braamfischerville. We excluded Eldorado Park, formerly a coloured area, which has not historically been regarded as part of Soweto. Because we were interested in opinions, it was decided to use individuals as the unit of analysis. We included all residents over the age of sixteen years.

Questionnaire

The questionnaire included more than 200 questions (although 'skip' clauses meant that no respondent was expected to answer all of these). It covered demographics, opinions, identities, lifestyle (including possessions and cultural activities), employment, households and support, plus a section for fieldworkers to record their observations of accommodation. We decided not to ask about HIV/AIDS and to estimate income through the proxy of the Living Standards Measure (LSM). Our questions were predicated on research problems and a critical reading of relevant literature that are discussed in Chapter 1. We designed the questionnaire so it could to be administered in about 45 minutes by a trained fieldworker. It was conceived and printed in English (but a professional isiZulu translation was also available). A copy of this questionnaire may be obtained from the website of the South African Research Chair in Social Change.

Multi-stage sampling

We aimed at the efficient use of resources, while also ensuring that, following a weighting exercise, the sample represented the population. To this end, our sampling involved the selection of, firstly, clusters; secondly, stands within a cluster; and, finally, an individual living on a stand.

SELECTION OF CLUSTERS

Each of the clusters was located within one of the small-area layers (SALs) demarcated for the 2001 Census. SALs, the smallest unit for which basic demographic data was made publicly available, were often the same as an enumerator area, but when such an area had a population of less than 500 it was merged with another to form an SAL. In terms of age and type of housing, individual SALs are mostly homogeneous. Operating on the assumption that population change had been even across Soweto, we could then use the 2001 population data to select the required number of SALs (and thence clusters). This was achieved according to the method described by Crankshaw, Welch and Butcher (2001). All SALs were listed with their population and cumulative population. We divided the total population by the required number of SALs in order to produce the sampling interval. Then, using a randomly selected starting point, we applied the sampling interval for the cumulative populations to selected SALs (see Photograph A1.1). So, if the sampling interval was 10 000 and one started with the SAL that includes person number 8 000, the selected SALs would be those with persons numbered 18 000, 28 000 and so on. In this way, the probability of selecting a particular SAL is proportionate to the size of its population, and a basic condition for representivity is fulfilled.

However, it was necessary to vary this procedure in two ways. Firstly, there were some areas in which the assumption of even population growth was erroneous. Comparing aerial photographs for 2001 and 2006, it was apparent that, while the removal of some informal (that is, shack) settlements had reduced the population of certain SALs, the building of new housing had, in effect, created novel ones. For the former cases, we approximated the reduction and applied this to the appropriate SAL. In the latter, we demarcated our own proto-SALs, roughly estimating populations in the first instance and adjusting these once we had more accurate information.

The second modification involved stratification of the sample. This was done to avoid under-representing those SALs in which there might be an extreme gender imbalance, or a high proportion of particularly poor or relatively well-off people. For this exercise we utilised a variety of SAL-level census data, including housing type, access to basic services, and ownership of goods such as computers and refrigerators. In practice, we worked with four categories: hostels, informal settlements, well-off areas and a large residual grouping we called 'mixed'.

SELECTION OF STANDS

For each of the selected SALs we chose fifteen 'stands' (that is, a single unit of property). In most cases this was achieved using SAL plans produced for the 2001

Census. We took a random starting point and chose each fifth stand to the left of it. The numbers fifteen and five were determined partly on grounds of efficiency – which was important given limited resources and a desire to obtain a sample large enough to capture variations within the population. Sampling every fifth stand minimised distortions that might arise from taking individuals who lived closer, and some SALs would have been too small to survey more than fifteen stands. Since each stand had an equal chance of selection, the objective of drawing a representative sample was sustained.

For new areas we adapted the procedure using the 2006 aerial photographs. Each roof was treated as if it were a stand, a reasonable assumption given the nature of these areas (which consisted of single-building houses). A similar procedure was adopted with informal settlements laid out in a formal manner. With the hostels and three of the informal settlements, it was necessary to undertake the selection of 'stands' in the field. Researchers, rather than fieldworkers, undertook this task. With hostels, we treated a room as a stand, and in informal settlements we used an individual shack in the same way. In one informal settlement where population density was especially high, we extended the sampling interval to every tenth shack.

A 'stand' was used as the unit of enquiry rather than a house or household, because in some parts of Soweto it is common to find shacks and/or extensions to a main house that may be rented to people who are not members of the household. It was important not to under-represent these individuals.

SELECTION OF INDIVIDUALS

Fieldworkers selected individuals using a Kish grid. The procedure was simple. Firstly, they listed everyone on the stand aged sixteen years or over. Then, they randomly selected the respondent using the grid, which had rows defined by the number of adults on the stand and columns defined by the last two digits in the number on the questionnaire. In the survey, no substitution was permitted. Where necessary, fieldworkers had to make appointments to meet the selected individuals, and they often had to go back on numerous occasions until this particular person was interviewed. In some cases, more than ten visits were made before giving up. This method reduced bias derived from substitution, which excludes individuals who are less likely to be at home (for example, workers). Because there were varying numbers of people on each stand, the chance of selecting a particular individual on a two-person stand was ten times as great as selecting a particular individual on a 20-person stand. As a consequence, it was necessary to undertake post-survey weighting in order to extrapolate from the survey to the population.

Data collection

RECRUITMENT OF FIELDWORKERS

We recruited 50 fieldworkers: 45 were University of Johannesburg (UJ) students and five came from the SECC, a community-based organisation. The students ranged from final-year undergraduates to master's students; most had a background in sociology; 41 had a South African vernacular language as their mother tongue; and the majority had grown up in a township. Nine of these were appointed as supervisors, each responsible for a team and a car. The SECC fieldworkers provided invaluable knowledge of local communities across Soweto. In addition, two students worked with one of the researchers on the selection of stands, the storage of data, the monitoring of completion and payments to fieldworkers.

FIELDWORKER TRAINING

Supervisors received four days of training, which included discussion of the project and its theoretical foundations, and other fieldworkers received two. The supervisors piloted the questionnaire with friends and family, which assisted with shortening its length. All fieldworkers participated in a discussion about the translation of particular terms, and then, following this and a field trial, final modifications were made to the questionnaire.

FIELDWORK PROBLEMS AND SOLUTIONS

It quickly became apparent that the pace of data collection was too slow to reach the desired sample size within the time allowed by our funding, thus compromising the representivity of our sample. On the third day we called a temporary halt to activities. After some negotiation the funder agreed to provide additional support; we changed the payment structure so that each fieldworker was expected to complete an agreed number of questionnaires per day; we created an extra team; and we brought in an additional researcher, giving us two fieldwork managers (each responsible for five teams). All changes were discussed with the fieldworkers and agreed by them. We also reduced the number of clusters from an initial 188 to 170. Because this was done at a very early stage, the re-selection of SALs could be accomplished without significantly undermining our sampling. The appointment of a second manager made it possible to check a higher proportion of samples.

The rejection rate was low (see Table A1.1). However, fieldworkers reported occasional difficulties, mainly with individuals who were physically or mentally ill. Mortality also posed a problem – selected individuals would be in mourning; others would be away attending funerals; and funeral processions would physically hinder movement across Soweto on Saturdays. Fieldworkers were taken aback by the extent of poverty that existed, and some gave apples and other small presents to needy individuals. There were two assaults on fieldworkers, both minor. Access to hostels and some informal settlements had to be negotiated with community leaders. In one hostel, there was serious faction fighting and fieldwork had to be delayed for several days.

RESPONSE RATE

In the last two days of the fieldwork, some colleagues assisted with data collection and fieldworkers put in extra hours to ensure that every stand was visited at least twice. After the three-week period set aside for the survey, one of the researchers undertook a 'mopping-up' exercise tracking down respondents hitherto recorded as 'could not trace'. In the end, the response rate was slightly over 90 per cent (see Table A1.1). There was no cluster in which the response rate was less than 80 per cent (that is, twelve completed questionnaires). Some SALs were oversampled in error, requiring an additional post-survey weighting exercise. This occurred because our survey maps were marked with two extra calling points – in case selected stands were associated with churches, shops or other buildings where nobody lived – and miscommunication lead to fieldworkers sampling at some of these extra locations. In total 2 340 questionnaires were completed.

Table A1.1 Response rate.

	Number	Percentage of full sample
Full sample	2 550	100.0
Oversample	*40*	*(1.6)*
Interviews completed minus oversample	2 300	90.2
Could not trace respondent	128	5.0
Rejection	116	4.5
Partially completed	6	0.2

We doubt that the response rate would have been as high in wealthier areas of Johannesburg, where people would have regarded their time as being more precious and where tighter security would have imposed physical barriers. A low level of employment among the population ensured that a high proportion of our respondents were available to answer questions, even without an appointment. Further, fieldworkers reported a general eagerness among respondents to have their opinions noted. The diligence and perseverance of fieldworkers, and their commitment to the project also contributed to success. Overall, we felt our decision to undertake our own fieldwork, rather than hire a survey company, was vindicated.

Post-survey considerations

DATA CAPTURE AND ANALYSIS

Data capture was organised through UJ's Statkon unit. It was analysed by team members using SPSS. Analysis involved a considerable amount of recoding, in particular to produce our occupational categories and LSM scores. This is discussed elsewhere in the book.

WEIGHTING

Analysis required two kinds of weighting. Firstly, we had to adjust for oversampling. Each respondent in an oversampled cluster was given a value arrived at by dividing fifteen by the actual number of completed questionnaires in the cluster. Secondly, we had to make allowance for stand size. For this we simply multiplied each answer by the number of adults living on the stand. In some instances there was an interaction between stand size and some other variable, for example, employment, and where this was significant it has been raised in the text.

GENDER

Extrapolating from our survey, it seemed that 59 per cent of the population were women and 41 per cent were men. It was unlikely that this was the actual gender balance in Soweto, and we undertook a follow-up survey to check the position. For this we selected 800 stands, randomly selected from our original sample. This time the aim was simply that of accurately determining the sex of everybody aged sixteen and over living on a stand, so it did not matter who on the stand was interviewed, and, indeed, it was even permissible to interview knowledgeable individuals on a neighbouring stand if necessary. A single team led by one of the researchers conducted this fieldwork. Because of the simplicity of the survey and the fact that results were not dependent on the presence of a selected individual, the response rate was exceptionally high – over 99.4 per cent. Extrapolating from our results, we concluded that the population comprises 52 per cent women and 48 per cent men.

These figures might be compared with those from the 2001 Census which showed that for the same areas we surveyed (that is, Soweto, Diepkloof, Meadowlands and Noordgesig) the population comprised 51 per cent women and 49 per cent men. However, our special survey probably provided a more accurate reflection of the true position at the time of our main survey. Firstly, it was closer in time – only seven months later. Secondly, we were content that our method of sampling, the limited purpose of special survey, the quality of the team conducting the survey and the excellent response rate ensured a high level of accuracy.

Given the difference between our main survey and the special gender survey, we compared the two sets of data for each stand researched on both occasions. There were discrepancies, of course, but there was no particular pattern – some teams had recorded the adults on a stand more accurately than others, but all had made occasional errors, and the difference between teams was marginal. The problem was general. Importantly, the researcher who undertook the mopping-up exercise said that nearly all the people he interviewed were men, so it is likely that this would also have been true of those who remained in the 'could not trace' list at the end. We also found that men were more likely to be in one-person households, thus they tended to be more difficult to locate than women.

Our procedure for dealing with the under-representation of men in the sample was to undertake our analysis for females and males both separately and together. Where the results were very similar, we have published one table; where there was a significant difference, we have presented them separately.

Further qualitative research

This had two main components: semi-structured interviews (referred to as the qualitative interviews in the book) and a documentary film. These were preceded by report-backs on quantitative findings to the SECC and the Meadowlands branch of the ANC. These provided opportunities for gathering additional information and developing new questions.

Qualitative survey

QUESTIONS

The new research addressed three concerns. Firstly, we wished to learn more about the way in which people derived their conception of class, including their own class identity. By this stage, we had discovered that a middle-class identity was ubiquitous, and wanted to know why. Secondly, we needed to plot work histories. For instance, had the people we recorded as 'unemployed' always been unemployed, or had they moved in and out of some kind of work? Thirdly, our occupational categories had 'grown out of the data', which enabled us to categorise the respondents, but did not give us the information we needed about their households. The new survey was aimed at filling these lacunae. These issues related to our interest in understanding the relationship between workers and those who were either unemployed or underemployed.

RESEARCH DESIGN

We had ended the quantitative survey by asking people if they would be prepared to answer further questions, and, if so, to provide us with contact information. We now drew on this data to develop a purposive sample. There was no intention to make a representative selection (as with the gender survey). The aim was to have a good spread of respondents in terms of gender, age, occupational category and housing type. If the person chosen was not available, a suitable substitute was found. Moreover, we were keen to interview two contrasting individuals from the same household, as this would assist us to make assessments about the salience of gender and generation differences, especially with regard to class identity. To this end, we selected 50 respondents with the intention of interviewing a total of 100 people. In practice, we recorded 72 interviews, all of which were undertaken in the language the respondent preferred. Six experienced fieldworkers conducted this research. The interview schedule that we used is available from the South African Research Chair in Social Change.

Research documentary

Finally, we made a 50-minute research documentary. This addressed the question: 'Why do 66 per cent of Sowetans consider themselves middle class?' Once again, sampling started with a list of the respondents from the quantitative survey who were available for further interviews. From this we selected 25 individuals, with these reflecting a range of employment categories. Lastly, we chose five diverse respondents who would be comfortable in front of a camera. The ensuing film, *Phakathi: Soweto's Middling Class,* was made together with two young filmmakers involved with Eyelight Productions. Data collected as part of this project was used in a dissertation prepared by the researcher who was mainly responsible for the film (Phadi 2010b). At the time of writing, the film had been shown publicly in South Africa, Germany, the United Kingdom, the United States, Russia and India. On each occasion it provoked a lively response, and discussions deepened our comparative understanding of 'class'.

Additional research

In addition to the research described above, we utilised a variety of other sources and modes of analysis. For example, we made extensive use of official census and labour force data; our interpretation of language draws, to some degree, on etymology; and the chapter on religion involved an additional round of semi-structured interviews. This is described in the relevant chapters.

Appendix 2

Sowetans in the Classifying Soweto survey

Claire Ceruti

This appendix outlines demographics that are not directly relevant to other chapters. Some of the data is useful background for the information in the chapters and all of it should be of broader interest for and beyond issues of class. This appendix sketches the distribution of Sowetans as they appear in our data regarding age, gender, education, language, politics and opinions. All the data is from the 2006 Classifying Soweto survey, except where otherwise indicated.

Age

Of Sowetans who were older than fifteen years at the time of the survey, more than half were younger than 36, and half again of those (a quarter of all Sowetans) were younger than 26. Table A2.1 shows the age distribution of Sowetans. To put this distribution into context, the life expectancy of black South Africans is approximately 48 years. The spread of ages in Soweto was very similar to the spread of ages in the census taken five years before our survey, and in both the Johannesburg Metro and Gauteng, the province in which Johannesburg is located, in the year following our survey (see Table A2.1).

In later sections we will see how age interacts with education and political opinions.

Women and men

Women slightly outnumber men in Soweto, making up 52 per cent of Sowetans in our special gender survey (see Appendix 1). This is similar to the 51 per cent in Stats SA figures for the Johannesburg Metro and Gauteng Province in 2007. The Classifying Soweto survey itself found a much smaller proportion of men, although if most of our missing respondents were men, the proportions are more like the

Table A2.1 Age distribution in Soweto in 2006, South Africa in 2001, and Johannesburg and Gauteng in 2007.

Age	Percentage of Sowetans, 2006	Percentage of South Africans, 2001	Percentage of Johannesburg Metro, 2007	Percentage of Gauteng, 2007
Older than 60	10	8.5	7	7
45–60	17	16.6	17	18
36–45	18	20.5	21	21
26–35	28	29.2	30	30
16–26	28	25.3	25	25
Total	101	100.1	100	101

Sources: Column 2 – Classifying Soweto survey 2006; Column 3 – Author's calculations from Stats SA Census 2001; Columns 4 and 5 – Author's calculations from Stats SA Community Survey 2007.

gender survey. The over-representation of women in our sample matters less when comparing women and men, because the comparison relies on relative proportion.

While women in Soweto were not significantly poorer than men of a similar age, as measured by the Living Standards Measure (LSM) scale (explained in Chapter 3), there were significant differences in the kinds of households in which they lived. Women tended to live in bigger households than men (a mean of 5.3 humans for women, compared to 4.6 for men) and a woman was less likely to live in a household in which she was the only adult. Women also tended to live in households with more children (a mean of 1.6 children in women respondents' households, compared to 1.1 children in men's). Also women tended to have had more children than men of a similar age (a mean of 2.2 children for women, 1.7 for men).

Women were marginally more likely than men to report that they depended on income from someone else (effect strength 0.10), and slightly more likely than men to depend on government funding – which includes old age pensions and child support grants – as their main means of income (effect strength 0.16). These differences did not hold, however, for men and women in the age category 16–26 years. Women were more likely than men to be unemployed with no alternative economic activity. (We use 'employed' and 'unemployed' here in the sense used in our employment categories developed in Chapter 4.) Employed women were marginally more likely than employed men to live in a household with a domestic worker, and employed women were more likely than other women to live in a household with a domestic worker. There were no similar differences among men. Women were moderately less likely than men to personally own a car, whether employed or otherwise (effect strength 0.25).

Households

Living in a nuclear family was a minority experience for Sowetans. In our survey, 44 per cent of adult Sowetans lived in households with three or more adults and a child or children. (We do not know what proportion of households this is, because our sampling unit was individuals.) A further 20 per cent of adult Sowetans lived in households with three or more adults, but no children. They were among the total 36 per cent who lived in households with no children. This left only 14 per cent of Sowetans in nuclear-like households with two adults and children. These two adults were not necessarily in a relationship. Less than 5 per cent of adult Sowetans lived in households composed of a child or children and a lone adult. Women make up the majority of such households.

Education

Students in South Africa normally complete secondary school at the age of eighteen years if they pass every year of their schooling. Fewer than half of Sowetans older than nineteen at the time of our survey had completed secondary school, while close to one-fifth of Sowetans older than sixteen had not gone beyond primary school. Overall, this nevertheless makes Sowetans better educated than their black counterparts in the whole city and the province, with proportions of matriculants similar to the proportions of white matriculants in the province (Table A2.2). However, Sowetans' continued disadvantage becomes apparent regarding primary and higher education. Table A2.2 shows that, like black people in the surrounding areas, fewer than 3 per cent had completed a degree. Not shown, only 5 per cent of Sowetans had even attended a university. By contrast, only 3 per cent of white people in Gauteng did not continue beyond primary school, while 18 per cent – almost one-fifth – had graduated from a university. Some of this disparity may be because graduates from Soweto generally achieve the means to move out of the township, but the disparity at the primary end of the educational scale also implies a legacy of unequal education.

Sowetan women and men of similar ages have similar levels of education, but women in all age categories were more likely than men to have completed a post-school diploma than to have *attended* university after school (effect strength 0.14). However, from 26 years and older, women from Soweto who attended university were strongly more likely to have *completed* a degree than men of a similar age who attended university (effect strength >0.40).

Figure A2.1 illustrates that younger Sowetans had received more education than had older Sowetans. This probably reflects the expansion of secondary

Table A2.2 Levels of education of Sowetans compared with the city and the province.

People aged 20 years and above	Percentage of Sowetans, 2006	Percentage of black people in Johannesburg Metro, 2007	Percentage of black people in Gauteng, 2007	Percentage of white people in Gauteng, 2007
No formal education	3	5	4	0
Primary school (Std 5/ Grade 7)	13	20	19	2
Some secondary (including O-levels)	37	44	45	29
Matric/Grade 12/A-levels	32	20	21	33
Post-school diploma (not university)	5	5	5	14
University degree	2	2	2	10
Postgraduate	0	1	1	8
Any other	2	3	3	3

Sources: Classifying Soweto survey 2006; Stats SA Community Survey 2007.

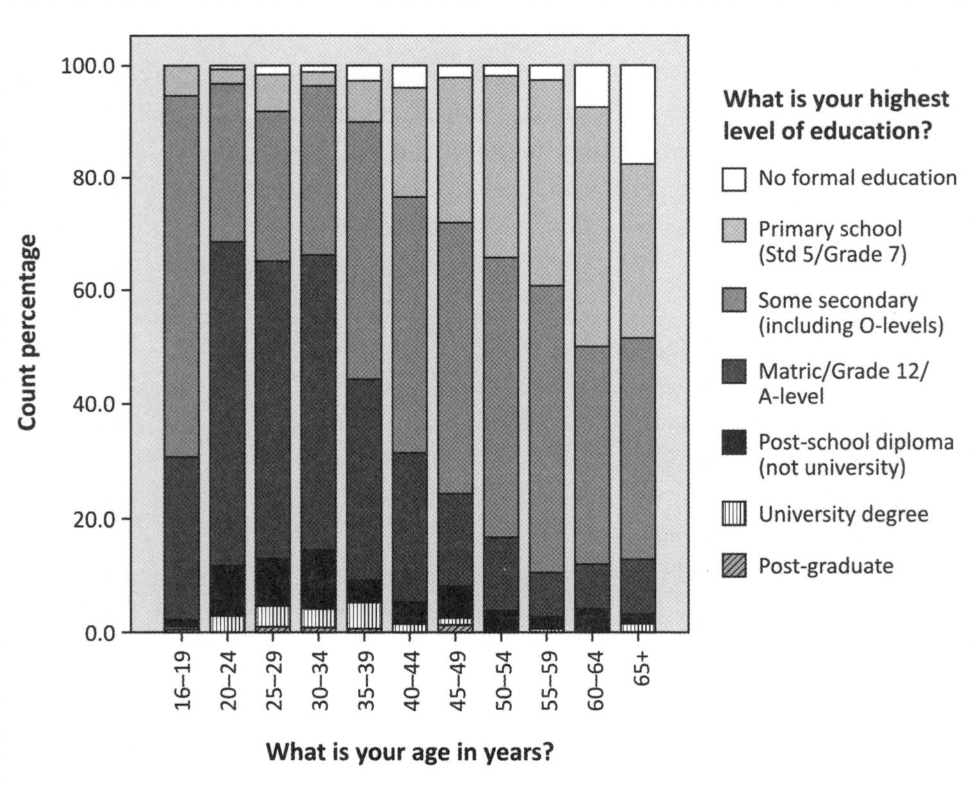

Figure A2.1 Education by age group among Sowetans aged sixteen years and older.
Source: Classifying Soweto survey 2006.

education in the early 1970s, plus the removal of racial restrictions on tertiary education at the end of the apartheid era.

The majority of Sowetans live in a household with a child who attends school. Just more than half live in a household with a child or children who attend school in Soweto. Some 13 per cent lived in a household with a child or children who attended school in a formerly white suburb and 5 per cent were in households that had children in school in another town. Sending children to suburban schools is understood to ensure a better education. The LSM score of households with children at school in the suburbs or in another town was substantially higher (<0.6640) than that of households whose children attended school in Soweto (0.4774), which makes sense, because suburban schools often charge higher fees than township schools.

Levels of education were associated with higher living standards. It is, of course, unclear whether more education leads to better living standards or whether better living standards 'cause' more education. Sowetans with any qualification beyond matric had a mean LSM score of 0.8466, while those who had completed high school had a score of 0.3673 and those who had completed only primary school had a mean LSM score of 0.0421. Sowetans with any education beyond completing secondary school were more likely to have been to a movie in the month before the survey (effect strength 0.174) and to have had a braai (barbeque) in the month before the survey (effect strength 0.107), more likely to have bought a birthday present for an adult in the month before the survey (effect strength 0.123), and more likely to personally own a car (effect strength 0.169). They were also more likely to speak English with their friends (effect strength 0.115). Sowetans with any kind of further education were less likely to live in an unrenovated council house (effect strength 0.106) and more likely to live in a bond house (effect strength 0.128). Figure A2.2 illustrates the spread of different housing types according to the level of education.

Finally, Figure A2.3 illustrates the interaction between education levels and the employment categories outlined in Chapter 4.

Language

The single most widely spoken language in Soweto was isiZulu, claimed by 39 per cent of Sowetans as their mother tongue, with Sesotho and Setswana each spoken as a mother tongue by close to a fifth. SiSwati, isiNdebele, Tshivenda, Shangaan, Afrikaans and English, each spoken by fewer than 5 per cent of Sowetans, are combined into 'other' in Figure A2.4.

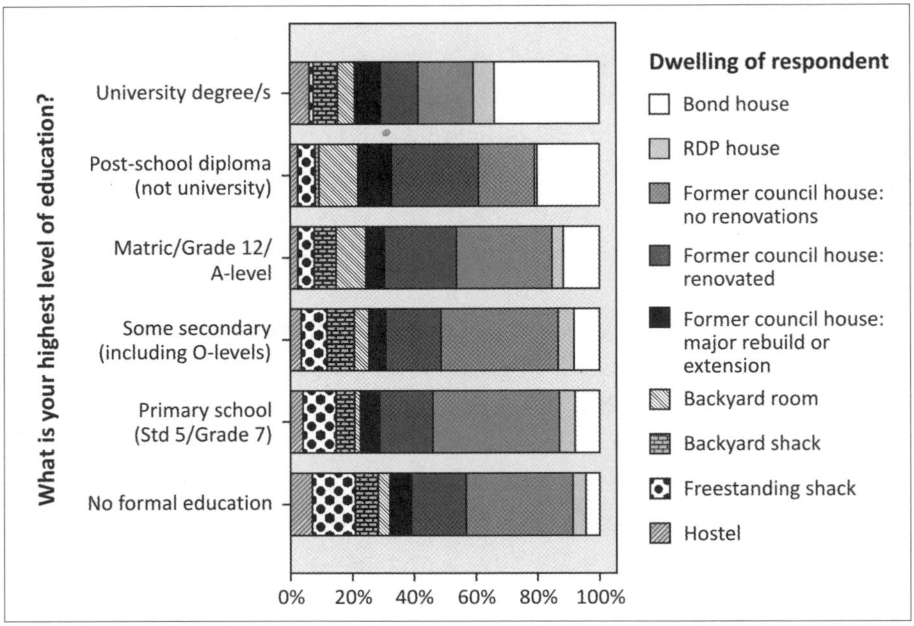

Figure A2.2 Education levels and dwelling type.
Source: Classifying Soweto survey 2006.

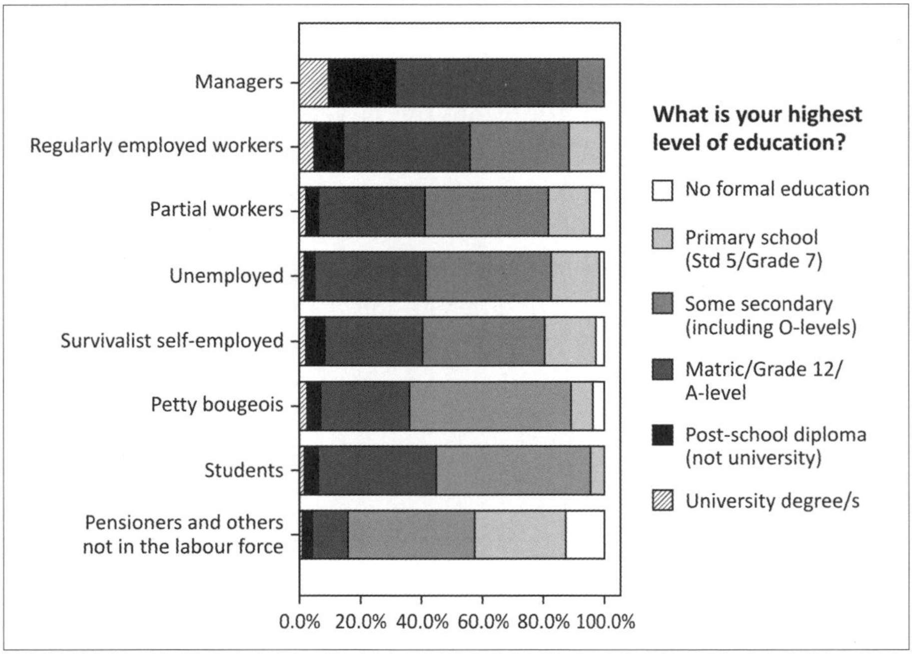

Figure A2.3 Education levels and employment categories.
Source: Classifying Soweto survey 2006.

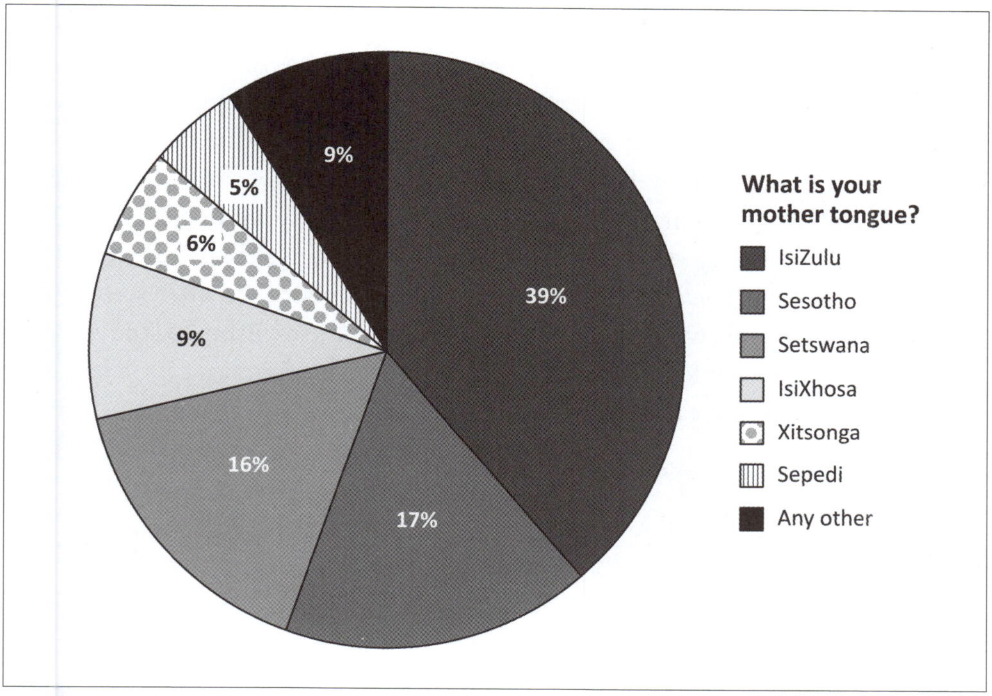

Figure A2.4 Mother tongue of Sowetans, 2006.
Source: Classifying Soweto survey 2006.

Exactly comparable data are not available from Stats SA for 2007, but the 2001 Census suggests that these proportions were similar five years before our survey, and that the proportion of isiZulu speakers in Soweto was somewhat greater than the proportion of isiZulu speakers among black Africans in the country and the province.

Table A2.3 Mother tongue in South Africa, Gauteng and Soweto, 2001.

	Percentage of black Africans in the whole country	Percentage of black Africans in Gauteng	Percentage of Sowetans
IsiZulu, isiNdebele	32.1	31.7	39.6
IsiXhosa	22.3	10.2	9.5
Sesotho	10.0	17.7	16.8
Setswana	10.3	11.3	14.4
All others	25.3	29.0	19.6

Source: Stats SA 2001 Census.

Just more than half of Sowetans spoke their mother tongue with their friends. About 10 per cent spoke English with their friends – taken by some to be a marker of being middle class – and 13 per cent spoke *tsotsitaal* – literally, gangsters language – which is a township dialect that mixes slang and several South African languages. Figure A2.5 illustrates how both age and levels of education influence languages spoken with friends. Younger people were more likely to speak English or *tsotsitaal* with their friends, but the proportions using these languages were even more pronounced among Sowetans of any age group with education after school. This may be because people would generally have to leave the township to study beyond school, where they would be more exposed to the need to communicate in languages other than their mother tongue.

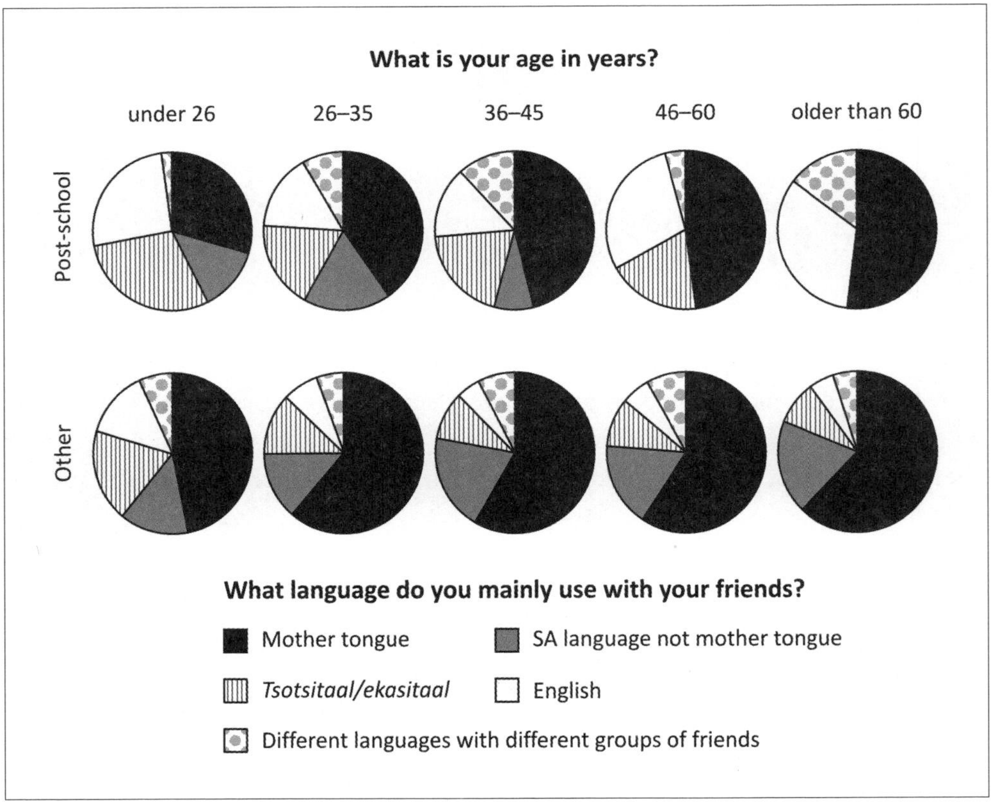

Figure A2.5 Language spoken with friends, age and level of education.

Source: Classifying Soweto survey 2006.

Politics and opinions

Soweto became world famous for the 1976 Soweto uprising, and some of its residents remain organised. For example, during our fieldwork, we witnessed several marches organised by the Soweto Electricity Crisis Committee (SECC), a group formed to oppose cut-offs of electricity and water for non-payment, which later extended its concerns to include evictions. While SECC membership is drawn from the sorts of people who would generally call themselves lower class in Soweto, members of the SECC tended to identify themselves as working class in our interviews, even when unemployed, indicating the importance of organisations in shaping class identities.[1]

On the whole, Sowetans were *mostly* not members of organisations in 2006. Approximately 65 per cent of Sowetans *supported* a political party, but only 13 per cent of those – about 8 per cent of all Sowetans – were *members* of a party. Members of a party were significantly older on average (mean age 44 years) than supporters (mean age 38 years).

Table A2.4 and Figure A2.6 show that in 2006 the African National Congress (ANC) had the largest support among political parties at the time of the survey – 59 per cent of Sowetans. However, they also show that nearly a third of Sowetans said that they did not support any political party.

Table A2.4 Support for political parties in Soweto (first choice party).

Which political party do you support?	Percentage of Sowetans
ANC	59
Explicitly does not support any party	27
Inkatha Freedom Party (IFP)	2
ANC Youth League	1
African Christian Democratic Party (ACDP)	1
Democratic Alliance (DA)	0
All other parties	2
Total	93
Did not answer/missing respondent	7

Source: Classifying Soweto survey 2006. Percentages rounded off.

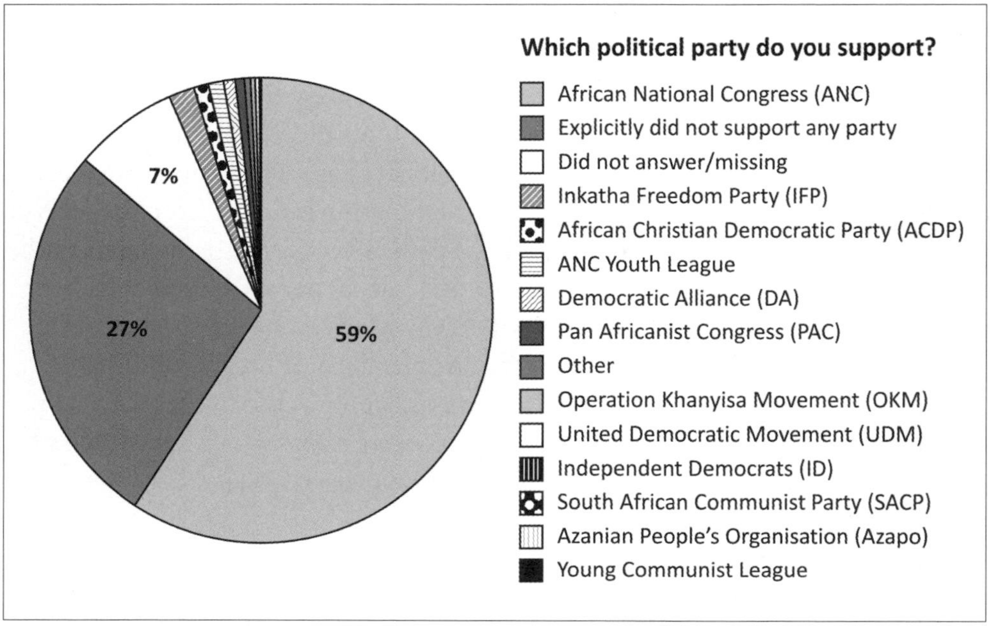

Figure A2.6 Sowetans' support for political parties.
Source: Classifying Soweto survey 2006.

Again, age affects support for political parties. The means plot in Figure A2.7 suggests that it had been easier for younger people to break from political parties that emerged from liberation movements in favour of abstention from party support, or support for the Democratic Alliance (DA) or the former Independent Democrats. However, this trend was complicated by the comparatively advanced average age of supporters of the Operation Khanyisa Movement (OKM), a left opposition to the ANC, and the United Democratic Movement (UDM), which broke from the ANC after 1994 under the leadership of former Bantustan army commander, Bantu Holomisa. The OKM supporters' age probably reflects the organisation's origins in organising against the cut-offs of water and electricity. Its support, therefore, tended to be among people who were old enough to be taking responsibility for their households, but who did not earn well enough to cover the bills – in particular, pensioners.

A third – 35 per cent – of Sowetans reported that they had 'talked about politics' in the week before the survey and another 9 per cent had talked about politics within the previous month, while 36 per cent said that they had never talked about politics. About two-thirds (60 per cent) said they had voted in the previous local

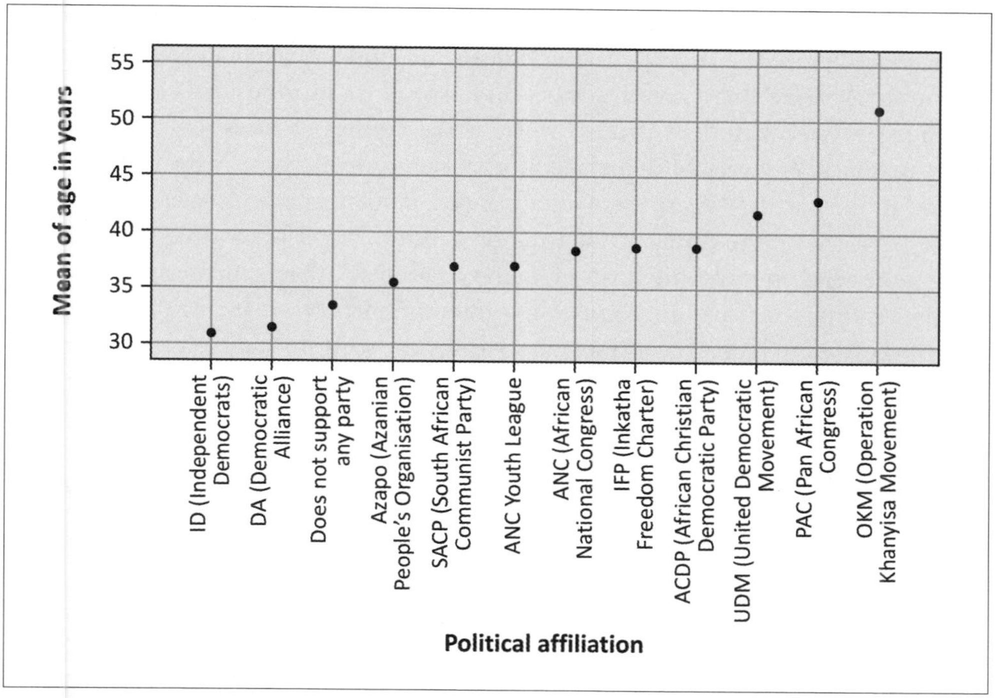

Figure A2.7 Age and political affiliation.
Source: Classifying Soweto survey 2006.

government elections and 45 per cent reported that they had attended a public meeting. An important minority has been more active still: 20 per cent said they had been on a march or demonstration and 20 per cent said they had been on strike. It is not surprising that there is an association among the last three of these activities, with the strongest association being between 'striking' and 'marching and demonstrating' (effect strength 0.442).

Age affected participation in these activities. The mean age of voters was significantly higher than the mean age of non-voters (42 years compared to 29), and this pattern remains for each of the political parties and among people who expressed no allegiance to a party. Strikers and people who had been to a public meeting were also, on average, older than people who had never been on strike, but these activities are less age polarised than voters and non-voters, at 38/36 years and 38/35 years, respectively. However, there is hardly an age difference between people who had marched or demonstrated and people who had not (37 and 36 years, respectively).

Of those who said they had been on strike, half of those had done so within the seven years before the survey, that is, since 2000, and a quarter in the year before the survey. 'Strike' here is not always understood in an industrial sense – people occasionally talk of student strikes or use 'strike' to mean a mass stayaway, such as those in the later years of apartheid. Forty per cent of those who had been on 'strike' in the past five years were unemployed, students or pensioners. We do not know what they were doing at the time of striking, but it is possible that some of them were referring to some form of 'delivery protest' (that is, protests demanding the provision of services and houses by government). Nevertheless, a substantial part of these were industrial strikers: a strike in the security industry at the time of our survey shows up clearly in our data, as do strikes among retail workers in 2005. The year 2000 marked a low point in industrial strikes, but from then until 2007 the level of strikes increased steadily (Ceruti 2008: 319).

Only 9 per cent of all Sowetans were members of a trade union, but 27 per cent of *employed* Sowetans were members of a trade union. This included Sowetans employed in partial work (see Chapter 4 for definition). Finally, approximately 15 per cent of Sowetans were involved in some kind of community organisation, although these may be the kind driven by government as much as self-organised. The single biggest category was community policing forums, which made up 20 per cent of those who were members of a community organisation, followed by self-help associations (12 per cent). The South African National Civic Organisation, formed around 'community issues' during apartheid, and the SECC each claimed 5 per cent of Sowetans who were members of community organisations. Once again, people involved in community organisations were, on average, older than people who were not. This may reflect not only different experiences historically, but also the likelihood that people generally acquire more responsibility for households as they grow older and therefore were more likely to get involved in organisations that take up issues of concern to householders.

In short, there was a sizeable interest in politics, but only a minority were organised. Men were slightly more likely to have been on strike (effect strength 0.1), but then they are also more likely to be employed. They were no more likely to have attended a public meeting. The *mean* age of people who had attended a public meeting was a little higher (39 years) than for those who had not (36 years), but mean age is no different for strikers and demonstrators compared to non-strikers and non-demonstrators. There was little difference between the have-been-active minority and the inactive majority on most of the twenty opinion questions in our survey (see Table A2.5). They differed on two of our questions: people who had been on strike or attended a public meeting were more likely to agree with the statement 'black empowerment is only enriching the few' (effect strength 0.1) and voters were more likely to agree with the statement 'we are suffering' (effect strength 0.1).

Table A2.5 Sowetans' opinions.

I am going to read you a statement. You tell me how much you agree or disagree.	**Strongly agree (%)**	**Agree (%)**	**Neutral (%)**	**Disagree (%)**	**Strongly disagree (%)**	**No answer/ don't know/ do not understand (%)**
e-Soweto siyafana ('we are all the same in Soweto').	5	25	4	53	15	2
A man's word should be final in a marriage.	13	32	5	37	13	1
Things were better under apartheid.	6	23	8	41	21	2
It is unfair when a manager who drives a BMW complains when a worker using a taxi comes five minutes late to work.	12	49	6	24	7	2
If one works hard enough, anyone can get rich.	14	44	5	30	6	1
We are suffering.	25	46	7	18	3	1
Jacob Zuma should be the next president.	26	33	7	16	12	7
Nurses must be allowed to strike.	6	24	5	39	25	1
Black empowerment is only enriching a few.	15	45	8	16	5	11
Same-sex marriage should be allowed.	5	13	4	31	46	2
Taxation is too high.	19	47	9	14	3	8
COSATU (Congress of South African Trade Unions) should split from the ANC.	5	21	11	36	14	13
People who have work should not complain about their wages.	5	15	4	45	31	2
Social grants encourage laziness.	19	33	6	26	14	3
They are rich because we are poor.	12	38	10	22	5	12

Source: Classifying Soweto survey 2006.

In general, Sowetans' opinions exhibited a strong sense of inequality: 71 per cent agreed with the statement '[w]e are suffering'; 60 per cent agreed that black empowerment is only enriching a few; and 50 per cent agreed that '[t]hey are rich because we are poor'. Close to one-third agreed with the statement, '[t]hings were better under apartheid' (which is not so much an endorsement of racial rule, necessarily, as a slur on the new government's broken promises, often uttered by people who had declared themselves dissatisfied with their current circumstances in our interviews). Such statements tended to correlate with the 60 per cent support for Jacob Zuma, who was then just beginning his rise to the Presidency (Ceruti 2007). The growing political tensions in the alliance between the ruling party and the main trade union federation were reflected in the opinion, held by a quarter of Sowetans, that COSATU should split from the ANC. Yet alongside the sense of social injustice runs a belief in the possibility of individual achievement: 58 per cent agreed with the statement '[i]f one works hard enough, anyone can get rich' (more pronounced among younger respondents) and more than half – 52 per cent – felt that '[s]ocial grants encourage laziness'. Nevertheless, perceptions of wealth creation retain a class edge: when asked '[i]n a company, who creates profits?', 52 per cent of Sowetans said workers, 25 per cent mentioned capital or capitalists (managers, bosses, capital), 8 per cent said external forces (like customers or market forces) and the remainder thought it was some combination of these. In response to the question, 'how close do you feel to the unemployed', 74 per cent said 'very' and a further 14 per cent said 'slightly'. While only one-fifth of Sowetans agreed with the statement that '[p]eople who have work should not complain about their wages', the majority – 64 per cent – opposed nurses' right to strike.

On issues of gender and sexuality, Sowetans were quite conservative: nearly half – 45 per cent – agreed with the statement '[a] man's word should be final in a marriage'. Unsurprisingly, women were much less likely to hold this opinion than men. Older people and the most recent arrivals to Soweto, regardless of age, were more likely to agree with it. Only 18 per cent of Sowetans agreed that same sex marriage should be allowed, but younger people were more likely to support the statement. Eight per cent of Sowetans said they had experienced discrimination because of their sexual orientation, and therefore may be assumed to be gay/lesbian/bisexual. Men were slightly more likely to oppose same-sex marriage than women.

Conclusion

The data presented above should have enriched the reader's sense of Sowetans, while highlighting some of the ways in which gender, age, education, living standards and the like may interact with one another. Although the Classifying Soweto database was created with the aim of investigating class, this appendix has demonstrated its capacity to sketch many other dimensions of Sowetan life.

Note

1. See Alexander (2005) for the demographics of SECC activists shortly before the survey.

Bibliography

Abercrombie, N. and Urry, J. (1983). *Capital, Labour and the Middle Classes*. London: George Allen and Unwin.

Adler, G. and Steinberg, J. (eds). (2000). *From Comrades to Citizens: The South African Civics Movement and the Transition to Democracy*. London: Macmillan.

Alexander, N. (2009). 'Language politics in South Africa'. In S. Bekker, M. Dodds and M. Khosa (eds). *Shifting African Identities*. Pretoria: HSRC Press.

Alexander, P. (1999). 'Coal, control, and class experience in South Africa's Rand Revolt of 1922'. *Comparative Studies of South Asia, Africa and the Middle East* 19(1): 31–45.

———. (2000). *Workers, War and the Origins of Apartheid: Labour and Politics in South Africa, 1939–48*. Oxford: James Currey.

———. (2005). 'New social movements and leadership: Trevor Ngwane and the Soweto Electricity Crisis Committee'. In C. Barker and M. Tyldesley (eds). *Tenth International Conference on Alternative Futures and Popular Protest, Vol. 1*. Manchester: Manchester Metropolitan University Faculty of Humanities and Social Science.

———. (2006a). 'Globalisation and new social identities: A jigsaw puzzle from Johannesburg'. In P. Alexander, M. Dawson and M. Ichharam (eds). *Globalisation and New Identities: A View from the Middle*. Johannesburg: Jacana Media.

———. (2006b). 'Is there only one working class? Racial division and unemployment in South Africa'. Paper presented at the international seminar on What is the Working Class? International Institute of Social History, Amsterdam.

———. (2007). 'History, internationalism and intellectuals: The case of Harold Wolpe'. *Transformation* 63: 109–26.

———. (2010a). 'Class, subjectivity and parochialism: A reflection and an introduction'. *South African Review of Sociology* 41(3): 1–23.

———. (2010b). 'Rebellion of the poor: South Africa's service delivery protests – a preliminary analysis.' *Review of African Political Economy* 123: 25–40.

———. (2012). 'Protests and police statistics: Some commentary'. *Mail and Guardian*, 13 April.

———. (forthcoming). 'Barricades, ballots and experimentation: Making sense of the 2011 local government election with a social movement lens'. In M. Dawson and L. Sinwell (eds). *Contesting Transformation: Popular Resistance in Twenty-First Century South Africa*. London: Pluto Press.

Alexander, P. and Chan, A. (2004). 'Does China have an apartheid pass system?' *Journal of Ethnic and Migration Studies* 30(4): 609–29.

Alexander, P. and Pfaffe, P. (2011). 'South Africa's rebellion of the poor: Balfour and the relationship to means of protest'. Paper presented to the South African Research Chair in Social Change Concept and Evidence Workshop, University of Johannesburg, 2–4 July.

———. (2012). 'Social relationships to the means and ends of protest in South Africa's ongoing rebellion of the poor'. Manuscript available from first author.

Aliber, M. (2003). 'Chronic poverty in South Africa: Incidence, causes and policy'. *World Development* 31(3): 473–90.

Altman, M. (2003). 'The state of employment and unemployment in South Africa'. In J. Daniel, A. Habib and R. Southall (eds). *State of the Nation South Africa 2003–2004*. Cape Town: HSRC Press.

Ambler, K. (2011). 'Bargaining with grandma: The impact of the South African pension on household decision making'. Manuscript available from author (ambler@umich.edu).

American National Election Studies (2010). 'Respondents' social class, self-identification 1956–2008'. *ANES Guide to Public Opinion and Electoral Behaviour.* http://www.electionstudies.org (accessed 23 May 2011).

Amoako, S. (2012) 'Teachers' unions and politics in Ghana and South Africa, 1900–2010'. MA dissertation, University of Johannesburg.

Anderson, A. (2000a). 'Pentecostals and apartheid in South Africa during ninety years, 1908–1998'. University of Birmingham. http://www.ocms.ac.uk/docs/Allanpercent20Andersonpercent20lecture20041005.pdf_(accessed 18 September 2010).

———. (2000b). *Zion and Pentecost: The Spirituality and Experience of Pentecostal and Zionist/Apostolic Churches in South Africa.* Pretoria: UNISA Press.

Ballard, R., Habib, A. and Valodia, I. (eds). (2006). *Voices of Protest: Social Movements in Post-apartheid South Africa*. Pietermaritzburg: University of KwaZulu-Natal Press.

Banaji, J. (2010). *Theory as History: Essays on Modes of Production and Exploitation*. Chicago: Haymarket Books.

Barchiesi, F. (2005). 'Social citizenship and the transformations of wage labour in the making of post-apartheid South Africa, 1994–2001'. PhD dissertation, University of the Witwatersrand.

———. (2010). *Precarious Liberation: Workers, the State, and Contested Social Citizenship in Post-apartheid South Africa*. Albany and Pietermaritzburg: State University of New York Press and University of KwaZulu-Natal Press.

Barchiesi, F. and Kenny, B. (2002). 'From workshop to wasteland: De-industrialization and fragmentation of the black working class on the East Rand (South Africa) 1990–1999'. In B. Altena and M. van der Linden (eds). *De-industrialization: Social, Cultural, and Political Aspects*. Cambridge: Cambridge University Press.

Baskin, J. (1991). *Striking Back: A History of COSATU*. Johannesburg: Ravan Press.

Bayat, A. (1998). *Street Politics: Poor People's Movements in Iran*. Cairo: American University in Cairo Press.

Beall, J., Crankshaw, O. and Parnell, S. (2002a). 'Social differentiation and urban governance in greater Soweto: A case study of post-apartheid reconstruction'. http://eprints.lse.ac.uk/2933/ (accessed 20 May 2011).

———. (2002b). *Uniting a Divided City: Governance and Social Exclusion in Johannesburg*. London: Earthscan.

———. (2003). 'Social differentiation and urban governance in greater Soweto'. In R. Tomlinson et al. (eds). *Emerging Johannesburg: Perspectives on the Postapartheid City*. New York: Routledge.

Beavon, K. (2004). *Johannesburg: The Making and Shaping of the City*. Pretoria: UNISA Press.

Behal, R. and Van der Linden, M. (eds). (2007). *India's Labouring Poor*. New Delhi: Cambridge University Press.

Beinart, W., Delius, P. and Trapido, S. (eds). (1986). *Putting a Plough to the Ground: Accumulation and Dispossession in Rural South Africa, 1850–1930*. Johannesburg: Ravan Press.

Bennett, T. et al. (2009). *Culture, Class, Distinction*. London and New York: Routledge.

Bezuidenhout, A. and Fakir, K. (2006). 'Maria's burden: Contract cleaning and the crisis of social reproduction in post-apartheid South Africa'. *Antipode* 38(3): 462–85.

Bhorat, H. and Leibbrandt, M. (1996). 'Understanding unemployment: The relationship between the employed and the jobless'. In J. Baskin (ed.). *Against the Current: Labour and Economic Policy in South Africa*. Johannesburg: Ravan Press.

Biko, S. (2004). *I Write what I Like*. Alfred Stubbs (ed.). London: Bowerdean Press.

Bloomquist, K.L. (2001). *Classism as an Ecclesial Matter*. Geneva: Department of Theology and Religious Studies, Lutheran World Federation.

Bompani, B. (2006). 'Mandela mania: Mainline churches in post-apartheid South Africa'. *Third World Quarterly* 27: 1137–49. http://www.jstor.org/stable/417744 (accessed 30 November 2010).

———. (2008). 'African independent churches in post-apartheid South Africa: New political interpretations'. *Journal of Southern African Studies* 34(3): 665–7.

———. (2010). 'Religion and development from below: Independent Christianity in South Africa'. *Journal of Religion in Africa* 40: 307–30.

Bond, P. (2000). *Elite Transition: From Apartheid to Neoliberalism in South Africa*. London: Pluto Press.

———. (2002). 'Power to the people in South Africa: Operation Khanyisa! and the fight against electricity privatization'. *Multinational Monitor*, January/February: 20–2.

Bonner, P. (1982). 'The Transvaal Native Congress, 1917–1920: The radicalisation of the black petty bourgeoisie on the Rand'. In S. Marks and R. Rathbone (eds). *Industrialisation and Social Change in South Africa: African Class Formation, Culture, and Consciousness, 1870–1930*. Harlow: Longman.

Bonner, P. and Nieftagodien, N. (2008). *Alexandra: A History*. Johannesburg: Wits University Press.

Bonner, P. and Segal, L. (1998). *Soweto: A History*. Cape Town: Maskew Miller Longman.

Bottero, W. (2005). *Stratification: Social Division and Inequality*. London: Routledge.

Bourdieu, P. (1984). *Distinction: A Social Critique of the Judgement of Taste*. Trans. by R. Nice. Cambridge, Mass.: Harvard University Press.

———. (1986). *Distinction: A Social Critique of the Judgement of Taste*. Abingdon: Routledge, Taylor and Francis Group.

———. (1990). *In Other Words: Essays Towards a Reflexive Sociology*. Trans. by M. Adamson. Bristol: The Polity Press.

Booysen, S. (2011). *The African National Congress and the Regeneration of Political Power*. Johannesburg: Wits University Press.

———. (2012). '"The ballot and the brick" – enduring under duress'. In S. Booysen (ed.). *Local Elections in South Africa: Parties, People, Politics*. Bloemfontein: Sun Press.

Boyer, G.R. (2004). 'The evolution of unemployment relief in Great Britain'. *Journal of Interdisciplinary History* 34(3): 393–433.

Brandel-Syrier, M. (1971). *Reeftown Elite: A Study of Social Mobility in Modern African Community on the Reef*. London: Routledge and Kegan Paul.

Breckenridge, K. (2002). 'From hubris to chaos: The making of the *bewysburo* and the end of documentary government'. Paper presented to the Institute for Social and Economic Research, University of the Witwatersrand.

Breen, R. (2005). 'Foundations of a neo-Weberian class analysis'. In E.O. Wright (ed.). *Approaches to Class Analysis*. Cambridge: Cambridge University Press.

Breman, J. (2003). *The Labouring Poor in India*. New Delhi: Oxford University Press.

Brewer, J. (1986). *After Soweto: An Unfinished Journey*. Oxford: Clarendon Press.

Bryant, A. (1905). *A Zulu-English Dictionary with Notes on Pronunciation*. Durban: Mariannhill Mission Press.

Buhlungu, S. (2006a). 'Cosatu and the first ten years of democratic transition in South Africa'. In S. Buhlungu (ed.). *Trade Unions and Democracy: Cosatu Workers' Political Attitudes in South Africa*. Cape Town: HSRC Press.

———. (2006b). 'Upstarts or bearers of traditions? The Anti-Privatisation Forum of Gauteng'. In R. Ballard, A. Habib and I. Valodia (eds). *Voices of Protest: Social Movements in Post-apartheid South Africa*. Pietermaritzburg: University of KwaZulu-Natal Press.

Bundy, C. (1979). *The Rise and Fall of the South African Peasantry*. Berkeley, CA: University of California Press.

Bureau of Democracy, Human Rights and Labour. (2008). 'South Africa's Population by Religion'. International Religious Freedom Report. Washington, DC: Bureau of Democracy, Human Rights and Labour, US Department of State. http://www.pards.org/infreports.html (accessed 29 November 2010).

Byrne, D. (2006). *Social Exclusion*. Milton Keynes: Open University Press.

Callinicos, A. (1988). *South Africa: Between Reform and Revolution*. London: Bookmarks.

———. (2006). 'What is the revolutionary subject today?' Paper presented at the international seminar on What is the Working Class? International Institute of Social History, Amsterdam.

CASE. (1998). *Determining Our Own Development: A Community-based Socio-economic Profile of Alexandra*. Report prepared for the CFBN Foundation, Johannesburg.

Castells, M. (1983). *The City and the Grassroots: A Cross-Cultural Theory of Urban Social Movements*. London: Edward Arnold.

CDE (Centre for Development and Enterprise). (2011). *A Fresh Look at Unemployment*. Johannesburg: CDE.

Ceruti, C. (2007). 'South Africa: Rebirth of a mass movement?' *International Socialism Journal* 116: 19–24.

———. (2008). 'Striking against a politically explosive background'. In P. Alexander, C. Ceruti and B. Kenny (eds). *Comprehending Class: Working Papers on Research in Soweto and the East Rand*. Centre for Sociological Research, University of Johannesburg.

———. (2011). 'The hidden element in the 2010 public-sector strike in South Africa'. *Review of African Political Economy* 38(127): 151–7.

———. (forthcoming). 'Unfolding contradictions in the "Zuma movement": The alliance of the public sector strikes of 2007 and 2011'. In M. Dawson and L. Sinwell (eds). *Contesting Transformation: Problematising Resistance in Post-apartheid South Africa*. London: Pluto Press.

Ceruti, C. and Phadi, M. (2008). 'What class identities are built from: Perceptions of class in Soweto: Qualitative and quantitative data'. Unpublished paper.

Chan, C.K. (2010). 'Class struggle in China: Case studies of migrant worker strikes in the Pearl River Delta'. *South African Review of Sociology* 41(3): 61–80.

Chan, T.W. and Goldthorpe, J. (2010). 'Social status and cultural consumption'. In T.W. Chan (ed.). *Social Status and Cultural Consumption*. Cambridge: Cambridge University Press.

Christopher, A.J. (1994). *The Atlas of Apartheid*. Johannesburg: Wits University Press.

Clogg, C.C. (1979). *Measuring Underemployment: Demographic Indicators for the United States*. New York: Academic Press.

Cobley, A. (1990). *Class and Consciousness: The Black Petty Bourgeoisie in South Africa, 1924 to 1950*. Westport, CT: Greenwood Press.

Cockburn, C. (1977). *The Local State: Management of Cities and People*. London: Pluto Press.

Colenso, J.W. (1905). *Zulu–English Dictionary*. Natal: Vause, Slatter.

COSATU (Congress of South African Trade Unions). (2012). *Workers Survey*. Johannesburg: COSATU.

Crankshaw, O. (1986). 'Theories of class and the African "middle class" in South Africa, 1969–1983'. *Africa Perspective* 1(1 and 2): 3–33.

———. (1993). 'On the doorstep of management: Upward mobility of African workers in the metal industry and its implications for trade union organisation'. *South African Sociological Review* 6(1): 1–18.

———. (1997). *Race, Class and the Changing Division of Labour under Apartheid*. London: Routledge.

———. (2005). 'Class, race and residence in black Johannesburg, 1923–1970'. *Journal of Historical Sociology* 18(4): 356–93.

———. (2008). 'Race, space and the post-Fordist spatial order of Johannesburg'. *Urban Studies* 45(8): 1692–711.

Crankshaw, O., Gilbert, A. and Morris, A. (2000). 'Backyard Soweto'. *International Journal of Urban and Regional Research* 24(4): 841–57.
Crankshaw, O., Welch, M. and Butcher, S. (2001). 'GIS technology and survey sampling methods: The Khayelitsha/Mitchell's Plain 2000 survey'. *Social Dynamics* 27(2): 79–103.
Crompton, R. (2008). *Class and Stratification*. Bristol: The Polity Press.
Crompton, R. and Scott. J. (2000). 'Introduction: The state of class analysis'. In R. Crompton et al. (eds). *Renewing Class Analysis.* Oxford: Blackwell.
CSS (Central Statistical Service). (1993). *October Household Survey 1992*. Pretoria: CSS.
Czegledy, A.P. (2008). 'A new Christianity for a new South Africa: Charismatic Christians and the post-apartheid order'. *Journal of Religion in Africa* 38: 284–311.
Dalla Costa, R. (1971). 'Women and the subversion of the community'. http://www.generation-online.org/p/fpdallacosta2.htm (accessed 27 August 2011).
Davies, R.H. (1973). 'The white working class in South Africa'. *New Left Review* 82: 40–59.
———. (1979). *Capital, State and White Labour in South Africa 1900–1960: An Historical Materialist Analysis of Class Formation and Class Relations*. Brighton: Harvester Press.
Davies, R.J. (1981). The spatial formation of the South African city. *GeoJournal Supplement* 2: 59–72.
Davis, M. (2006). *Planet of Slums*. London and New York: Verso.
Dawson, H. (2012). 'Youth and political unrest: Waiting and envy in a South African informal settlement'. MA dissertation, Oxford University.
Dawson, M.C. (2010). 'Phansi privatisation! Phansi': The Anti-Privatisation Forum and ideology in social movements'. In W. Beinhart and M. Dawson (eds). *Popular Politics and Resistance Movements in South Africa*. Johannesburg: Wits University Press.
Dawson, M.C. and Sinwell, L. (forthcoming). *Contesting Transformation: Popular Resistance in Twenty-First Century South Africa*. London: Pluto Press.
De Gruchy, J.W. (1978). *The Church Struggle in South Africa*. Cape Town: David Philip.
De Vaus, D. and McAllister, I. (1987). 'Differences in religion: A test of the structural location theory'. *American Sociological Review* 52: 472–81.
Dent, G.R. and Nyembezi, C.L. (1995). *Scholar's Zulu Dictionary*. New York: Hippocrent Books.
Department of Housing. (2000). *National Housing Code*. Pretoria: Department of Housing.
Deshpande, S. (2003). *Contemporary India.* New Delhi: Penguin.
Devine, F. (2005). 'Middle-class identities in the United States'. In F. Devine et al. *Rethinking Class: Culture, Identities and Lifestyle.* Basingstoke: Palgrave.
Dhawan, N.D. (2010). 'The married "new Indian woman": Hegemonic aspirations in new middle-class politics'. *South African Review of Sociology* 41(3): 45–60.
Doke, C.M. et al. (1990). *English–Zulu, Zulu–English Dictionary*. Johannesburg: Wits University Press.
Dolby, N. (2001). *Constructing Race: Youth Identity and Popular Culture in South Africa.* Albany, NY: SUNY Press.

Dooley, D. and Prause, J. (2004), *The Social Costs of Unemployment*. Cambridge: Cambridge University Press.

Dorsey, M. and Thulani, G. (2002). 'Conclusion: Environmentalism, the WSSD, and uneven political development'. In P. Bond. *Unsustainable South Africa: Environment, Development, and Social Protest*. Pietermaritzburg: University of KwaZulu-Natal Press.

Draper, H. (1977). *Karl Marx's Theory of Revolution, Part 1: State and Bureaucracy*. New York and London: Monthly Review Press.

———. (1978). *Karl Marx's Theory of Revolution, Part 2: The Politics of Social Classes*. New York and London: Monthly Review Press.

Du Toit, A. (2004). '"Social exclusion" discourse and chronic poverty: A South African case study'. *Development and Change* 35(5): 987–1010.

Du Toit, A. and Neves, D. (2007). 'In search of South Africa's second economy'. *Africanus* 37(2): 2–19.

Dyers, C. (2009). 'From *ibharu* to *amajoin*: Translocation and language in a new South African township'. *Language and Intercultural Communication* 9(4): 256–70.

Edgell, S. (1993). *Class*. London: Routledge.

Egan, A. and Wafer, A. (2006). 'Dynamics of a "mini-mass movement": Origins, identity and ideological pluralism in the Soweto Electricity Crisis Committee'. In R. Ballard, A. Habib and I. Valodia (eds). *Voices of Protest: Social Movements in Post-apartheid South Africa*. Pietermaritzburg: University of KwaZulu-Natal Press.

Eidelberg, P. (1999). 'Guerrilla warfare and the decline of urban apartheid: The shaping of a new middle class and the transformation of the African National Congress (1975–1985)'. *Comparative Studies of South Asia, Africa and the Middle East* 19(1): 53–65.

Engels, F. (1884). *Origins of the Family, Private Property and the State (preface to the first edition).* http://www.Marxists.org (accessed 24 June 2012).

———. (1969). (First published 1887.) *The Condition of the Working-class in England*. London: Panther Books.

Escobar, A. (1997). 'The making and unmaking of the third world through development'. In M. Rahnema and V. Bawtree (eds). *The Post Development Reader*. London: Zed Books.

Esteva, G. (1992). 'Development'. In W. Sachs (ed.). *The Development Dictionary*. London: Zed Books.

Fanon, F. (1965). *Black Skins, White Masks.* London: Pluto Press.

———. (1988). *Cultures of Solidarity: Consciousness, Action and Contemporary American Workers*. Berkeley, CA: University of California Press.

Feagin, J.R. (1972). 'Poverty: We still believe that God helps those who help themselves'. *Psychology Today* November: 109–29.

Fiil-Flynn, M. (2001). *The Electricity Crisis in Soweto*. Johannesburg: Municipal Services Project.

Freston, P. (2005). 'The Universal Church of the Kingdom of God: A Brazilian church finds success in Southern Africa'. *Journal of Religion in Africa* 35: 33–65.

Furnham, A. (1988). *Lay Theories: Everyday Understanding of Problems in the Social Sciences*. Oxford: Pergamon Press.

Furnham, A. and Procter, E. (1989). 'Belief in a just world: Review and critique of the individual difference literature'. *British Journal of Social Psychology* 28(4): 365–84.

Future Foundation. (2006). *Middle Britain: Summary Report: Class Membership and Money in 21st Century Britain*. N.p.: Future Foundation.

Gaffney Group. (2012). *Gaffney's Local Government in South Africa: Official Yearbook.* Sandton: Gaffney Group.

Garner, R.C. (2000). 'Religion as a source of social change in the new South Africa'. *Journal of Religion in Africa* 30(3): 310–43.

Garuba, H. (2009). 'Language and identity in Nigeria'. In S. Bekker, M. Dodds and M. Khosa (eds). *Shifting African Identities.* Pretoria. HSRC Press.

Gerth, H.H. and Mills, C.W. (1991). From Max Weber: Essays in Sociology. Oxon: Routledge.

Goldthorpe, J. (2000). *On Sociology: Numbers, Narratives, and the Integration of Research and Theory*. Oxford: Oxford University Press.

———. (2008). 'Two oppositions in studies of class: A reflection'. In A. Lareau and D. Conley (eds). *Social Class: How Does It Work?* New York: Russell Sage Foundation.

Goldthorpe, J. and Chan, T.W. (2007). 'Class and status: The conceptual distinction and its empirical relevance'. *American Sociological Review* 72: 512–32.

Goldthorpe, J. and Marshall, G. (1992). 'The promising future of class analysis'. *Sociology* 26(3): 381–400.

Goodhew, D. (2000a). 'Growth and decline in South Africa's churches, 1960–91'. *Journal of Religion in Africa* 30(3): 344–69.

———. (2000b). 'Working class respectability: The example of the western areas of Johannesburg, 1930–55'. *Journal of African History* 41(2): 241–66.

Gramsci, A. (1971). *Selections from the Prison Notebooks*. Ed. and trans. by Q. Hoare and G. Novell Smith. London: Lawrence and Wishart.

Hankela, E. (2006). 'The church must become the people of Soweto: Manas Buthelezi's existential-Christocentric understanding of the church'. http://www.doria.fi/bitstream/handle/10024/59574/thechurc.pdf?sequence=1 (accessed 30 November 2010).

Harper, D.J. et al. (1990). 'Lay causal perceptions of third world poverty and the just world theory'. *Social Behavior and Personality* 18: 235–8.

Hart, G. (2007) 'Changing concepts of articulation, part one: Historical, theoretical and empirical diagnostics'. *Africanus* 37(2): 46–65.

Harvey, D. (2012). *Rebel Cities: From the Right to the City to the Urban Revolution*. London: Verso.

Hastings, A. (1994). *Oxford History of the Christian Church: The Church in Africa (1940–1950)*. Oxford: Clarendon Press.

Hauser, P.M. 1974. 'The measurement of labor utilization'. *Malayan Economic Review* 19: 1–17.

Hellmann, E. (1971). *Soweto: Johannesburg's African City*. Johannesburg: South African Institute of Race Relations.

Hendriks, J. and Erasmus, J. (2005). 'Religion in South Africa: The 2001 population census data'. *Journal of Theology for Southern Africa* 3(121): 88–111.

Hindson, D. (1981). 'Pass offices and labour bureaux: An analysis of the development of a national system of pass controls in South Africa 1923–1980'. DPhil dissertation, University of Sussex.

———. (1987). *Pass Controls and the Urban African Proletariat*. Johannesburg: Ravan Press.

Hirschsohn, P. (2011). 'The "hollowing out" of trade union democracy in COSATU? Members, shop stewards and the South African Communist Party'. *Law, Democracy and Development* 13: 1–31.

Hirson, B. (1979). *Year of Fire, Year of Ash. The Soweto Revolt: Roots of a Revolution?* London: Zed Books.

———. (1989). *Yours for the Union: Class and Community Struggles in South Africa*. Johannesburg: Wits University Press.

Hope, M. and Young, J. (1983). *The South African Churches in a Revolutionary Situation*. New York: Orbis Books.

Horn, P. (2005). 'New forms of collective bargaining: Adapting to the informal economy and new forms of work'. *Labour, Capital and Society* 38(1/2): 208–24.

Hout, M. (2008). 'How class works: Objective and subjective aspects of class since the 1970s'. In A. Lareau and D. Conley (eds). *Social Class: How Does It Work?* New York: Russell Sage Foundation.

Human, P. (1981). *Quality of Life in Soweto: A Sociological View*. Pretoria: Centre for Sociological Research, UNISA.

Hussmanns, R. (2007). *Measurement of Employment, Unemployment and Underemployment: Current International Standards and Issues in Their Application.* Geneva: ILO Bureau of Statistics.

Iliffe, J. (1987). *The African Poor*. New York: Cambridge University Press.

ILO (International Labour Organisation). (2007). *Beyond the Employment/Unemployment Dichotomy: Measuring the Quality of Employment in Low-income Countries: Key Indicators of the Labour Market Programme*. Geneva: ILO Publications.

———. (2010). 'Underemployment'. In *ILO Overview and Topics 2010.* Geneva: ILO. http://www.ilo.org/global/statistics-and-databases/ (accessed 15 May 2011).

———. (2012a). *Global Employment Trends 2011: Preventing a Deeper Jobs Crisis*. Geneva: ILO Publications.

———. (2012b). LABORSTA Internet: Strikes and Lockouts. http://laborsta.ilo.org/STP/guest (accessed 24 May 2012).

Independent. (2004). 'We sleep in the suburb but we live in Soweto'. 14 October. http://www.independent.co.uk/opinion/commentators/we-sleep-in-the-suburb-but-we-live-in-soweto-543714.html (accessed 20 May 2011).

IOL (*Independent Online*). (2008). 'Migration hits housing delivery'. 27 May. http://www.iol.co.za (accessed 20 May 2011).

Jameson, F. (2011). *Representing Capital: A Reading of Volume One*. London: Verso.

Jenkins, R. (2002). *Pierre Bourdieu*. London: Routledge.

Jensen, L. and Slack, T. (2003). 'Underemployment in America: Measurement and evidence'. *American Journal of Community Psychology* 32(1/2): 21–31.

Joburg News. (2006). 'Mall boom in Soweto'. 5 July. http://joburgnews.co.za/2006/july/jul5_malls.stm (accessed 20 May 2011).

Jochelson, K.J. (2001). *The Colour of Disease*. Basingstoke: Palgrave.

Johnstone, F. (1976). *Class, Race and Gold: A Study of Class Relations and Racial Discrimination in South Africa*. London: Routledge and Kegan Paul.

Jones, G.S. (1983). *Language of Class: Studies in English Working Class, 1832–1982*. Cambridge: Cambridge University Press.

Jowell, R. et al. (1993). *British Social Attitudes Survey: Ninth Report*. Aldershot: Ashgate.

Kane-Berman, J. (1978). *Soweto: Black Revolt, White Reaction*. Johannesburg: Ravan Press.

Katznelson, I. (1982). *City Trenches: Urban Politics and the Patterning of Class in the United States*. Chicago, IL: University of Chicago Press.

Keegan, T. (1987). *Transformation in Industrializing South Africa: The South African Highveld to 1914*. Basingstoke: Macmillan.

Kelly, J. (2012). 'Workdays lost to the economy'. Email communication, 7 June. Kelly is employed by Andrew Levy Employment Publications.

Kenny, B. (2003). 'Labour market flexibility in the retail sector: Possibilities for resistance'. In T. Bramble and F. Barchiesi (eds). *Rethinking the Labour Movement in the 'New' South Africa*. Aldershot: Ashgate.

Kingdon G. and Knight, J. (2000). 'The incidence of unemployment in South Africa'. Unpublished paper presented to the Trade and Industrial Secretariat Annual Forum, held at Muldersdrift, Johannesburg.

Khan, F. and Pietersen, E. (2006). 'The Homeless People's Alliance: Purposive creation and ambiguated realities'. In A. Ballard, A. Habib and I. Valodia (eds). *Voices of Protest: Social Movements in Post-apartheid South Africa*. Pietermaritzburg: University of KwaZulu-Natal Press.

Koltko-Rivera, M. (2004). 'The psychology of worldviews'. *Review of General Psychology* 8(1): 3–58.

Kuper, L. (1949). 'The South African native: Caste, proletariat or race?' *Social Forces* 28(3): 146–53.

———. (1965). *An African Bourgeoisie: Race, Class, and Politics in South Africa*. New Haven, CT: Yale University Press.

Langa, M. and Von Holdt, K. (forthcoming). 'Insurgent Citizenship, Class Formation and the Dual Nature of a Community Protest: A Case Study of "Kungcatsha"'. In M.C. Dawson and L. Sinwell (eds). *Contesting Transformation: Popular Resistance in Twenty-First Century South Africa*. London: Pluto Press.

Laurie, A. (1998). Document no. 04044-1A.E98. Geneva: ILO. H:\WPWIN\WP6WE\MEETINGS\ICLS\04044-1A.E98 (accessed 5 May 2011).

Legassick. M. (2011). Email communication, 20 April.

Legassick, M. and Wolpe, H. (1976). 'The Bantustans and capital accumulation in South Africa'. *Review of African Political Economy* 3(7): 87–107.

Lehulere, O. (2005). 'The new social movements, Cosatu and the "new UDF"'. *Khanya Journal* 11: 18–40.
Leibbrandt, M. (2010). 'Trends in South African income distribution and poverty since the fall of apartheid'. *OECD Social, Employment and Migration Working Papers* 101. Paris: OECD.
Leibbrandt, M., Bhorat, H. and Woolard, I. (2001). 'Household inequality and the labour market in South Africa'. *Contemporary Economic Policy* 19(1): 73–86.
Lerner, M.J. (1980). *The Belief in a Just World*. New York: Plenum Press.
Lerner, M.J. and Miller, D.T. (1978). 'Just world research and the attribution process: Looking back and ahead'. *Psychological Bulletin* 85: 1030–51.
Levi, M. and Olson, D. (2000). 'The battles in Seattle'. *Politics and Society* 28(3): 309–29.
Lindell, I. (2010). *Africa's Informal Workers Collective Agency: Alliances and Transnational Organizing in Urban Africa*. London and New York: Zed Books and Nordiska Afrikainstitutet.
Lings, K. (2011). 'LFS shows turn-around'. *Citizen*, 4 May.
Lipton, M. (1986). *Capitalism and Apartheid: South Africa, 1910–1986*. Aldershot: Wildwood House.
Lodge, T. (1991). 'Other political forces'. In T. Lodge and B. Nasson (eds). *All, Here, and Now: Black Politics in South Africa in the 1980s*. Cape Town: David Philip.
Mabin, A. and Smit, D. (1997). 'Reconstructing South Africa's cities? The making of urban planning 1900–2000'. *Planning Perspectives* 12: 193–223.
Maboea, S.I. (2002). *The Influence of Life Giving Power in the African Traditional Religion and the Zionist Churches*. Pretoria: CB Powell Bible Centre, UNISA.
MacDonald, M. (2006). *Why Race Matters in South Africa*. Boston, MA: Harvard University Press.
MacShane, D., Plaut, M. and Ward, D. (1984). *Power! Black Workers, Their Unions and the Struggle for Freedom in South Africa*. Nottingham: Spokesman.
Makhulu, W.P.K. (1998). 'The future task and place of the African independent churches in a new South Africa'. In C. du Toit and N. Ngada (eds). *Hearing the AIC Voice*. Pretoria: Research Institute for Theology and Religion, UNISA.
Malikane, C. (2010). 'Income distribution, persistent unemployment, and the classical growth cycle: Evidence from South Africa'. *Journal of Developing Areas* 44(1): 187–99.
Manda, O, 2009. 'Race and class in East Rand industries'. Unpublished conference paper. Available from author.
Mandy, N. (1984). *A City Divided: Johannesburg and Soweto*. Johannesburg: Macmillan.
Maphumlo, S. (2002). 'Soweto's whites face uneasy times'. *IOL news*. http://www.iol.co.za/news/south-africa/soweto-s-whites-face-uneasy-times-1.97537#.T9h17lLWkwc (accessed 13 June 2012).
Maree, J. (1975). 'Current labour utilisation and underemployment in South Africa'. In W.H. Thomas (ed.). *The Conditions of the Black Worker*. London: African Publication Trust.

Mariz, C.L. (1992). 'Religion and poverty in Brazil: A comparison of Catholic and Pentecostal communities'. *Sociological Analysis* 53: 63–70.

———. (1996). 'Pentecostalism and confrontation with poverty in Brazil'. In D.A. Smith and B.F. Gutierrez (eds). *The Power of the Spirit*. Louisville: AIPRAL/CELEP.

Marx, A.W. (1992). *Lessons of Struggle*. Cape Town: Oxford University Press.

Marx, K. (1954). (First published 1867.) *Capital: A Critique of Political Economy, Vol. I*. Trans. by S. Moore and E. Aveling. London: Lawrence and Wishart.

———. (1976). (First published 1867.) *Capital, Vol. I: A Critique of Political Economy*. Trans. by B. Fowkes. London: Penguin.

Marx, K. and Engels, F. (1965). (First published 1848.) Trans. by S. Moore. *Manifesto of the Communist Party*. Peking: Foreign Languages Press.

Marks, M. (1995). '"We are fighting for the liberation of our people": Justification of violence by activist youth in Diepkloof, Soweto'. Seminar paper no. 385, Institute for Advanced Social Research, University of the Witwatersrand.

Marks, S. and Rathbone, R. (eds). (1982). *Industrialisation and Social Change in South Africa: African Class Formation, Culture, and Consciousness, 1870–1930*. Harlow: Longman.

Massey, D. (1994). *Space, Place and Gender*. Minneapolis: University of Minnesota Press.

May, J. (1998). *Experience and Perceptions of Poverty in South Africa*. Durban: Praxis.

May, J. and Meth, C. (2007). 'Dualism or underdevelopment in South Africa: What does quantitative assessment of poverty, inequality and employment reveal?' *Development Southern Africa* 24(2): 271–87.

Mayer, P. (1977). *Soweto People and Their Social Universe*. Pretoria: HSRC Press.

———. (1979). 'Class, status and ethnicity as perceived by Johannesburg Africans'. In A.P. Hare, G. Wiendieck and M.H. von Broembsen (eds). *South Africa: Sociological Analysis*. Cape Town: Oxford University Press.

Mbembe, A., Dlamini, N. and Khunou, G. (2008). 'Soweto now'. In S. Nuttall and A. Mbembe (eds). *Johannesburg: The Elusive Metropolis*. Johannesburg: Wits University Press.

Mbiti, J.S. (1975). *Introduction to Africa Religion*. London: Heinemann.

McCloud, S. (2007). 'Putting some class into religious studies: Resurrecting an important concept'. *Journal of the American Academy of Religion* 75(4): 840–62.

McIver, R.K. and Currow, S. (2001). 'A provocative study of tithing trends in Australia'. http://www.ministrymagazine.org/archive/2001/August/a-provocative-study-of-tithing-trends-in-australia.html (accessed 11 November 2011).

McKinley, D. and Naidoo, P. (eds). (2004). *Mobilising for Change: The Rise of the New Social Movements in South Africa*. Development Update Series. Johannesburg: Interfund.

McLellan, D. (1987). *Marxism and Religion*. Basingstoke: Macmillan.

Meintjies, H. (2001). 'Washing machines make lazy women'. *Journal of Material Culture* 6(3): 345–63.

Meth, C. (2006a). 'Income poverty in 2004: A second engagement with the recent van der Berg et al. figures'. Durban: School of Development Studies, University of KwaZulu-Natal.

———. (2006b). 'What was the poverty headcount in 2004 and how does it compare to recent estimates by Van der Berg et al.?' Southern Africa Labour and Development Research Unit, University of Cape Town.

———. (2010). 'What do we know? Professor Servaas van der Berg's poverty estimates'. Durban: School of Development Studies, University of KwaZulu-Natal.

Miles, M. and Huberman, M. (1994). *Qualitative Data Analysis*. Thousand Oaks, CA: Sage Publishers.

Miller, M.E. and West, A.M. (1993). 'Influences of worldview on personality, epistemology and choice of profession'. In J. Demick and P.M. Miller (eds). *Development in the Workplace*. Hillsdale, NJ: Earlbaum Publishers.

Mills, W. (1953). *White Collar: The American Middle Classes*. New York: Oxford University Press.

Miraftab, F. (2003). 'The perils of participatory discourse: Housing policy in postapartheid South Africa'. *Journal of Planning Education and Research* 22: 226–39.

Mncube, T. (2007). 'Anglican Church Dioceses of Jabavu Central (Soweto)'. Unpublished Anglican Church attendance report.

Mndende, N. (1997). 'From racial oppression to religious oppression: African religion in the new South Africa'. *Dialogue and Alliance* 11(1): 39–50.

Modisha, G. (2007). 'A contradictory class location? The African corporate middle class and the burden of race in South Africa'. *Transformation* 65: 120–45.

Monyokolo, M.B. (1990). 'Soweto's 3 year rent boycott: How the class aspect affects people's perception of and response of the rent boycott – a case study of Pimville-Klipspruit sub-township'. Honours dissertation, University of the Witwatersrand.

Moodie, T.D. (2010). 'Comprehending class compromise in the history of class struggle on the South African gold mines: Variations and vicissitudes of class power'. *South African Review of Sociology* 41(3): 99–116.

Moody, K. (1997). *Workers in a Lean World: Unions in the International Economy*. London and New York: Verso.

Moore, E. (1953). 'The exportability of the "labour force" concept'. *American Sociological Review* 18(1): 68–72.

Morris, A. et al. (1999). *Change and Continuity: A Survey of Soweto in the Late 1990s*. Johannesburg: Department of Sociology, University of the Witwatersrand.

Mosoetsa, S. (2003). 'Re-emerging communities in post-apartheid South Africa: Mpumalanga township, KwaZulu-Natal, Durban'. Paper presented at the Workshop on Crisis States, University of the Witwatersrand, 14–18 July.

———. (2011). *Eating from One Pot: The Dynamics of Survival in Poor South African Households*. Johannesburg: Wits University Press.

Mufson, S. (1991). 'Introduction'. In T. Lodge and B. Nasson (eds). *All, Here, and Now: Black Politics in South Africa in the 1980s*. Cape Town: David Philip.

Munck, R. (1999). 'Labour dilemmas and labour futures'. In R. Munck and P. Waterman (eds). *Labour Worldwide in the Era of Globalisation: Alternative Union Models in the New World Order*. Basingstoke: Macmillan.

Muthwa, S. (1994). 'Female household headship and household survival in Soweto'. *Journal of Gender Studies* 3(2): 165–75.

Myrdal, G. (1968). *Asian Drama: An Enquiry into the Poverty of Nations*. New York: Twentieth Century Fund.

Narunsky-Laden, S. (2008). 'Identity in post-apartheid South Africa: "Learning to belong" through the (commercial) media'. In A. Hadland et al. (eds). *Power, Politics and Identity in South African Media*. Cape Town: HSRC Press.

———. (2010). 'Introduction: Cultural economy in post-transitional South Africa'. *Critical Arts* 24(1): 1–30.

National Planning Commission. (2011). *Diagnostic Report.* Pretoria: National Planning Commission.

National Treasury. (2007). *A National Poverty Line for South Africa*. Pretoria: National Treasury.

Nelsen, H.M. and Potvin, R.H. (1980). 'Towards disestablishment: New patterns of social class, denomination and religiosity among youth?' *Review of Religious Research* 22(2): 137–54.

Ngwane, T. (2003). 'A movement of movements? Sparks in the township'. *New Left Review* 22: 37–56.

———. (2010). 'Some thoughts without consulting the lexicon'. Unpublished document.

———. (2011). 'Ideology and agency in protest politics: Service delivery struggles in post-apartheid South Africa'. MA dissertation, University of KwaZulu-Natal.

Niebuhr, H.R. (1929). *The Social Sources of Denominationalism*. New York: Meridian Books.

Nkuna, L. (2007). '"Fitting-in" to a "classy place"'. In P. Alexander, M. Dawson and M. Ichharam (eds). *Globalisation and New Identities: A View from the Middle*. Johannesburg: Jacana Media.

Norton, G.R. (1940). 'The emergence of new religious organizations in South Africa: A discussion of causes'. *Journal of the Royal African Society* 39(157): 348–53.

Nthambeleni, B. (1999). 'The role of civil society in sustaining democracy: A case study of the Soweto Civic Association'. MA dissertation, Rand Afrikaans University.

———. (2009). 'The South African National Civic Organisation: A two-tiered social movement'. DLitt et Phil dissertation, University of Johannesburg.

Nuttall, S. (2004). 'Stylizing the self: The Y generation in Rosebank, Johannesburg'. *Public Culture* 16(3): 430–52.

Nycquist, T.E. (1983). *African Middle Class Elite*. Grahamstown: Institute of Social and Economic Research, Rhodes University.

Nzimande, B. (1986). 'Managers and the new middle class'. *Transformation* 1: 39–62.

———. (1990). 'Class, national oppression and the African petty bourgeoisie: The case of the African traders'. In R. Cohen, Y. Muthien and A. Zegeya (eds). *Repression and Resistance: Insider Accounts of Apartheid*. London: Hans Zell.

Nzimande, E.B. (1991). '"The corporate guerillas": Class formation and the African petty bourgeoisie in post-1973 South Africa'. PhD dissertation, University of Natal, Durban.

O'Meara, D. (1983). *Volkskapitalisme: Class, Capital and Ideology in the Development of Afrikaner Nationalism, 1924–1948*. Johannesburg: Ravan Press.

ONS (Office of National Statistics). (2008). 'Detailed category distinctions and operational issues'. http://www.ons.gov.uk (accessed 1 July 2010).

Ortiz, J. (2009). 'Does religion distribution matter in the economic growth of Latin America?' *International Journal of Business and Economics* 8(3): 183–99.

Palmer Development Group et al. (2005). *Soweto Retail Strategy*. Johannesburg: City of Johannesburg Economic Development Unit.

Parnell, S. (1988). 'Racial segregation in Johannesburg: The Slums Act, 1934–1939'. *South African Geographical Journal* 70(2): 112–26.

Payne, G. and Grew, C. (2005). 'Unpacking "class ambivalence": Some conceptual and methodological issues in accessing class cultures'. *Sociology* 39(5): 893–910.

Pernegger, L. and Godehart, S. (2007). 'Keynote address: Townships in the South African Geographic Landscape: Physical and Social Legacies and Challenges'. Pretoria: South African Treasury. http://www.treasury.gov.za/divisions/bo/ndp/TTRI/TTRI%20Oct%202007/Day%201%20-%2029%20Oct%202007/1a%20Keynote%20Address.pdf (accessed 11 June 2012)

Phadi, M. (2010a). 'Meaning of "middle class": The case of Soweto'. MA dissertation, University of Johannesburg.

Phadi, M. (narrator). (2010b). *Phakhati: Soweto's Middling Class*. Documentary made by Eyelight Productions and the Centre for Sociological Research, University of Johannesburg.

Phadi, M. and Ceruti, C. (2011). 'Multiple meanings of the middle class in Soweto, South Africa'. *African Sociological Review* 15(1).

———. (forthcoming). 'Why did two-thirds of Sowetans call themselves middle class? How multiple meanings of "middle" link to classed experience'. *African Sociological Review*.

Phadi, M. and Manda, O. (2010), 'The language of class: Southern Sotho and Zulu meanings of "middle class" in Soweto'. *South African Review of Sociology* 41(3): 81–98.

Piazza-Georgi, B. (2000). *A Profile of the Self-employed in Soweto in mid-1999, with Gender Disaggregation: A Report on a Field Survey*. Johannesburg: Department of Economics, University of the Witwatersrand.

Pieterse, J.N. (2002). 'Global inequality: Bringing politics back in'. *Third World Quarterly* 23(6): 21–4.

Pillay, D. (2006). 'Cosatu, alliances and working class politics'. In S. Buhlungu (ed.). *Trade Unions and Democracy: Cosatu Workers' Political Attitudes in South Africa*. Cape Town: HSRC Press.

———. (2008). 'Globalisation and the informalisation of labour: The case of South Africa'. In A. Bieler, I. Lindberg and D. Pillay (eds). *Labour and the Challenges of Globalisation*. London: Pluto Press.

Piven, F.F. and Cloward, R.A. (1979). *Poor People's Movements: Why they Succeed, How they Fail*. New York: Vintage Books.

Pfaffe, P. (2011). 'A protest event analysis of South Africa's rebellion of the poor'. MA dissertation, Berlin School of Economics and Law.

Posel, D. (1991). *The Making of Apartheid, 1948–1961: Conflict and Compromise*. Oxford: Clarendon Press.

———. (2010). 'Races to consume: Revisiting South Africa's history of race, consumption and the struggle for freedom'. *Ethnic and Racial Studies* 33(2): 157–75.

Poulantzas, N. (1975). *Class in Contemporary Capitalism*. London: Verso.

Presidency, South Africa. (2007). *Development Indicators: Mid-term Review*. Pretoria: Government Printer.

———. (2009). *Development Indicators 2009*. Pretoria: National Planning Commission. http://www.thepresidency.gov.za/learning/me/indicators/2009/indicators.pdf (accessed 20 June 2012).

Pretorius, H. and Jafta, L. (1993). 'African initiated churches'. In R. Elphick and R. Davenport (eds). *Christianity in South Africa: A Political, Social, and Cultural History*. Berkeley, CA: University of California Press.

Proctor, A. (1979). 'Class struggle, segregation and the city: A history of Sophiatown, 1905–1940'. In B. Bozzoli (ed.). *Labour, Townships and Protest*. Johannesburg: Ravan Press.

Rex, J. (1986). 'The role of class analysis in the study of race relations: A Weberian perspective'. In J. Rex and D. Mason (eds). *Theories of Race and Ethnic Relations*. Cambridge: Cambridge University Press.

Roberts, D. (2011). *Reading the Riots*. London: Guardian Books (with LSE). Kindle edition.

Roberts, K. (2001). *Class in Modern Britain*. Basingstoke: Palgrave.

Robinson, J. (1936). 'Disguised unemployment'. *Economic Journal* 46(182): 225–37.

Rogers, D.T. (1987). *Contested Truths: Keywords in American Politics since Independence*. New York: Basic Books.

Rosenthal, K. (2010). 'New social movements as civil society: The case of past and present Soweto'. In W. Beinhart and M. Dawson (eds). *Popular Politics and Resistance Movements in South Africa*. Johannesburg: Wits University Press.

Rudwick, S. (2005). 'Township language dynamics: IsiZulu and isiTsotsi in Umlazi'. *Southern African Linguistics and Applied Language Studies* 23(3): 305–17.

Runciman, C. (2012) 'Mobilisation and insurgent citizenship of the Anti Privatisation Forum, South Africa: An ethnographic study'. PhD dissertation, Glasgow University.

Runciman, C., Ngwane, T. and Alexander, P. (2012). 'A protest event analysis of South Africa's rebellion of the poor: Initial results'. PowerPoint presentation to South African Sociological Association Conference, University of Cape Town.

SAARF (South African Advertising Research Foundation). n.d. Website. http://www.saarf.co.za (accessed 20 May 2011).

SAHO (South African History Online). (n.d.). 'The Mass Democratic Movement, February 1988–January 1990'. http://www.sahistory.org.za (accessed 16 November 2011).

SAIRR (South African Institute of Race Relations). (1976). *Survey of Race Relations in South Africa*. Johannesburg: SAIRR.

———. (1977). *Survey of Race Relations in South Africa*. Johannesburg: SAIRR.
———. (1978). *Survey of Race Relations in South Africa*. Johannesburg: SAIRR.
SA Local Government Briefing. (2012). '56% of black metro adults unhappy with service delivery: TNS Surveys. *SA Local Government Briefing* July (additional edition): 32.
Santos, J.A.F. (2010). 'Comprehending the class structure specificity in Brazil'. *South African Review of Sociology* 41(3): 24–44.
Saul, T. and Gelb, S. (1981). *The Crisis in South Africa*. New York: Monthly Review Press.
Savage, M. (2000). *Class Analysis and Social Transformation*. Buckingham: Open University Press.
Savage, M., Bagnall, G. and Longhurst, B. (2001). 'Ordinary, ambivalent and defensive: Class identities in northwest of England'. *Sociology* 35(4): 875–92.
Schlemmer, L. (2005). 'Lost in transformation? South Africa's emerging African middle class'. *CDE Focus Occasional Paper* no. 8. Johannesburg: Centre for Development and Enterprise.
Scully, B. (2011). 'Isolated or interdependent? Livelihoods of workers and the unemployed in South Africa's jobs crisis'. Paper presented to the South African Sociological Association Congress, Pretoria, 10–13 July.
Seekings, J. (1992). ' "Trailing behind the masses": The United Democratic Front and township politics in the Pretoria-Witwatersrand-Vaal region, 1983–84'. *Journal of Southern African Studies* 18(1): 93–114.
———. (2000). *The UDF: A History of the United Democratic Front in South Africa, 1983–1991*. Cape Town: David Philip.
———. (2003a). 'Do South Africa's unemployed constitute an underclass?' *CSSR Working Paper* 32. Cape Town: Centre for Social Science Research, University of Cape Town.
———. (2003b). 'Social stratification and inequality in South Africa at the end of apartheid'. *CSSR Working Paper* 31. Cape Town: Centre for Social Science Research, University of Cape Town.
———. (2004). 'Trade unions, social policy and class compromise in post-apartheid South Africa'. *Review of African Political Economy* 100: 299–312.
———. (2007a). 'Perceptions of Class in Post-Apartheid Cape Town'. *CSSR Working Paper* 198. Cape Town: Centre for Social Science Research, University of Cape Town.
———. (2007b). *Poverty and Inequality after Apartheid*. Cape Town: Centre for Social Science Research, University of Cape Town. http://www.sarpn.org/documents/d0003024/Poverty_inequality_Seekings_Sep2007.pdf (accessed 20 June 2012).
———. (2008a). 'Beyond "fluidity": Kinship and households as social projects.' *CSSR Working Paper* 237. Centre for Social Science Research, University of Cape Town.
———. (2008b). 'Unemployment, chance and class in South Africa'. Draft paper for presentation at Stanford University.
———. (2009). 'The rise and fall of the Weberian analysis of class in South Africa between 1949 and the early 1970s'. *Journal of Southern African Studies* 35(4): 865–81.
———. (2010). 'Weber, Marx and South African studies'. Paper for festschrift for Gavin Williams.

———. (2011). 'Race, class, and inequality in the South African city'. In G. Bridge and S. Watson (eds). *The New Blackwell Companion to the City*. Chichester: Blackwell Publishing.

Seekings, J. and Natrass, N. (2005). *Class, Race and Inequality in South Africa*. New Haven, CT: Yale University Press.

Sharpe, M.R.L. (1952). *Everyday Sesotho Reader*. Morija: Morija Sesotho Book Depot.

Shubane, K. (1991). 'Soweto'. In T. Lodge and B. Nasson (eds). *All, Here, and Now: Black Politics in South Africa in the 1980s*. Cape Town: David Philip.

Silver, B. (2003). *Forces of Labour: Workers' Movements and Globalization since 1870*. Cambridge: Cambridge University Press.

Simkins, C. (1981). 'The demographic demand for labour and institutional context of African unemployment in South Africa'. *SALDRU Working Paper* 32. Cape Town: SALDRU, University of Cape Town.

———. (2004). 'Employment and unemployment in South Africa'. *Journal of Contemporary African Studies* 22(2): 253–78.

Simkins, C. and Desmond, C. (1978). 'Introduction'. In C. Simkins and C. Desmond (eds). *South African Unemployment: A Black Picture*. Pietermaritzburg: Development Studies Research.

Simon, D. (1989). 'Crisis and change in South Africa: Implications for the apartheid city'. *Transactions of the Institute of British Geographers* 14(2): 189–206.

Simson, H. (1973). 'Fascism in South Africa'. *African Review* 3(3).

Skeggs, B. (2004). *Class, Self, Culture*. London: Routledge.

Sono, M. (2011). 'Grace Bible Church: Mission and outreach methods'. http://www.gbcsoweto. org.za/index.php?nav=pagesandview=24andPHPSESSID (accessed 30 September 2011).

Southall, R. (2004). 'Political change and the black middle class in democratic South Africa'. *Canadian Journal of African Studies* 38(3): 521–42.

Stadler, A.W. (1979). 'Birds in the cornfields: Squatter movements in Johannesburg, 1944–1947'. In B. Bozzoli (ed.). *Labour, Townships and Protest*. Johannesburg: Ravan Press.

Standing, G. (1999). *Global Labour Flexibility: Seeking Distributive Justice*. Basingstoke: Macmillan.

———. (2011). *The Precariat: The New Dangerous Class*. London: Bloomsbury Academic.

Stark, R. (1972). 'The economics of piety'. In G. Thielbar and S. Feldman (eds). *Issues in Social Inequality*. Boston: Little, Brown.

Stats SA (Statistics South Africa). (1996). *October Household Survey 1995*. Pretoria: Stats SA.

———. (1999). *October Household Survey 1996*. Pretoria: Stats SA.

———. (2006). *Labour Force Survey 2006*. http://www.statssa.gov.za/publications/P0210/P0210September2006.pdf (accessed 19 March 2010).

———. (2007). *Community Survey 2007: Basic Report*. Pretoria: Stats SA.

———. (2008a). *Labour Force Survey September 2007*. Pretoria: Stats SA.

———. (2008b). *Quarterly Labour Force Survey: Additional Aspects of the Labour Market in South Africa: Informal Employment; Underemployment and Underutilised Labour; Unemployment*. Pretoria: Stats SA.

———. (2008c). *Quarterly Labour Force Survey, Quarter 3, 2008*. Pretoria: Stats SA.

———. (2008d). *Report on the Responses of Statistics South Africa to Recommendations of the International Monetary Fund on Improvements to the Labour Force Survey*. Pretoria: Stats SA.

———. (2009a). *Changes in Standard of Living among Population Groups in South Africa, 1998–2006*. Pretoria: Stats SA.

———. (2009b). *Labour Force Survey Historical Revision September Series 2000 to 2007*. Pretoria: Stats SA.

———. (2009c). *Quarterly Labour Force Survey, Quarter 3, 2009*. Pretoria: Stats SA.

———. (2009d). *Quarterly Labour Force Survey, Quarter 4, 2008*. Pretoria: Stats SA.

———. (2010a). *Quarterly Labour Force Survey, Quarter 1, 2010*. Pretoria: Stats SA.

———. (2010b). *Quarterly Labour Force Survey, Quarter 3, 2010*. Pretoria: Stats SA.

———. (2011a). *Mid-year Population Estimates 2011*. Pretoria: Stats SA.

———. (2011b). *Quarterly Labour Force Survey, Quarter 2, 2011*. Pretoria: Stats SA.

———. (2012a). *Quarterly Labour Force Survey, Quarter 1, 2012*. Pretoria: Stats SA.

———. (2012b). *Quarterly Labour Force Survey, Quarter 2, 2012*. Pretoria: Stats SA.

Stedman Jones, G. (1983). *Language of Class: Studies in English Working Class, 1832–1982*. Cambridge: Cambridge University Press.

Stewart. A. (2008). 'Praying with the hand that you are dealt'. *ILLUMINE: Journal of the Centre for Studies in Religion and Society* 7(1): 35–52.

Streeten, P. (1981). *First Things First: Meeting Basic Human Needs in Developing Countries*. Oxford: World Bank and Oxford University Press.

Stuber, J.M. (2006). 'Talk of class: The discursive repertoires of white working- and upper-middle-class college students'. *Journal of Contemporary Ethnography* 35(3): 285–318.

Sundkler, B.G.M. (1961). *Bantu Prophets in South Africa*. Oxford: Oxford University Press.

Surridge, P. (2007). 'Class boundaries: A quantitative exploration of identity and consciousness'. *British Journal of Sociology* 58(2): 207–26.

Swatos, W.H. (ed.). (2001). 'Stratification'. *Encyclopedia of Religion and Society*. Hartford: Hartford Institute for Religion Research, Hartford Seminary.

Swilling, M. and Phillips, M. (1989). 'The emergency state: Its structure, power and limits'. In *South African Review, Vol. 5*. Johannesburg: Ravan Press.

Swilling, M. and Shubane, K. (1992). *The Soweto Experience: Urban Popular Movements in 'Post Apartheid' South Africa*. Montreal: CIDMAA.

Tamney, J.B. (1991). 'Social class composition of congregations and pastoral support for liberal activism'. *Review of Religious Research* 33(1): 18–32.

Tarrow, S. 2011. 'What's in a word?' Unpublished manuscript. Available from author.

Tema, N. and Nyhodo, B. (2007). 'Food inflation: A South African overall picture from the National Agricultural Marketing Council database'. Pretoria: National Agricultural Marketing Council.

Terreblanche, S. (2002). *A History of Inequality in South Africa 1965–2002*. Pietermaritzburg: University of Natal Press.

Thompson, E.P. (1968). *The Making of the English Working Class*. Harmondsworth: Penguin.

Tilly, C. and Tilly, C. (1998). *Work under Capitalism*. Boulder, CO: Westview Press.

Tomlinson, R., Beauregard, R., Bremner, L. and Mangcu, X. (2003). 'The postapartheid struggle for an integrated Johannesburg'. In R. Tomlinson, R. Beauregard, L. Bremner and X. Mangcu (eds). *Emerging Johannesburg*. New York: Routledge.

Turnham, D. (1971). *The Employment Problem in Less Developed Countries*. Paris: Development Centre of the OECD.

UN-HABITAT (United Nations Human Settlements Programme). (2010). *State of the World's Cities 2010/2011: Bridging the Urban Divide*. London and Washington, DC: Earthscan.

Van den Bergh, P. (1965). *South Africa: A Study in Conflict*. Berkeley, CA: University of California Press.

Van der Berg, S. et al. (2005). 'Trends in poverty and inequality since the political transition'. Paper presented at the TIPS/DPRU/WIDER Conference, Stellenbosch, 30–31 November.

Viljoen, R. (1995). 'Moravian missionaries, Khoisan labour and colonists'. In H. Bredekamp and R. Ross (eds). *Missions and Christianity in South African History*. Johannesburg: Wits University Press.

Vollgraaff, R. (2011). 'SA strike rate highest in the world'. *Sunday Times Business Times Supplement*, 7 August: 4.

Von Holdt, K. et al. (2011). *The Smoke that Calls: Insurgent Citizenship, Collective Violence and the Struggle for a Place in the new South Africa*. Johannesburg: Centre for the Study of Violence and Reconciliation, and Society, Work and Development Institute, University of the Witwatersrand.

Von Holdt, K. and Webster, E. (2005). 'Work restructuring and the crisis of social reproduction'. In E. Webster and K. von Holdt (eds). *Beyond the Apartheid Workplace*. Pietermaritzburg: University of KwaZulu-Natal Press.

Wale, K. and Alexander, P. (2009). '"Too poor to be unemployed": Underemployment in South Africa'. Unpublished paper.

Washington Post. (2012). 'News summary: Spain's unemployment rate hits 24.6 percent in 2nd-qtr, 5.7 million out of work'. 27 July.

Weber, M. (1924). 'Class, status, party'. In H.H. Gerth and C.W. Mills. (1948). *From Max Weber*. London: Routledge and Kegan Paul.

———. (1967). *The Protestant Ethic and the Spirit of Capitalism*. Trans. by T. Parsons. London: Unwin University Books.

———. (1978). 'The distribution of power within the political community: Class, status, party'. In *Economy and Society, Vols. 1 and 2*. Trans. by E. Fischoff et al. Berkeley, CA: University of California Press.

———. (2010). 'The distribution of power within the community: Classes, *stände*, parties'. Trans. by D. Waters et al. *Journal of Classical Sociology* 10(2): 137–52.

Webster, E. (ed.). (1978). *Essays in Southern African Labour Studies*. Johannesburg: Ravan Press.

———. (2005). 'Making a living, earning a living: Work and employment in Southern Africa'. *International Political Science Review* 26(1): 55–71.

———. (2006). 'Trade unions and the challenge of informalisation of work'. In S. Buhlungu (ed.). *Trade Unions and Democracy: Cosatu Workers' Political Attitudes in South Africa*. Cape Town: HSRC Press.

West, M. (1975). *Bishops and Prophets in a Black City: African Independent Churches in Soweto, Johannesburg*. Cape Town: David Philip.

White, F. (2008). 'Strengthening democracy? The role of social movements as agents of civil society in post-apartheid South Africa'. PhD dissertation, University of London.

Williams, J.J. (2006). 'South Africa's ten years of democracy: Development and media discourse'. *Development Southern Africa* 23(3): 427–43.

Williams, R. (1976). *Keywords: A Vocabulary of Culture and Society*. New York: Oxford University Press.

Wilson, M. and Mafeje, A. (1963). *Langa: A Study of Social Groups in an African Township*. Cape Town: Oxford University Press.

Wolpe, H. (1972). 'Capitalism and cheap labour-power in South Africa: From segregation to apartheid'. *Economy and Society* 1(4): 425–56.

———. (1976). 'The "white working class" in South Africa'. *Economy and Society* 5(3): 197–240.

———. (1986). 'Class concepts, class struggle and racism'. In J. Rex and D. Mason (eds). *Theories of Race and Ethnic Relations*. Cambridge: Cambridge University Press.

———. (1988). *Race, Class and the Apartheid State*. London: James Currey.

Woolard, I. and Leibbrandt, M. (2006). 'Towards a poverty line for South Africa'. Background note. Southern Africa Labour and Development Research Unit, University of Cape Town.

Wright, E.O. (1978). *Class, Crisis and the State*. London: Verso.

———. (1995). 'The class analysis of poverty'. *International Journal of Health Services* 25(1): 85–100.

———. (2000). *Class Counts: Student Edition*. Cambridge: Cambridge University Press.

———. (2002). 'Alternative foundation of class analysis'. http://www.ssc.wisc.edu (accessed August 2011).

———. (2005). *Approaches to Class Analysis*. Cambridge: Cambridge University Press.

———. (2008). 'Logics of class analysis'. In A. Lareau and D. Conley (eds). *Social Class: How Does It Work?* New York: Russell Sage Foundation.

Zeilig, L. and Ceruti, C. (2007). 'Slums, resistance and the African working class'. *International Socialism Journal* 117. http://www.isj.org.uk/index.php4?id=398andissue=117.

Zuern, E. (2011). *The Politics of Necessity: Community Organizing and Democracy in South Africa*. Madison, WI: University of Wisconsin Press.

Zussman, R. 1985. *Mechanics of the Middle Class*. Berkeley, CA: University of California Press.

Notes on Contributors

Peter Alexander is professor of sociology at the University of Johannesburg, where he is the South African Research Chair in Social Change. He has a doctorate from London University, did post-doctoral research at Oxford University, has published widely on labour history, and is currently working on South Africa's 'rebellion of the poor'. His most recent book is the co-authored *Marikana: a View from the Mountain and a Case to Answer* (Jacana 2012, Bookmarks 2013).

Claire Ceruti is completing her doctorate on public sector workers' strikes for the University of Johannesburg. She holds an MA from the University of the Witwatersrand and has worked as a researcher on farmworker and land issues, as a journalist and as an editor of a socialist magazine. She was employed by UJ as a researcher.

Keke Motseke now works as a research manager in the commercial environment. She gained an MA from the University of Johannesburg and worked for Statistics South Africa before returning to UJ as a researcher.

Mosa Phadi is completing her doctorate for the University of Johannesburg on the topic of views and experiences of blackness among Black South Africans. Her MA was from UJ, and she was employed by UJ as a researcher.

Kim Wale is completing her doctorate on memories of squatter violence at the School of Oriental and African Studies in London. She has an MA from the University of Cape Town, and she was employed by UJ as a researcher.

Index